A TEXT BOOK OF
DATABASE MANAGEMENT SYSTEMS

For

SEMESTER – I

THIRD YEAR DEGREE COURSE IN INFORMATION TECHNOLOGY

As Per New Revised Syllabus of
Savitribai Phule Pune University, 2014

Mrs. Sheetal Gujar-Takale
M. E. (C.S.E)
Head and Assistant Professor,
Department of Information Technology,
Vidya Pratishthan's College of Engineering,
Baramati, Pune.

Mr. Sahil K. Shah
M. E. (Computer Engg.)
Assistant Professor,
Department of Information Technology,
Vidya Pratishthan's College of Engineering,
Baramati, Pune.

N 3183

Database Management System - II ISBN 978-93-5164-147-6

Second Edition : June 2015
© : Authors

The text of this publication, or any part thereof, should not be reproduced or transmitted in any form or stored in any computer storage system or device for distribution including photocopy, recording, taping or information retrieval system or reproduced on any disc, tape, perforated media or other information storage device etc., without the written permission of Authors with whom the rights are reserved. Breach of this condition is liable for legal action.

Every effort has been made to avoid errors or omissions in this publication. In spite of this, errors may have crept in. Any mistake, error or discrepancy so noted and shall be brought to our notice shall be taken care of in the next edition. It is notified that neither the publisher nor the authors or seller shall be responsible for any damage or loss of action to any one, of any kind, in any manner, therefrom.

Published By :
NIRALI PRAKASHAN
Abhyudaya Pragati, 1312, Shivaji Nagar,
Off J.M. Road, Pune – 411005
Tel - (020) 25512336/37/39, Fax - (020) 25511379
Email : niralipune@pragationline.com

Printed By :
REPRO INDIA LTD
Mumbai.

☞ **DISTRIBUTION CENTRES**

PUNE
Nirali Prakashan : 119, Budhwar Peth, Jogeshwari Mandir Lane, Pune 411002, Maharashtra
Tel : (020) 2445 2044, 66022708, Fax : (020) 2445 1538
Email : bookorder@pragationline.com, nirlilocal@pragationline.com
Nirali Prakashan : S. No. 28/27, Dhyari, Near Pari Company, Pune 411041
Tel : (020) 24690204 Fax : (020) 24690316
Email : dhyari@pragationline.com, bookorder@pragationline.com

MUMBAI
Nirali Prakashan : 385, S.V.P. Road, Rasdhara Co-op. Hsg. Society Ltd.,
Girgaum, Mumbai 400004, Maharashtra
Tel : (022) 2385 6339 / 2386 9976, Fax : (022) 2386 9976
Email : niralimumbai@pragationline.com

☞ **DISTRIBUTION BRANCHES**

JALGAON
Nirali Prakashan : 34, V. V. Golani Market, Navi Peth, Jalgaon 425001,
Maharashtra, Tel : (0257) 222 0395, Mob : 94234 91860

KOLHAPUR
Nirali Prakashan : New Mahadvar Road, Kedar Plaza, 1st Floor Opp. IDBI Bank
Kolhapur 416 012, Maharashtra. Mob : 9850046155

NAGPUR
Pratibha Book Distributors : Above Maratha Mandir, Shop No. 3, First Floor,
Rani Jhanshi Square, Sitabuldi, Nagpur 440012, Maharashtra
Tel : (0712) 254 7129

DELHI
Nirali Prakashan : 4593/21, Basement, Aggarwal Lane 15, Ansari Road, Daryaganj
Near Times of India Building, New Delhi 110002
Mob : 08505972553

BENGALURU
Pragati Book House : House No. 1, Sanjeevappa Lane, Avenue Road Cross,
Opp. Rice Church, Bengaluru – 560002.
Tel : (080) 64513344, 64513355,Mob : 9880582331, 9845021552
Email:bharatsavla@yahoo.com

CHENNAI
Pragati Books : 9/1, Montieth Road, Behind Taas Mahal, Egmore,
Chennai 600008 Tamil Nadu, Tel : (044) 6518 3535,
Mob : 94440 01782 / 98450 21552 / 98805 82331,
Email : bharatsavla@yahoo.com

niralipune@pragationline.com | www.pragationline.com
Also find us on www.facebook.com/niralibooks

Dedicated affectionately to a multifarious personality who is constantly striving for World Peace and is a driving force for the Betterment of education in India

Respected Sir

Dr. Vishwanathrao D. Karad

Executive President and Director
Maharashtra Academy of Engineering and Educational Research
MIT, PUNE

PREFACE TO THE SECOND EDITION

We are glad and excited to announce that the First Edition of this book received an overwhelming response from the engineering student community, compelling us to release its Second Edition within a very short period of time.

This thoroughly revised Second Edition has been updated with additional matter, many solved problems, including solutions to all university examination papers (Nov./Dec. 2014 and May 2015).

Special care has been taken to maintain high degree of accuracy in the theory and numericals throughout the book.

We take this opportunity to express our sincere thanks to Dineshbhai Furia of Nirali Prakashan, a reputed pioneer in the publication field. Our special thanks to Jignesh Furia for their effective cooperation and great care in bringing out this revised edition. We also appreciate the efforts of M. P. Munde and the entire staff of Engineering Books Deptt. of Nirali Prakashan namely Mrs. Deepali Lachake (Co-ordinator) and Mrs. Shilpa Kale for bringing this book to the students in a timely manner.

We sincerely hope that this " Second Edition" will also be warmly received by all concerned as in the past.

Valuable suggestions from our esteemed readers to improve the book are most welcome and highly appreciated.

Pune **Authors**

PREFACE FOR THE FIRST EDITION

Database technology is one of the most rapidly growing areas of computer and information technology. Basically, Database Management systems is nothing more than a computer based record keeping system that is a system whose overall purpose is to record and maintain information.

The objective of Database Management Systems is to provide a convenient and effective method of defining, sorting and retrieving the information stored in the database. In addition, the database management system is responsible for the safety of information.

The book introduces the basic concepts of Database Management Systems. These concepts are presented through various examples in Data modeling and design. It covers aspects of Database design, Database languages and Database system implementation. It also covers various Database architectures, introduction to new Database technologies such as MySQL, NOSQL, MongoDB, XML Databases, Tera Data RDBMS and Hadoop. Its focus is on the facets of a course in Database Management Systems that are of importance and interest to the students of Information Technology and related fields.

Finally and hopefully, use of this book will uplift the reader's interest in continuing the education.

The support provided by the Publisher Shri. Dineshbhai Furia and staff of Nirali Prakashan particularly Shri. M. P. Munde has been invaluable in this venture and I am deeply indebted to them.

Valuable suggestions communicated by the students and teachers will be given effect in the second edition.

Pune   **Authors**
June 2015

SYLLABUS......

Unit – I   Introduction   **6 Hours**

Database Concepts, Database System Architecture, Data Modeling : Data Models, Basic Concepts, entity, attributes, relationships, constraints, keys, E-R and EER diagrams: Components of E-R Model, conventions, converting E-R diagram into tables, EER Model components, converting EER diagram into tables, legacy system model, Relational Model: Basic concepts, Attributes and Domains, Codd's Rules, Relational Integrity: Domain, Entity, Referential Integrities, Enterprise Constraints, Views, Schema Diagram, Database Design : Functional Dependency,

Purpose of Normalization, Data Redundancy and Update Anomalies, Functional Dependency-Single Valued Dependencies. Single Valued Normalization: 1NF, 2NF, 3NF, BCNF. Decomposition: lossless join decomposition and dependency preservation, Multi valued Normalization (4NF), Join Dependencies and the Fifth Normal Form.

Unit - II   SQL and PL/SQL   **6 Hours**

Introduction to SQL: Characteristics and advantages, SQL Data Types and Literals, DDL, DML, DCL, TCL, SQL Operators, Tables: Creating, Modifying, Deleting, Views: Creating, Dropping, Updating using Views, Indexes, Nulls SQL DML Queries: SELECT Query and clauses, Set Operations, Predicates and Joins, Set membership, Tuple Variables, Set comparison, Ordering of Tuples, Aggregate Functions, Nested Queries, Database Modification using SQL Insert, Update and Delete Queries, concept of Stored Procedures, Cursors, Triggers, assertions, roles and privileges Programmatic SQL: Embedded SQL, Dynamic SQL, Advanced SQL-Programming in MYSQL,SQL 2.0/SQL for OODB, No SQL- MongoDB

Unit - III   Database Transactions   **6 Hours**

Basic concept of a Transaction, Transaction Management, Properties of Transactions, Concept of Schedule, Serial Schedule, Serializability: Conflict and View, Cascaded Aborts, Recoverable and Nonrecoverable Schedules, Concurrency Control: Need, Locking Methods, Deadlocks, Time-stamping Methods, Optimistic Techniques, Recovery methods : Shadow-Paging and Log-Based Recovery, Checkpoints, Performance Tuning, Query Optimization with respect to No SQL Database

Unit - IV   Advance and Emerging Database Concept   **8 Hours**

Database Architectures: Centralized and Client-Server Architectures, 2 Tier and 3 Tier Architecture, Introduction to Parallel Databases, Key elements of Parallel Database Processing, Architecture of Parallel Databases, Introduction to Distributed Databases, Architecture of Distributed Databases, Distributed Database Design, Internet Databases, Database Connectivity using Mongo databases

Unit - V   Large Scale Data Management   **6 Hours**

Introduction to Big Data, XML: DTD, XML Schemas, XQuery, XPath, JSON: Overview, Data Types, Objects, Schema, JSON with Java/PHP/Ruby/Python, Hadoop : HDFS, HBase : Overview, HBase Data Model, HBase Region, Hive, SSD

Unit – VI   Data Warehousing and Data Mining   **8 Hours**

Teradata RDBMS, Teradata Technology, Data Warehousing : Introduction, Evolution of Data Warehouse, Characteristics, Benefits, Limitation of Data Warehousing, Main Components of Data Warehouse, Conceptual Models, Data Mart, OLAP, Data Mining : Process, Knowledge Discovery, Goals of Data Mining, Data Mining Tasks, Machine learning for Big Data, Business Intelligence, Business analytics.

Emerging Database Technologies: Introduction, Cloud Computing and Data Management, Mobile Databases, Dealing with Massive Datasets-Map Reduce and Hadoop. Introduction to SQLite database, XML databases.

CONTENTS ......

Unit - I Introduction

1.	Introduction	1.1 - 1.20
2.	Data Modeling	2.1 - 2.48
3.	Relational Model	3.1 - 3.12
4.	Relational Database Design	4.1 - 4.36

Unit - II SQL and PL/SQL

5.	Introduction to SQL	5.1 - 5.28
6.	SQL DML Queries	6.1 - 6.28
7.	Advanced SQL Programming	7.1 - 7.14

Unit - III Database Transactions

8.	Transaction Management	8.1 - 8.56

Unit - IV Advance and Emerging Database Concept

9.	Database Systems Architecture & MONGODB	9.1 - 9.20

Unit - V Large Scale Data Management

10.	XML and JSON	10.1 - 10.20
11.	HADOOP	11.1 - 11.10

Unit – VI Data Warehousing and Data Mining

12.	Data Warehousing and Data Mining	12.1 - 12.20
13.	Emerging Database Technologies	13.1 - 13.10

- **Proficiency Examination** — P. E. 1 - P. E. 14
- **Glossary** — G. 1 – G. 16
- **SQL** — SQL 1 – SQL 14
- **Solved University Question Papers (Nov./Dec. 2014 & May 2015)** — P.1-P.14

◊ ◊ ◊

Unit - I

CHAPTER 1
INTRODUCTION

1.1 Introduction
1.2 File processing system and Disadvantages of File Processing System
1.3 Advantages of Database Management System (DBMS).
1.4 Disadvantages of DBMS
1.5 Data Abstraction
1.6 Data Models
1.7 Instances and Schemas
1.8 Data Independence
1.9 Database Languages
1.10 Database Terminologies
1.11 Components of DBMS and Overall Structure of DBMS
1.12 Multi-user DBMS Architecture
    1.12.1 Teleprocessing :
    1.12.2 File Server :
    1.12.3 Client Server :
        1.12.3.1 Transaction Processing Monitors :
1.13 System Catalogue
- Review Questions on Instructional Objectives
- University Questions

1.1 INTRODUCTION

Database is a collection of data. It contains information about one particular enterprise.
Examples of enterprise and its database are : Manufacturing company which stores product data.
1. Bank : Which stores customers banking data.
2. Hospital : Which stores patient data.
3. University : Which stores student data.
- **Database Management System** (DBMS) is collection of interrelated data and a set of programs to access the data.
The objective of DBMS is to provide convenient and effective method of defining, storing and retrieving the information contained in the database.

- In addition, the DBMS must provide for the safety of the information stored. It should protect the data from system crash or attempt at unauthorized access. If the data are to be shared among several users, the system must avoid possible anomalous results.

Examples of DBMS :
- Oracle
- Microsoft Access
- Foxpro etc.

1.2 FILE PROCESSING SYSTEM AND DISADVANTAGES OF FILE PROCESSING SYSTEM

Before the advent of DBMS, information was stored using file-processing system. In this system, data is stored in permanent system files. Different application programs are written to extract the data from these files and to add records to these files. But, there are number of major disadvantages in using file processing system, to store the data.

1. Data Redudancy and Inconsistency : Since the data files and application programs are created by different programmers over a long period.

- The data files are likely to have different formats.
- Programs may be written in several programming languages.
- The same information may be duplicated in several plates.

This results in data redundancy and inconsistency.

Consider following two data files :

- Savings account data file : Stores information about customer {account_no, name, social_security, address, telephone_no}.
- Checkings account data file : Stores information about customer {account_no, name, social_security, address, telephone_no}.

Fields {name, social_security, address and telephone_no} are same in both the files i.e. duplication of data is there which results in data redundancy. Data redundancy increases the cost of storing and retrieving the data.

If the values of these common fields are not matching for some records in both files, then it results in inconsistency of data.

2. Difficulty in Accessing the Data : Conventional file processing system does not allow needed data to be retrieved in a convenient and efficient manner.

For example : Consider a data file.

Savings account data file with fields {acc_no, name, social_security, address, balance}.

Application programs to access the data are written. But if user wants to display only those records for which balance is greater than Rs. 10,000. And if that program is not written, then it is difficult to access that data.

3. **Data Isolation :** Because data are scattered in various files and file may be in different formats, it is difficult to write new application programs to retrieve the appropriate data.

4. **Integrity Problems :** The data values stored in the database must satisfy certain types of consistency constraints. Application programmers enforce these consistency constraints by adding appropriate code in the various application programs. However, when a new constraint is to be added, it is difficult to change the programs to enforce the new constraint.

5. **Atomicity Problem :** A computer system is subject to failure. In many applications it is crucial to ensure that once a failure has occurred and has been detected, the data are stored to the consistent state that existed prior to the failure. It is difficult to ensure this property in a conventional file-processing system.

For example : Consider a program to transfer Rs. 500 from account A to account B.

If failure occurs after removing Rs. 500 from account A and before adding Rs. 500 to account B.

This results in inconsistent state.

6. **Concurrent Access Anomalies :** In case of file-processing system, data is not centralized. If two or more users want to access the database at the same time, interaction of concurrent updates may result in inconsistent data.

7. **Security Problem :** Since application programs are added to the system in an ad hoc manner it is difficult to enforce security constraints.

1.3 ADVANTAGES OF DATABASE MANAGEMENT SYSTEM (DBMS)

1. **Centralized Management and Control Over Data :** Database administrator is the person having central control over the system.
2. **Reduction of Redundancies :** Centralized control of data by DBA avoids unnecessary duplication of data.
3. **Shared Data :** DBMS allows the sharing of data under its control by any number of application programmers and users.
4. **Integrity :** Centralized control also ensures that adequate checks are incorporated in the database to provide data integrity.
5. **Security :** The DBA can ensure that proper access procedures are followed, including proper authentication schemes for access to the DBMS and additional checks before permitting access to sensitive data.
6. **Conflict Resolution :** DBA resolves the conflicting requirements of various users and applications.

7. **Data Independence :** DBA can modify the structure of data record. This modification do not affect other applications.

1.4 DISADVANTAGES OF DBMS

- Number of problems are associated with centralization of data.
- Cost of software and hardware.
- Complexity of back-up and Recovery is increased.

1.5 DATA ABSTRACTION

A major purpose of DBMS is to provide users with an abstract view of the data. Many database system users are not computer-trained, hence the complexity is hidden from them through several levels of abstraction.

Data abstraction means to hide certain details of how the data is stored and maintained.

Following are the levels of abstractions :

Physical Level : It is the lowest level of abstraction. It describes how the data is actually stored and describes the data structures and access methods to be used by the database. At the physical level, complex low-level data structures are described in detail. The internal view is expressed by the internal schema which contains the definition of stored record, the method of representing the data fields and the access aids used.

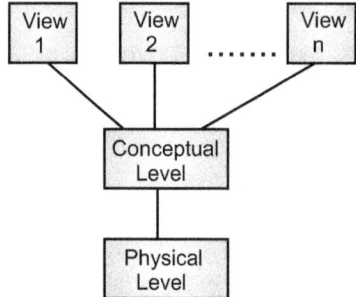

Fig. 1.1 : Interrelationship among the three-levels of abstraction

Conceptual Level : It is the next higher level of abstraction. It describes what data are actually stored in the database and the relationship that exist among the data.

Here, the entire database is described in terms of small number of relatively simple structures.

The conceptual level of abstraction is used by database administrators, who must decide what information is to be kept in the database. One conceptual view represents entire database. It is defined by conceptual schema.

View Level : It is the highest level of abstraction. It describes only a part of the entire database.

Many users of the database system will not be concerned with all of the information. They may need only a part of the entire database. To simplify their interaction with the database, view level is defined. The system may provide many views for the same database.

It is defined by physical/external schema.

An example to Distinguish among Levels of Abstraction :

Consider a data record defined using a structure in C.

```
struct customer
{
char customer_name [50];
char social_security [50];
char customer_street [50];
char customer_city [50];
} cust;
```

customer defines a structure with 4 fields. Each field has a name and data type associated with it.

Physical Level :

In case of programming language, at the physical level customer structure can be described as a block of (200 bytes) consecutive memory locations. The language compiler hides this level of detail from programmers.

Similarly, the database system hides, many of the lowest level storage details from the database programmers. Database administrators may be aware of certain details of the physical organization of the data.

Conceptual Level :

Programmers using programming language define work at this level of abstraction and define structure by a type definition and the interrelationship among these structures is defined.

Similarly, database administrators usually work at this level of abstraction and define database schema.

View Level :

At this level users can see the final result of the program for different inputs. Similarly, at the view level, several views of the database are defined and database users can get the required output.

1.6 DATA MODELS

Data Model is the collection of conceptual tools for describing :
1. Data
2. Data Schema
3. Consistency Constraints

Data models are classified into following three categories :
1. Object Based Logical Data Model
2. Record Based Logical Data Model
3. Physical Data Model

1. Object-Based Logical Model

Object-based logical models are used in describing data at :
- Logical Level
- View Level

Following are the object based logical models :
1. Entity Relationship Model
2. Object Oriented Model
3. Semantic Data Model
4. Functional Data Model.

Entity Relationship (E-R) model consist of a collection of basic objects, called entities and relationships among these objects. An Entity is an object that is distinguishable from other objects by a specific set of attributes. A Relationship is an association among several entities.

An object may contain, in addition to relations and entities, ER model also represents certain constraints to which the contents of a database must conform. One important constraint is Mapping Cardinality, which express the number of entities to which another entity can be associated via a relationship set.

Object Oriented Model is based on a collection of objects. An Object contains values stored in instance variables within the object and bodies of code that operate on the object. These bodies of code are called 'Methods'.

Objects that contain the same type of values and the same methods are grouped together into classes. A Class may be viewed as a type definition for objects. The only way in which one object can access the data of the another object is by invoking a method of that other object. This is called Sending Messages to the object.

2. Record-Based Logical Model :

Record based logical models are used in describing data at :
- Logical Level
- View Level

In record-based models, database is structured in fixed format records of several types. Each type defines a fixed number of fields or attributes and each field is usually of fixed length.
Following are the record based data models :

Relational Model :
It uses a collection of tables to represent both data and relationship among those data. Each table has multiple columns and each column has a unique name.

Network Model :
In Network Model, data is represented as collection of records and relationship among data are represented by links, which can be viewed as pointers. The records in databases are organized as collection of arbitrary graphs.

Hierarchical Model :
It is similar to Network Model, in the sense that data and relationship among data are represented by records and links respectively. But in this model the records in databases are organized as collections of trees rather than arbitrary graphs.

3. Physical Data Model :
It is used to describe data at the lowest level. Following are the physical models.
- Unifying model
- Frame memory model.

1.7 INSTANCES AND SCHEMAS

Collection of information stored in the database at a particular (instance of time) moment is called an instance of the database.

The overall design of the database is called the database schemas.

Analogy to the concept of data types, variables and values in programming language :
Consider a structure in C.

```
struct customer
{
char customer_name [50];
char social_security [50];
char customer_street [50];
char customer_city [50];
} cust;
```

Here, cust is a variable of type customer structure. A database schema corresponds to the programming language type definition.

A variable of a given type has a value at a given instance. The value of the variable in programming languages corresponds to an instance of a database schema.

Database system supports three database schemas :
1. **Physical Schema :** It is at the lowest level. i.e. at Physical level.
2. **Logical Schema :** It is at the next or intermediate level i.e. at Logical level.
3. **Sub-Schema :** It is at the highest level i.e. at the View level.

1.8 DATA INDEPENDENCE

The ability to modify a schema definition in one level without affecting a schema definition in the next higher level is called data independence. There are two levels of data independence:
1. Physical Data Independence.
2. Logical Data Independence.

1. Physical Data Independence :
It is the ability to modify the physical schema without causing application programs to be rewritten.

2. Logical Data Independence :
It is the ability to modify the logical schema without causing application programs to be rewritten.

Logical data independence is more difficult to achieve than is the physical data independence.

1.9 DATABASE LANGUAGES

Data sublanguage consists of two parts :
1. **Data Definition Language :** To specify the database schema.
2. **Data Manipulation Language :** To express database queries and updates.

1. Data Definition Language :

Database schema is specified by a set of definitions which are expressed by a special language called **Data Definition Language** (DDL).

Data Dictionary : The result of compilation of DDL statements is a set of tables, which is stored in a special file called **Data Dictionary** or **System Catalogues**. This file contain **meta data** i.e. data about data.

Data Storage and Definition Language : The storage structure and access methods used by the database system are specified by a set of definitions in a special type of DDL called Data Storage and Definition Language.

2. Data Manipulation Language :

DML is a language that enables users to access or manipulate data as organized by the appropriate data model.

Data manipulation means :
- To retrieve the information from database.
- To insert information into database.
- To delete information from database.
- To modify information from database.

There are two types of DML :

1. **Procedural DML :** It requires a user to specify what data are needed and how to get those data.
2. **Non-procedural DML :** It requires a user to specify what data are needed without specifying how to get those data.

Query is a statement requiring or requesting the retrieval of information.

Query language is the portion of DML that involves information retrieval.

1.10 DATABASE TERMINOLOGIES

1. **Transaction Management :**

Transaction is a collection of operations that perform a single logical function in a database application. It accesses and possibly updates the data items.

Transaction management ensures the atomicity and durability properties.

2. **Database Manager or Storage Manager :**

It is a program module which provides the interface between low level data stored in the database and the application programs and queries submitted to the system.

Following are responsibilities of database manager :

- **Interaction with the file manager :** Actual data is stored in the file system. The database manager translates the various DML statements into low level file system commands. This database manager is responsible for actual storing, retrieving and updating of data in the database.
- **Integrity enforcement :** Consistency constraints are specified by database administrator. But the responsibility of database manager is to enforce, implement or check those constraints.
- **Security enforcement :** It is the responsibility of database manager to enforce the security requirements.
- **Backup and recovery :** It is the responsibility of database manager to detect system failures and restore the database to a consistent state.
- **Concurrency control :** Interaction among the concurrent users is controlled by database manager.

The storage manager or database manager is thus responsible for :
- Storing the data,
- Retrieving the data and
- Updating of data in the database.

3. **Database Administrator :**

The person having central control over the system is called database administrator.

- **Schema Definition :** Database schemas are written by database administrator. These database schemas are translated by DDL complier to a set of tables, that are permanently stored in the data dictionary.
- **Storage structure and Access method definition :** The DBA creates appropriate storage structures and access methods by writing a set of definitions which is translated by data storage and data definition language compiler.
- **Schema and Physical organization modification :** DBA writes a set of definitions to modify the database schema or description of physical storage organization.
- **Granting of authorization for data access :** DBA is responsible for granting the access to the database.
- **Integrity-constraint specification :** Integrity constraints are written by DBA and they are stored in a special file, which is accessed by database manager, while updating the data.

4. **Database Users :**

There are four different types of database users :

- **Application Programmers :** These are computer professionals who interact with the system through DML calls, which are embedded in a program written in a host language. These programs are commonly referred to as application programs.
- **Sophisticated Users :** They interact with the system through their requests written using a database query language. This request is referred to as a query.
- **Specialized Users :** They are sophisticated users who write specialized database applications that do not fit into the traditional data processing framework. Examples of specialized database applications are :
  (i) Knowledge based,
  (ii) Expert system,
  (iii) Computer Aided Design System.
5. **Naive Users :** They are unsophisticated users who interact with the system by involving one of the permanent application programs that have been written previously.

1.11 COMPONENTS OF DBMS AND OVERALL STRUCTURE OF DBMS

Components of DBMS are broadly classified as follows :

1. **Query Processor :**
   (a) DML Compiler
   (b) Embedded DML pre-compiler
   (c) DDL Interpreter
   (d) Query Evaluation Engine

2. **Storage Manager :**
   (a) Authorization and Integrity Manager
   (b) Transaction Manager
   (c) File Manager
   (d) Buffer Manager

3. **Data Structure :**
   (a) Data Files
   (b) Data Dictionary
   (c) Indices
   (d) Statistical Data

1. **Query Processor Components :**

- **DML Pre-compiler :** It translates DML statements in a query language into low level instructions that query evaluation engine understands.

  It also attempts to transform user's request into an equivalent but more efficient form.

- **Embedded DML Pre-compiler :** It converts DML statements embedded in an application program to normal procedure calls in the host language.

  The Pre-compiler must interact with the DML compiler to generate the appropriate code.

- **DDL Interpreter :** It interprets the DDL statements and records them in a set of tables containing meta data or data dictionary.

- **Query Evaluation Engine :** It executes low-level instructions generated by the DML compiler.

2. **Storage Manager Components :**

  They provide the interface between the low-level data stored in the database and application programs and queries submitted to the system.

- **Authorization and Integrity Manager :** It tests for the satisfaction of integrity constraints checks the authority of users to access data.

- **Transaction Manager :** It ensures that the database remains in a consistent state despite the system failures and that concurrent transaction execution proceeds without conflicting.

- **File Manager :** It manages the allocation of space on disk storage and the data structures used to represent information stored on disk.

- **Buffer Manager :** It is responsible for fetching data from disk storage into main memory and deciding what data to cache in memory.

3. Data Structures :

Following data structures are required as a part of the physical system implementation.

- **Data Files :** It stores the database.
- **Data Dictionary :** It stores meta data (data about data) about the structure of the database.
- **Indices :** Provide fast access to data items that hold particular values.
- **Statistical Data :** It stores statistical information about the data in the database. This information is used by query processor to select efficient ways to execute query.

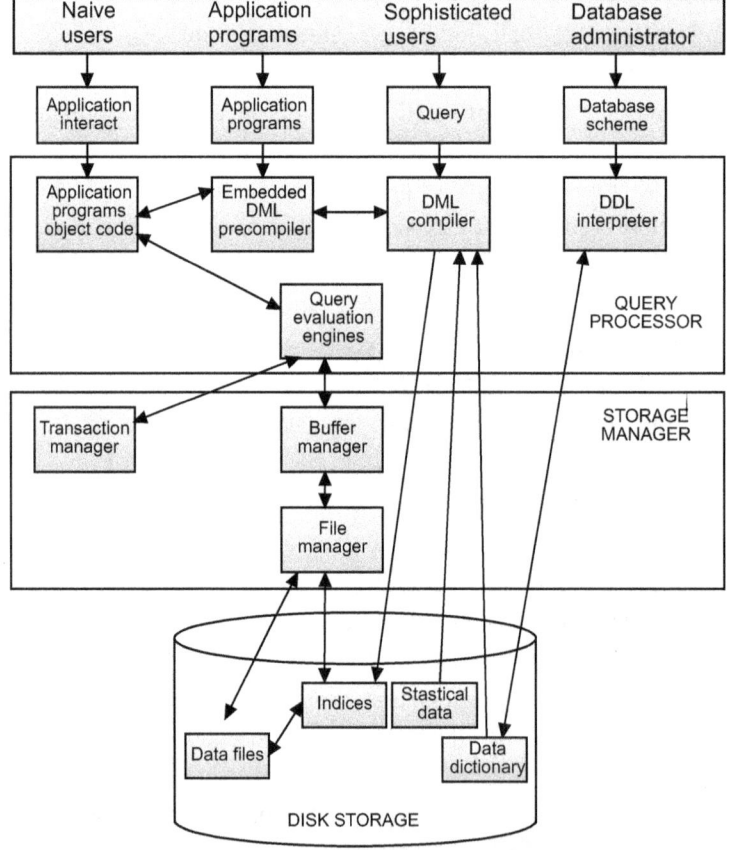

Fig. 1.2 : System structure

1.12 MULTI-USER DBMS ARCHITECTURE

The architectures that are used to implement multi-user database management systems are :
- Teleprocessing
- File Server
- Client Server

1.12.1 Teleprocessing :

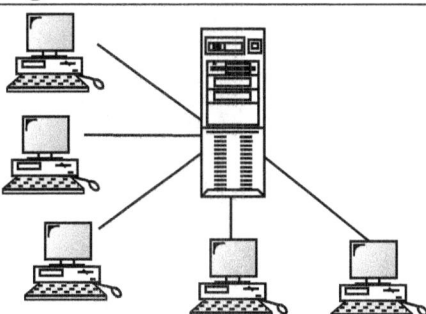

Fig. 1.3 : Teleprocessing

The traditional architecture for multi-user systems was Teleprocessing, where there is :
- One computer with a single Central Processing Unit (CPU) and
- A number of terminals.

All processing is performed within the boundaries of the same physical computer.

User terminals are typically the **'Dumb Terminals'**. They are incapable of functioning at their own and they are attached by cable to the central computer.

The terminals send messages via. the communication control sub-system.

1.12.2 File Server :

In a file server environment, the processing is distributed about the network, typically the Local Area Network (LAN). The file server holds the files required by the application and the DBMS. However, the applications and DBMS run on each workstation, requesting files from the file server when necessary.

The file server acts simply as a shared data disk. The DBMS on each workstation sends requests to the file server for all data that the DBMS requires that it is stored on disk.

This approach can generate significant amount of network traffic, which can lead to performance problems.

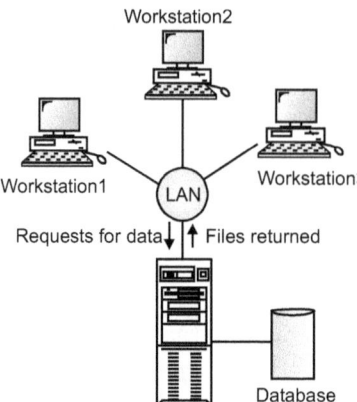

Fig. 1.4 : File server

The file server architecture has three main disadvantages :
- There is a large amount of network traffic.
- A full copy of DBMS is required on each workstation.
- Concurrency, Recovery and Integrity control are more complex because there can be multiple DBMS accessing the same files.

1.12.3 Client Server :

To overcome the disadvantages of the first two methods the client-server architecture was developed. As the name suggests there is :

A **client process**, which requires some resource,

A **server process**, which provides the resource.

There is no requirement that the client and server must reside on the same machine. In the database context, the client manages the user interface and the application logic.

- It takes the user requests.
- Checks the syntax.
- Generates database requests in SQL or another database language.
- Transmits the message to the server, waits for response and formats the response for the end-user.

The server process :
- Accepts and processes the database requests.
- Transmits the result to the client.

   Processing of the requests involves checking authorization, ensuring integrity, maintaining the system catalog, and performing query and update processing.

   In addition, it also provides concurrency and recovery control.

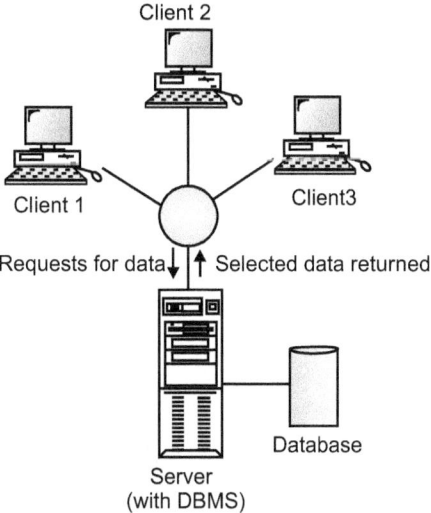

Fig. 1.5 : Client server

Following are the advantages of Client Server architecture :

1. It enables wider access to existing databases.
2. **Increased Performance :** If the clients and the server reside on different computers then different computers can be processing application in parallel.
3. **Hardware Costs may be Reduced :** It is the only server that requires the storage and processing sufficient to store and manage the database.
4. **Communication Costs are Reduced :** Applications carry out part of operations on the client and send only the requests for database access over the network.
5. **Increased Consistency :** The server can handle integrity checks, so that constraints need be defined and validated only in one place.
6. **It Maps on to Open :** System architecture quite naturally.

Summary of Client Server Functions :

Client	Server
1. Manages the user interface.	1. Accepts and processes database requests from clients.
2. Accepts and checks syntax of user input.	2. Checks authorization.
3. Generates database requests and transmits to the server.	3. Ensures integrity constraints not violated.
4. Passes response back to user.	4. Performs query/update processing and transmits response to the client.
	5. Maintains system catalogue.
	6. Provides concurrent database access.
	7. Provides recovery control.

Alternative client server topologies are :
1. Single Client, Single Server.
2. Multiple Client, Single Server.
3. Multiple Client, Multiple Server.

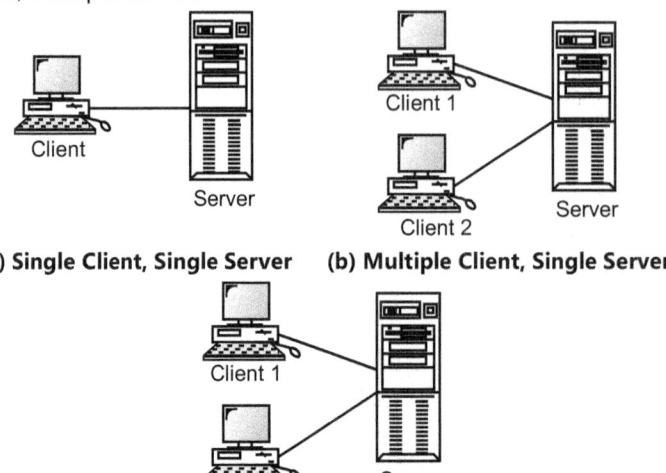

(a) Single Client, Single Server (b) Multiple Client, Single Server

(c) Multiple Client, Multiple Server

Fig. 1.6 : Alternative client-server topologies

1.12.3.1 Transaction Processing Monitors :

A program that controls data transfer between clients and servers in order to provide a consistent environment, particularly for online transaction processing.

The transaction processing monitor is a middleware component that provides access to the services of a number of resource managers and provides uniform interface for programmers who are developing the transactional software.

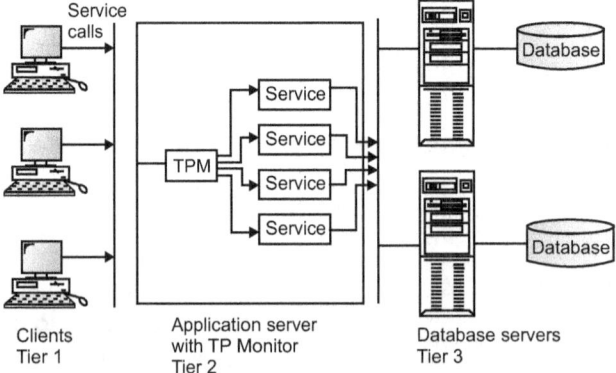

Fig. 1.7 : Transaction processing monitor

Transaction Processing monitor provides significant advantages :

1. **Transaction Routing :** The transaction processing monitor can increase the scalability by directing the transactions to specific DBMS.
2. **Managing Distributed Transactions :** The transaction processing monitor can manage transactions that require access to data held in multiple DBMS.
3. **Load Balancing :** The transaction processing monitor can balance client requests across multiple DBMSs on one or more computers by directing client calls to the least loaded server.
4. **Funneling :** In environments with a large number of users, it may sometimes be difficult for all users to be logged on simultaneously to the DBMS. The transaction processing monitor can establish connections with DBMSs as and when required and can funnel user requets through these connections.
5. **Increased Reliability :** The TP monitor acts as transaction manager, performing the necessary actions to maintain the consistency of the database, with the DBMS acting as the resource manager.

1.13 SYSTEM CATALOGUE

System Catalogue : A repository of information describing the data in the database, that is the meta-data or data about data.

Data Dictionary (also called system catalogue) stores meta-data that is, data about data, such as :

Information about relations
- Names of relations.
- Names and Types of attributes of each relation.
- Names and Definitions of views.
- Integrity constraints.

User and accounting information, including passwords.
- Names of authorized users.
- Accounting information about users.
- Passwords or other information used to authenticate Statistical and Descriptive data.
- Number of tuples in each relation.
- Method of storage for each relation.
  Physical file organization information.
- How relation is stored (sequential/hash/...).
- Physical location of relation.
  (a) Operating system file name or
  (b) Disk addresses of blocks containing records of the relation.

Information about indices

- Name of the index.
- Name of relation being indexed.
- Attributes on which the index is defined.
- Types of index formed.

Catalog structure can use either specialized data structures designed for efficient access or a set of relations, with existing system features used to ensure efficient access.

A Possible Catalogue Representation : primary keys are underlined

Relation-meta-data = (relation-name, number-of-attributes, storage-organization, location)

Attribute-meta-data = (attribute-name, relation-name, domain-type, position, length)

User-meta-data = (user-name, encrypted-password, group)

Index-meta-data = (index-name, relation-name, index-type, index-attributes)

View-meta-data = (view-name, definition)

REVIEW QUESTIONS ON INSTRUCTIONAL OBJECTIVES

1. Define following terms :
   - (a) Meta-data
   - (b) DDL
   - (c) DML
   - (d) Transaction
   - (e) View
   - (f) Sub schema
   - (g) Instance and schema
   - (h) Data model
   - (i) DBMS
   - (j) Database
   - (k) Database manager
   - (l) DSL
   - (m) Data independence
   - (n) Query language.
2. State the advantages of DBMS.
3. Draw a diagram to show database architecture.
4. Draw the three layered database management system architecture.
5. What are the major responsibilities of database manager module of DBMS system ?
6. Distinguish between Physical data independence and Logical data independence.
7. Write a short note on :
   - (a) Traditional file based database.
   - (b) Database manager.
   - (c) Database users.
   - (d) Data model.
   - (e) Database administrator.
   - (f) DBMS components and System structure.
8. What are the disadvantages of DBMS ?

UNIVERSITY QUESTIONS

1. Explain : **(Dec. 2004)**
   (a) Data abstraction.
   (b) Data independence.
2. Draw and explain system structure.
3. Explain with example DDL and DML.
4. Define :
   (a) Meta data   (b) Data model   **(May 2004)**
5. Compare DBMS and File processing system.   **(May 2004)**
6. Consider a two-dimensional integer array of size m × n that is to be used in 'C' programming language. Using the arrays as an example, Illustrate difference between the three levels of abstraction.   **(May 2004)**
7. Define following :
   (a) Tuple   (b) Attribute
   (c) Schema   (d) Domain   **(May 2003)**
8. State in brief how following disadvantages of File processing system are eliminated in DBMS :   **(May 2003)**
   (a) Data Redundancy   (b) Integrity
9. Explain various components of DBMS.   **(May 2003)**
10. Differentiate between following :   **(May 2003)**
    (a) Logical and Physical data independence   (b) DDL and DML.
11. Define :
    (a) Domain   (b) Assertions
    (c) Trigger   (d) Primary key   **(Dec. 2003)**
12. Write a short note on Data model.
13. Define :
    (a) Entity,   (b) Transaction,
    (c) Query,   (d) Candidate key.   **(Dec. 2002)**
14. Compare File processing system and DBMS based on following points : Data Isolation, Integrity, Atomicity, Security.   **(Dec. 2002)**
15. Compare the data models : Relational, Network, Hierarchical.   **(Dec. 2002)**
16. Explain data independence in detail.   **(May 2002)**
17. Define :
    (a) Schema   (b) Instance
    (c) Primary key   (d) Super key   **(May 2002)**
18. Define :
    (a) Entity   (b) Procedural DML
    (c) Non-procedural DML   (d) DBA   **(Dec. 2001)**

DATABASE MANAGEMENT SYSTEMS (T.E. IT) INTRODUCTION

19. What are the disadvantages of storing organizational information in file processing system ? **(Dec. 2001)**
20. Compare different data models. **(Dec. 2001)**
21. Define the following terms :
    (a) Schema (b) Query
    (c) Candidate key (d) Foreign key **(May 2001)**
22. What is the difference between Physical data independence and Logical data independence ? **(May 2001)**
23. Explain various components of DBMS. **(May 2001)**
24. Differentiate between DBMS and a File processing system. **(Dec. 2000)**
25. Explain in brief different levels of abstraction.
    Consider a two-dimensional integer array of size m × n that is to be used In 'C' programming language. Using the arrays as an example, illustrate difference between the three levels of abstraction.
26. Define :
    (a) DBMS (b) DDL
    (c) DML (d) Transaction **(May 2000)**
27. Explain various components of DBMS. **(May 2000)**
28. Write a note on Conventional File Processing System. **(April 03, Oct. 02)**
29. What are the drawbacks of conventional file processing system ? **(April 04, 03)**
30. What is the difficulty in accessing data ? **(April 04)**
31. Explain :
    (1) Database Languages **(April 03, Dec. 06)**
    (2) Data Definition Language **(May 05)**
    (3) Data Administrator **(May 05)**
32. Explain in brief data models. **(April 01, Oct. 03, April 04, May 05, May 06)**
33. Write a detail note on data base system structure.
    (Oct. 03, Dec. 04, May 05, April 01, 03, Nov. 04, May 06, 07)
34. Explain various Data Models used in DBMS **(Nov. 12, May .13)**

CHAPTER 2
DATA MODELING

2.1 Introduction
2.2 Entity-Relationship Model : Basic Concepts
    2.2.1 Entity
    2.2.2 Entity Set
    2.2.3 Attribute
    2.2.4 Relationship
    2.2.5 Relationship Set
2.3 Constraints
    2.3.1 Mapping Cardinality
    2.3.2 Existence Dependencies
    2.3.3 Participation Constraint
2.4 Keys
    2.4.1 Super Key
    2.4.2 Candidate Key
    2.4.3 Primary Key
2.5 Entity-Relationship Diagram
2.6 Extended E-R Features
2.7 Reduction of E-R Schema to Tables
2.8 Solved Examples
2.9 Network Model
    2.9.1 Data Structure Diagrams
    2.9.2 DBTG CODASYL Model
    2.9.3 Implementation Techniques
2.10 Hierarchical Model
    2.10.1 Tree Structure Diagram
    2.10.2 Implementation Techniques
    2.10.3 The IMS Database System
- Review Questions on Instructional Objectives
- University Questions

2.1 INTRODUCTION

Data model is a collection of conceptual tools for describing :
- Data;
- Data Relationship;
- Data Semantics; and
- Consistency Constraints.

Data models are classified into three categories.
1. Object Based Logical Data Model
2. Record Based Logical Data Model
3. Physical Data Model

In this chapter we study :
(1) E–R Model,
(2) Network Model,
(3) Hierarchical Model.

2.2 ENTITY–RELATIONSHIP MODEL : BASIC CONCEPTS

E–R model is based on a perception of a real world that consists of a set of basic objects called entities and relationship among these objects.

2.2.1 Entity

- An entity is an object in the real world that is distinguishable from all other objects.
- An entity is a thing in the real world with an independent existence.
- An entity has a set of properties or attributes and the values for some set of attributes or properties may uniquely identify an entity.
- An entity can be concrete or abstract.

For example : Student, Account, Person are the entities.

Student is an entity with properties (attributes) roll_no and class, of a student uniquely identifies the student (entity).

Student is concrete entity whereas Day, Class are abstract entities.

Entity Student :

| Ashwin | 4320 | S.E. |

2.2.2 Entity Set

- Entity set is a set of entities of the same type that share the same properties or attributes.
- Entity sets need not be disjoint.

For example : The set of all students is defined as entity set student.

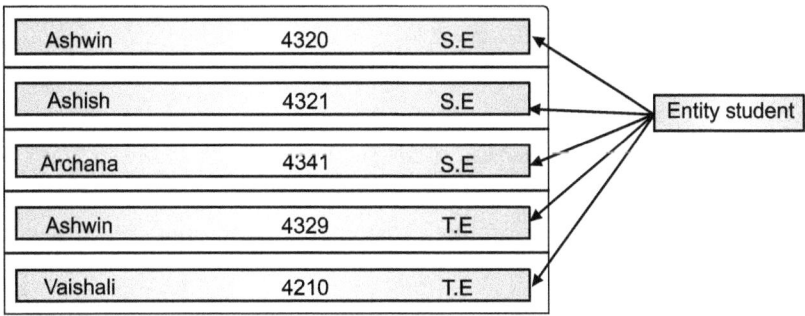

Fig. 2.1 : Student Entity Set

2.2.3 Attribute

Each entity has a set of **Attributes**. Each attribute has a domain from which the values for this attribute are drawn. Following are the attribute types :

1. Simple and Composite Attribute : Simple attributes can not be divided into subparts, on the other hand composite attributes can be divided into subparts.

For example : Consider customer entity with following attributes :

- customer_no.
- customer_address

Here, customer_no. is simple attribute, and customer_address is composite attribute, which can be further divided into following components.

- street_address
- street_no.
- apt_number

2. Single-valued and Multi-valued Attributes : Single-valued attribute has single value for a particular entity.

Multi-valued attribute has a set of values for a specific entity.

For example, Consider the entity customer with attributes.

  customer_no.
  customer_address

Where, one may have two addresses.

Here, customer_no. is a single-valued attribute. It refers to only one customer.

But customer_address is multi-valued attribute. customer_address may have any number of values.

3. Null Attribute : Null value is used when an entity does not have a value for an attribute. Null can also designate that an attribute is unknown (i.e. missing or not known).

4. Derived Attribute : The value for this type of attribute can be derived from the values of other related attributes or entities.

2.2.4 Relationship

Relationship is an **association** among several **entities.**

Consider two entity sets,

Customer with attributes : (name, address, social_security).

Account with attributes : (acc_no., balance, type).

cust_acc is a relation between two entities customer and account, which specifies which account belongs to which customer.

2.2.5 Relationship Set

- It is a set of relationships of same type.
- Formally, it is mathematical relation on n ≥ 2 (possibly non-distinct) entity sets.

If $E_1, E_2, ..., E_n$ are entity sets, then a relationship set R is a subset of $\{(e_1, e_2, ..., e_n) \mid e_1 \in E_1, e_2 \in E_2, e_n \in E_n\}$ where $(e_1, e_2, ..., e_n)$ is a relationship.

Consider the following two entity sets,

Account = {acc_no., balance, type}

Customer = {name, city, social_security}

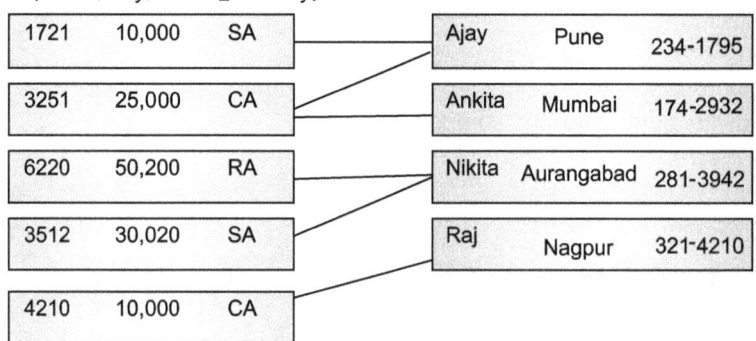

Fig. 2.2 : cust_acc relationship set

Binary Relationship Set relates two entity sets. n-ary Relationship Set relates 'n' number of entity sets. n-ary relationship set can be replaced by binary relationship set.

2.3 CONSTRAINTS

E-R enterprise schema may define certain constraints to which the contents of a database must conform.

In this section we examine following constraints :

- Mapping Cardinalities
- Existence Dependencies
- Participation Constraints.

2.3.1 Mapping Cardinality

Mapping cardinality or cardinality ratio expresses the number of entities to which another entity can be associated via a relationship set. Mapping cardinalities are most useful in describing binary relationship sets.

For a binary relationship set R between two entity sets A and B, the mapping cardinality must be one of the following.

(1) One-to-One : An entity in 'A' is associated with at most one entity in 'B' and an entity in 'B' is associated with at most one entity in 'A'.

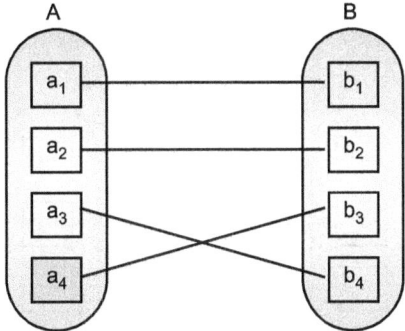

Fig. 2.3 : One-to-one

(2) One-to-Many : An entity in 'A' is associated with any number of entities in 'B'. An entity in 'B' however, can be associated with at most one entity in 'A'.

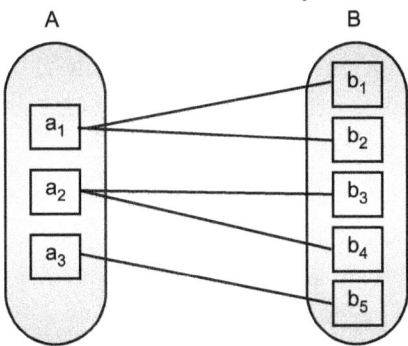

Fig. 2.4 : One-to-many

(3) Many-to-One : An entity in 'A' is associated with at most one entity in 'B'. An entity in 'B' however can be associated with any number of entities in 'A'.

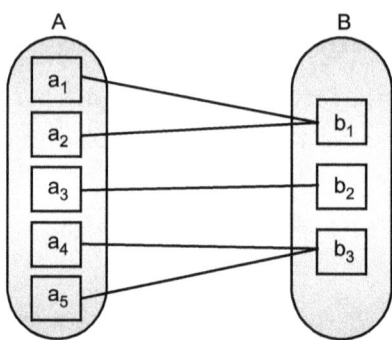

Fig. 2.5 : Many-to-one

(4) Many-to-Many : An entity in 'A' is associated with any number of entities in 'B' and an entity in 'B' is associated with any number of entities in 'A'.

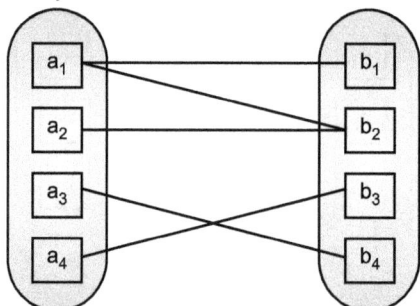

Fig. 2.6 : Many-to-many

2.3.2 Existence Dependencies

If existence of entity x depends on the existence of entity y, then x is said to be existence dependent on y. If y is deleted, x should also be deleted. Entity y is said to be dominant entity and x is said to be sub-ordinate entity.

Example : Consider the entity sets account and transaction and relationship set log. log relates account and transaction entities. This relation is one-to-many, i.e. one account may have n transactions, but every transaction is associated with only one account.

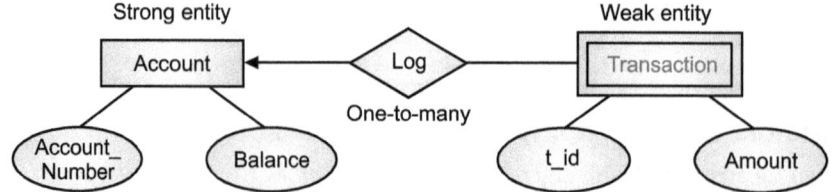

Fig. 2.7 : One-to-many

Account			Log			Transaction	
Acc_No	Balance		Acc_No	T_id		T_id	Amount
6532	10,000		6532	1		1	+ 300
6239	5020		6532	2		2	+ 4000
			6532	3		3	− 200
			6239	4		4	+ 5000
			6532	5		5	− 100
			6532	6		6	− 200

If an account entity is deleted, then all the transactions associated with entity account must be deleted. Account is a dominant entity and transaction is a subordinate entity. Transaction entity is existence dependent on account entity.

2.3.3 Participation Constraint

The participation of an entity set E in a relationship set R is said to be total if every entity in E participates in at least one relationship in R. If only some entities in E participate in relationships in R, the participation of entity set E in relationship is said to be partial.

2.4 KEYS

Individual entities and relationships are distinct but it is important to distinguish entities within entity sets and relationships within relationship sets. The concept of keys helps us to distinguish the entities and relationships.

2.4.1 Super Key

Super key is a set of one or more attributes which taken collectively allows us to identify uniquely an entity in the entity set.

Consider the entity set account with attributes {acc_no., cust_name, bank_name, balance, address}.

Here, acc_no is super key of account entity set. Similarly, (acc_no, cust_name) is a super key and (acc_no., bank_name) is a super key. But cust_name and bank-name independently are not the super keys.

Super key may contain extra attributes i.e. if k is a super key, then any super set of k is also a Super key.

2.4.2 Candidate Key

Candidate Key is a **Minimal Super Key.** No proper subset of a candidate key is super key.

For account entity set acc_no is the candidate key. If combination of cust_name and branch_name is sufficient to distinguish among members of the account then {cust_name, account_number branch_name} is also a candidate key.

But cust_name and branch_name independently are not the candidate keys.

2.4.3 Primary Key

- Primary key is a candidate key chosen by the database designer as the principal means of identifying entities within an entity set.
- An entity set which doesn't have sufficient attributes to form a primary key is called **weak entity set.**
- An entity set which has a primary key is called as **strong entity set**. Member of strong entity set is dominant entity and member of weak entity set is **subordinate entity**.
- Members of weak entity set are distinguished by a set of attributes which is called as **discriminator** of that weak entity set.
- The **primary key** of weak entity set is formed by the primary key of strong entity set on which it is existence dependent plus the discriminator.
- **Relationship Set :** Let R be a relationship set involving entity sets $E_1, E_2, E_3, ..., E_n$. Let $P(E_i)$ denote primary key of E_i entity set. If R has no attributes associated with it, then the set of attributes of R is given as :

$$P(E_1) \cup P(E_2) \cup P(E_3) \cup .... \cup P(E_n).$$

- If R has attributes $a_1, a_2, ... a_n$, associated with it then the set of attributes of R is,

$$P(E_1) \cup P(E_2) \cup .... \cup P(E_n) \cup \{a_1, a_2, ..., a_n\}$$

In both the above cases $P(E_1) \cup P(E_2) \cup P(E_3) \cup .... \cup P(E_n)$ form a super key of the relationship.

- The primary key of relationship set depends on the mapping cardinality of the relationship set.

Case 1 : If the relationship is many-to-many, primary key of relationship set is union of primary key of both entity sets.

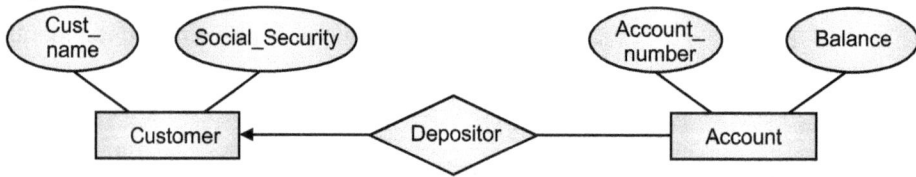

Fig. 2.8 : Many-to-many

Primary key of customer is social_security, primary key of account is acc_no, attributes of depositor are {social_security, acc_no}.

Primary key of depositor is {social_security, acc_no}

Case 2 : If the relationship is one-to-many or many-to-one, primary key of relationship set is primary key of one entity set.

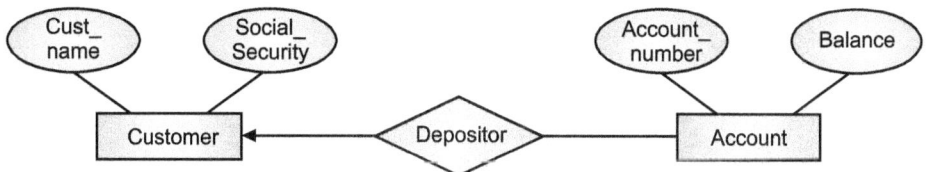

Fig. 2.9 : One-to-many

Primary key of depositor is {acc_no}

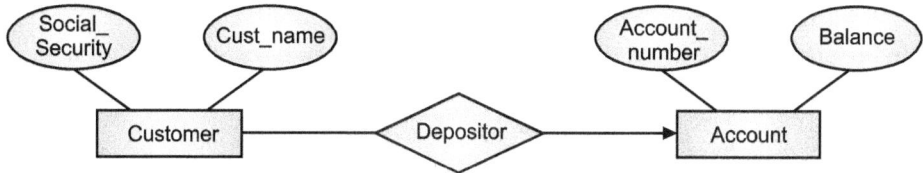

Fig. 2.10 : Many-to-one

Primary key of depositor is {social_security}.

Case 3 : In case of one-to-one relationship, relationship set has no primary key.

2.5 ENTITY-RELATIONSHIP DIAGRAM

Overall logical structure of database can be expressed graphically by an E-R diagram.
Following are the components of E-R diagram.

1. Rectangles   : Represent entity set.
2. Ellipses   : Represent attributes.
3. Diamonds   : Represent relationship set.
4. Lines   : Link attributes to entity sets and relationship sets.
5. Double ellipse   : Represent multi-valued attribute.
6. Dashed ellipse   : Represent derived attribute.
7. Double lines   : Indicate total participation of an entity in a relationship set.
8. Double rectangle : Represent weak entity set.

Representation of Mapping Cardinalities :

Mapping cardinality is indicated by directed line (→) or undirected line (—).

Consider two entities,

Customer – { cust_name, social_security, address}

Account – { acc_no, balance}

Relationship set is depositor with attributes {social_security, acc_no}.

1. If the relationship is many-to-many i.e. one customer may have any number of accounts and one account can be shared by any number of customers, then this cardinality is represented as follows.

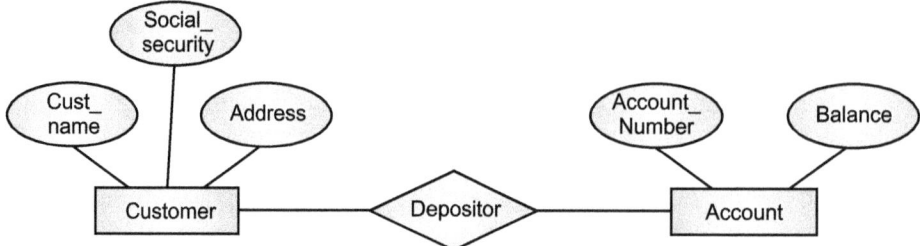

Fig. 2.11 : Many-to-many

2. If the relationship is one-to-many i.e. one customer may have any number of accounts, but one account belongs to only one customer then this cardinality is represented as follows:

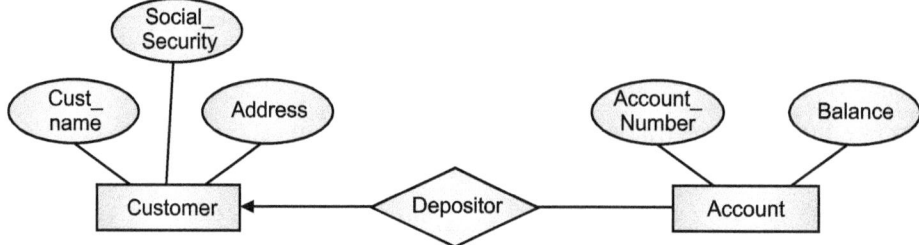

Fig. 2.12 : One-to-many

3. If the relationship is many-to-one i.e. many customers can share one account, then this cardinality is represented as follows :

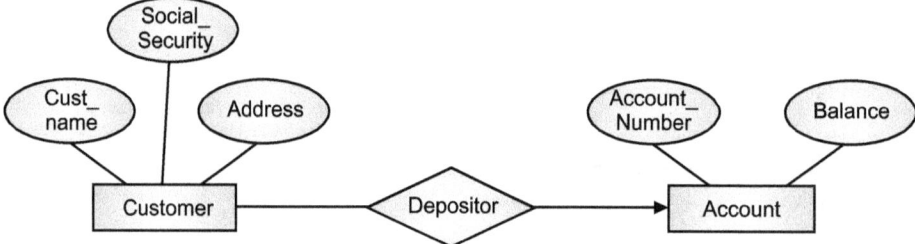

Fig. 2.13 : Many-to-one

4. If the relationship is one-to-one i.e. each customer has one account and each account belongs to one customer, then this cardinality is represented as follows :

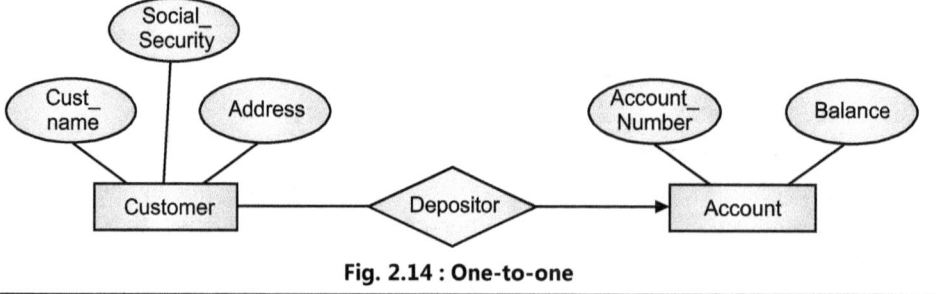

Fig. 2.14 : One-to-one

Representation of Role :

Role of a given entity is indicated by labelling the lines that connect the entities and relationship set.

Consider an entity Employee which stores information about all customers who work for some given factory. An employee may be a worker or a manager. These are the roles of entity employee, which can be represented as follows :

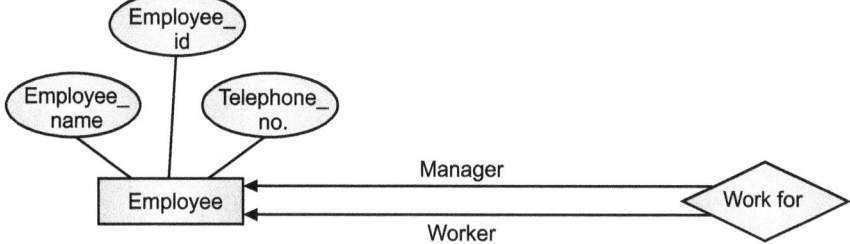

Fig. 2.15 : E-R Diagram with role of employee entity

Representation of Non-Binary Relationship :

Consider a ternary relationship set CAB which relates 3 entities.

Customer – {cust_name, social_security, street, city}

Account – {acc_no, balance}

Branch – {branch_name, city, assets}

Here, one customer may have several accounts, one account may belong to several customers and each account is in a specific branch.

This relationship can be represented as :

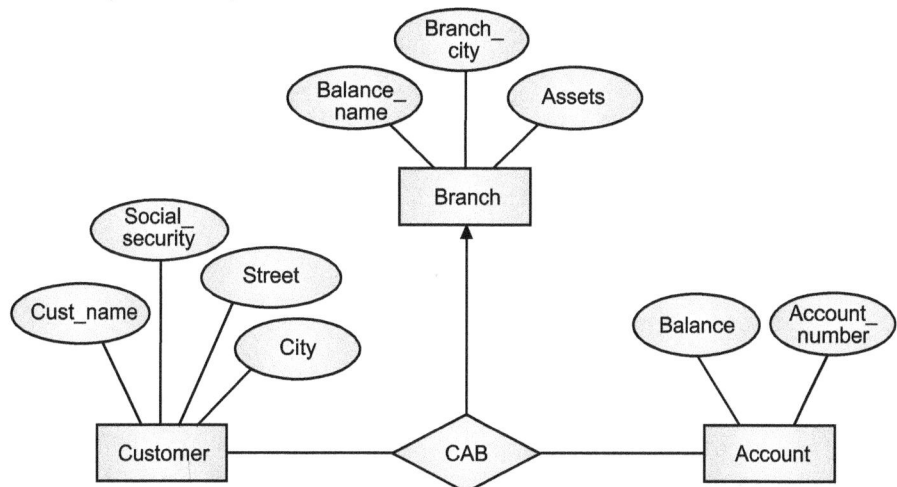

Fig. 2.16 : Non-binary relationship with three entity set

Representation of Weak Entity Set :

Weak entity sets are represented by a doubly outlined box.

Consider entity sets,

Account – {account_no, balance}.

Transaction – {transaction_no, date, amount}.

Where, transaction is a weak entity set which is dependent on account entity. This can be represented as :

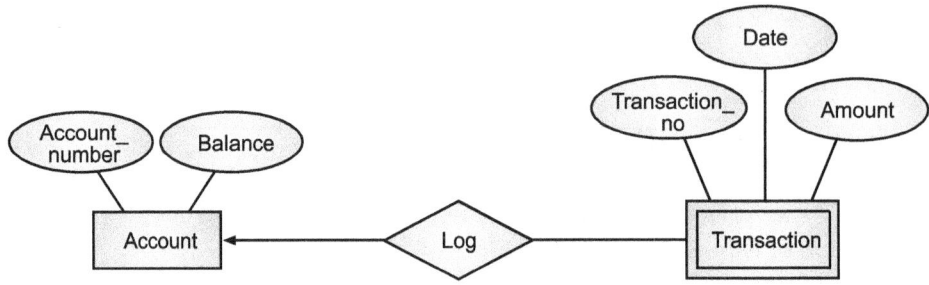

Fig. 2.17 : Week entity set

Weak entity set can also be represented as a multi-valued composite attribute of strong entity set.

2.6 EXTENDED E-R FEATURES

Following are the extended entity relationship features of E-R model.

1. Specialization.
2. Generalization.
3. Aggregation.
4. Attribute Inheritance.

1. Specialization :

It is the process of designating sub groupings within an entity set.

Consider an account entity which can be classified into :

- Savings account
- Checkings account.

Checking account can further be classified into :

- Standard checking account
- Gold checking account
- Senior checking account.

Hence, specialization of account entity is savings account and checking account.

Specialization of checking account is standard checking account, gold checking account and senior checking account.

In E-R diagram, specialization is depicted by a triangle component labelled ISA.

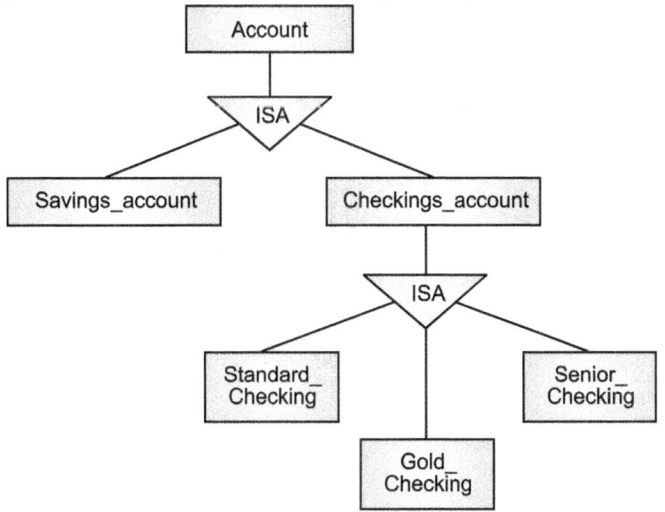

Fig. 2.18 : Specialization

Account is higher level entity and savings account and checkings account are lower level entities.

Checking account is higher level entity and standard checking, gold checking and senior checking are lower-level entities.

2. Generalization :

It is a containment relationship that exits between a higher level entity set and one-or-more lower level entity sets. Attributes of higher level entity set and of lower level entity set are common. This commonality is expressed by generalization.

For example : Attributes of account entity set are {account_no, balance}.

Attributes of saving account are {acc_no, balance, interest_rate}

Attributes of checkings account are {acc_no, balance, overdraft_amount}.

Attributes of standard checking account are :

{acc_no, balance, overdraft_amount, number_check}

Attributes of gold checking account are, {acc_no, balance, overdraft_amount, inter_pay, min_balance}

Attributes of senior account are, {acc_no, balance, overdraft_amount, date_of_birth}

The generalization can be shown using E-R diagram as follows :

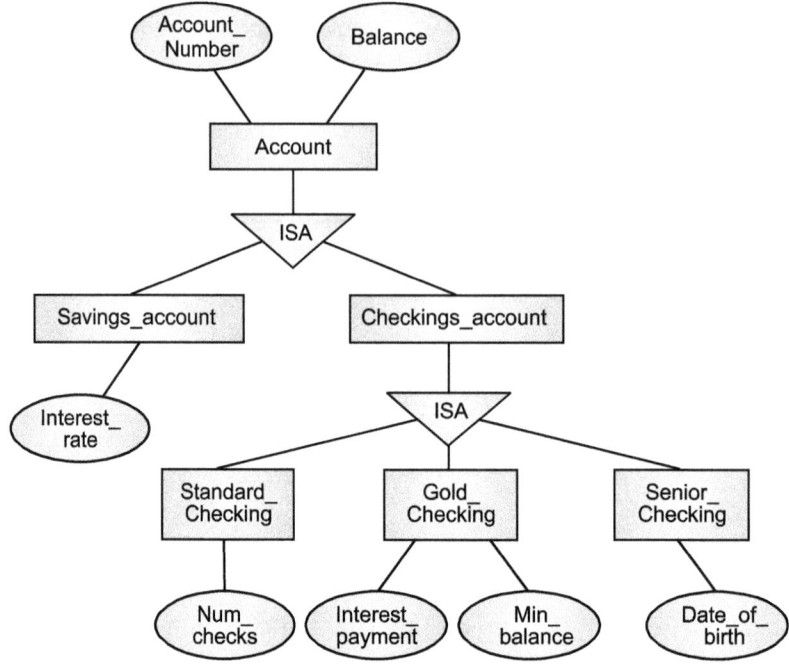

Fig. 2.19 : Generalization

Comparison of Generalization and Specialization :
1. Generalization is a simple inversion of specialization.
2. Specialization emphasizes difference among several entities within the set by creating distinct lower level entity sets.
3. Generalization is used to emphasize the similarities among lower-level entity sets and to hide the differences.
4. While designing E-R schema we apply both processes.
5. E-R diagram does not distinguish between specialization and generalization.
6. New levels of entity representation are distinguished (specialization) or synthesized (generalization) so that the database schema fully expresses the application of database and the user requirements of database.

Note : Higher level and lower level entity sets can also be designated by the terms super class and subclass.

Constraints on Generalization :

First type of constraints involves determining which entities can be members of a given lower-level entity set. Such membership may be one of the following :

1. **Condition-defined** : In condition defined lower-level entity sets, membership is evaluated on the basis of whether or not an entity satisfies an explicit condition or predicate.
2. **User-defined** : In user defined lower level entity sets are not constrained by a membership condition; rather, the database user assigns entities to a given entity set.

   Second type of constraint relates to whether or not entities may belong to more than one lower level set within a single generalization. The lower level entity sets may be one of the following.
3. **Disjoint** : A disjointness constraint requires that an entity belong to no more than one lower level entity set.
4. **Overlapping** : In overlapping generalizations, the same entity may belong to more than one lower level entity set within a single generalization.

Completeness Constraint on generalization or specialization, specifies whether or not an entity in higher level entity set must belong to at least one of the lower level entity sets within the generalization/specialization. This constraint may be one of the following :

- **Total Generalization or Specialization :** Each higher level entity must belong to a lower level entity set.
- **Partial Generalization or Specialization** : Some higher level entities may not belong to any lower level entity set.

3. **Attribute Inheritance :**

The attributes of higher level entity sets are inherited by the lower level entity sets.

A lower level entity set also inherits participation in relationship sets in which its higher level entity set participates.

For example : Attributes of account entity are inherited by savings_account entity, checking-account entity sets and standard, gold and senior entity set.

If an entity set is a lower-level entity set in more than one ISA relationship, the resulting structure is said to be a lattice.

4. **Aggregation :**

Aggregation is an abstraction through which relationships are treated as higher-level entities.

It helps to express relationship among relationships. To illustrate the need of aggregation consider the database describing information about employees who work on a particular project and use a number of different machines in their work.

E-R Diagram : To represent the database without using aggregation is :

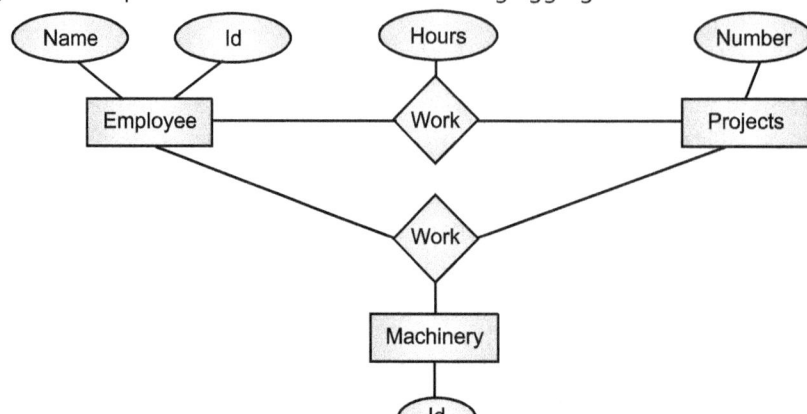

Fig. 2.20 : E-R diagram without aggregation

Here, work relation allocates projects to employees. One employee may work on any number of projects and on one project any number of employees may be working. Work relation relates employee and project correctly.

Uses relation which is ternary relationship can not relate machines, projects and employees correctly. Each machine is associated with a project and the employees working on that project.

To represent this relation correctly, consider the relation work as one entity and machinery as another entity.

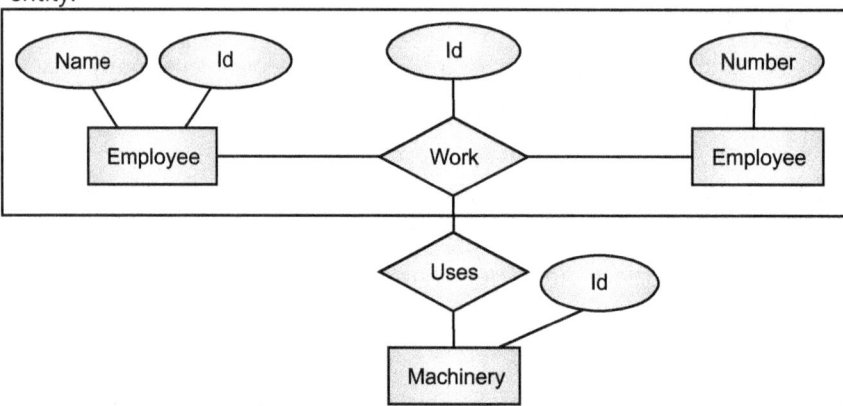

Fig. 2.21 : E-R diagram including aggregation

Here, attributes of work relationship are {emp_id, number_hours} and primary key is {emp_id, number}.

Uses is relationship which relates work and machinery.

Hence, attributes of uses are :

{emp_id, number, machine_id}

Primary key of uses is
  {emp_id, number, machine_id}
This correctly expresses the uses relationship.

2.7 REDUCTION OF E-R SCHEMA TO TABLES

E-R database schema can be a collection of tables. For each entity set and for each relationship set, there is unique table. Each table has multiple columns; each of which corresponds to attribute of that set.

1. Representation of Strong Entity Set :
Let 'A' is a strong entity set with attributes $a_1, a_2, a_3, ..., a_n$.
'A' entity is represented by a table with n - columns, each of which correspond to attribute of 'A'. Each row in this table corresponds to one entity of the entity set 'A'.

2. Representation of Weak Entity Set :
Let 'A' be a weak entity set with attributes $a_1, a_2, ..., a_n$ and 'B' is the strong entity set on which 'A' is dependent. Primary key of 'B' is $b_1, b_2, ..., b_k$.
'A' can be represented by a table with one column for each attribute of the set $\{a_1, a_2, ..., a_n\} \cup \{b_1, b_2, ..., b_k\}$

3. Representation of Relationship Set :
Let R be a relationship set with attributes $c_1, c_2, ..., c_n$ which relates A and B. Primary key of A is $a_1, a_2, ..., a_k$ and primary key of B is $b_1, b_2, ..., b_m$.
Relationship set R can be represented by a table with columns corresponding to each of the attribute in the set
$\{c_1, c_2, ... c_n\} \cup \{a_1, a_2, ..., a_k\} \cup \{b_1, b_2, ..., b_m\}$.

4. Representation of Generalization :
There are two methods for transforming E-R diagram which includes generalization. Consider the E-R diagram using generalization.

Fig. 2.22 : E-R diagram with generalization

Method 1 : Create a table for the higher level entity set. For each lower-level entity set, create a table which includes a column for each attribute of the primary key of the higher-level entity set and one column for each attribute of that entity set.

For the E-R diagram, we have three tables.

Entity account with columns account_number, balance, entity savings_account with columns account_number and interest_rate.

Entity checkings_account with columns account_number and overdraft amount.

Method 2 : Create table for each lower-level entity which includes columns for each of the attributes of that entity set plus column for each attribute of the higher-level entity set.

For the E-R diagram we have two tables.

Entity savings-account with columns account_number, balance, interest_rate. Entity checking_account with columns account_number, balance, over-draft_amount.

5. Representation of Aggregation :

Create table for each entity set and relationship set. Consider the E-R diagram using aggregation.

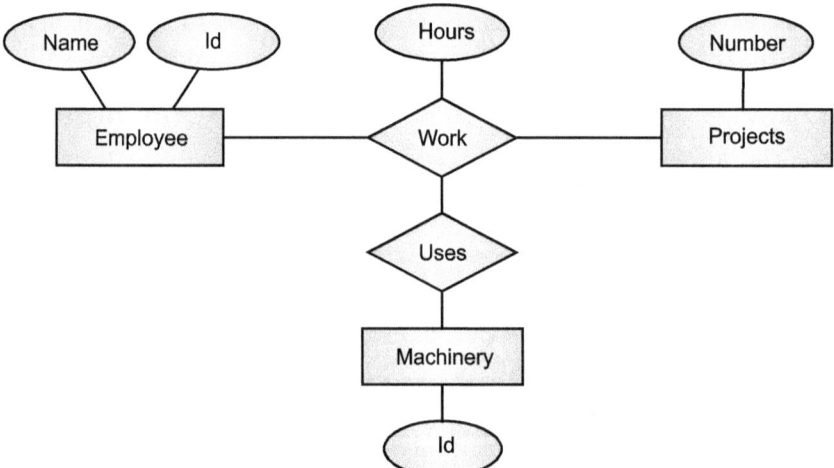

Fig. 2.23 : E-R diagram with aggregation

Employee table columns are emp_name, emp_id

Project table column is project_number

Machinery table columns are machine_id

Work table has columns : emp_id, project_number, hours.

Uses table has attributes emp_id, project_id, machine_id

2.8 SOLVED EXAMPLES

Ex. 1 : An information system is to be designed for keeping the records of Universe cup cricket tournament. In all, there are teams from 10 countries participating in the tournament. Each country sends 15 players and 4 other members. For players, the runs he scored and the number of wickets taken (so far) is to be recorded. For non-players, the role (manager, coach etc.) and the number of years of experience in that capacity is to be recorded. There are matches scheduled amongst and teams on several grounds on fixed dates. Each ground has a fixed seating capacity and a size. For 38 matches, 11 referees have been assigned duties. Every match will have 3 referees working for it. The performance of every player in every match is to be recorded in terms of the runs he scored and the wickets he took. Draw an E-R model of the system.

Design table layouts from E-R model.   **(Dec. 98, 16 Marks)**

Solution :

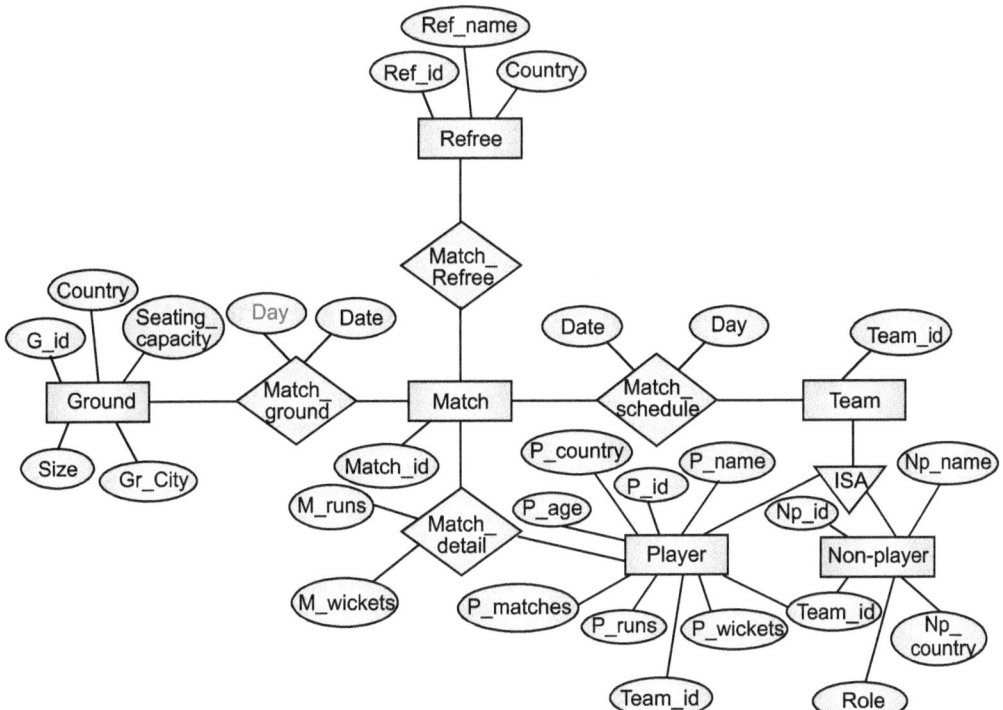

Fig. 2.24 : E-R diagram

Description of Entities in E-R diagram :
1. Match – {match_id} primary key match_id.
2. Ground entity set with attributes,
   {g_id, country, city, size, sealing_capacity}

Primary key – g_id
3. Referee entity set with attributes
   {ref_id, ref_name, country}
   Primary key – ref_id
4. Team entity set with attributes {Team_id}
   Primary key – Team_id
5. Player entity set with attributes,
   {P_id, Team_id, P_name, P_age, P_country,
   P_wickets, P_runs, P_matches,
   Primary key – {P_id, Team_id}
6. Non-player entity set with attributes,
   {Np_id, Team_id, Np_name, Np_country, role}
   Primary key – {Np_id, Team_id}.

Description of Relationship Sets in E-R Diagram :

1. Match-ground is relationship set that relates Ground and Match entities. This relation is many-to-many. Attributes of this relationship set are -
   {g_id, match_id}
2. Match-referee is relationship set that relates referee and match entities. This relation is many-to-many. Attributes of this relationship set are :
   {ref_id, match_id}
3. Match-schedule is a relationship set that relates Team and match entity sets. This is many-to-many relationship. Attributes of this set are -
   {match_id, team_id, day, date}
4. Match-detail is a relationship set that relates match and player entities.
   This is many-to-many relationship with attributes.
   {match_id, p_id, m_runs, m_wickets, team_id}.

Tables for each set.

(1) Match Table :

M_id
001
002

(2) Ground Table :

g_id	Country	Gr_city	Size	Capacity
101	India	Bombay	1000	20,000
201	Australia	Melbourne	2000	15,000

(3) Referee Table :

Ref_id	Ref_name	Ref_country
011	XYZ	England
021	PQR	India

(4) Player Relation :

Team_id	Player_id	Ply_age	Ply_name	Ply_runs	P_wick	Ply_match
1001	01	24	Sachin	8000	75	250
2001	01	34	Mark	6000	5	220

(5) Non-player Table :

Team_id	NP_id	NP_name	NP country	NP Exp	NP Role
1001	111	Gaikwad	India	2	Manager
2001	112	Kapil	India	1	Coach

(6) Match Ground :

M_id	Gr_id	Day	Date
001	10L	Monday	12/2/98
002	20L	Tuesday	13/3/98

(7) Match Referee :

m_id	Ref_id
001	011
001	021

(8) Match Schedule :

m_id	team_id	m_day	m_date
001	1001	Monday	12/3/98
001	2001	Monday	12/3/98

(9) Match Detail :

m_id	p_id	team_id	m_runs	m_wickets
001	01	1001	100	2
001	01	2001	57	0

Ex. 2 : Assume you are to compose database requirements of a wholesale dealer for audio, video consumer equipment from different manufacturers (brands). Customers are the various retail outlets (retailers). Wholeseller extends credit to old customer and special discounts are offered to new customers (retailers). You have to generate an E-R model for above DBMS application with the scope restricted to details (queries on) of customers (retailers), products stocked and their prices discounts and credits offered etc. **(Dec. 97, 8 marks)**

Solution : Description of Entities :
1. Consumer-equipment with attributes {equip_id}
2. Audio-equipment with attributes {a_id, equip_id, brand}
3. Video equipment with attribute {V_id, equip_id, brand}
4. Wholesale-dealer with attributes {dealer_id}
5. Customer with attributes {c_id, c_name}
6. New with attributes {c_id, c_name, discount}
7. Old with attributes {c_id, c_name, credit}

Description of Relationships :

Cons-whole with attributes {equip_id, dealer}

Equip-cost with attributes {equip_id, dealer, cust_id, cust_name}

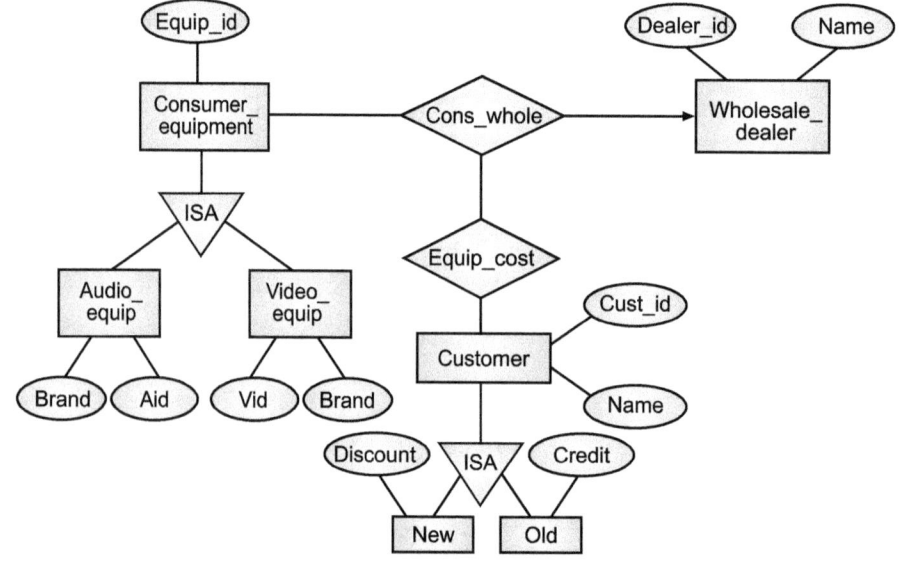

Fig. 2.25 : E-R diagram

Ex. 3 : A movie studio wishes to institute a database to manage their files of movies, actors and directors. The following facts are relevant. Each actor has appeared in many movies.
➢ Each director has directed many movies.
➢ Each movie has had one director and one or more actors.
➢ Each actor and director may have several addresses and telephone numbers.

Identify the entities and attributes.

Draw E-R diagram. **(May 94, 12 Marks)**

Solution :

Description of Entities and Relationships :
1. Actor is an entity with attributes {a_name, a_id }
2. Movie is an entity with attributes {m_id, a_name}
3. Director is an entity with attributes {d_id, name}
4. Act movie is a relationship with attributes {a_id, m_id}
5. Dir_Movie is a relationship with attributes {d_id, m_id}
6. Dir_add is a relationship with attributes {d_id, a_id}
7. Act_add is a relationship with attributes {a_id, add_id}
8. Act_address is an entity set with attributes {ad_id, city, street}
9. Dir_address is an entity set with attributes {add_id, city, street}

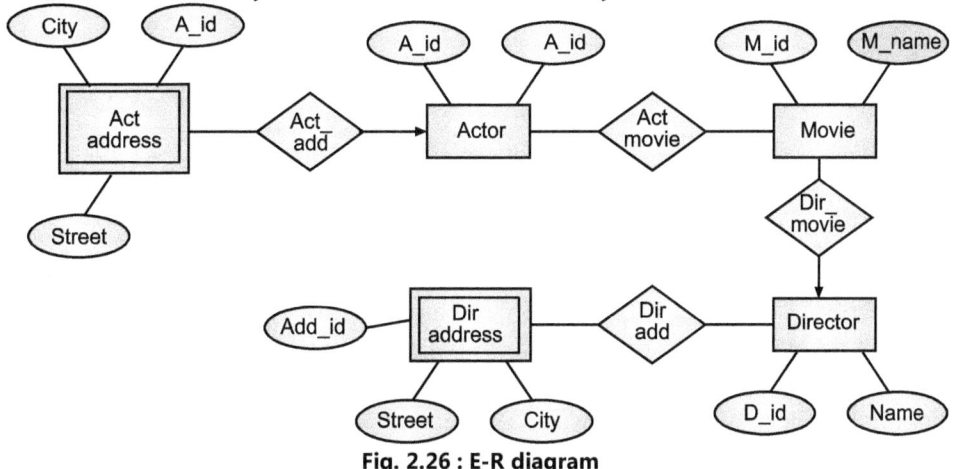

Fig. 2.26 : E-R diagram

Ex. 4 : Construct an E-R diagram for a car-insurance company that has a set of customers, each of whom owns one or more cars. Each car has associated with it zero to any number of recorded accidents. **(Dec. 2002)**

Solution :

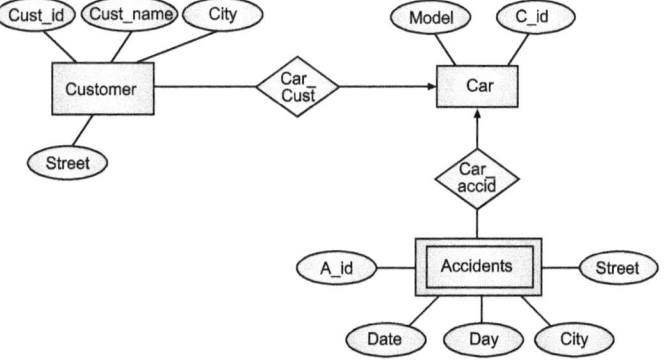

Fig. 2.27 : E-R diagram

Ex. 5 : Construct an E-R diagram for a hospital with a set of patients and a set of medical doctors. Associate with each patient a log of the various tests and examination conducted. **(May 2001)**

Solution :

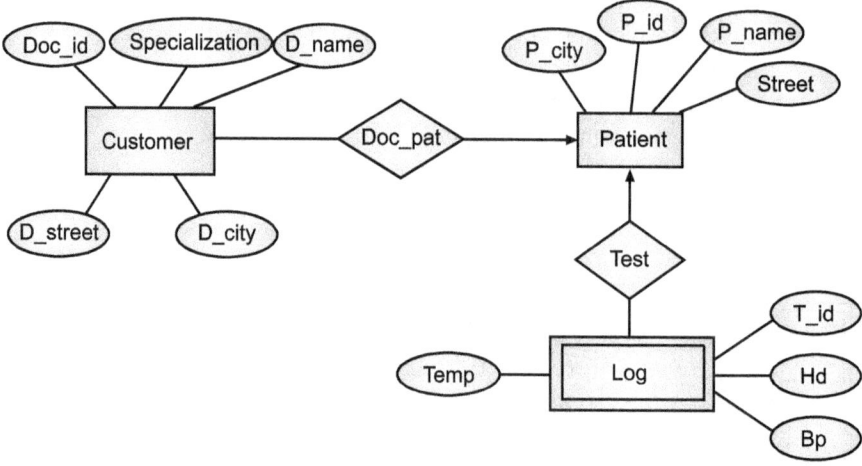

Fig. 2.28 : E-R diagram

Ex. 6 : Videobec is the leading corporation in the growing video rental business. It has the largest number of stores and prides itself on having the most comprehensive list of video movies and games. It also rents VCR and video cameras to its members. As a convenience, it repairs video equipment, the actual work being contracted out to a number of repair shops who reap 80% of repair charges. Each videobec's store is run by a manager and assistant manager who are full-time employees. In addition, each store hires its own part-time help who are paid on hourly basis. The membership priviledge is extended to customers for a period of 1 year and is renewable unless a member has habitually tardy in returning items borrowed. A member is allowed to rent upto 12 movies, 6 video games, 1 VCR and 1 video camera simultaneously. Movies and games can be returned to any store but VCR and video camera has to be returned to the store from which it was borrowed. Members have access to the on-line catalogue of titles and may reserve titles. A reserved title has to be picked before 6 p.m., after which time the reservation is automatically cancelled. Item are charged per day and borrowed items are to be returned before noon. Any late return bears a charge of 1 additional day. A discount of 20% is awarded on week days for all items rented and a total discount of 33% is also given on movie rentals on week days, when more than 3 titles are borrowed at a time. Movies are held by videobec in both VHS and Beta format. The catalogue of movies contain title of movie, producer, director, 2 leading actors, categories of movies number of cassette of available and charge per day. The video games catalogue contains the name of the game, game system and charger per day. Videobec carries multiple copies of same title and a store would have been assigned any number of copies of each title. A store that has more copies will return these at the end of each week to videobec's head office which redistributes them to appropriate stores. Draw E-R diagram.

Solution :

Description of Entities :

- Videobec is an entity with attributes name, address, e-mail, phone no., number of stores, number of movies, number of games, number of cameras, number of VCRs, number of members and number of repairs.
- Store entity set with attributes store_id, number of games, number of movies, number of cameras, number of VCRs, number of employees.

  Primary key : store_id

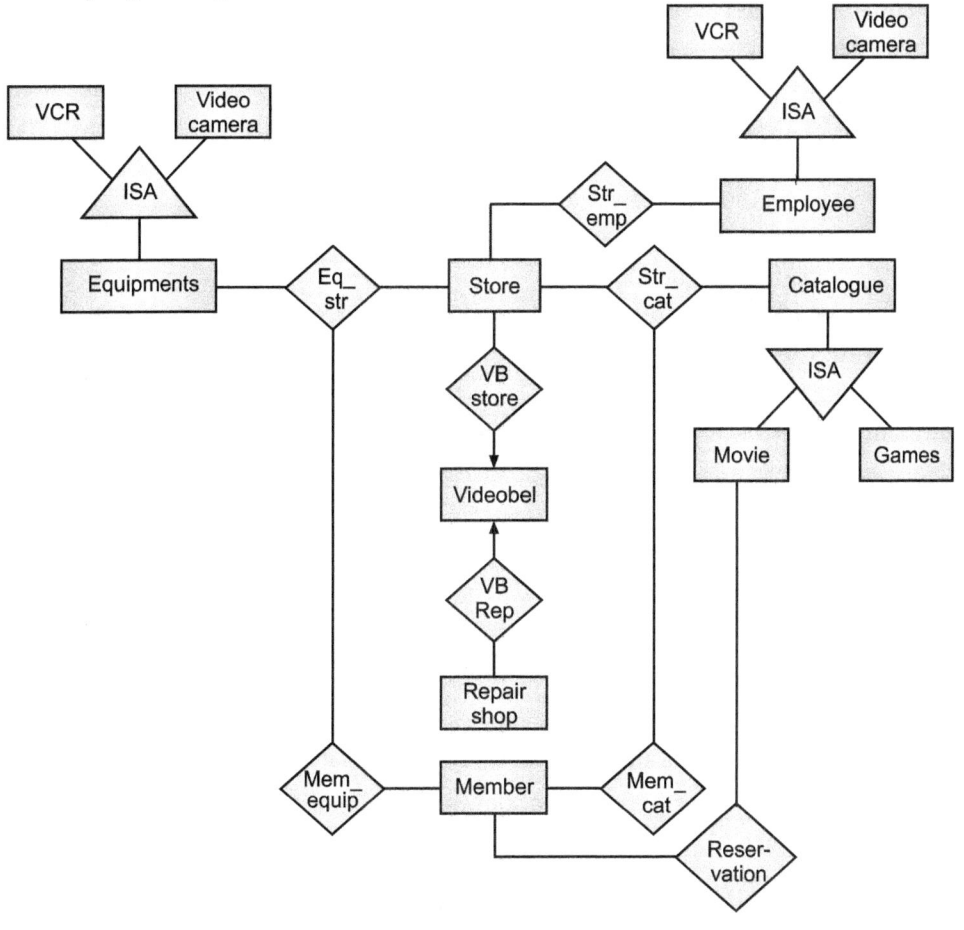

Fig. 2.29 : E-R diagram

- Catalogue entity set with attributes catalogue_id, number of movies and number of games.
  Primary key : catalogue_id
- The movies and games entity sets which we get as a result of generalization of catalogue entity set.
  Attributes of movie entity set are :
  movie_id, movie_title, movie_actor, movie_actress,
  movie_dir, number of copies, movie_type and charge-per-day.
  Primary key : catalogue_id, movie_id
  Attributes of game entity set are : game charge, game_id, game_system.
  Primary key : game_id, catalogue_id.
- Equipment entity set attribute is equipment_id
  Primary key : equipment_id
- VCR and Video Equipment are entity sets derived by generalization of Equipment entity set.
  Attributes of VCR are : VCR_id, VCR_company, and VCR_ent.
  Primary key – VCR_id, equipment_id
  Attributes of video equipment are -
  V_id, V_company and V_rent
- Employee entity set attributes are emp_id
  Primary key is emp_id
- Generalization of Employee set results in part-time and full-time.
  Attribute of these entity sets are id, name, salary, work.
- Member entity set attributes are :
  member_id, name, date, rem.

Description of Relationship Sets :
- Reservation entity set having attributes :
  movie_id, member_id
- Vbstore – is one-to-many relationship between videobec and store.
  Attributes are store_id.
- Vbrep – is one-to-many relationship between videobec and repair shop.
- Eq_str is many-to-many relationship between Equipment and store with attributes equip_id, store_id.
- Str_emp is many-to-many relationship between store and employee with attributes store_id and emp_id.

- Str_cat is many-to-many relationship between store and catalogue with attributes store_id and cat_id.
- Mem_equp is aggregation which relates eq_str, relationship and member entity with attributes num-mid, equip_id, store_id.
- Mem_cat is aggregation which relates str_cat and member entity.
  Attributes of this relationship set are store_id, cat_id, mem_id.

Ex. 7 : An insurance agent sells insurance policies to clients. Policies can be of different types such as vehicle insurance, life insurance, accident insurance etc. The agent collects monthly premiums on the policies in the form of cheques of local banks. Appropriate attributes must be assumed for various entities such as agents, vehicles, policy.

Draw an E-R model for above system. Your E-R model should take advantage of extended E-R notation where relevant. **(June 2000, 12 Marks)**

Solution :

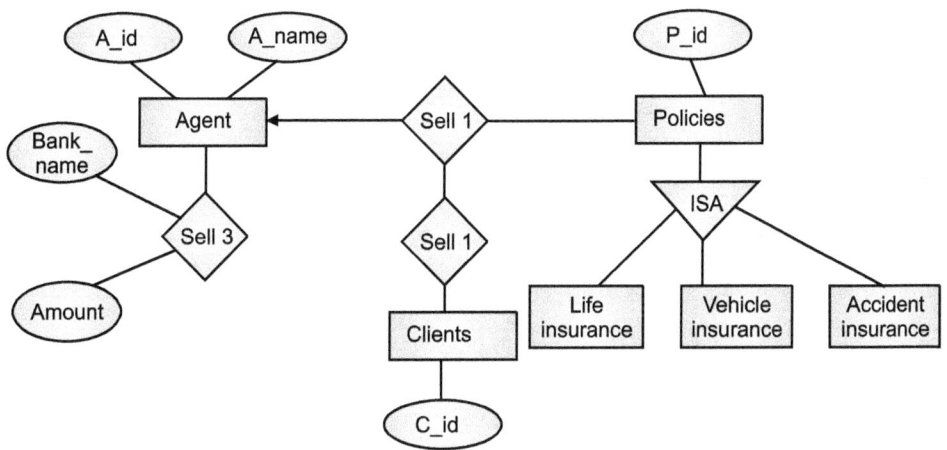

Fig. 2.30 : E-R diagram for Ex. 7

Ex. 8 : Following information is maintained manually in a library.

Books (Accession_number, name, authors, price, book_type, publisher)

Borrowers (membership_no, name, address,
  category, max_no of books that can be issued,
  Accession_number of books borrowed)

The following constraints are observed

- Each book has unique accession_number.
- A book may have more than one author.

- There may be more than one copy of a book.
- The category of borrower determines the max. Number of books that may be issued to borrower.

Identify the entities, relationship and draw E-R diagram.

Provide for issue and return of book, fine calculation and claiming of a issued book.

Solution : (Dec. 96, 8 Marks)

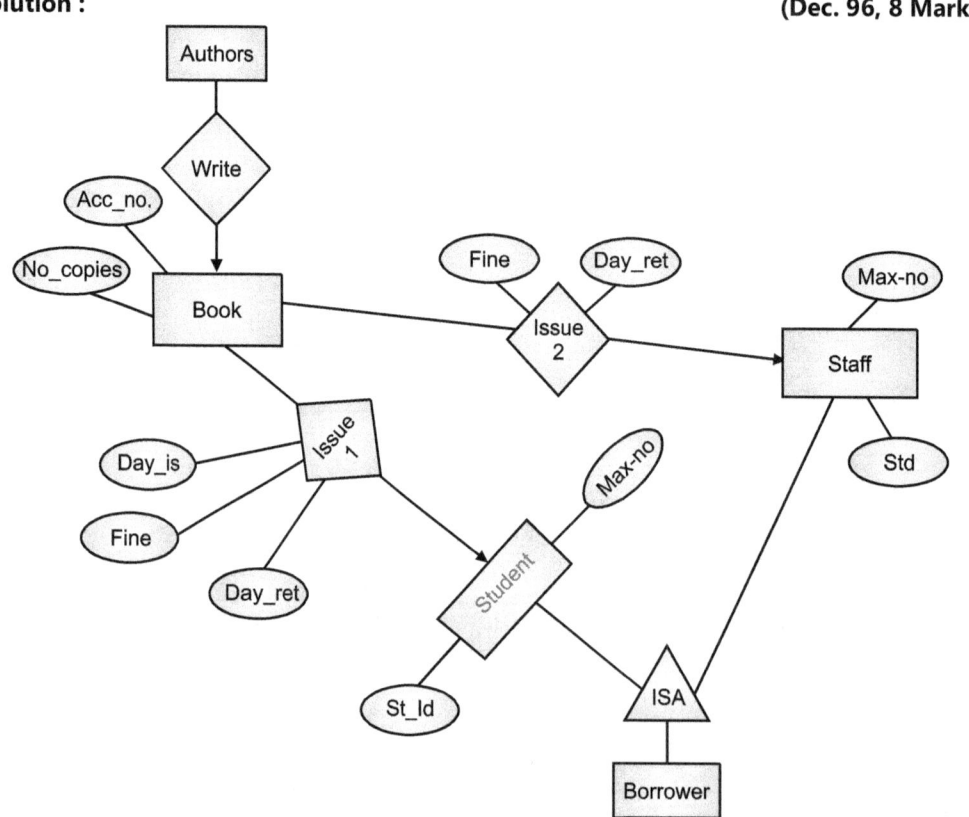

Fig. 2.31 : E-R diagram for Ex. 8

Ex. 9 : It is required to set-up medical record database system, given the following data
- Patients identification number name, address date of birth, blood group.
- Physician identification number name, address and their specialties
- Data about patients visit to physician like the date of visit, the medicine prescribed, the dose of each medicine, tests ordered at the visit, result of those tests, temperature, blood pressure.

Give an E-R diagram for the database.

Solution :

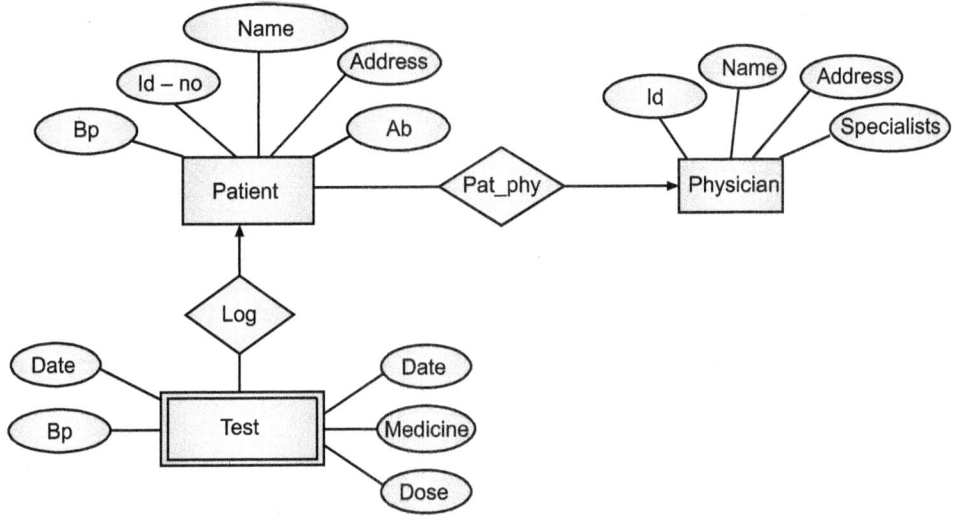

Fig. 2.32 : E-R diagram for Ex. 9

Ex. 10 : A Post office has few postmen who go everyday to distribute letters. Every morning post office receives a large number of registered letters. The post office intends to create a database to keep track of these letters.

➢ Every letter has a sender, an origin post office from where it was sent, a destination post office to which it is to be sent, a date of registration, date of arrival at destination post office, receiver and a status.

➢ Every sender has a name, an address.

➢ Every receiver has a name and an address.

➢ Every postman has a designated area where he delivers letters.

➢ The area consists of a set of streets under the jurisdiction of the post office.

➢ Every street consists of a set of buildings.

➢ Every building has a number and may be a name. It may be housing more than one family.

➤ The status of the letter can be not yet taken for delivery, delivered, addressee not available, address not known, addressee did not accept the letter, redirected to the new address of the addressee and sent to the sender.

Draw the E-R Diagram

Solution :

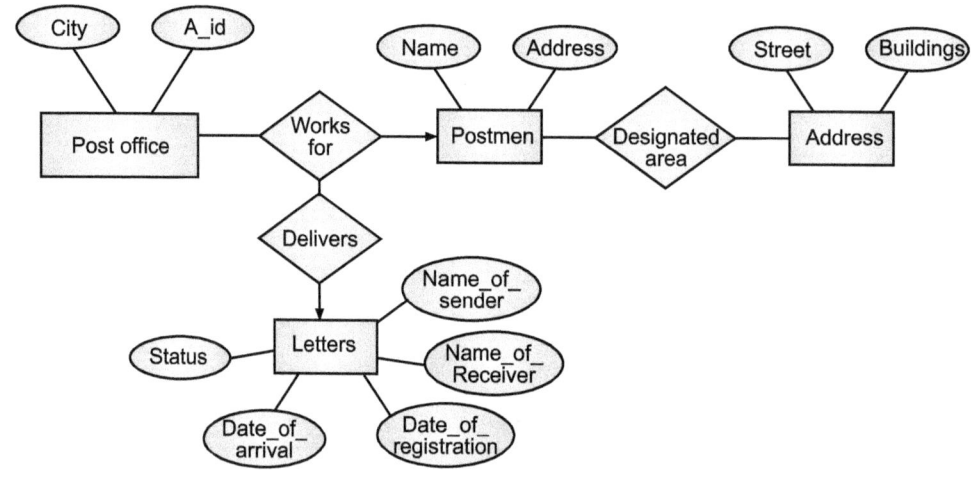

Fig. 2.33 : E-R diagram for Ex. 10

Ex. 11 : A university database contains information about professors and courses. For each of the following situations, draw an E-R diagram that describes it.

➤ Professors can teach the same course in several semesters, and only the most recent such offerings need to be recorded.

➤ Professors can teach the same course in several semesters, and each offering is to be recorded.

➤ Every professor must teach some course.

➤ Every professor teaches exactly one course.

➤ Every professor teaches exactly one course and each course must be taught by one professor.

➤ Now suppose that team of professors can teach certain courses jointly, but it is possible that no one professor in a team can teach the course. Model this situation, introducing additional entity sets and relationship sets if necessary.

Solution :

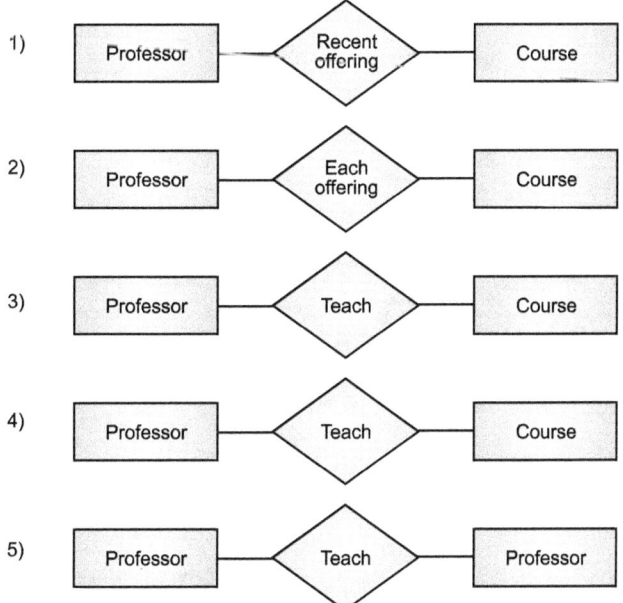

Fig. 2.34 : University database with courses and professors information

Ex. 12 : Consider the following information about a university database.

➢ Professors have an id, a name, an age, a rank and a research area.
➢ Projects have a project number, a funding agency, a starting date, and finish data and a budget.
➢ Under-graduate students have an id, a name, an age, a course.
➢ Each project is managed by one professor, called as Principal Investigator.
➢ One or more professors, called as Co-investigators, work each project on.
➢ When graduate students work on a project, a professor must supervise their work on the project.
➢ Graduate students can work on multiple projects in which case they will have different supervisor for each one.
➢ Departments have a department number, department name, and an office.
➢ Departments have a professor known as HOD.

Design and draw the E-R Diagram.

Solution :

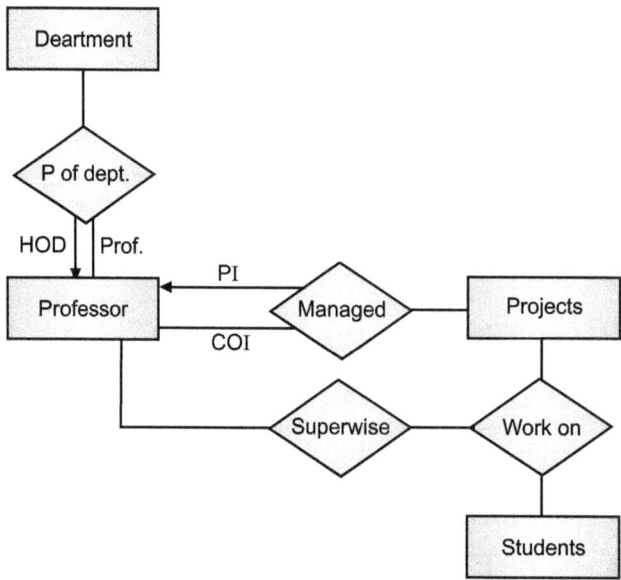

Fig. 2.35 : E-R diagram of university database

Ex. 13 : Draw an E-R diagram for a relational database that represents the current term enrollment at Pune University with following assertions. There are 2000 instructors, 4000 courses and 30,000 students.
- An instructor may teach none, one or more courses in a given term (average 2.0 courses).
- An instructor must direct the research of at least one student (average 2.0 students).
- A course may have none, one or two prerequisite courses.
- A course may exists even if no student has currently enrolled for that.
- All courses are taught by only one instructor.
- The average enrollment in E-R a course is 30 students.
- A student must select at least one course per term.   **(May 2002)**

Solution :

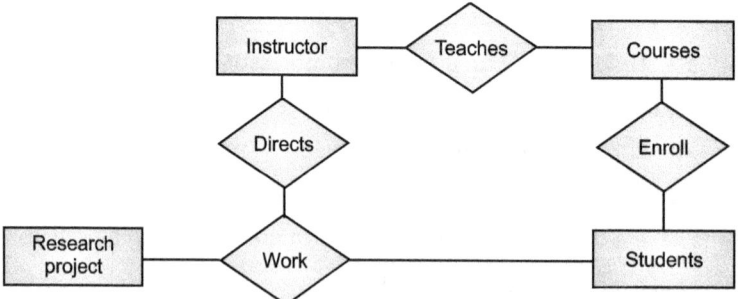

Fig. 2.36 : E-R diagram of team controller

Ex. 14 : The people's bank offer five types of accounts : Loan, Checking, Premium savings, Daily interest saving and Money market. It operates a number of accounts. Account can be joint, i.e. more than one client may be able to operate a given account.

Identify entities and draw E-R Diagram. **(Dec. 2004)**

Solution :

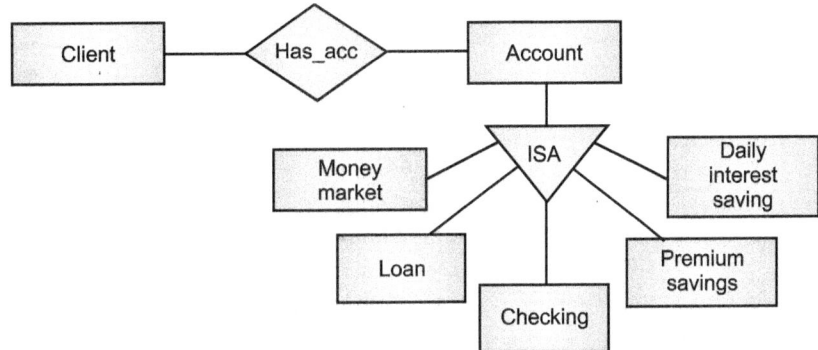

Fig. 2.37 : E-R diagram of five bank accounts

Ex. 15 : Design a generalization – specialization hierarchy for a motor – vehicle sales. The company sells motorcycles, passenger cars, vans and busses. Justify placement of attributes at each level of hierarchy. **(May 2003)**

Solution :

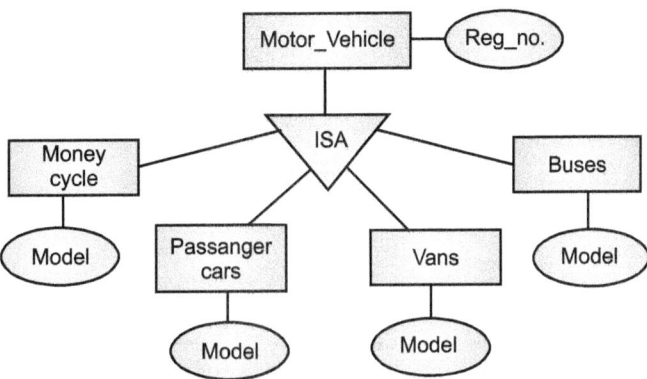

Fig. 2.38 : E-R diagram of motor vehicle

2.9 NETWORK MODEL

Network model is a record based data model. Data in network model are represented by collections of records and relationships among data are represented by links, which can be viewed as pointers. The records in the database are organized as collection of arbitrary graphs.

A record is in many respects similar to an entity in the Entity-Relationship (E-R) model. A link can be viewed as a restricted (binary) form of relationship in the sense of the E-R model.

As an illustration consider a database representing customer_account relationship in a banking system.

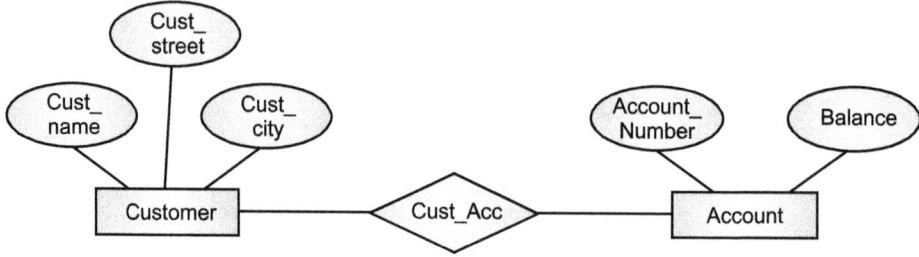

Fig. 2.39 : E-R diagram of banking system with customer_account relationship

There are two records in the database : customer and account.

Record customer is represented by the record type customer with fields.

Customer_name, Customer_street, Customer_city.

Record-type customer can be defined as follows :

    type customer = record
    cust_name : string;
    cust_street : string;
    cust_city : string;
    end

Record account is represented by the record type account with fields acc_no, balance

Record account can be defined as follows :

    type account = record
    acc_no : string;
    balance : integer;
    end

A sample database is given in Fig. 2.40.

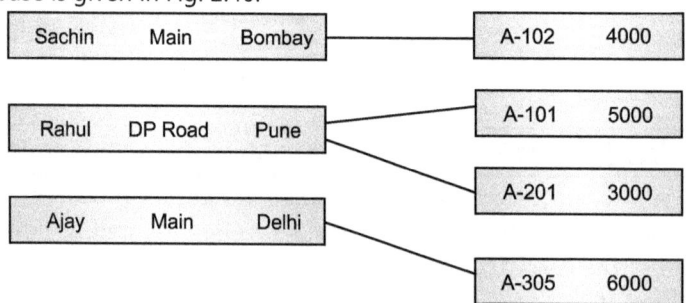

Fig. 2.40 : Network database

2.9.1 Data Structure Diagrams

A data structure diagram is a schema representing the design of a network database.

Such a diagram consists of two basic components :

1. **Boxes :** Which correspond to record types
2. **Lines :** Which correspond to links

A data structure diagram serves the same purpose as an E-R diagram. It specifies the overall logical structure of the database. E-R diagrams can be translated into corresponding data structure diagrams.

Example 1 :

Consider the E-R diagram given in Fig. 2.39.

In the given E-R diagram the entity sets customer, and account are related through a binary many-to-many relationship cust_acc, with no descriptive attributes.

This diagram specifies that a customer may have several accounts and an account may belong to more than one customer.

The corresponding data structure diagram is given in Fig. 2.41.

Customer				Account	
Cust_name	Cust_street	Cust_city	Cust_account	Account_no	Balance

Fig. 2.41 : Data structure diagram

Record type customer corresponds to entity customer. It includes three fields.

cust_name, cust_street, cust_city

Record type account corresponds to the entity account. It includes two fields – acc_no, balance

The relationship cust_acc has been replaced with link cust_acc.

If the relationship cust_acc were one-to-many from customer to account, then the link would have an arrow pointing to customer record_type.

Similarly, if the relationship cust_acc were one-to-one, then the link cust_acc would have two arrows :

One pointing to account record and one pointing to customer record_type.

Example 2 :
Consider the E-R diagram given in Fig. 2.42 :

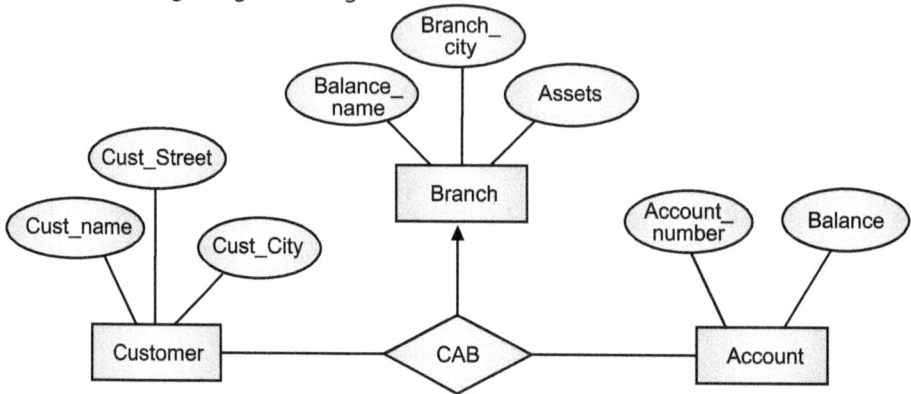

Fig. 2.42 : E-R diagram

The E-R diagram consists of three entities : Customer, account and branch. They are related through a relationship CAB with no descriptive attributes :

This diagram specifies that a customer may have several accounts, each located in a specific branch and that account may belong to several different customers.

Since a link can connect precisely two different record types, we need to connect these three record types through a new record type that is linked to each of them directly.

A new record type Rlink it is created. It may have no fields or have a single field containing unique identifier. This identifier is supplied by the system, and is not used directly by the application program. This new record type is also called as dummy (or link or junction) record type.

In the network data-structure for the given E-R diagram, Rlink record type is used to represent the CAB relationship. In addition to Rlink, three many-to-one links, custRlink, AcctRlink and BranchRlink are also a created.

If the relationship CAB had any descriptive attributes, they would become fields of the record type Rlink.

The network data structure diagram is shown in Fig. 2.43

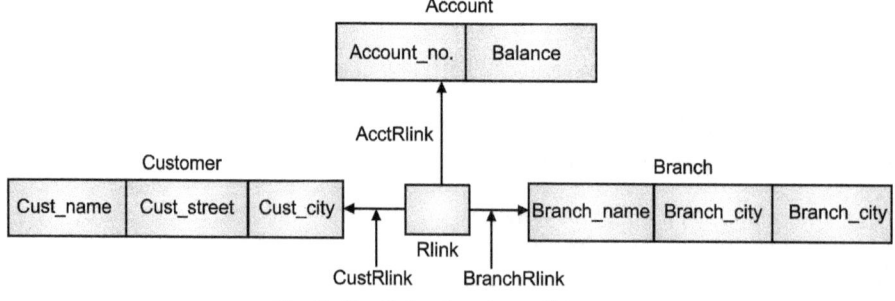

Fig. 2.43 : Data structure diagram

2.9.2 DBTG CODASYL Model

First database standard, called CODASYL DBTG was written in late 1960's by the database Task Group.

In the DBTG model only many-to-one links can be used. One-to-one links are represented as many-to-one links. Many-to-many links are disallowed to simplify the implementation.

Hence, according to DBTG CODASYL model, the E-R diagram shown in Fig. 2.44 can be transformed to a network data structure diagram on next page.

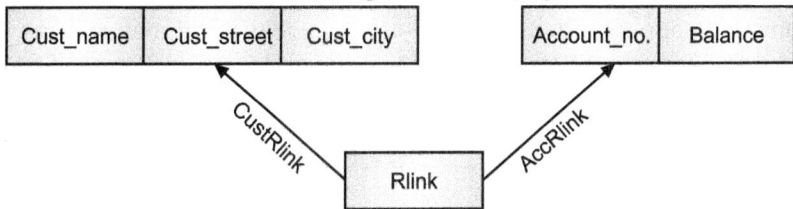

Fig. 2.44 : E-R diagram

The many-to-many relationship cust_acc is represented by two many-to-one relationships custRlink and AcctRlink.

A data structure diagram consisting of two record types that are linked together has a general form as shown in Fig. 2.45.

Fig. 2.45 : DBTG set

This structure is referred to in the DBTG model as a DBTG set. The name of the set is usually chosen to be the same as the name of the link connecting the two record types.

In DBTG set, the record-type A is designated as the owner of the set, and record type B is designated as the member (or child) of the set.

Each DBTG set can have any number of set occurence i.e. actual instances of linked records.

Fig. 2.46 given below shows three set occurences of corresponding to DBTG set shown in Fig. 2.46.

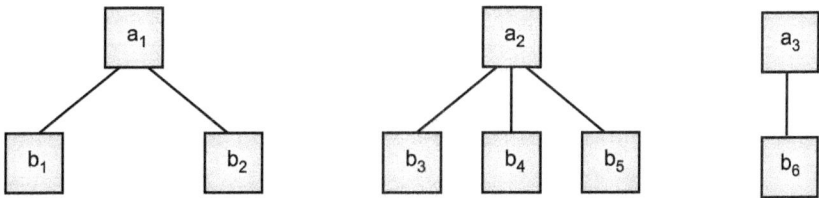

Fig. 2.46 : Three set occurrences of corresponding DBTG

Since many-to-many links are disallowed, each set occurrence has precisely one owner, and has zero or more member records. In addition no member record of a set can participate in more than one occurrence of the set at any point. A member record, however, can participate simultaneously in several set occurrences of different DBTG sets.

The data manipulation language of DBTG model consists of commands that are embedded in a host language. The commands enable the programmer to select records from the database based on the value of a specified field and to iterate over the selected records by repeated commands to get the next record.

The programmer is also provided with commands to find the owner of a set in which a record participates and to it iterate over the members of the set. And also the commands to update the database.

2.9.3 Implementation Techniques

Links are implemented in the DBTG model by adding pointer-field to records that are associated via link.

Consider the bank account and customer example. The account and customer are linked with many-to-one relationship. An account record can be associated with only one customer record. Thus using one pointer in the account record pointing to customer record, the relationship can be represented. However multiple pointers are required in the customer record to represent number of accounts of each customer.

Rather than using multiple pointers in the customer record, a ring structure can be used to represent the entire occurrence of DBTG set. In a ring structure, the records of both the owner and member types for a set occurrence are organised into a circular list. There is one circular list for each set occurence i.e. for each record of the owner type.

Fig. 2.47 shows the ring structure for the customer_account example.

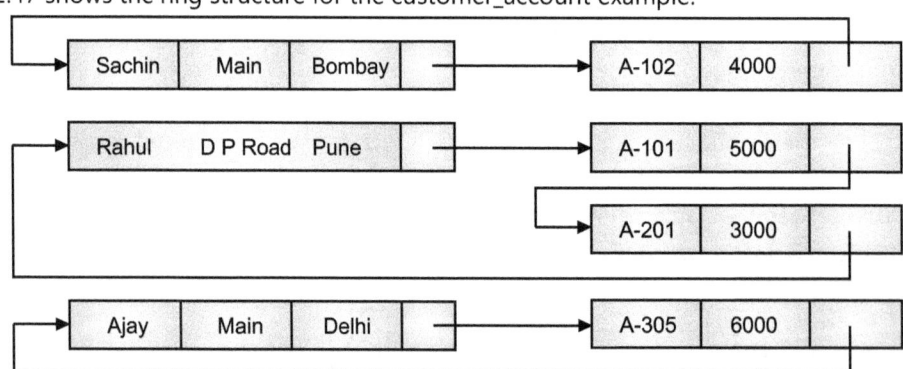

Fig. 2.47 : A ring structure

It is significantly hard to implement many-to-many links using pointers. Hence, DBTG model is restricted to many-to-one links.

2.10 HIERARCHICAL MODEL

Hierarchical model is a record based data model. It is similar to the network model. In this model, data and relationships are represented by records and links respectively.

It differs from network model in that; the records are organised as collections of trees rather than arbitrary graphs.

A hierarchical database consists of a collection of records that are connected to each other through links. A record in hierarchical model is similar to a record in the network model. Each record is a collection of fields (attributes), each of which contains only one data value. A link is an association between precisely two records. Thus, a link in hierarchical model is similar to a link in network model.

As an illustration consider a database that represents a customer_account relationship in a banking system, which is shown below Fig. 2.48 using E-R model.

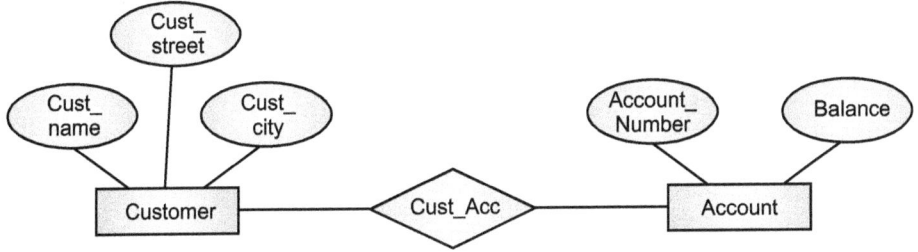

Fig. 2.48 : E-R diagram with customer_account relationship

The database represents two record types :

Customer and account.

A sample database is given in Fig. 2.49.

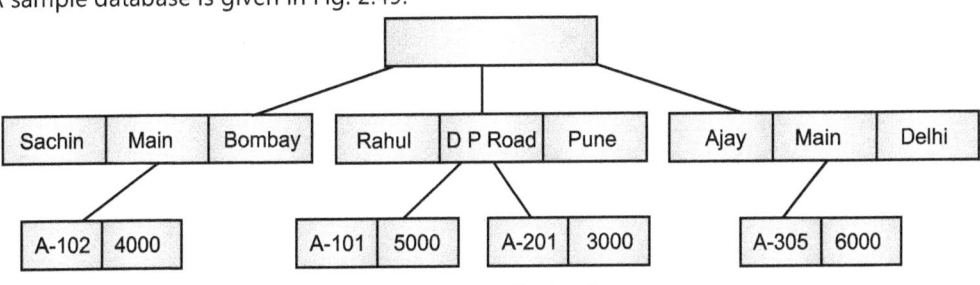

Fig. 2.49 : Sample database

In above given hierarchical database, all customers and accounts records are organised in the form of a rooted tree, where the root of the tree is dummy node.

A hierarchical database is a collection of such rooted trees, and hence, it forms a forest. Each such rooted tree is referred as a database tree.

2.10.1 Tree-Structure Diagram

A Tree-structure diagram is the schema for representing a hierarchical database.

This diagram consists of two basic components :

1. **Boxes :** Which correspond to record_types.
2. **Lines :** Which correspond to links.

A tree-structure diagram serves the same purpose as does an E-R diagram. It specifies the overall logical structure of the database.

A tree-structure diagram of hierarchical database is similar to the Data-structure diagram in the network model.

But the main difference is that : in the tree-structure diagram record types are organised in the form of a rooted tree, whereas in the data structure diagram, record types are organised in the form of an arbitrary graph. There can be no cycles in the tree-structure diagram. However, still the E-R diagram can be transformed into corresponding tree-structure diagram.

For example : Consider the E-R diagram given below in Fig. 2.50.

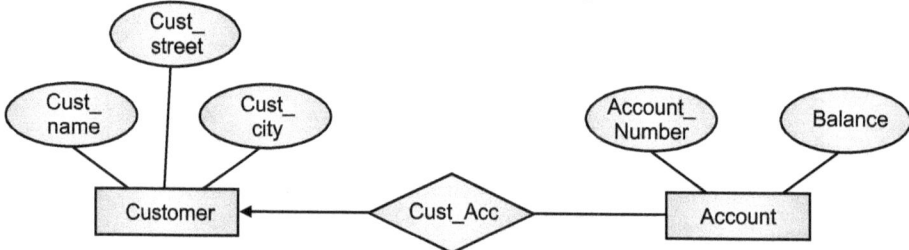

Fig. 2.50 : E-R diagram

It consists of the two entity sets customer and account related through a binary one-to-many relation cust_acc, with no descriptive attributes. This diagram specifies that a customer can have several accounts, but an account can belong to only one customer.

The corresponding tree-structure diagram can be given as :

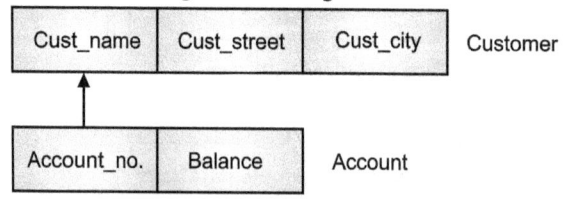

Fig. 2.51 : Tree-structure diagram

The record type customer corresponds to the entity set customer. It includes three fields : cust_name, cust_street, cust_city.

Similarly, account is the record type corresponding to the entity set account. It includes two fields : acc_no, balance.

The relationship cust_acc is replaced with the link cust_acc, with an arrow pointing to customer record type.

Only one-to-many and one-to-many relationship can be directly represented in the hierarchical model.

If the relationship is many-to-many, then the transformation from an E-R diagram to a tree structure diagram is more complicated.

An E-R diagram with many-to-many relationship is given in Fig. 2.52.

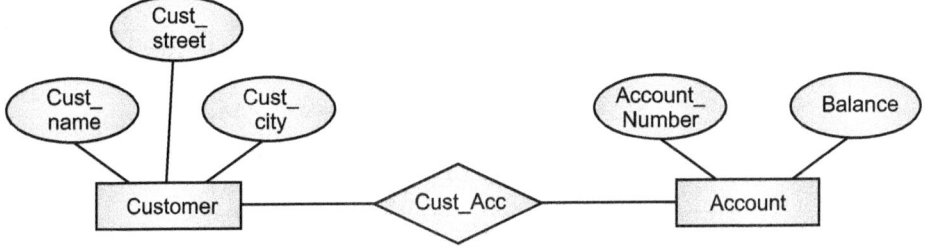

Fig. 2.52 : E-R diagram

To transform this E-R diagram to a tree structure diagram, we do the following :

1. Create two separate tree-structure diagram T_1 and T_2, each of which has the customer and account record types. In tree T_1 customer is the root; in tree T_2, account is the root.
2. Create the following two links :
   (i) Customer_account a many-to-one link from account record type to customer record in T_1.
   (ii) Account - customer a many-to-one link from customer record type to account record type in T_2.

The resulting tree-structure is given in Fig. 2.53.

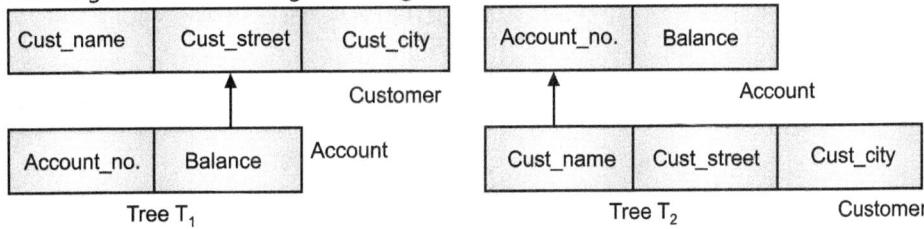

Fig. 2.53 : Tree-structure

The database schema is represented as a collection of tree-structure diagrams. For each such diagram, there exists one single instance of a database tree. The root of this tree is dummy node. The children of that node are instances of the appropriate record type. Each such child instance may in turn, have several instances of various record types, as specified in the corresponding tree-structure diagram.

A sample database corresponding to the tree-structure (T_1) diagram of Fig. 2.47 is shown below in Fig. 2.54.

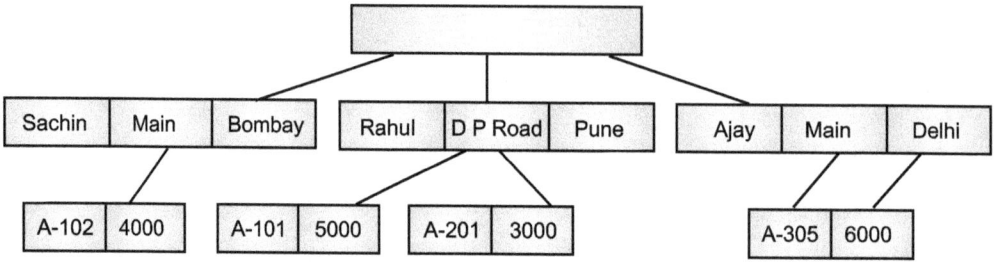

Fig. 2.54 : Sample database with tree-structure

A sample database corresponding to the tree-structure diagram T_2 of Fig. 2.53 is shown in Fig. 2.55.

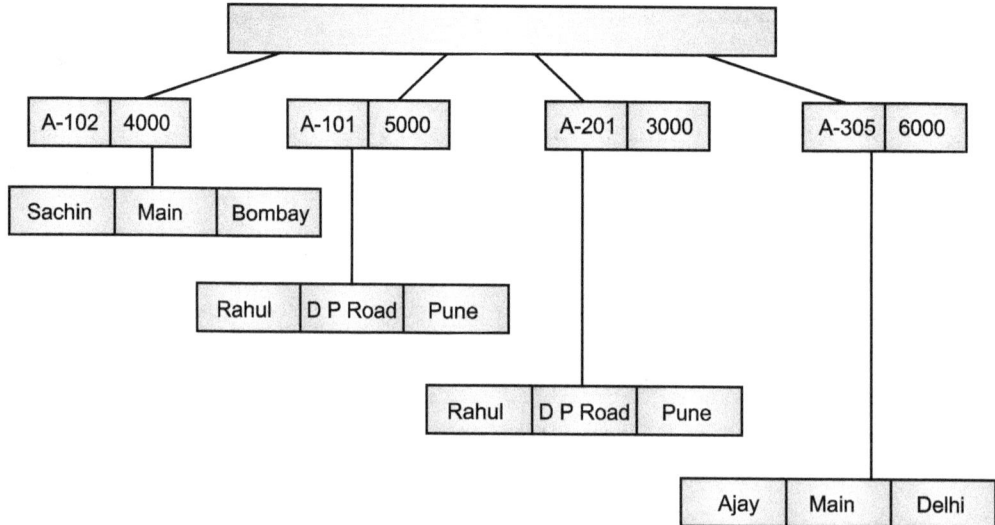

Fig. 2.55 : Tree-structure of Fig. 2.53

Consider the E-R diagram of Fig. 2.56

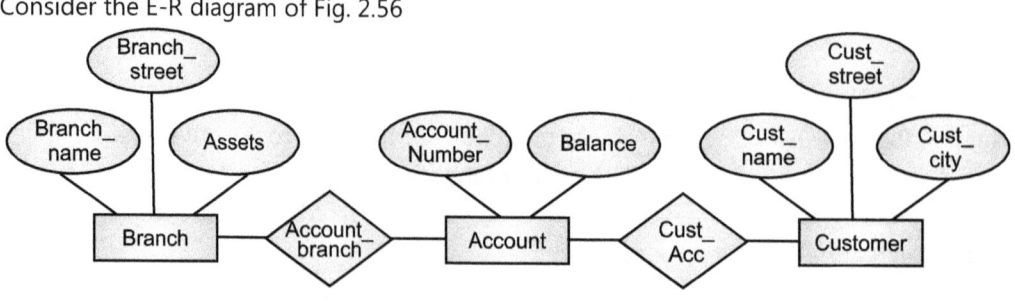

Fig. 2.56 : E-R diagram

A tree-structure diagram for the E-R diagram can be obtained using the algorithm which is described before as follows :

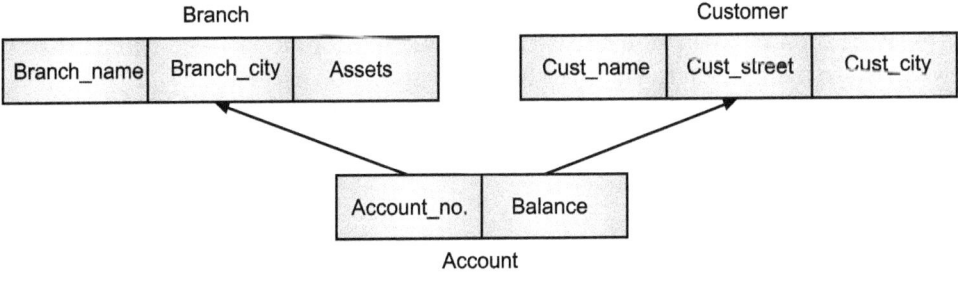

Fig. 2.57

This is not a rooted tree, since the only possible root can be record type account, but this record type has many-to-one relationships with both its children, and that violates our definition of a rooted tree.

It can be transformed to a rooted-tree form by replication the account record type, to create two separate trees as shown in Fig. 2.58.

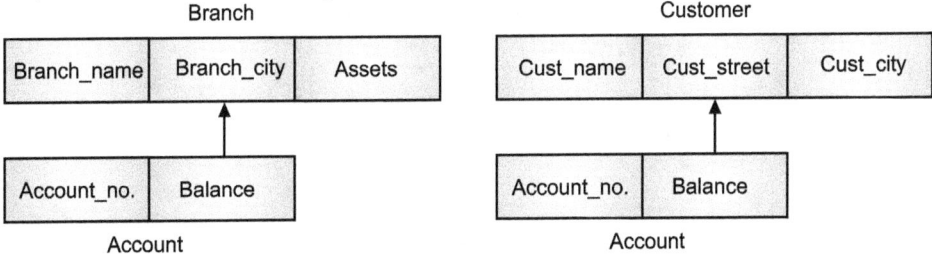

Fig. 2.58

2.10.2 Implementation Techniques

Record replication (For example : Replication of record type account in the above example) has two major drawbacks :

1. Data inconsistency may result when updating takes place.
2. Waste of space is unavoidable.

The solution to this problem is to introduce a virtual record. Such a record contains no data value; it does contain a logical pointer to a particular physical record.

When a record is to be replicated in several database trees, we keep a single copy of that record in one of the trees, and replace every other record with a virtual record containing a pointer to that physical record.

As an example, consider the E-R diagram of Fig. 2.50 and its corresponding tree structure diagram of Fig. 2.51, which comprises two separate trees each consisting of both customer and amount record types.

To eliminate data replication, we create two virtual record types : Virtual-customer and virtual-account. We then replace record type account with record type virtual-account in the first tree T_1 and replace record type customer with virtual-customer record in the second tree T_2. The association between virtual record and physical record is specified by a dashed line drawn between them. The resulting tree structure is shown on next page.

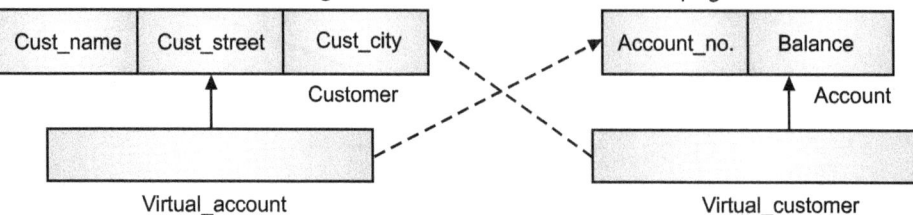

Fig. 2.59

An instance of a tree-structure diagram can be implemented using leftmost child and next-siblings pointers. A record has only two pointers. The left-most child pointer points to one child. The next-sibling pointer points to another child of the same parent.

This structure is shown in Fig. 2.60 for the database tree of Fig. 2.54.

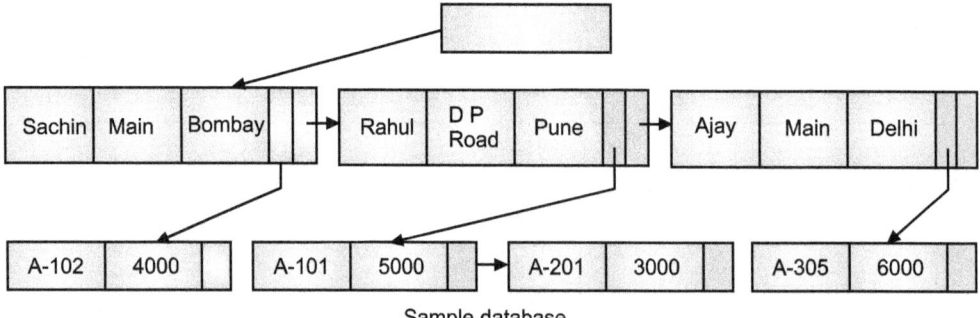

Sample database

Fig. 2.60 : Tree-structure of Fig. 2.54

Data manipulation language for hierarchical databases consists of commands that are embedded in a host language. It is similar to the data manipulation language for network databases, although there are differences in the facilities provided. The data manipulation language of the IMS database system is called DL/I.

2.10.3 The IMS Database System

The hierarchical model is significant because of the importance of IBM's IMS database system.

The IBM Information Management System is one of the oldest and most widely used database systems.

Since, the IMS databases have historically been among the largest, the IMS developers were among the first to deal with such issues as concurrently, recovery, integrity and efficient query processing.

The need for high performance transaction processing led to the introduction of the IMS fast path. Fast path uses an alternative physical data organisation designed to allow the most active parts of the database to reside in main memory and is fore runner of work in main-memory database systems.

REVIEW QUESTIONS ON INSTRUCTIONAL OBJECTIVES

1. Define following terms :
   (a) Association
   (b) Relationship
   (c) Aggregation
   (d) Specialization
   (e) Generalization
   (f) Entity set
   (g) Attribute.

2. Are weak entities necessary ? What is the distinction between a weak entity set and a strong entity set ? Can a weak entity set be converted to strong entity ?

3. Write a note on :
   (a) E-R model
   (b) Representation of E-R model in tabular form
   (c) Mapping constraints.

4. Draw an E-R diagram for following enterprises :
   (a) College
   (b) University
   (c) Library
   (d) Hospital
   (e) Fast food restaurant
   (f) Departmental store.

5. Reduce the E-R diagram in Example 4 to tabular form.

6. Show with your own appropriate examples the Entity Relationship. E-R model notation for cases stated.
   (a) Weak entity/strong entity relationship

(b) Multiplicity of relationship

(c) Specialization/generalization relationship

(d) Entities and their attributes

(e) Attributes of a relationship.

7. Define the terms : entity of attribute. Explain different types of attribute.

8. Explain different attribute types with respect to E-R model.

9. What is generalization ?

10. Define the concept of aggregation. Give two examples of where this concept is useful.

11. Explain the distinction among the terms primary key, candidate key, and super key.

12. Write a note on :

(a) E-R diagrams to database table design conversion.

(b) Hierarchical model.

13. Network model.

14. Compare Network and Relational data model.

15. Define following terms :

(a) View

(b) Database trigger.

16. How do you represent many-to-many relationships in :

(a) Network model ?

(b) Hierarchical model ?

17. Represent the following relationship in both models :

A teacher teaches many subjects. A subject may be shared by more than one teacher for teaching.

18. Explain the hierarchical data model and explain the virtual record in the context of implementation of hierarchical databases. Describe a way of mapping many-to-many relationships using virtual records.

19. What is DBTG set ? Explain why a member record of a set occurrence cannot participate in more than one occurrence of the set at any point.

20. What is meant by pinned record ? Describe how insertion and deletions of database records is implemented in hierarchical model.

DATABASE MANAGEMENT SYSTEMS (T.E. IT) DATA MODELING

UNIVERSITY QUESTIONS

1. There is a business that owns a softball complex. It organize league and tournament play over several seasons per year. The people associated with this business are represented as players or employees. An employee may also be a player. Most of these people play for teams that compose the leagues of the organization. These several leagues are not allowed to register into multiple leagues. These several leagues and teams, with each team playing several games each season. Once a team and a league have entered the organization, they are invited to participate in each season thereafter.
   Construct E-R Diagram. **(May 2004)**

2. Draw an E-R Diagram for Online Book Stores. Clearly mention your assumptions. **(Dec. 2003)**

3. Write a note on Hierarchical Data Model. **(April 2003)**

4. What do you mean by entity and entity sets ? **(Oct. 2000, May 07)**

5. Explain : Attributes. **(Oct 2000, Dec. 05, May 07)**

6. Write a note on :
   (a) Mapping Cardinalities. **((May 05 T.E. Comp.), Oct. 02, Oct. 03 (T.E.I.T.))**
   (b) Participation constraints. **(Oct. 03)**

7. Write a note on :
   (1) Candidate key **(April 01, Oct. 02)**
   (2) Candidate key **(Oct. 03, Oct 02)**
   (3) Foreign key **(April 01, Dec. 05)**

8. What do you mean by Dependency ? **(April 01, 03)**

9. Write a note on Existence dependencies. **(Oct. 03)**

10. What is specialization ? **(Oct 02)**
    (Oct. 2000, Nov. 04, Oct. 02, Oct. 03, Dec. 06)

12. Write a note on Generaliszation constraints. **(April 01, Oct.03)**

13. Write a note on aggregation. **(Dec. 04, Dec. 06)**

14. Explain : how the reduction of an E-R schema to tables will be done.
    (Dec. 05, May 04, Dec. 06)

15. Write how generalization will represent in tabular form. **(May 06)**

16. How following problems are handled with DBMS

(a) Data Isolation

(b) Data Redundancy

(c) Data Integrity **(Dec.10, May.12, Dec.13)**

17. Explain with example, how ER diagrams are converted to tables.

(Dec.11, May.13, Dec.13)

18. Explain need of following

(a) Foreign key

(b) Views

CHAPTER 3
RELATIONAL MODEL

3.1 Introduction

3.2 Basic Concepts

3.3 Codd's Rules

3.4 Relational Integrity

3.5 Views

3.6 Schema Diagram

- Review Questions on Instructional Objectives
- University Questions

3.1 INTRODUCTION

Record-based data model describes data at logical and view levels. Database in this model is structured in a fixed format records of several types. Each record type defines a fixed number of attributes and each attribute is of fixed length.

Record-based model is classified into following three categories :

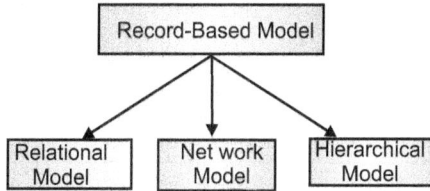

In this chapter we shall study Relational model. Database management systems based Relational data model are popularly called as RDBMS.

It uses a collection of tables to represent both data and relationship among those data.

Each table has multiple columns, each column represents an attribute and each row represents the relationship among the set of values (data).

What is a Relation ?

Lets consider the situation of a bank :

In a bank there are 50 saving account which belong to 60 customers. The following tables illustrate the above said data :

Table 3.1 : Account

acc_no	acc_type	balance
31001	saving	10,000
31002	saving	60,000
.	.	.
.	.	.
.	.	.
31009	saving	8,000
31000	saving	4,000

Table 3.2 : Customer

ss_no	name	city	phone_no
10924	Rohit Khanna	Pune	020-25432755
57951	Renu Patel	Mumbai	022-25452798
10702	Raj Kulkarni	Pune	020-25482767
10832	Neeta Joshi	Mumbai	022-25452859
.	.	.	.
.	.	.	.
.	.	.	.
67890	Ashwini R.	Pune	020-26442755

Table 3.3 : Account_customer

acc_no	ss_no
31001	57951
31002	10702
.	.
.	.
.	.
31049	10702
31050	10832

Thus, we can organize the data in the form of set of tables.

Relational model follows this method of organizing the data. A database in a relational database is essentially a collection of two-dimensional tables having a set of rows and columns. These tables are called as relations in this context. The rows of the table are called tuple.

To summarize we can say :

Relations represent facts describing a set of real world entities. In a relation, we represent one entity per row and one attribute per column. The table name and column name are used to help in interpreting the meaning of the values in each row of the relation.

3.2 BASIC CONCEPTS

Attributes : Attribute is the name of a column in a table.

The attributes of relation Account are acc_no, acc_type, balance. The numbers of attributes of a relations is called as arity (or degree or order) of the relation.

No two attributes of a relation can have same name.

Domain : Domain (D) is the set of values of the same data type.

Domain of an attribute is defined as the set of allowable values for the attribute.

Domain is a set having "homogeneous" members and it is conceptually similar to the data type concept in programming languages.

According to the set of values, domain is classified into four categories :

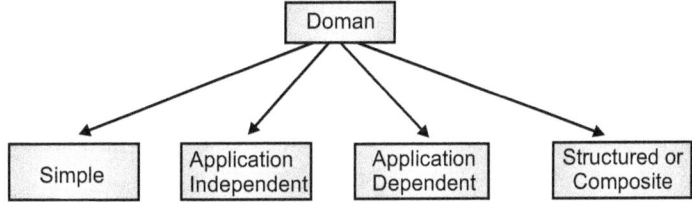

Domain (D) is said to be simple if all its elements are non-decomposable.

Application Independent or Atomic domain is the general set of integers, real numbers or character strings.

Application Dependent domain is having the values permitted in the database.

Structured or Composite domain can be specified as a set consisting of non-atomic values.

For example : Attribute address which specifies street, city.

It is possible that several attributes in a relation can have same domain.

Tuple : Every row of a relation is called as tuple.

Tuple is comparable to a record in a conventional file processing systems and an entity in E-R model. It is defined as 'an ordered set of attributes'.

Number of tuples in an relation is called as cardinality of the relation.

Tuples are generally denoted by lower-case letters r, s, t, ... of alphabet.

An n-tuple t (having n attributes) can be represented as t ($a_1, a_2, ..., a_n$) where a_i is a value of ith attribute in tuple t. In tuple representation, the order of attributes is significant and fixed.

Relation : Relation is a collection of homogeneous tuples.

A relation with n attributes is a subset of Cartesian Product of domains of those attributes.

Consider the Account relation in Table 3.1 with attributes : (acc_no, acc_type, balance).

Domain of acc_no is {31001, 31002, 31003, ..., 31049, 31050}

Domain of acc_type is {saving, current}

Domain of Balance is {10000, 60000, ..., 4000, 8000}

Relation Account is subset of Cartesian Product of domains of all these attributes.

Relation has two parts :
1. Relation schema
2. Tuples

Properties of Relation :

A relation has following properties :
- The relation has a name that is distinct from all other relation names.
- Each cell of the relation contain exactly one atomic single value.
- Each attribute has a distinct name.
- The values of an attribute are no duplicate tuples.
- The order of attributes has no significance.
- The order of tuples has no significance.

Intension and Extension : The structure of relation together with a specification of the domains and any other restriction on possible values, is called its intension, which is usually fixed unless the meaning of the relation is changed to include additional attributes. The tuples are called the extension (or state) of the relation which changes over time.

Degree : The degree of a relation is the number of attributes it contains.

A relation with only one attribute would have a degree of one is called an Unary Relation, A relation with two attributes is called a Binary Relation and with n attributes is called an n-ary relation.

Cardinality : The cardinality of relation is the number of tuples it contains.

The cardinality is the property of the extension of the relation and is determined from the particular instance of the relation at any given moment.

Relation Schema : It defines the set of attributes of that relation. It can be represented as R-schema ($A_1, A_2, A_3, ..., A_n$) where the domain of each attribute A_i is D_i and the relation R over the set of attributes R-schema is denoted as R (R-schema) and R (R-schema) $\subseteq D_1 \times D_2 \times D_3, ..., \times D_n$.

The Account relation in Table 3.1 can be represented as Account (Account_schema), were Account_schema (acc_no, acc_type, balance).

Relational Database : A collection of normalized relations with distinct relation names is called as relational database.

Relational Database Schema : A set of relation schemas, each with distinct name is called as relational database.

NULL Value : Null Value indicates that the value for corresponding attribute is either not available or not applicable.

It is distinct from empty character string and it is distinct from zero or any other number.

Relational Keys :

Super Key : An attribute, or a set of attributes, that uniquely identifies a tuple in within a relation is called as super key.

A super key uniquely identifies each tuple within a relation. However, a super key may contain additional attributes that are not necessary for unique identification.

Candidate Key : A super key such that no proper subset is a super key (minimal super key) within a relation is called as candidate key.

A candidate key K for a relation R has two properties :

- **Uniqueness :** In each tuple of R, the values of K uniquely identify that tuple.
- **Irreducibility :** No proper subset of k has the uniqueness property.

There may be several candidate keys for a relation.

When the key consists of more than one attribute, we call it a composite key.

Primary Key : The candidate key that is selected to identify tuples uniquely within the relation is called as primary key.

The candidate key that is not selected to be primary key is called as **alternate Key.**

Foreign Key : An attribute, or a set of attributes, within one relation that matches the candidate key of some relation is called as foreign key.

3.3 CODD'S RULES

In 1985 Codd proposed an informal set of twelve rules by which a database could be evaluated to see how relational it is. Very few commercial databases exist which meet or satisfy all twelve rules.

All twelve rules are built on the following foundation rule RULE 0.

Rule 0 : Any truly relational database must be manageable entirely through its own relational capabilities.

Rule 1 : The Information Rule

All information in a relational database is represented explicitly at the logical level and in exactly one way – by values in tables.

In simple terms this means that if an item of data doesn't reside in a table in the database then it doesn't exist. This can be extended to the point where even such information as table, view and column etc. should be contained somewhere in table form.

Rule 2 : The Rule of Guaranteed Access

Each and every datum in relational database is guaranteed to be logically accessible by restoring to a combination of table name, primary key value and column value.

If a database conforms to Rule 2, every atomic value should be easily retrievable.

Rule 3 : The Systematic Treatment of NULL Values

Null Values are supported in a fully relational DBMS for representing missing information in a systematic way, independent of data type.

Rule 4 : The Database Description Rule

The description of the database is held and maintained using the same logical structures used to define the data, thus allowing users with appropriate authority to query such information in the same ways and using the same language as they would query any other data in database.

Rule 4 states that there must be a data dictionary within the RDBMS that is constructed of tables and/or views that can be examined using SQL.

Rule 5 : The Comprehensive Sub Language Rule

There must be at least one language whose statements can be expressed as character strings conforming to some well defined syntax, that is comprehensive in supporting the following :

- Data definition
- View definition
- Data manipulation
- Integrity constraint
- Authorization
- Transaction boundaries.

This means that the RDBMS must be completely manageable through its own dialect of SQL.

Rule 6 : The View Updating Rule

All views that can be updated in theory can be updated by the system.

Rule 7 : The Insert And Update Rule

The capability of handling a base relation, or in fact a derived relation, as a single operand must hold good for all retrieve, update, delete, and insert activity.

Rule 8 : The Physical Independence Rule

User access to the database, via terminal monitors or application programs, must remain logically consistent whenever changes to the storage representation, or access methods to the data, are changed.

Rule 9 : The Logical Data Independence Rule

Application programs and terminal activities must remain logically unimpaired whenever information preserving changes of any kind, that are theoretically permitted, are made to the base table.

Rule 10 : Integrity Independence Rule

All integrity constraints defined for a database must be definable in the language referred to in Rule 5 and stored in the database as data in tables.

The following integrity rules should apply to every relational database :
- Entity Integrity : No component of a primary key can have missing values.
- Referential Integrity : For each distinct foreign key value there must exist a matching primary key value in the same domain.

Rule 11 : Distribution Rule

An RDBMS must have distribution independence.

It states that applications running on a non-distributed database must remain logically unimpaired that data if that data should then become distributed in the context of a distributed relational database.

Rule 12 : No Subversion Rule

If an RDBMS supports a lower level language that permits for example row-at-a-time processing, then this language must not be able to bypass any integrity rules or constraints defined in the higher level, set-at-a-time, relational language.

3.4 RELATIONAL INTEGRITY

1. Domain Constraint :

We have seen that a domain of possible values must be associated with every attribute. The standard domain types such as integer types, character types and date types are defined in SQL. Declaring an attribute to be of a particular domain acts as a constraint on the values that it can take. Domain constraints are the most elementary form of integrity constraints. They are tested easily by the system whenever a new data item is entered into the database.

It is possible for several attributes to have same domain.

Example :

customer_name and employee_name might have same domain : the set of all person names.

However, the domains of balance and branch_name are distinct. At the implementation level both customer names and branch names are character strings. But at conceptual level, customer_name and branch_name have distinct domains.

From the above discussion we can see that a proper definition of domain constraints allow us to test values inserted in the database and also permits us to test queries to ensure that the comparison made make sense.

The create domain clause can be used to define new domains.
Example :
> create domain dollars numeric (12, 2)
> create domain pounds numeric (12, 2)

The statement define the domain dollars and pounds to be decimal numbers with total 12 digits, two of which are placed after the decimal point.

An attempt to assign a value of type dollars to a variable of type pounds would result in a syntax error, although both are of the same numeric type.

Values of one domain can be cast to another domain. If the attribute A of relation r is of type dollars, we can convert it to pounds by writing

> cast r.A as pounds

SQL also provides
> drop domain

and,
> alter domain

Causes to drop or to modify domains that have been created earlier.

Check clause in SQL permits domains to be restricted in powerful ways that most programming language type system does not permit. Specifically, the check clause permits the schema designer to specify a predicate that must be satisfied by value assigned to a variable whose type is the domain.

Example :
> Create domain Hourlywage numeric (5, 2)
> Constraint wage_value_test
> Check (value>=4.00)

Which ensures that an hourly wage domain allows only values greater than 4.00.

The check clause can also be used to restrict a domain to not contain any null values.
> Create domain acc_no char (10)
> Constraint acc_no_null_test
> check (value not null)

The domain can be restricted to contain only a specified set of values by using the clause in clause.
> Create domain acc_type char (10)
> Constraint acc_type_test
> Check (value in ('checking', 'saving'))

2. Nulls :

Represent a value for an attribute that is currently unknown or is not applicable for this tuple. A null can be taken to mean the logical value 'unknown'. It can mean that a value is not applicable to a particular tuple, or it could mean that no value has yet been supplied. Nulls are a way to deal with incomplete or exceptional data. However a null is not the same as a zero numeric value or a text string filled with spaces; zeros and spaces are value but null represents the absence of values.

3. Integrity Rules :

Integrity Rules are the constraints or restrictions that apply to all instances of the database. There are two integrity rules :

I. Entity Integrity Rule :

In a base relation, no attribute of a primary key can be **NULL**.

By definition primary key is a minimal identifier that is used to identify tuples uniquely. This means that no subset of a primary key is sufficient to provide unique identification of tupels. If we allow a null for any part of primary key, we are implying that not all the attributes are needed to distinguish between the tuples, which contradicts the definition of primary key.

II. Referential Integrity Rule :

If a foreign key exists in a relation, either the foreign key value must match a candidate key value of some tuple in its home relation or the foreign key value must be wholly **NULL**.

4. Enterprise Constraints :

These are the additional rules specified by the users or database administrators of a database.

3.5 VIEWS

Base Relation : A named relation corresponding to an entity in the conceptual schema, whose tuples are physically stored in the database.

View : The dynamic result of one or more relational operations operating on the base relations to produce another relation. A view is a virtual relation that does not necessarily exist in the database but can be produced on request by a particular user, at that time of request.

A view is a relation that appears to the user to exist, can be manipulated as if it were a base relation, but does not necessarily exists in storage.

The contents of view are defined as a query on one or more base relations.

Any operations on the view are automatically translated into the operations on the base relation from which it is derived.

Views are dynamic, meaning that changes made to the base relations that affect the view are reflected in the view.

When user makes permitted changes to the view, these changes are made to the underlying relations.

Purpose of relation :

The view is desirable for following reasons :

- It provides a powerful and flexible security mechanism by hiding parts of the database from the view.
- It permits users to access data in a way that is customized their needs, so that the same data can be seen by different users in a different way at the same time.
- It can simplify complex operations on the base relations.

Updating views :

All updates to the base relation must be immediately reflected in all views that reference that base relation. Similarly, if a view is updated, then the underlying base relation should reflect the change.

However, there are restrictions on the types of updates that can be made through the view.

- Updates are not allowed through a view defined using a simple query involving a single base relation and containing the primary key or the candidate key of the base relation.
- Updates are not allowed through views involving multiple base relations.
- Updates are not allowed through views involving aggregation or grouping operations.

Following are the classes of views :
- Theoretically not Updateable.
- Theoretically Updateable.
- Partially Updateable.

3.6 SCHEMA DIAGRAM

A database schema, along with primary key and foreign key dependencies, can be depicted pictorially by the **Schema Diagram**.

- Each relation appears as a box, with attributes listed inside shown in Fig. 3.1 it and the relation name above it.
- If there are primary key attributes, a horizontal line crosses the box, with the primary key listed above the line.
- Foreign key dependencies appear as arrows from the foreign key attributes of the referencing relation to the primary key attributes of the referenced relation.

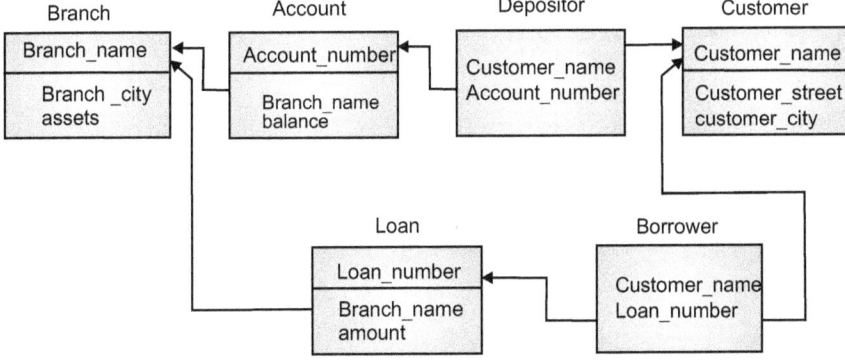

Fig. 3.1 : Schema Diagram

REVIEW QUESTIONS ON INSTRUCTIONAL OBJECTIVES

1. Discuss the following concepts in the context of relational model :
   (i) Relation
   (ii) Domain
   (iii) Attribute
   (iv) Tuple
   (v) Intension and extension
   (vi) Degree
   (vii) Cardinality.

2. Define the two integrity rules.
3. What is a view ? Discuss the difference between a view and a base relation.
4. Discuss the difference between primary key and foreign key.
5. What are the properties of relation ?
6. What is the difference between schema diagram and E-R diagram ?
7. Specify the twelve Codd's rules.

UNIVERSITY QUESTIONS

1. Write short notes on : Schema diagram. **(May 2003)**
2. Explain in Codd's rule and relational integrity. **(Oct. 2000, Dec. 2006)**
3. What are the principle components of Relational Model ? **(Oct. 02, Oct. 03)**
4. Explain Relational Data Structure. **(April 03, Oct. 03)**
5. What is the referential integrity ? **(Nov 04, May 05, Dec. 06)**
6. Explain referential integrity in SQL. **(Dec. 05)**
7. Write a note on :
   (i) Nulls **(Dec. 05)**
   (ii) Entity Integrity **(April 04)**
   (iii) View **(April 01, May 05, Oct. 03, Dec. 05)**
   (iv) Updating Views **(April 03, Dec. 05)**
8. Explain need of following:
   (a) Views
   (b) Primary Key
   (c) Foreign Key

CHAPTER 4
RELATIONAL DATABASE DESIGN

- 4.1 Introduction
- 4.2 Good Database Design Properties
- 4.3 An Example of Bad Design and its Consequences
- 4.4 Decomposition
- 4.5 Desirable Properties of Decomposition
    - 4.5.1 Loss-Less-Join Decomposition
    - 4.5.2 Dependency Preserving
- 4.6 Purpose of Normalization
- 4.7 Data Redundancy and Update Anomalies
- 4.8 Functional Dependency
- 4.9 Dependencies and Logical Implications
- 4.10 Normalization Using Functional Dependencies
    - 4.10.1 First Normal Form (1NF)
    - 4.10.2 Second Normal Form (2NF)
    - 4.10.3 Boyce - Codd Normal Form (BCNF)
    - 4.10.4 Third Normal Form (3NF)
    - 4.10.5 Solved Examples
    - 4.10.6 Comparison of BCNF and 3NF
- 4.11 Multivalued Dependency
- 4.12 Axioms for Functional and Multivalued Dependencies
- 4.13 Loss-Less and Dependency Preserving Decomposition
- 4.14 Normalization using Multivalued Dependency
    - 4.14.1 Fourth Normal Form (4NF)
- 4.15 Join Dependencies
    - 4.15.1 Project Join Normal Form (PJNF)
    - 4.15.2 Domain Key Normal Form (DKNF)
- • Review Questions on Instructional Objectives
- • University Questions

4.1 INTRODUCTION

A relation in a relational database is based on a relation schema, which consists of a number of attributes.

A relational database is made up of a number of relations and corresponding relational database schema.

This chapter deals with issues involved in design of database schema using relational model.

The goal of a relational database design is to generate a set of relation schema that allows us to store information without unnecessary redundancy and also to retrieve information easily.

One approach is to design schemas that are in an appropriate normal forms. The normal forms are used to ensure that various types of anomalies and inconsistencies are not introduced into the database.

4.2 GOOD DATABASE DESIGN PROPERTIES

A good database design must possess following properties :

1. **Content Preserving :** The design is content preserving if the original relation can be derived from the relations resulting from the design process.

2. **Dependency Preserving :** The relation design is dependency preserving if the original set of constraints can be derived from the dependencies in the output of the design process. The design is minimally dependency preserving if there are no extraneous dependencies in the output of the design process and the original dependencies cannot be derived from a subset of the dependencies in the output of the design process.

3. **Interrelation Join Constraint :** The relation is free from interrelation join constraints if there are no dependencies that can only be derived from the join of two or more relations in the output of the design process.

4.3 AN EXAMPLE OF BAD DESIGN AND ITS CONSEQUENCES

A relation schema to store the information concerning loans is given as :

Lending_schema = (branch_name, branch_city, assets, customer_name, loan_no., amount)

The relation lending is given in Table 4.1.

Table 4.1 : Lending relation

Branch_name	Branch_city	Assets	Customer_name	Loan_number	Amount
SBI	Bombay	4,00,000	Sachin	L - 15	10,000
ICICI	Pune	34,00,000	Rahul	L - 31	20,000
HDFC	Delhi	4,90,000	Raj	L - 29	1,50,000
Bank of India	Bombay	1,00,000	Ajay	L - 25	29,000
City Bank	Delhi	25,00,000	Anil	L - 69	3,00,000
BOM	Pune	32,00,000	Rahul	L - 93	10,000
HDFC	Delhi	4,90,000	Ramesh	L - 21	1,50,000
BOH	Aurangabad	20,000	Sachin	L - 51	20,000

Suppose that we wish to add a new loan to the database.

The loan is made by SBI to Sachin in the amount of 15,000 Rs. The loan_no. is L - 32.

In our lending relation we need to add the tuple with values on all attributes of lending-schema.

(SBI, Bombay, 4,00,000, Sachin, L - 32, 15,000)

Thus in general we must repeat asset and city data for a branch, for each loan made by that branch.

Suppose that we wish to update the data in the database. Suppose that SBI bank moves from Bombay to Madras. To update lending relation we must ensure that every tuple pertaining to SBI branch is updated, otherwise the database will show two cities for SBI branch which is undesirable.

Suppose that there is a branch ICICI which doesn't have any loan at that branch.

We cannot represent this branch information in the lending relation.

Tuples in lending relation require values for loan_no., amount, and customer_name. Otherwise null values can be inserted for these attributes, but the null values are difficult to handle.

Thus the above database design has following undesirable properties.

1. **Repetition of Information or Redundancy :**

The aim of the database system is to reduce the redundancy i.e. the information stored must not be repeated. Repetition of information wastes space. But the above database design repeats information for asset and city attributes.

2. **Various Types of Anomalies :**

Multiple copies of same data result in update anomalies.

The above database results in insertion anomaly.

(**For example :** Insertion of loan tuple).

It results in deletion anomaly. **For example :** if user wants to delete a loan tuple, and the branch_name in that tuple will also get deleted. If that is the only loan made by that branch, the database will not lose that branch information.

3. **Inability to Represent Certain Information :**

For example : cannot store branch information which has made no loan

4.4 DECOMPOSITION

The above mentioned problems can be solved using decomposition.

Decomposition is defined as :

The decomposition of a relation schema,

$$R = (A_1, A_2, ..., A_n)$$ its replacement by a set of relation schemas $\{R_1, R_2, ..., R_n\}$ such that,

$$R_i \subseteq R \text{ for } 1 \leq i \leq n \text{ and}$$

$$R_1 \cup R_2 \ ...... \ \cup R_n = R.$$

A relation R can be decomposed into a collection of relation schema $\{R_1, R_2, ..., R_n\}$ to eliminate some of the anomalies contained in the original relation R.

Example : Consider the relation_schema for relation lending and the relation lending shown in Table 4.1.

Lending schema = (branch_name, city, asset, customer_name, loan_no., amount)

The lending_schema is decomposed into the following two schemas.

Branch_cust_schema = (branch_name, branch_city, assets, customer_name)

Customer_loan_schema = (customer_name, loan_no., amount)

The new relations are constructed using lending relation as follows :

Branch_customer = $\pi_{branch\_name, branch\_city, assets, customer\_name}$ (lending)

Customer_loan = $\pi_{customer\_name, loan\_no., amount}$ (lending)

Two relations are shown in Tables 4.2 and 4.3.

Table 4.2 : Branch_Customer Relation

Branch_name	Branch_city	Assets	Customer_name
SBI	Bombay	4,00,000	Sachin
ICICI	Pune	34,00,000	Rahul
HDFC	Delhi	4,90,000	Raj
Bank of India	Bombay	1,00,000	Ajay
City Bank	Delhi	25,00,000	Anil
BOM	Pune	32,00,000	Rahul
HDFC	Delhi	4,90,000	Ramesh
BOH	Aurangabad	20,000	Sachin

Table 4.3 : Customer_loan relation

Customer_name	Loan_number	Amount
Sachin	L - 15	10,000
Rahul	L - 31	20,000
Raj	L - 29	1,50,000
Ajay	L - 25	29,000
Anil	L - 69	3,00,000
Rahul	L - 93	10,000
Ramesh	L - 21	1,50,000
Sachin	L - 51	20,000

We can reconstruct the original lending relation as follows :

branch_customer ⋈ cost_loan

The result of this is shown in Table 4.4. If this relation (branch_customer ⋈ customer_loan) is compared with lending relation, we can observe that,

- Every tuple that appears in lending relation appears in branch_customer ⋈ customer_loan.
- There are tuples in branch_customer ⋈ customer_loan relation which are not there in lending relation.

branch_customer ⋈ customer_loan relation has the following additional tuples :

(SBI, Bombay, 4,00,000, Sachin, L - 51, 20,000)

(ICICI, Pune, 3,40,000, Rahul, L - 93, 10,000)

(BOM, Pune, 3,20,000, Rahul, L - 31, 20,000)

(UTI, Aurangabad, 20,000, Sachin, L - 15, 10,000).

Table 4.4

Branch_name	Branch_city	Assets	Customer_name	Loan_number	Amount
SBI	Bombay	4,00,000	Sachin	L - 15	10,000
SBI	Bombay	4,00,000	Sachin	L - 51	20,000
ICICI	Pune	34,00,000	Rahul	L - 31	20,000
ICICI	Pune	34,00,000	Rahul	L - 93	10,000
HDFC	Delhi	4,90,000	Raj	L - 29	1,50,000
BOI	Bombay	1,00,000	Ajay	L - 25	29,000
City Bank	Delhi	25,00,000	Anil	L - 69	3,00,000
BOM	Pune	32,00,000	Rahul	L - 31	20,000
BOM	Pune	32,00,000	Rahul	L - 93	10,000
HDFC	Delhi	4,90,000	Ramesh	L - 21	1,50,000
BOH	Aurangabad	20,000	Sachin	L - 15	10,000
BOH	Aurangabad	20,000	Sachin	L - 51	20,000

Consider the query : Find the branch name of all branches that have made loan in an amount less than Rs. 15,000.

The result of this query using lending relation is SBI, BOM.

The result of same query using branch_customer ⋈ customer_loan relation is : (SBI, ICICI, BOM, BOH) i.e. two additional branch_names are there.

Suppose that a customer is having several loans from different branches, we cannot tell which loan belongs to which branch i.e. we are not able to represent in the database information about which customers are borrowers from which branch.

From the above two cases it is clear that the given decomposition results in bad database design. It results in loss of information and repetition of information.

Consider another database decomposition.

Branch_loan_schema = (branch_name, branch_city, assets)

Loan_info_schema = (branch_name, customer_name, loan_no., amount)

4.5 DESIRABLE PROPERTIES OF DECOMPOSITION

A relation schema R can be decomposed into a collection of relation schemas to eliminate anomalies contained in the original relation schema R. However, any such decomposition requires that the information contained in the original relation be maintained.

This in turn requires that the decomposition must be :

- Loss-less join decomposition
- Dependency preserving
- Without any repetition of information.

4.5.1 Loss-less Join Decomposition

Let R be a relation schema and let F be a set of functional dependencies on R. Let R_1 and R_2 form a decomposition of R. This decomposition is a loss-less join decomposition of R if at least one of the following functional dependencies are in F^+.

- $R_1 \cap R_2 \rightarrow R_1$
- $R_1 \cap R_2 \rightarrow R_2$

Loss-less join decomposition can also be defined as :

A decomposition of a relation schema R into the relation schemas R_i ($1 \leq i \leq n$) is said to be a loss-less join decomposition if

$$r = (\pi_{R_1}(r) \bowtie \pi_{R_2}(r) \bowtie \pi_{R_3}(r) \bowtie \text{-----} \bowtie \pi_{R_n}(r))$$

where, r is relation on relation_schema R.

Examples

1. Let R (A, B, C) and F = {A → B}. Then the decomposition of R into R_1 (A, B) and R_2 (A, C) is loss-less-join decomposition, because :

$$A \rightarrow B \text{ is the FD in F.}$$

By augmentation, it gives

$$A \rightarrow AB$$

Which is equal to,

$$R_1 \cap R_2 \rightarrow R_1.$$

2. Let R (A, B, C) and F = {A → B}. The decomposition of R into R_1 (A, B) and R_2 = (B, C) is not loss-less join decomposition because, F^+ does not contain

$$R_1 \cap R_2 \rightarrow R_1 \text{ or}$$
$$R_1 \cap R_2 \rightarrow R_2$$

i.e. common attribute does not functionally determine either A or C. i.e. it is not a key of R_1 or R_2.

3. Let R = (A, B, C, D, E) and

$$F = \{ A \rightarrow BC$$
$$CD \rightarrow E$$
$$B \rightarrow D$$
$$E \rightarrow A \}$$

Then the decomposition of R into,

$$R_1 = (A, B, C) \text{ and}$$
$$R_2 = (A, D, E) \text{ is loss-less join decomposition because } F^+ \text{ contain}$$
$$A \rightarrow ABC \text{ (obtained by augmentation of } A \rightarrow BC)$$

which is equivalent to,

$$R_1 \cap R_2 \rightarrow R_1$$

4. Let R = (A, B, C, D, E) and

$$F = \{ A \rightarrow BC,$$
$$CD \rightarrow E$$
$$B \rightarrow D$$
$$E \rightarrow A \}$$

Then the decomposition of R into,

$$R_1 = (A, B, C) \text{ and}$$
$$R_2 = (C, D, E)$$

is not a loss-less join decomposition because F^+ does not contain,

$$R_1 \cap R_2 \rightarrow R_1 \text{ or}$$
$$R_1 \cap R_2 \rightarrow R_2$$

4.5.2 Dependency Preserving

Given a relation schema R and set of functional dependencies associated with it F. R is decomposed into the relation schemas $R_1, R_2, ..., R_n$ with functional dependencies $F_1, F_2, ..., F_n$. Then the decomposition is dependency preserving if the closure of F' (where $F' = F_1 \cup F_2 \cup ... \cup F_n$) is identical to F^+ i.e.

$$F'^+ = F^+$$

Example 1 : Let R (A, B, C, D) and

$$F = \{A \rightarrow B, A \rightarrow C, C \rightarrow D\}$$

R is decomposed into,

R_1 = (A, B, C) with the FDs
F_1 = { A → B, A → C }
R_2 = (C, D) with FDs
F_2 = {C → D}
$F' = F_1 \cup F_2$ = {A → B, A → C, C → D}

Hence, $F'^+ = F^+$

Hence the decomposition is dependency preserving, and also loss-less.

Example 2 : R (A, B, C, D) and

$F = \{A \rightarrow B, A \rightarrow C, C \rightarrow D\}$ is decomposed into
R_1 = {A, B, D} with functional dependencies
F_1 = { A → B, A → D } and
R_2 = {B, C} with functional dependencies
F_2 = { }

This is not a dependency preserving decomposition. Also it is not loss-less join decomposition.

The relations branch_loan and loan_info are given in Tables 4.5 and 4.6.

Table 4.5 : Branch_loan relation

Branch_name	Branch_city	Assets
SBI	Bombay	4,00,000
ICICI	Pune	34,00,000
HDFC	Delhi	4,90,000
Bank of India	Bombay	1,00,000
City Bank	Delhi	25,00,000
BOM	Pune	32,00,000
BOH	Aurangabad	20,000

Table 4.6 : Loan_info relation

Branch_name	Customer_name	Loan_number	Amount
SBI	Sachin	L - 15	10,000
ICICI	Rahul	L - 31	20,000
HDFC	Raj	L - 29	1,50,000
HDFC	Ramesh	L - 21	1,50,000
Bank of India	Ajay	L - 25	29,000
City Bank	Anil	L - 69	3,00,000
BOM	Rahul	L - 93	10,000
BOH	Sachin	L - 51	20,000

This is a good database design. It has :
- no repetition of information
- no anomalies
- no inability to represent information
- no loss of information.

4.6 PURPOSE OF NORMALIZATION

Normalization : It is a technique for producing a set of relations with desirable properties given the data requirements of an enterprise.

Normalization means to represent database design in a normal form.

A normal form represents a good database design. It is used to eliminate various anomalies and inconsistencies.

There are two approaches to represent the database design in a normal form :
1. Decomposition
2. Synthesis.

The decomposition approach starts with one relation and associated set of constraints in the form of :
- Functional dependencies
- Multivalued dependencies
- Join dependencies.

A relation that has any undesirable properties in the form of insertion, deletion or update anomalies, repetition of information or loss of information, is replaced by its projections. This results in a normal form.

This chapter deals with decomposition approach and following normal forms :

1. First Normal Form (1NF)
2. Second Normal Form (2NF)
3. Third Normal Form (3NF)
4. Boyce Codd Normal Form (BCNF)
5. Fourth Normal Form (4NF)
6. Project Normal Form (PJNF)
4. Domain Key Normal Form (DKNF)

The second approach is synthesis approach. It starts with a set of functional dependencies on a set of attributes. It then synthesizes relations of Third Normal Form (3NF).

The database design resulting from any of the above approach always is a good design with all the properties of good database design.

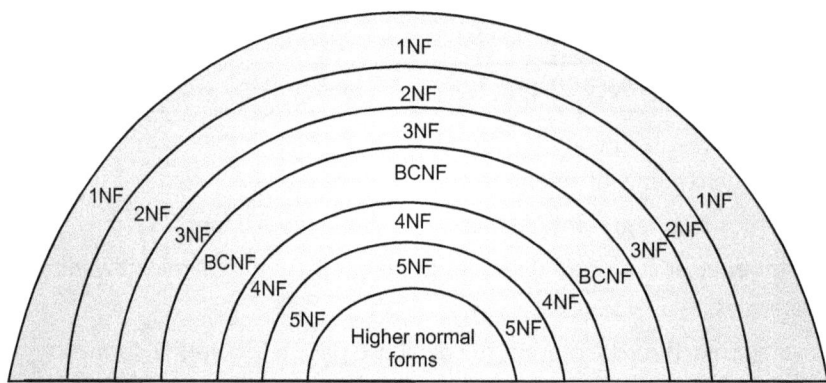

Fig. 4.1 : Diagrammatic illustration of the relationship between the normal forms

4.7 DATA REDUNDANCY AND UPDATE ANOMALIES

Data Redundancy :

The major aim of relational database design is to group attributes into relations to minimize data redundancy and thereby reduce the file storage space required by the implemented base relations.

The problems associated with data redundancy are illustrated by comparing the staff, branch relations with StaffBranch relation.

Table 4.7 : Staff Table

Staff_no	S_name	Position	Salary	Branch_no
SL21	Rima Sinha	Manager	30000	B005
SG34	Raj Varma	Assistant	12000	B003
SG14	Varun S.	Supervisor	18000	B003
SA9	Neeta K.	Assistant	9000	B004
SG5	Ram Shetty	Manger	24000	B003
SL41	Riya Khanna	Assistant	9000	B005

Table 4.8 : Branch Table

Branch_no	B_Address
B005	22, MIDC Road, Baramati
B004	16, Law College Road, Pune
B003	34, 4 Street Road, Delhi

Table 4.9 : Staff Branch

Staff_No	S_name	Position	Salary	Branch_no	Address
SL21	Rima Sinha	Manager	30000	B005	22, MIDC Road, Baramati
SG34	Raj Varma	Assistant	12000	B003	34, 4 Street Road, Delhi
SG14	Varun S.	Supervisor	18000	B003	34, 4 Street Road, Delhi
SA9	Neeta K.	Assistant	9000	B004	16, Law College Road, Pune
SG5	Ram Shetty	Manger	24000	B003	34, 4 Street Road, Delhi
SL41	Riya Khanna	Assistant	9000	B005	22, MIDC Road, Baramati

The relations have the form :

Staff (staff_No, s_Name, position, salary, branch_No)

Branch (branch_No, address)

StaffBranch (staff_No, s_Name, position, salary, branch_No, address)

In StaffBranch relation there is redundant data; the details of branch are repeated for every member.

Relations that have redundant data may have problems called **update anomalies**, which are classified as insertions, deletions or modification anomalies.

Insertion Anomalies :

There are two main types of insertion anomalies, which can be illustrated using StaffBranch relation :

- To insert the details of new members of staff into StaffBranch relation, we must include the details of the branch at which the staff are to be located.

    For example : To insert the details of new staff located at branch number B004, we must enter correct details of branch number B004, so that branch details are consistent with values for branch B004 in other tuples of the SaffBranch relation. The relations Staff and Branch do not suffer from this problem

- To insert details of a new branch that currently has no members of staff into the StaffBranch relation, it is necessary to enter nulls into the attributes for Staff, such as staffNo. However staffNo is the primary key for the StaffBranch relation. Attempting to enter NULL violates the entity integrity and is not allowed. We therefore can not enter a tuple for a new branch into the StaffBranch relation.

Deletion Anomalies :

If we delete a tuple from the StaffBranch relation and that was the last member of the staff located at a branch, the details of the branch are also lost from the database.

For example : If we delete the tuple for staff number SA9, the details regarding B004 are lost from the StaffBranch relation.

Modification Anomalies :

If we want to change the value of one of the attributes of a particular branch in the StaffBranch relation.

For example : The address for branch number B003, we must update the tuples for all staff located at that branch.

4.8 FUNCTIONAL DEPENDENCY

Functional dependencies are constraints on the set of legal relations. They allow us to express facts about the enterprise that we are modeling with our database. The notion of functional dependency generalises the notion of super key.

A super key can be defined as follows :

Let R be a relation schema. A subset K of R is a super key of R if in any legal relation r (R), for all pairs t_1 and t_2 of tuples in r such that $t_1 \neq t_2$, then $t_1 [K] \neq t_2 [K]$ i.e. no tuples in legal relation r (R) can have same values on attribute set K.

The functional dependency can be defined as follows :

Let $\alpha \subseteq R$ and $\beta \subseteq R$. The functional dependency $\alpha \rightarrow \beta$ holds on R if in any legal relation r (R), for all pairs of tuples t_1 and t_2 in r such that $t_1[\alpha] = t_2[\alpha]$ it is also the case that, $t_1[\beta] = t_2[\beta]$.

Using functional dependency notation, we say that K is a super key if whenever $t_1[K] = t_2[K]$, it is also the case that, $t_1[R] = t_2[R]$.

Functional dependencies allow us to express constraints that we cannot express using super keys.

We shall use the functional dependencies in following two ways.

- To specify constraints on the set of legal relations.
- To test relations to see whether the relations are legal under a given set of functional dependencies.

Let r be a relation schema for relation r (R). r satisfies the functional dependency $\alpha \rightarrow \beta$ if a given set of values for each attribute in α uniquely determines each of the values of the attributes in β. β is said to be functionally dependent on α.

In order to verify if a given FD $\alpha \rightarrow \beta$ is satisfied by a relation r on a relation schema R, we find any two tuples with the same α value; if the FD $\alpha \rightarrow \beta$ is satisfied in r, then the β values in these tuples must be same. We repeat this procedure until we have examined all such pairs of tuples with the same α value. A simpler approach is to order the tuples of R on the α values, so that all tuples with the same α values are together. Then it is easy to verify if the corresponding β values are also same and verify if R satisfies the FD $\alpha \rightarrow \beta$.

Example 1 : Consider the following relation and relation - schema.

Schedule_schema = (Prof., Cource, Room, Max_enrol, Day, Time)

Table 4.10

Prof.	Cource	Room	Max_Enroll	Day	Time
Sachin	353	A 532	40	Mon	1145
Sachin	353	A 532	40	Wed	1145
Sachin	351	C 320	60	Tue	115
Sachin	351	C 320	60	Thu	115
Rahul	355	H 940	300	Tue	845
Ajay	456	B 248	45	Thu	1015
Rahul	355	H 940	300	Mon	845
Ajay	456	B 248	40	Tue	1015

The FD Cource $\rightarrow$ Prof. is satisfied by this relation. But Prof. $\rightarrow$ cource is not satisfied.

Example 2 :

Consider theloan_info_schema = (branch_name, loan_no., customer_name, amount) and the loan_info relation (Table)

The set of functional dependencies that hold on relation schema is :

$$loan\_no \to amount$$
$$loan\_no \to branch\_name$$

it cannot hold,

$$loan\_no \to customer\_name$$

Example 3 :

Consider the relation student_info table and the relation schema.

Student info_schema = (Name, Cource, Phone_No., Major, Prof., grade)

The functional dependencies satisfied by the relation schema are :

$$Name \to Phone\_no.$$
$$Name \to Major$$
$$Name\ Cource \to Grade$$
$$Course \to Prof.$$

Table 4.11 : Student_info Relation

Name	Course	Phone_No.	Major	Prof.	Grade
Ajay	353	234 – 4539	Comp	Ashish	A
Sachin	329	424 - 4390	Chemistry	Sunil	B
Ajay	328	234 - 4539	Comp	Kapil	B
Rahul	456	388 - 5183	Physics	Rajesh	A
Anil	293	341 - 6259	Decision sci.	Sagar	C
Raj	491	823 - 4293	Maths	Ankit	B
Raj	356	823 - 4293	Maths	Salil	in prog
Ajay	492	234 - 4539	Comp	Sunil	in prog
Ramesh	349	839 - 0824	English	Kapil	C

Table 4.12 : Relation r on Schema R (A, B, C, D)

A	B	C	D	E
a_1	b_1	c_2	d_1	e_1
a_2	b_2	c_1	d_2	e_2
a_3	b_1	c_2	d_1	e_3
a_3	b_3	c_3	d_3	e_4
a_1	b_2	c_1	d_2	e_5
a_4	b_4	c_4	d_4	e_6
a_3	b_2	c_1	d_2	e_4
a_5	b_4	c_4	d_4	e_8

4.9 DEPENDENCIES AND LOGICAL IMPLICATIONS

Given relation schema R and a set of functional dependencies F, let us consider a functional dependency $X \rightarrow Y$ which is not in F. F can be said to logically imply $X \rightarrow Y$, if for every relation r on the relation schema R that satisfies the functional dependencies in F, r also satisfies $X \rightarrow Y$.

F logically implies $X \rightarrow Y$ is written as $F \models X \rightarrow Y$.

To determine whether a functional dependency $X \rightarrow Y$ is logically implied by F, we use a set of rules or axioms. The axioms are numbered F_1 through F_6.

Here we consider that r is a relation on the relation schema R ($A_1, A_2, ..., A_n$), and W, X, Y, Z are subsets of R.

- F_1 : Reflexivity   : $(X \rightarrow X)$
- F_2 : Augmentation   : $(X \rightarrow Y) \models (XZ \rightarrow Y \text{ and } XZ \rightarrow YZ)$
- F_3 : Transitivity   : $(X \rightarrow Y \text{ and } Y \rightarrow Z) \models (X \rightarrow Z)$
- F_4 : Additivity   : $(X \rightarrow Y \text{ and } X \rightarrow Z) \models (X \rightarrow YZ)$
- F_5 : Projectivity   : $(X \rightarrow YZ) \models (X \rightarrow Y \text{ and } X \rightarrow Z)$
- F_6 : Pseudotransitivity : $(X \rightarrow Y \text{ and } YZ \rightarrow W) \models (XZ \rightarrow W)$

To illustrate above inference axioms consider the relation r given in Table 4.12.

F_1 : reflexivity : $(X \rightarrow X)$

This is obvious since any set of attributes implies the same set of attributes.

Augmentation : $(X \rightarrow Y) \models (XZ \rightarrow Y \text{ and } XZ \rightarrow YZ)$

The FD $B \rightarrow C$ is satisfied and by augmentation we find that the FDs

$$AB \rightarrow C$$
$$BC \rightarrow C$$
$$BD \rightarrow C$$
$$BE \rightarrow C$$
$$ABC \rightarrow C$$
$$BCD \rightarrow C \text{ etc. are also satisfied.}$$

Additivity : $(X \rightarrow Y \text{ and } X \rightarrow Z) \models (X \rightarrow YZ)$

From relation r, the FDs

$$B \rightarrow C$$
$$B \rightarrow D \text{ imply that}$$
$$B \rightarrow CD \text{ is also satisfied by relation schema.}$$

Projectivity : $(X \rightarrow YZ) \models (X \rightarrow Y \text{ and } X \rightarrow Z)$

From relation r, the FD

$$B \rightarrow CD$$

Imply that $B \rightarrow C$ and $B \rightarrow D$ are also satisfied.

Transitivity : From the relation r the FDs B → C and C → D are satisfied and hence by transitivity, B → D.

Pseudotransitivity : The relation r satisfies the FDs, C → B and AB → E so by pseudotransitivity, the FD CA → E is also satisfied.

Closure of Set of Functional Dependencies :

The set of functional dependencies that is logically implied by F is called the closure of F and is written as F^+.

$$F^+ = \{X \to Y \mid F \models X \to Y\}$$

An FD f in F^+ is logically implied by F, since any relation R on the relation schema R that satisfies the FDs in F also satisfies the FD in F^+ and hence f.

Example :

Let $\qquad F = \{W \to X, X \to Y, W \to XY\}$

then $\qquad F^+ = \{X \to X, Y \to Y, W \to W, W \to X, X \to Y, W \to XY, W \to Y\}$.

First three are from F_1.

Next three are copied from F.

W → XY, hence according to F_5, W → X and W → Y.

Canonical Cover :

A set of functional dependencies F_c is a canonical cover if every FD in F_c satisfies the following :

1. Each FD in F_c is simple. In a simple FD the right-hand side has a single attribute i.e. each FD is of the form X → A.
2. For no FD X → A with Z ⊂ X is $\{(F_c - (X \to A)) \cup (Z \to A)\} \models F_c$.

   In other words, the left-hand side of each FD doesn't have any extraneous attributes or the FDs in F_c are left reduced.
3. No FD X → A is redundant i.e. $\{F_c - (X \to A)\}$ does not logically imply F_c.

   A canonical cover is sometimes called minimal.

Full Functional Dependency :

Given a relational schema R and an FD X → Y, Y is fully functionally dependent on X if there is no Z, where Z is a proper subset of X, such that Z → Y. The dependency X → Y is left reduced, there being no extraneous attributes in the left-hand side of the dependency.

Example :

In the relation schema R (ABCDEH) with FDs

$$F = \{A \to BC, CD \to E, E \to C, CD \to AH, ABH \to BD, DH \to BC\},$$

the dependency A → BC is left reduced and BC is fully functionally dependent on A.

Partial Dependency : Given a relation schema R with the functional dependencies F defined on the attributes of R and K as a candidate key, if X is a proper subset of K and if, F ⊨ X → A, then A is said to be partially dependent on K.

Example 1 :

Given R (A, B, C, D) and F = {AB → C, B → D}, the key of this relation is AB and D is partially dependent on the key.

Example 2 :

In the relation schema,

Student_info schema = (Name, Course, Grade, Phone_no., Major, Course_Dept.) with FDs

F = {Name → Phone_no., Major, course → course_Dept., Name Course → Grade}

{Name, Course} is a candidate key. Name and course are prime attributes. Grade is fully functionally dependent on the candidate key.

Phone_no, Course_Dept, and Major and partially dependent on the candidate key.

Transitive Dependency : Given a relation schema R with the functional dependencies F defined on the attributes of R, let X and Y be subsets of R and let A be an attribute of R such that X ⊄ Y, A ⊄ XY. If the set of functional dependencies {X → Y, Y → A} is implied by F (i.e. F ⊨ X → Y → A and F → ⊨ Y → X) then A is transitively dependent on X.

Example 1 : Given R (A, B, C, D, E) and the functional dependencies F = {AB → C, B → D, C → E}, AB is the key and E is transitively dependent on the key since AB → C → E.

Example 2 : In the relation schema,

Prof_info_schema = (Prof_name, Dependent, Chairperson)

and the functional dependencies

F = {Prof_name → Department
Department → Chair person}

Prof_name is the key and chair person is transitively dependent on prof_name since

Prof_name → Department → Chair person

Prime Attribute and Non-prime Attribute :

An attribute A in a relation schema R is a prime attribute or simply prime if A is a part of any candidate key of the relation. If A is not a part of any candidate key of R, A is called a non-prime attribute or simply non-prime.

Example :

If, R (A, B, C, D, E, H) and

F = {A → BC, CD → E, E → C, AH → D}

then AH is the candidate key of R. The attributes A and H are prime and the attributes B, C, D and E are non-prime.

Unnormalized Relation :

An unnormalized relation contain non-atomic values.

4.10 NORMALIZATION USING FUNCTIONAL DEPENDENCIES

4.10.1 First Normal Form (1NF)

A relation schema is said to be in first normal form (1NF) if the values in the domain of each attribute of the relation are atomic. In other words, only one value is associated with each attribute and the value is not a set of values or a list of values.

A database schema is in First Normal form (1NF) if every relation schema indicated in the database schema is in 1NF.

Example : Cource_prof relation shown in table 4.13 is not in 1NF but shown in table 4.14 is in 1NF.

Table 4.13 : Course_Prof. relation

Fac_Dept	Prof.	Course preferences	
		Course	Course_Dept.
Comp-sci	Sachin	353	Comp sci
		349	Comp sci
		221	Decision
	Raj	353	Comp sci
		351	Comp sci
		349	Maths
Chemistry	Rajesh	353	Comp sci
		456	Maths
		242	Chemistry
Mathematics	Rahul	353	Comp sci
		349	Comp sci
		221	Maths
		456	Maths

Table 4.14 : Course_Prof. relation

Fac_Dept	Prof_home	Course	Course_Dept.
Comp sci	Sachin	353	Comp sci
Comp sci	Sachin	349	Comp sci
Comp sci	Sachin	321	Decision sci
Comp sci	Raj	353	Comp sci
Comp sci	Raj	351	Comp sci
Comp sci	Raj	349	Maths
Chemistry	Rajesh	353	Comp sci
Chemistry	Rajesh	456	Maths
Chemistry	Rajesh	242	Chemistry
Mathematics	Rahul	353	Comp sci
Mathematics	Rahul	349	Comp sci
Mathematics	Rahul	221	Maths
Mathematics	Rahul	456	Maths

4.10.2 Second Normal Form (2NF)

A relation schema R (S, F) is in second Normal Form (2NF) if it is in the 1NF and if all non-prime attributes are fully functionally dependent on the relation key (s).

A database schema is in second normal form if every relation schema included in the database schema is in second normal form.

Example : Consider the teachers relation shown in Table 4.15.

$\quad$ Teaches_schema = (course, prof, room, room_cap, enrol_lmt).

This relation is in 1NF since, it contains only atomic values.

Functional dependencies in this relation are :

$\quad$ {Course $\rightarrow$ (Prof, Room, Room_cap, enrol_limit),

$\quad$ Room $\rightarrow$ Room_cap}

A course is scheduled in a given class_room and since each room has the given maximum number of available seats i.e. the functional dependency.

$\quad$ Room $\rightarrow$ Room_cap

One course will be conducted in one class_room.

$\quad$ i.e. course $\rightarrow$ room. Hence, there is a transitive dependency.

$\quad$ course $\rightarrow$ room $\rightarrow$ room_cap, also there is other transitive dependency.

$\quad$ room $\rightarrow$ room_cap $\rightarrow$ enrol_lmt

The presence of these transitive dependencies cause following problems.

The capacity of a room cannot be entered in the database unless a course is scheduled in that room.

The capacity of the room in which only one course is scheduled will be deleted if the only course scheduled in that class_room is deleted.

Because the same class_room can appear more than once in the database, these could be inconsistencies between multiple occurrences of attribute pair room and room_cap.

From the above discussions it is clear that teachers relation is in 1NF but still its not a good database design. It is not in 2NF.

Consider the decomposition of teaches relation into the relations

    Course_details_schema = (course, prof, room, enrol_lmt)

and   Room_details_schema = (Room, Room_cap)

The set of functional dependencies in course_detail is :

    {Course → prof, course → Room, Course → enrol_lmt}

The set of functional dependencies in Room-details is :

    {Room → Room_cap}

These relations do not have any partial dependencies. Each of the attributes is fully functionally dependent on key attributes, course and room respectively. Hence the two are in 2NF.

Table 4.15 : Teachers relation

Course	Prof	room	enrol_lmt	Room_cap
353	Sachin	A 532	40	45
351	Sachin	C 320	60	100
355	Raj	H 940	300	400
456	Rahul	B 248	45	50
459	Ajay	D 110	45	50

Table 4.16 : Course_details

Course	Prof	Room	Enrol_lmt
353	Sachin	A 532	40
351	Sachin	C 320	60
355	Raj	H 940	300
456	Rahul	B 248	45
459	Ajay	D 110	45

Table 4.17 : Room_details

Room	Room_cap
A 532	45
C 320	100
H 940	400
B 248	50
D 110	50

However, the relation course_details has a transitive dependency since

$$Course \rightarrow Room \rightarrow Enrol\_lmt$$

and in addition there is an interrelation join dependency between the relation. Course_details and room_details to enforce the constraint that the enrol_lmt be less than or equal to the room_cap.

4.10.3 Boyce - Codd Normal Form (BCNF)

A relation schema R is in BCNF with respect to a set F of functional dependencies if for all functional dependencies in F^+ of the form $\alpha \rightarrow \beta$, where $\alpha \subseteq R$ and $\beta \subseteq R$, at least one of the following holds.

- $\alpha \rightarrow \beta$ is a trival functional dependency (i.e. $\beta \subseteq \alpha$).
- α is a super key for schema R.

A database design is in BCNF if each member of the set of relation schema's that constitutes the design is in BCNF.

Consider the following relation schemas and their respective functional dependencies :

1. Customer_schema = (customer_name, customer_street, customer_city)
   Customer_name $\rightarrow$ customer_street, customer_city

This relation schema is in BCNF.

Customer_name $\rightarrow$ customer_street, customer_city

is a non-trival functional dependency but the candidate key for this schema is customer_name.

2. Branch_schema = (branch_name, assets, branch_city)
   branch_name $\rightarrow$ assets branch_city

This schema is in BCNF.

branch_name $\rightarrow$ assets branch_city

is a non-trival functional dependency but branch_name is the candidate key.

3. Loan_info_schema = (branch_name, customer_name, loan_no., amount)
   loan_no $\rightarrow$ amount branch_name

This schema is not in BCNF, because loan no. is not a super key and loan_no → amount branch_name is not a trival functional dependency.

The loan_info schema is not in a desirable form since it suffers from repetition of information. To eliminate this redundancy, the relation schema can be decomposed in those schemas which are in BCNF.

Consider the decomposition of loan_info_schema into two schemas :

    loan_schemas = (branch_name, loan_no., amount)
    borrower_schema = (customer_name, loan_no.)

The decomposition is loss-less join decomposition because

    loan_no. → amount branch_name

holds on loan_schema.

    loan_no. is candidate key of loan_schema.

Only trival dependencies hold on borrower schema. This both schemas of decomposition are in BCNF.

Algorithm for BCNF decomposition :

If relation schema R is not in BCNF, we can decompose R into a collection of BCNF schemas $R_1, R_2, ..., R_n$. Using the algorithm given below :

```
result:={R}
done:=false;
Compute F⁺;
while (not done) do
if(there is a schema Rᵢ in result that is not in BCNF)
then
begin
    let α → β be a non_trival functional dependency that holds on Rᵢ such that
    α → Rᵢ is not in F⁺, and α ∩ β = φ;
    result:=(result-Rᵢ) ∪ (Rᵢ-β) ∪ (α, β);
end
else
    done := true
```

BCNF decomposition algorithm.

This algorithm generates BCNF decomposition which is also loss-less-join decomposition.

Example 1 :

Let,
    R = (A, B, C, D) and
    F = { AB → C,
          C → A }

Find BCNF decomposition of R using the algorithm.

Consider,
$$AB \to C$$
$$R_1 = (A, B, C)$$
$$F_1 = \{ AB \to C, C \to A \}$$
$$R_2 = (A, B, D)$$
$$F_2 = \{ \}$$

R_2, can be again decomposed using,
$$C \to A$$
$$R_{11} = (A, C)$$
$$F_{11} = \{ C \to A \}$$
$$R_{12} = \{ B, C \}$$
$$F_{12} = \{ \}$$

Example 2 :

Find BCNF decomposition of the relation schema shipping with the following set of functional dependencies.

$$\text{Shipping\_schema} = (\text{ship, capacity, Data, Cargo, Value})$$
$$\text{Ship} \to \text{Capacity}$$
$$\text{Ship Date} \to \text{Cargo}$$
$$\text{Cargo capacity} \to \text{Value}$$

Consider cargo capacity → Value FD.

It gives
$$R_1 = (\text{Cargo, Capacity, Value})$$
$$R_{11} = (\text{Cargo, Capacity, Ship, Date})$$

Now using ship → capacity FD,

R_{11} can be decomposed as :
$$R_2 = (\text{Ship, Capacity})$$
$$R_3 = (\text{Ship, date, cargo})$$

Hence, the shipping is decomposed as follows :

R_1 (Cargo, Capacity, Value) with F.D.
$$\text{Cargo capacity} \to \text{Value}$$

R_2 (Ship, Capacity) with the FD
$$\text{Ship} \to \text{Capacity}$$

R_3 (Ship, Date, Cargo) with FD
$$\text{Ship Date} \to \text{Cargo}$$

This decomposition is loss-less-join decomposition and also dependency preserving.

Not every Decomposition is Dependency Preserving :

Consider the Banker_schema and set of functional dependencies.

$$\text{Banker\_schema} = (\text{branch\_name, customer\_name, banker\_name})$$

$$\text{Banker\_name} \rightarrow \text{branch\_name}$$

branch_name customer_name → banker_name

The above given Banker_schema is not in BCNF since, banker_name is not a super key.

Using BCNF decomposition algorithm and banker name → branch_name dependency it can be decomposed into :

$$\text{Banker\_branch\_schema} = (\text{banker\_name, branch\_name})$$

With FD F_1 = banker_name→branch_name

Customer_banker_schema = (customer_name, banker_name)

and FD $F_2 = \{\}$.

$$F' = F_1 \cup F_2 = \{\text{banker\_name} \rightarrow \text{branch\_name}\}$$

The decomposed schema preserve only,

banker_name → branch_name

F'^+ does not contain,

Customer_name branch_name → banker_name.

$$F'^+ \neq F^+$$

Hence, it is not a dependency preserving decomposition.

This example demonstrates that not every BCNF decomposition is dependency preserving.

We cannot always satisfy all three design goals :

1. BCNF
2. Loss-less Join
3. Dependency Preservation

4.10.4 Third Normal Form (3NF)

In those cases where we cannot meet all three design criteria, we abandon BCNF and accept a weaker normal form called Third Normal Form (3NF).

A decomposition in 3NF is always :

- Loss-less join decomposition, and
- Dependency preserving decomposition.

BCNF requires that all non-trival dependencies be of the form $\alpha \rightarrow \beta$ where α is a super key. 3NF relaxes this constraint slightly by allowing non-trival functional dependencies whose left side is not a super key.

A relation schema is in 3NF with respect to a set F of functional dependencies if, for all functional dependencies in F^+ of the form $\alpha \to \beta$ where $\alpha \subseteq R$ and $\beta \subseteq R$, at least one of the following holds.

- $\alpha \to \beta$ is a trivial functional dependency.
- α is a super key for R.
- Each attribute A in $\beta - \alpha$ is contained in a candidate key for R.

An Algorithm for Decomposition into Third Normal Form :

```
Let F_c be a canonical cover for F;
i := 0;
For each functional dependency α → β in F_c do
    if none of the schemas R_j  j = 1, 2, ..., i contains αβ then
    begin
        i := i + 1;
        R_i := αβ;
    end
if none of the schemas R_j; j = 1, 2, ..., i contains a candidate key for R then
    begin.
        i := i+1;
        R_i := any candidate key for R;
    end
return (R_1, R_2, ..., R_i)
```

This algorithm generates decomposition into 3NF of a given relation schema. The decomposition is dependency preserving and loss-less join decomposition.

4.10.5 Solved Examples

Example 1 :

Find 3NF decomposition of given relation schema and FDs.

Banker_info_schema = (branch_name, customer_name, banker_name, office_no.)

Functional dependencies are :

banker_name → branch_name office_no.

customer_name branch_name → banker_name

Solution :

Using the algorithm and FD

Result of for loop :
- banker_name → branch_name office_no.
  - α = banker_name, β = branch_name office_no.
  - R_1 = (banker_name, branch_name, office_no)
- Customer_name, branch_name → banker_name
  - R_2 = (customer_name, branch_name, banker_name)
- Second if condition is not satisfied since, candidate key for R is {customer name, branch_name}

which is present in R_2.

R_1 and R_2 given 3NF decomposition of schema which is loss-less and dependency preserving.

Example 2 :

Find 3NF decomposition of given relation schema.

Shipping (ship, capacity, Date, Cargo, value)

Functional dependencies :

$$Ship \rightarrow Capacity$$
$$Ship\ date \rightarrow Cargo$$
$$Cargo\ capacity \rightarrow Value.$$

Solution : Using the algorithm and functional dependencies.

- ship → capacity
  - R_1 = (ship, capacity)
- ship date → Cargo
  - R_2 = (ship, Date, Cargo)
- Cargo capacity → value
  - R_3 = (Cargo, Capacity, value)

R_1, R_2 and R_3 give 3NF decomposition which is loss-less and dependency preserving.

4.10.6 Comparison of BCNF and 3NF

1. Decomposition Properties :

3NF design is always dependency preserving and loss-less.

But, it is difficult to achieve all three design goals : BCNF, loss-less-join and dependency preservation.

2. Transitive Dependencies :

BCNF schema cannot have transitive dependencies.

But, if we do not eliminate transitive dependencies in 3NF, we may have to use null values to represent some of the possible meaningful relationships among data items and there is a problem of repetition of information.

It is generally preferable to output for 3NF with dependency preservation. If we cannot test for dependency preservation efficiently, we either pay high penalty in system performance or risk, the integrity of the data in our database.

If A relation schema is in BCNF, then it is also in 3NF :

From the definitions of BCNF and 3NF, it is clear that a relation schema which is in BCNF can satisfy at least one of the first two conditions of 3NF definition. Hence, it is also in 3NF.

If a relation schema is in BCNF then all functional dependencies are of the form **"super key determines a set of attributes"** or the dependency is trival. Thus, a BCNF schema cannot have any transitive dependencies. As a result, every BCNF schema is also in 3NF.

4.11 MULTIVALUED DEPENDENCY

If A $\rightarrow$ B is a functional dependency on given relation schema, then we cannot have two tuples with the same A value, but different B values i.e. a FD rules out existence of seven tuples where as Multivalued dependency does not rule out existence of certain tuples.

For this reason, functional dependencies are sometimes referred to as equality-generating dependencies and multivalued dependencies are referred to as tuple-generating dependencies.

Multivalued Dependency :

Let R be a relation schema and let $\alpha \subseteq R$ and $\beta \subseteq R$. The multivalued dependency,

$$\alpha \rightarrow\rightarrow \beta$$

holds on R if, in any legal relation r (R), for all pairs of tuples t_1 and t_2 in r such that $t_1[\alpha] = t_2[\alpha]$ there exist tuples t_3 and t_4 in r such that

$$t_1[\alpha] = t_2[\alpha] = t_3[\alpha] = t_4[\alpha]$$
$$t_3[\beta] = t_1[\beta]$$
$$t_4[\beta] = t_2[\beta]$$
$$t_3[R-\beta] = t_2[R-\beta]$$
$$t_4[R-\beta] = t_1[R-\beta]$$
$$t_1[R-\alpha-\beta] = t_4[R-\alpha-\beta]$$
$$t_2[R-\alpha-\beta] = t_3[R-\alpha-\beta]$$

The multivalued dependency,

$$\alpha \rightarrow\rightarrow \beta$$

can be represented in tabular form as follows.

Tuples	α	β	$R - \alpha - \beta$
t_1	$a_1 \dots a_i$	$a_{i+1} \dots a_j$	$a_{j+1} \dots a_n$
t_2	$a_1 \dots a_i$	$b_{i+1} \dots b_j$	$b_{j+1} \dots b_n$
t_3	$a_1 \dots a_i$	$a_{i+1} \dots a_j$	$b_{j+1} \dots b_n$
t_4	$a_1 \dots a_i$	$b_{i+1} \dots b_j$	$a_{j+1} \dots a_n$

The multivalued dependency $\alpha \twoheadrightarrow \beta$ says that the relationship between α and β is independent of the relationship between α and $R - \beta$.

If the multivalued dependency $\alpha \twoheadrightarrow \beta$ is satisfied by all relations on schema R, then $\alpha \twoheadrightarrow \beta$ is a trival multivalued dependency on schema R. Thus $\alpha \twoheadrightarrow \beta$ is a trival functional dependency if $\beta \subseteq \alpha$ or $\beta \cup \alpha = R$.

Multivalued dependencies can be used in following two ways :
1. To test relations to determine whether they are legal under a given set of functional and multivalued dependencies.
2. To specify constraints on the set of legal relations.

4.12 AXIOMS FOR FUNCTIONAL AND MULTIVALUED DEPENDENCIES

To design a relational database, a given relation schema R with functional and multivalued dependencies, we need a set of rules or axioms that will allow us to determine all the dependencies implied by a given set of known dependencies. We need these axioms to verify whether a given relation schema is legal (i.e. loss-less and dependency preserving) under a set of functional and multivalued dependencies.

Here consider that W, X, Y and Z are subsets of R.

F_1 : Reflexivity : $X \rightarrow X$

F_2 : Augmentation : $(X \rightarrow Y$ and $Y \rightarrow Z)$
    $\models (XZ \rightarrow Y$ and $XZ \rightarrow YZ)$

F_4 : Additivity : $(X \rightarrow Y$ and $X \rightarrow Z) \models (X \cdot YZ)$

M_1 : Replication : $(X \rightarrow Y) \models (X \cdot Y)$

The replication axiom leads to the following versions of axioms F_1 through F_3 for multivalued dependencies.

M_2 : Reflexivity : $X \twoheadrightarrow X$

M_3 : Augmentation : $X \twoheadrightarrow Y \models XZ \twoheadrightarrow Y$

If $(X \twoheadrightarrow Y$ and $Y \subseteq W)$ then $WX \twoheadrightarrow WY$

M_4 : Additivity or Union : $(X \twoheadrightarrow Y$ and $X \twoheadrightarrow Z) \models X \twoheadrightarrow YZ$.

M_5 : Complementation : $X \twoheadrightarrow Y \models X \twoheadrightarrow (R - X - Y)$

M_6 : Transitivity : $(X \twoheadrightarrow Y$ and $Y \twoheadrightarrow Z) \models X \twoheadrightarrow (Z - Y)$

M_4 : Coalescence : Given that $W \subseteq Y$ and $Y \cap Z = \cdot$ and if $X \twoheadrightarrow Y$ and $Z \twoheadrightarrow W$, then $X \twoheadrightarrow W$.

M_8 : Decomposition or projectivity :
    If $X \twoheadrightarrow Y$ and $X \twoheadrightarrow Z$, then
    $X \twoheadrightarrow (Y \cap Z)$, $X \twoheadrightarrow (Y - Z)$ and $X \twoheadrightarrow (Z - Y)$.

M_9 : Mixed (Pseudo) Transitivity :
    If $X \twoheadrightarrow Y$ and $XY \twoheadrightarrow Z$ then $X \twoheadrightarrow (Z - Y)$

4.13 LOSS-LESS AND DEPENDENCY PRESERVING DECOMPOSITION

Loss-less Join Decomposition :

Let R be a relation schema and let D be a set of functional and multivalued dependencies on R. Let R_1 and R_2 form a decomposition of R. This decomposition is loss-less join decomposition of R if and only if at least one of the following multivalued dependencies is in D^+.

$$R_1 \cap R_2 \rightarrow\rightarrow R_1$$
$$R_1 \cap R_2 \rightarrow\rightarrow R_2$$

Dependency Preservation :

Let R be a relation schema and let $R_1, R_2, ..., R_n$ be a decomposition of R. D is the set of functional and multivalued dependencies. The restriction of D to R_i is the set D_i consisting of :

- All functional dependencies in D^+ that include only attributes of R_i,
- All multivalued dependencies of the form,

$$\alpha \rightarrow\rightarrow \beta \cap R_i$$

where $\alpha \subseteq R_i$ and $\alpha \rightarrow\rightarrow \beta$ is in D^+.

The decomposition of R into schemas $R_1, R_2, ..., R_n$ is a dependency preserving decomposition with respect to a set D of functional and multivalued dependencies if for every set of relations $r_1(R_1), r_2(R_2), ..., r_n(R_n)$ such that for all i, r_i satisfies D_i, there exists a relation r (R) that satisfies D and for which $r_i = \pi_{R_i}(r)$ for all i.

4.14 NORMALIZATION USING MULTIVALUED DEPENDENCY

4.14.1 Fourth Normal Form (4NF)

A relation schema is in Fourth Normal Form (4NF) with respect to a set D of functional and multivalued dependencies if, for all multivalued dependencies in D^+ of the form $\alpha \rightarrow\rightarrow \beta$, where $\alpha \subseteq R$ and $\beta \subseteq R$ at least one of the following holds.

- $\alpha \rightarrow\rightarrow \beta$ is a trival multivalued dependency.
- α is a super key for schema R.

A database design is in 4NF if each member of the set of relation schema's that constitutes the design is in 4NF.

4NF and BCNF : 4NF is more restrictive than BCNF.

4NF differ from the definition of BCNF in only the use of multivalued dependencies instead of functional dependencies.

Every 4NF schema is in BCNF.

If schema R is not in BCNF, then it cannot be in 4NF :

If a schema R is not in BCNF, then there is a non-trival functional dependency $\alpha \rightarrow \beta$ holding on R, where α is not a super key.

$\alpha \rightarrow \beta$ implies $\alpha \rightarrow\rightarrow \beta$ by replication rule.

Hence $\alpha \rightarrow\rightarrow \beta$ is a non-trival functional dependency and α is not a super key, which means that R is not in 4NF.

But there are BCNF schemas that are not in 4NF. 4NF eliminates the problem encountered in BCNF.

Fourth Normal Form Decomposition Algorithm :

```
result:={R};
done:=false;
compute D⁺;
while (not done) do
    if (there is a schema Rᵢ in result that is not in 4
    NF) then
    begin
        let α → β be a non-trival multivalued dependency that holds on Rᵢ such that α
        → Rᵢ is not D⁺ and α ∩ β = φ'. result := (result - Rᵢ) ∪ (Rᵢ - β) ∪ (α, β);
    end
    else
        done:=true.
```

It generates loss-less join decomposition.

Example : Let R = (A, B, C, G, H, I) with

$$D = \{A \rightarrow\rightarrow B, B \rightarrow\rightarrow HI, CG \rightarrow H\}$$

R is not in 4NF. Lets apply 4NF decomposition algorithm and test resulting decomposition for dependencies preservation.

$A \rightarrow\rightarrow B$ is non-trival dependency and A is not a super key. The first iteration of while loop will replace R with two schemas :

(A, B) and (A, C, G, H, I)

(A, B) is in 4NF since all multivalued dependencies that hold on (A, B) are trival. But (A, C, G, H, I) is not in 4 NF.

Applying the multivalued dependency $CG \rightarrow\rightarrow H$ which follows from $CG \rightarrow H$ functional dependency, second iteration of while loop will replace the (A, C, G, H, I) schema into two schemas :

(C, G, H) and (A, C, G, I). Schema (C, G, H) is in 4NF, but schema (A, G, C, I) is not in 4NF.

Now using the productions,

$$A \rightarrow\rightarrow B$$

$$B \twoheadrightarrow HI$$

And transitivity rule,
$$A \twoheadrightarrow HI$$

i.e. $\quad A \twoheadrightarrow H$ and $A \twoheadrightarrow I$

Using $\quad A \twoheadrightarrow I$ (A, C, G, I) can be decomposed into (A, I) (A, C, G)

Thus the algorithm terminates resulting in following relation schemas in 4NF.

$\quad$ (A, B) {A $\twoheadrightarrow$ B}

$\quad$ (C, G, H) {G $\twoheadrightarrow$ H}

$\quad$ (A, I) {A $\twoheadrightarrow$ I}

$\quad$ (A, C, G) { } .

This decomposition is loss-less join decomposition. But, it is not a dependency preserving decomposition, since it fails to preserve the multivalued dependency B $\twoheadrightarrow$ HI.

If we are given a set of multivalued and functional dependencies, it is advantageous to find database design that meets the three criteria of :

1. 4NF
2. Dependency Preservation
3. Loss-less Join

But, if all dependencies are the functional dependencies, then the first criteria is just BCNF.

When we cannot achieve all three goals, we compromise on 4NF and accept BCNF or even 3NF with dependency preservation.

4.15 JOIN DEPENDENCIES

Let R be a relation schema and $R_1, R_2, ..., R_n$ be a decomposition of R. A relation r (R) satisfies the join dependency $(R_1, R_2, ..., R_n)$ if and only if

$$r = \pi_{R_1}(r) \bowtie \pi_{R_2}(r) \bowtie \pi_{R_3}(r) \bowtie \text{-----} \bowtie \pi_{R_n}(r)$$

A necessary condition for a relation schema R to satisfy a join dependency * $(R_1, R_2, ..., R_n)$ is that,

$$R = R_1 \cup R_2 ...... \cup R_n.$$

A join dependency is trival if one of the R'_1 is R itself.

A join dependency is the assertion that the decomposition of R into $R_1, R_2, ..., R_n$ is a loss-less join decomposition of R.

Consider the join decomposition * (R_1, R_2) on schema R. This decomposition requires that, for all legal r (R),

$$r = \pi_{R_1}(r) \bowtie \pi_{R_2}(r)$$

Let r contains two tuples t_1 and t_2 defined as follows :

	$R_1 - R_2$	$R_1 \cdot R_2$	$R_2 - R_1$
t_1	$a_1, a_2, ..., a_i$	$a_{i+1}, ..., a_j$	$a_{j+1}, ..., a_n$
t_2	$b_1, b_2, ..., b_j$	$a_{i+1}, ..., a_j$	$b_{j+1}, ..., b_n$

$t_1 [R_1 \cap R_2] = t_2 [R_1 \cap R_2]$, but t_1 and t_2 have different values on all other attributes.

Let us compute $\pi_{R_1}(r) \bowtie \pi_{R_2}(r)$ Table 4.18. Shows $\pi_{R_1}(r)$ and $\pi_{R_2}(r)$.

Table 4.18

$\pi_{R_1}(r)$

	$R_1 - R_2$	$R_1 \cap R_2$
$\pi_{R_1}(t)$	$a_1, ..., a_i$	$a_{i+1}, ..., a_j$
$\pi_{R_1}(t)$	$b_1, ..., b_i$	$a_{i+1}, ..., a_j$

$\pi_{R_2}(r)$

	$R_1 \cap R_2$	$R_2 - R_1$
$\pi_{R_2}(t)$	$a_{i+1}, ..., a_j$	$a_{j+1}, ..., a_n$
$\pi_{R_2}(t)$	$a_{i+1}, ..., a_j$	$b_{j+1}, ..., b_n$

The join $\pi_{R_1}(r) \pi_{R_2}(r)$ can be given as follows :

Table 4.19

	$R_1 - R_2$	$R_1 \cap R_2$	$R_2 - R_1$
t_1	$a_1, ..., a_i$	$a_{i+1}, ..., a_j$	$a_{j+1}, ..., a_n$
t_2	$b_1, ..., b_i$	$a_{i+1}, ..., a_j$	$b_{j+1}, ..., b_n$
t_3	$a_1, ..., a_i$	$a_{i+1}, ..., a_j$	$b_{j+1}, ..., b_n$
t_4	$b_1, ..., b_i$	$a_{i+1}, ..., a_j$	$a_{j+1}, ..., b_n$

Join contains two additional tuples t_3 and t_4 as shown in above Table 4.19.

From the above Table 4.16 we can say that, * (R_1, R_2) is equivalent to,

$$R_1 \cap R_2 \twoheadrightarrow R_1 \text{ and}$$
$$R_1 \cap R_2 \twoheadrightarrow R_2.$$

According to the definition of loss-less join decomposition, the above statement proves that join dependency *(R_1, R_2) forms loss-less join decomposition of R into R_1 and R_2.

Every join dependency of the form * (R_1, R_2) is therefore equivalent to a multivalued dependency. However, there are join dependencies that are not equivalent to any multivalued dependency.

Consider the relation schema R = (A, B, C). The join dependency *((A, B), (B, C), (A, C)) is not equivalent to any collection of multivalued dependencies. The tabular representation of join-dependency is given in Table 4.20.

Consider relation r (A, B, C) as shown in Table 4.20.

Table 4.20 : Tabular Representation of * ((A, B), (B, C), (A, C))

A	B	C
a_1	b_1	c_2
a_2	b_1	c_1
a_1	b_2	c_1
a_1	b_1	c_1

Table 4.21 : Relation r (A, B, C)

A	B	C
a_1	b_1	c_2
a_2	b_1	c_1
a_1	b_2	c_1
a_1	b_1	c_1

The relation r satisfies the join dependency * ((A, B), (B, C), (A, C)). It can be easily verified that

$\pi_{AB}(r) \bowtie \pi_{BC}(r) \bowtie \pi_{AC}(r)$ is exactly equal to r.

But r does not satisfy any non-trival multivalued dependency. It fails to satisfy any of

A $\twoheadrightarrow$ B, A $\twoheadrightarrow$ C, B $\twoheadrightarrow$ A, B $\twoheadrightarrow$ C, C $\twoheadrightarrow$ A, or C $\twoheadrightarrow$ B.

4.15.1 Project Join Normal Form : (PJNF)/5NF

A relation schema is in PJNF with respect to a set D of functional, multivalued and join dependencies if, for all join dependencies in D^+ of the form * (R_1 R_2 ... R_n) where each $R_i \subseteq R$ and R = $R_1 \cup R_2 \cup ... \cup R_n$ at least one of the following holds.

- * (R_1, R_2 ... R_n) is a trival join dependency.
- Every R_i is a super key for R.

A database design is in PJNF if each member of the set of relation schemas that constitutes the design is in PJNF.

PJNF is also known as Fifth Normal Form (5NF).

Example : The loan_info_schema is decomposed into following three relations.

loan_info_schema = (branch_name, customer_name, loan_no., amount)

R_1 - schema (loan_no., branch_name)

R_2 - schema (loan_no., customer_name)

R_3 - schema (loan_no., amount)

with the join dependency

*((loan no., customer_name) (loan_no., branch_name) (loan_no., amount))

This decomposition is in PJNF.

Because every multivalued dependency is also a join dependency, it is easy to see that every PJNF schema is also in 4NF. Thus, we may not be able to find a dependency preserving decomposition into PJNF for a given schema.

4.15.2 Domain Key Normal Form (DKNF)

Before we define DKNF, let us define two additional types of dependencies, domain constraints and key constraints and the concept of general constraints.

Domain Constraint (DC) : Each attribute A_i of a relation schema R (A_1, A_2, ... , A_n) is assigned a domain constraint of the form IN (A_i, S_{Ai}). This means that the attribute A_i of relation r, defined on the relation schema R, must have value from set S_{A1}.

Key Constraint (KC) : For the relation schema R (A_1, A_2, A., ...) the key constraint KEY (K), where K is a subset of R; is the restriction that no two tuples of relation r defined on the relation schema R have the same values for the attributes in K.

General Constraint (GC) : A general constraint is expressed as a simple statement or predicate and specifies some special requirements. Each tuple of a relation must specify this predicate for it to be a valid tuple.

The DKNF is not defined in terms of FD, MVD or JD. The central requirements of DKNF are the basic concepts of domains, keys and general constraints.

A relation schema is in DKNF if every general constraint can be inferred from the knowledge of the attributes involved in the schema, their underlying domains, and the sets of attributes that forms the keys.

The DKNF is considered to be the highest form of normalization, since all insertion and deletion anomalies are eliminated and all general constraints can be verified by using only DCs and KCs.

A relation that is in DKNF, is also in PJNF and therefore 4NF and BCNF.

Advantage of DKNF is that all constraints could be satisfied by ensuring that tuples of the relations satisfy the corresponding domain and key constraints. Since, this is easy to implement, relations in DKNF are preferable.

REVIEW QUESTIONS ON INSTRUCTIONAL OBJECTIVES

1. State the basic concept of the theory of normalization with respect to relational database. Explain in detail various normal forms, giving examples.

2. What are the desirable properties of decomposition ?
3. Illustrate inference axioms with appropriate examples.
4. Define :
   (i) Prime attribute (ii) Transitive Dependency
   (iii) Partial Dependency (iv) Full Functional dependency
   (v) Canonical cover (vi) Unnormalized relation.
5. Specify algorithm for BCNF decomposition.
6. Specify algorithm for 3NF decomposition.
7. Specify algorithm for 4NF decomposition.
8. With an example prove that : Not every BCNF decomposition is dependency preserving.
9. Specify conditions for decomposition to be loss-less join decomposition and dependency preserving decomposition.
10. State and prove Armstrong's axioms for functional dependency.
11. Specify need of normalization.
12. Write a note on :
    (i) Multivalued dependency (ii) Normalization using functional dependency.
13. Given an example of relation which is in 2NF but not in 3NF. Explain.
14. What is normalization ? Explain with example that 4NF is more desirable normal form than BCNF ?
15. Define normalization rules for :
    (i) BCNF (ii) 5NF (iii) FNF (iv) DKNF (v) PJNF.

UNIVERSITY QUESTIONS

1. Compare BCNF, 3NF and 4NF. **(May 2003)**
2. What are the pitfalls in relational-database Design. **(Nov. 04, Oct. 02, April 04)**
3. Explain the functional dependencies. **(Oct. 03, Nov. 04, Oct. 02, 03, Dec. 05)**
4. What is the closure of a set of functional dependencies ? **(Oct. 02)**
5. Write a note on :
   (i) Armstrong's Axioms **(Oct. 2000, April 01, April 03)**
   (ii) Canonical Cover **(May 06)**
   (iii) Normalization **(Oct. 2000, April 03)**
6. Write properties of decomposition. **(Oct. 03, April 04)**
4. What is the purpose of normalization. **(Oct. 2000)**

8. Explain why 4 NF is more desirable than BCNF. Rewrite the definition of 4NF and BCNF using the notions of domain constrains and general constraints. **(May.13)**
9. Explain various operators in relational algebra.
10. Given relation schema: R(A,B,C), S(D,E,F).

    Let relation r(R) and s(S) be given.

    Convert following SQL Statements in relational algebra form.

    1. Select * from r where B = 14
    2. Select A,F from r,s where r.C = s.D
    3. Update r, set B = B*15 where A='aaa'
    4. Select * from s where E < 20 **(May.13)**

Unit - II

CHAPTER 5
INTRODUCTION TO SQL

5.1 Introduction
5.2 Subdivisions of SQL
5.3 Data Definition Language
   1. Create table Command
   2. Alter table Command
   3. Drop table Command
5.4 Data Manipulation Language Commands
   1. Insert Command
   2. Delete Command
   3. Update Command
   4. Select Command
   5. Views in SQL
   6. Indexes in SQL
5.5 Data Control Language
   1. Grant Command
   2. Revoke Command
   3. Commit Command
   4. Rollback Command
- Review Questions on Instructional Objectives
- University Questions

5.1 INTRODUCTION

In this chapter we study the query language : Structured Query Language (SQL) which uses a combination of Relational Algebra and Relational Calculus.

It is a data sub language used to organize, manage and retrieve data from relational database, which is managed by Relational Database Management System (RDBMS).

Vendors of DBMS like Oracle, IBM, DB2, Sybase, and Ingress use SQL as programming language for their database.

SQL originated with the system R project in 1974 at IBM's San Jose Research Centre.

Original version of SQL was SEQUEL which was an Application Program Interface (API) to the system R project.

The predecessor of SEQUEL was named SQUARE. SQL-92 is the current standard and is the current version.

The SQL language can be used in two ways :
1. Interactively or
2. Embedded inside another program.

The SQL is used interactively to directly operate a database and produce the desired results. The user enters SQL command that is immediately executed. Most databases have a tool that allows interactive execution of the SQL language. These include SQL Base's SQL Talk, Oracle's SQL Plus and Microsoft's SQL server 7 Query Analyzer.

The second way to execute a SQL command is by embedding it in another language such as Cobol, Pascal, BASIC, C, Visual Basic, Java etc. The result of embedded SQL command is passed to the variables in the host program, which in turn will deal with them. The combination of SQL with a fourth-generation language brings together the best of two worlds and allows creation of user interfaces and database access in one application.

5.2 SUBDIVISIONS OF SQL

Regardless of whether SQL is embedded or used interactively, it can be divided into three groups of commands, depending on their purpose.
- Data Definition Language : (DDL).
- Data Manipulation Language : (DML).
- Data Control Language : (DCL).

Data Definition Language (DDL) :

Data Definition Language is a part of SQL that is responsible for the creation, updation and deletion of tables. It is responsible for creation of views and indexes also. The list of DDL commands is given below :

    CREATE TABLE
    ALTER TABLE
    DROP TABLE
    CREATE VIEW
    CREATE INDEX

Data Manipulation Language (DML) :

Data manipulation commands manipulate (insert, delete, update and retrieve) data. The DML language includes commands that run queries and changes in data. It includes the following commands :

    SELECT
    UPDATE
    DELETE
    INSERT

Data Control Language (DCL) :

The commands that form data control language are related to the security of the database performing tasks of assigning privileges so users can access certain objects in the database.

The DCL commands are :
- GRANT
- REVOKE
- COMMIT
- ROLLBACK

5.3 DATA DEFINITION LANGUAGE

The SQL DDL provides commands for defining relation schemas, deleting relations, creating indices, and modifying relation schemas.

The SQL DDL allows the specification of not only a set of relations but also information about each relation including :

- The schema for each relation.
- The domain of values associated with each attribute.
- The integrity constraints.
- The set of indices to be maintained for each relation.
- The security and authorization information for each relation.
- The physical storage structure of each relation on disk.

Domain/Data types in SQL :

The SQL-92 standard supports a variety of built-in domain types, including the following :

(1) Numeric data types include :

- Integer numbers of various sizes,
  INT or INTEGER
  SMALLINT
- Real numbers of various precision,
  REAL
  DOUBLE PRECISION
  FLOAT (n)
- Formatted numbers can be represented by using,
  DECIMAL (i, j) or
  DEC (i, j)
  NUMERIC (i, j) or NUMBER (i, j)

where, i - the precision, is the total number of decimal digits.

and j - the scale, is the number of digits after the decimal point.

The default for scale is zero and the default for precision is implementation defined.

(2) Character String Data Types : are either fixed - length or varying - length.

CHAR (n) or CHARACTER (n) - is fixed length character string with user specified length n.

VARCHAR (n) - is a variable length character string, with user - specified maximum length n. The full form of CHARACTER VARYING (n), is equivalent.

(3) Date and Time Data Types :

There are new data types for date and time in SQL-92.

DATE :   It is a calendar date containing year, month and day typically in the form yyyy : mm : dd

TIME :   It is the time of day, in hours, minutes and seconds, typically in the form HH : MM : SS.

Varying length character strings, date and time were not part of the SQL - 89 standard.

In this section we will study the three Data Definition Language Commands :

    CREATE TABLE
    ALTER TABLE
    DROP TABLE

1. CREATE TABLE Command :

The CREATE TABLE command is used to specify a new relation by giving it a name and specifying its attributes and constraints.

The attributes are specified first and each attribute is given a name, a data type to specify its domain of values and any attribute constraints such as NOT NULL. The key, entity integrity and referential integrity constraints can be specified within the CREATE TABLE statement, after the attributes are declared.

Syntax of Create Table Command :

```
CREATE TABLE table_name (
Column_name 1 data type [NOT NULL],
    :
    :
Column_name n data_type [NOT NULL])
```

The variables are defined as follows :

If NOT NULL is not specified, the column can have NULL values.

table_name - is the name for the table.

column_name 1 to column_name n - are the valid column names or attributes.

NOT NULL : It specifies that column is mandatory. This feature allows you to prevent data from being entered into table without certain columns having data in them.

Examples of CREATE TABLE Command :

1. **Create Table_Employee**
   (E_name   Varchar2 (20) NOT NULL,
   B_Date   Date,
   Salary   Decimal (10, 12)
   Address   Varchar2 (50));

2. **Create Table Student**
   (Student_id Varchar2 (20) NOT NULL,
   Last_Name   Varchar2 (20) NOT NULL,
   First_name   Varchar2 (20),
   B_Date   Date,
   State   Varchar2 (20),
   City   Varchar2 (20));

3. **Create Table Course**
   (Course_id   Varchar2 (5),
   Department_id Varchar2 (20),
   Title   Varchar2 (20),
   Description   Varchar2 (20));

Constraints in CREATE TABLE Command :

CREATE TABLE Command lets you enforce several kinds of constraints on a table : primary key, foreign key and check condition, unique condition.

A constraint clause can constrain a single column or group of columns in a table. There are two ways to specify constraints :

- As part of the column definition i.e. a column constraint.
- Or at the end of the create table command i.e. a table constraint.

Clauses that constrain several columns are the table constraints.

The Primary Key :

A table's primary key is the set of columns that uniquely identifies each row in the table. CREATE TABLE command specifies the primary key as follows :

CREATE TABLE table_name (
Column_name 1 data_type [NOT NULL],
      :
      :
Column_name n data type [NOT NULL],
[Constraint constraint_name]
[Primary key (Column_name A, Column_name B... Column_name X)]);

Variables are defined as follows :
table_name is the name for the table.
column_name 1 through column_name n are the valid column names
data_type is valid datatype
constraint which is optional
constraint_name identifies the primary key
column_name A through column_name X are the table's columns that compose the primary key.

Example :

1. **Create Table Employee**

(E_name	Varchar2 (20),
B_Date	Date,
Salary	Decimal (10, 2),
Address	Varchar2 (80),
Constraint	PK_Employee
Primary key (E_name));	

2. **Create Table Student**

(Student_id	Varchar2 (20),
Last_name	Varchar2 (20) NOT NULL,
First_name	Varchar2 (20),
B_Date	Date,
State	Varchar2 (20),
City	Varchar2 (20),
Constraint	PK_Student
Primary key	Student_id));

3. **Create Table Course**

Course_id	Varchar2 (5),
Department_id	Varchar2 (20),
Title	Varchar2 (20),
Description	Varchar2 (20),
Constraint	PK_Course
Primary key (Course_id, Department_id));	

Note : We do not specify NOT NULL constraint for those columns which form the primary key, since those are the mandatory columns by default. Primary keys are subject to several restrictions.

(i) A column that is a part of the primary key cannot be NULL.

(ii) A column that is defined as LONG, or LONG RAW (ORACLE data types) cannot be a part of primary key.

(iii) The maximum number of columns in the primary key is 16.

Foreign Key : A foreign key is a combination of columns with values based on the primary key values from another table. A foreign key constraint also known as a referential integrity constraint, specifies that the values of the foreign key correspond to actual values of primary key in other table.

CREATE TABLE Command specifies the foreign key as follows :

```
Create Table table_name(
(Column_name 1        data type [NOT NULL],
    :
    :
Column_name N         data type [NOT NULL],
[constraint           constraint_name
Foreign key (column_name F_1 ... Column_name F_N) references referenced-table
(column_name P_1, ... column_name P_N)]);
```

table_name - is the name for the table.

column_name 1 through column_name N are the valid columns.

constraint_name is the name given to foreign key.

referenced_table - is the name of the table referenced by the foreign key declaration.

column_name F_1 through column_name F_N are the columns that compose the foreign key.

Column_name P_1 through column_name P_N are the columns that compose the primary key in referenced_table.

Examples :

1. **Create Table Department**

```
(Department_id        Varchar2 (20),
Department_name       Varchar2 (20),
Constraint            PK_Department
Primary key           (Department_id));
```

2. **Create Table Course**

```
(Course_id            Varchar2 (20),
Department_id         Varchar2 (20),
Title                 Varchar2 (20),
Description           Varchar2 (20),
Constraint            PK_course
Primary key (Course_id, Department_id),
Constraint            FK_course
Foreign key (Department_id) references Department (Department_id));
```

Thus, primary key of course table is (Course_id, Department_id).

The primary key of Department table is (Department_id).

Foreign key of course table is (Department_id) which references the department table.

When you define a foreign key, the DBMS verifies the following :

1. A primary key has been defined for table referenced by the foreign key.
2. The number of columns composing the foreign key matches the number of primary key columns in the referenced table.
3. The datatype and width of each foreign key columns matches the datatype and width of each primary key column in the referenced table.

Unique Constraint or Candidate Key :

A candidate key is a combination of one or more columns, the values of which uniquely identify each row of the table. Create table command specifies the unique constraint as follows :

```
CREATE TABLE Table_name(
(column_name 1        data_type     [NOT NULL],
    :
    :
column_name n         data_type     [NOT NULL],
[constraint      constraint_name
Unique (Column_name A,......... Column_nameX)]);
```

Example:
1. **Create Table Student**

(Student_id	Varchar2 (20),	
Last_name	Varchar2 (20),	NOT NULL,
First_name	Varchar2 (20),	NOT NULL,
BDate	Date,	
State	Varchar2 (20),	
City	Varchar2 (20),	
Constraint	UK-student	
Unique	(last_name, first_name),	
Constraint	PK-student	
Primary key	(Student_id));	

A unique constraint is not a substitute for a primary key. Two differences between primary key and unique constraints are:

1. A table can have only one primary key, but it can have many unique constraints.
2. When a primary key is defined, the columns that compose the primary key are automatically mandatory. When a unique constraint is declared, the columns that compose the unique constraint are not automatically defined to be mandatory, you must also specify that the column is NOT NULL.

Check Constraint :

Using CHECK constraint SQL can specify the data validation for column during table creation. CHECK clause is a Boolean condition that is either TRUE or FALSE. If the condition evaluates to TRUE, the column value is accepted by database, if the condition evaluates to FALSE, database will return an error code.

The check constraint is declared in CREATE TABLE statement using the syntax:

`column_name datatype [constraint constraint_name] [CHECK (Condition)]`

The variables are defined as follows:
   column_name - is the column name
   data_type - is the column's data type

constraint_name - is the name given to check constraint condition is the legal SQL
Condition that returns a Boolean value.

Examples :
1. **Create Table Worker**

   (Name   Varchar2 (25) NOT NULL,
   Age   Number   Constraint CK_worker
   CHECK (Age Between 18 AND 65));

2. **Create Table Instructor**
   ```
   (Instructor_id        Varchar2 (20),
   Department_id         Varchar2 (20) NOT NULL,
   Name                  Varchar2 (25),
   Position              Varchar2 (25)
   Constraint       CK_instructor
   CHECK (Position in ('ASSISTANT PROFESSOR', 'ASSOCIATE PROFESSOR', 'PROFESSOR')),
   Address               Varchar2 (25),
   Constraint       PK_instructor
   Primary key (Instructor_id));
   ```

If the position of the instructor is not one of the three legal values, DBMS will return an error code indicating that a check constraint has been violated.

More than one column can have check constraint.

Create table Patient
```
(Patient_id        Varchar2 (25)      Primary key,
Body_Temp          Number (4, 1)
Constraint         Patient_BT
CHECK (Body_Temp >= 60.0 and Body_Temp <= 110.0),
Insurance_Status Char(1)
Constraint Patient_IS
CHECK (Insurance-Status in ('Y', 'y', 'N', 'n')));
```

One column can have more than one CHECK constraint.

Create table Loan - application
```
(loan_app_no  number (6) primary key,
Name Varchar2 (20),
Amount_requested number (9, 2) NOT NULL,
Amount_approved number (9, 2)
Constraint Amount_approved_limit
Check (Amount_approved<=10,00,000)
Constraint Amount_Approved_Interval
Check (Mod (Amount-Approved, 1000) = 0));
```

Establishing a Default Value for a Column :
By using DEFAULT clause when defining a column, you can establish a default value for that column. This default value is used for a column, whenever, row is inserted into the table without specifying the column in the INSERT statement.

Example :
Create table student
  (Student_id   Varchar2 (20),
  Last_name   Varchar2 (20)   NOT NULL,
  First_name   Varchar2 (20)   NOT NULL,
  BDate   Date,
  State   Varchar2 (20),
  City   Varchar2 (20),   DEFAULT 'PUNE'.
  Constraint   PK_student
  Primary key   (Student_id);

2. ALTER TABLE Command :
You can modify a table's definition using ALTER TABLE command. This statement changes the structure of a table, not its contents. Using ALTER TABLE command, you can make following changes to the table.

1. Adding a New Column to an Existing Table.

ALTER TABLE table_name
ADD (Column_name datatype
     :
     :
  Column_name n datatype);

Example :

SQL> Describe Department;

Name	Null ?	Type
Department_id		Varachar2 (20)
Department_name		Varachar2 (20)

SQL> Alter table Department
     ADD (University   Varchar2 (20),
          No_of_student   Number (3));

SQL> Describe Department;

Name	Null	Type
Department_id		Varachar2 (20)
Department_Name		Varachar2 (20)
University		Varachar2 (20)
No_of_student		Varachar2 (20)

2. Modify an Existing Column in The Existing Table.

```
ALTER TABLE table_name
MODIFY (Column_name      datatype : constraint,
... Column_name          datatype : constraint);
```

A column in the table can be modified in following ways -

(i) Changing a column definition from NOT NULL to NULL i.e. from mandatory to optional
Consider a table ex_table.

```
SQL> describe ex_table;
    Name            NULL ?          Type
    Record_no       NOT NULL        Numbers (38)
    Description                     Varchar2 (40)
    Current_value   NOT NULL        Number
SQL> Alter Table ex_table;
    modify (current_value number     Null);
    Table altered
SQL> Describe ex_table;
    Name            NULL ?          Type
    Record_No       NOT NULL        Number (38)
    Description                     Varchar2 (40)
    Current_value                   Number
```

(ii) Changing a column definition from NULL to NOT NULL.

If a table is empty, you can define a column to be NOT NULL. However, if table is not empty, you cannot change a column to NOT NULL unless every row in the table has a value for that particular column.

(iii) Increasing and Decreasing a Column's Width :

You can increase a character column's width and can increase the number of digits in a number column at any time.

Example :

```
SQL> Describe ex_table;
    Name            NULL ?          Type
    Record_No       NOT NULL        Number (38)
    Description                     Varchar2 (40)
    Current_value   NOT NULL        Number
SQL> Alter table ex_table
    modify (Description     Varchar2 (50));
    Table altered
SQL> Describe ex_table;
    Name            NULL ?          Type
```

Record_No	NOT NULL	Number (38)
Description	Varchar2 (50)	
Current_value	NOT NULL	Number

You can decrease a column's width only if the table is empty or if that column is NULL for every row of table.

3. Adding a Constraint to an Existing Table :

Any constraint i.e. a primary key, foreign key, unique key or check constraint can be added to an existing table using ALTER TABLE command.

ALTER TABLE table_name
ADD (constraint)

Example :

```
SQL> Create Table ex-table
     (Record_No      Number (38),
      Description    Varchar2 (40),
      Current_value  Number);
     Table created
SQL> Alter Table ex_table add
     (Constraint PK_ex_table primary key (Record_No));
     Table Altered.
```

4. Dropping the Constraints;

ALTER TABLE table_name
DROP Primary key

Using this you can drop primary key of table.

ALTER TABLE Table_name
DROP constraint constraint_name

Using this you can drop any constraint of the table.

Rules for Adding or Modifying A Column :

Following are the rules for adding column to a table :

(1) You may add a column at any time if NOT NULL is not specified.
(2) You may add a NOT NULL column in three steps :
   (i) Add a column without NOT NULL specified.
   (ii) Fill every row in that column with data.
   (iii) Modify the column to be NOT NULL.

Following are the rules to modify a column.

(1) You can increase a character column's width at any time.

(2) You can increase the number of digits in a NUMBER column at any time.

(3) You can increase or decrease the number of places in a NUMBER column at any time.

If a column is NULL for every row of the table, you can make following changes.

(i)   You can change its data type

(ii) You can decrease a character column's width

(iii) You can decrease the number of digits in a NUMBER column.

3. DROP TABLE Command :

Dropping a table means to remove the table's definition from the database. DROP TABLE command is used to drop the table as follows :

DROP TABLE table_name;

Example :

1. SQL > Drop table student;
   Table dropped
2. SQL > Drop table instructor;
   Table dropped.

You drop a table only when you no longer need it.

Note : The truncate command in ORACLE can also be used to remove only the rows or data in the table and not the table definition.

Example :

Truncate student

Table truncated.

Truncating cannot be rolled back.

5.4 DATA MANIPULATION LANGUAGE COMMANDS

The SQL DML includes commands to insert tuples into database, to delete tuples from database and to modify tuples in the database.

It includes a query language based on both relational algebra and tuple relational calculus.

In this section we will study following SQL DML commands.

INSERT

DELETE

UPDATE

SELECT

1. INSERT Command :

The syntax of insert statement is :

```
INSERT INTO table_name
[(column_name [ , column_name] ...... [ , column_name])]
VALUES
(column_value [ , column_value] ...... [ , column_value]);
```

The variables are defined as follows :

Table_name - is the table in which to insert the row.

column_name - is a column belonging to table.

column_value - is a literal value or an expression whose type matches the corresponding column_name.

The number of columns in the list of column_names must match the number of literal values or expressions that appear in parenthesis after the keyword *values*.

Example :

```
SQL> Insert into Employee
     (E_name, B_Date, Salary, Address)
     Values
     ('Sachin', '21-MAR-73', 50000.00, 'Mumbai');
     row created
SQL> Insert into student
     (Student_id, Last_name, First_name)
     Values
     ('SE201', 'Tendulkar', 'Sachin');
     row created
```

If the column names specified in Insert statement are more than values, then it returns an error.

Column and value datatype must match.

According to the syntax of INSERT statement, column list is an optional element. Therefore, if you do not specify the column names to be assigned values, it (DBMS) by default uses all the columns. The column order that DBMS uses is the order in which the columns were specified, when the table was created. However, use of Insert statement without column list is dangerous.

For example :

```
SQL> Describe ex_class;
     Name                    NULL ?              Type

     Class-building          NOT NULL            Varchar2 (25)
     Class-room   NOT NULL   Varchar2 (25)
     Seating-capacity                            Number (38)
SQL> Insert into ex_class
     Values
     ('250', 'Kothrud Pune', 500);
     1 row created.
```

The row is successfully inserted into the table, because, value and column data types were matching.

But the value 250 is not a correct value for column class_building.

The use of insert without column list may cause following problems.

1. The table definition might change, the number of columns might decrease or increase, and the INSERT fails as a result.
2. The INSERT statement might succeed but the wrong data could be entered in the table.

2. DELETE Command :

The syntax of delete statement is :

    DELETE FROM table_name
    [WHERE condition]

The variables are defined as follows :

table_name - is the table to be updated.

condition - is a valid SQL condition.

DELETE Command without WHERE clause will empty the table completely.

Example :

```
SQL>    Delete from Student
        Where Student_id = 'SE 201';
        1 row deleted.
SQL>    Detete from student
        Where first_name = 'Sachin' and
        Student_id = 'SE 202';
        1 row deleted.
```

3. UPDATE Command :

If you want to modify existing data in the database, UPDATE command can be used to do that. With this statement you can update zero or more rows in a table.

The syntax of UPDATE command is :

```
UPDATE table_name
SET  column_name :: expression
    [, column_name :: expression]
    [, column_name :: expression]
    [where condition]
```

The variables are defined as follows :

table_name is the table to be updated.

column_name is a column in the table being updated.

expression is a valid SQL expression.

condition is a valid SQL condition.

The UPDATE statement references a single table and assigns an expression to at least one column. The WHERE clause is optional; if an UPDATE statement does not contain a WHERE clause, the assignment of a value to a column will be applied to all rows in the table.

Example :

```
SQL> Update Student
     Set
     City = 'Pune',
     State = 'Maharashtra';
SQL> Update Instructor
     Set
     Position = 'Professor'
     where
     Instructor_id = 'P3021';
```

SQL Grammar :

Here, are some grammatical requirements to keep in mind when you are working with SQL.

1. Every SQL statement is terminated by a semicolon.
2. An SQL statement can be entered on one line or split across several lines for clarity.
3. SQL is not case sensitive. You can mix uppercase and lowercase when referencing SQL keywords (Such as SELECT and INSERT), table names, and column names.

However, case does matter when referencing to the contents of a column.

For Example : If you ask for all customers whose last names begin with 'a' and all customer names are stored in uppercase, you won't receive any rows at all.

4. SELECT Command :

The basic structure of an SQL expression consists of three clauses :

select, from and where.

- The select clause corresponds to the projection operation of the relational algebra. It is used to list the attributes desired in the result of a query.
- The from clause corresponds to the cartesian product operation of the relational algebra. It lists the relations to be scanned in the elevation of the expression.
- The where clause corresponds to the selection predicate of the relational algebra. It consists of predicate involving attributes of the relations that appear in the from clause.

Simple SQL query i.e. select statement has the form :

$$\text{select } A_1, A_2, ..., A_n$$
$$\text{from } r_1, r_2, ..., r_m$$
$$\text{where P is predicate.}$$

The variables are defined as follows :

$A_1, A_2, ..., A_n$ represent the attributes.

$r_1, r_2, ..., r_m$ represent the relations from which the attributes are selected.

P - is the predicate.

This query is equivalent to the relational algebra expression

$$\pi_{A_1, A_2, ... A_n} (\sigma_P (r_1 \times r_2 \times r_3 ... \times r_m))$$

Where clause is optional. If the where clause is omitted, the predicate P is true.

Select clause forms the cartesian product of relations named in the **from** clause, performs a relational algebra selection using the where clause and then projects the results onto the attributes of the select clause.

A Simple Select Statement :

At a minimum, select statement contains the following two elements.

1. The select list, the list of columns to be retrieved.
2. The from clause, the tables from which to retrieve the rows.

Examples : Consider the student database table.

1. A simple select statement - a query that retrieves only student_id from the student table is given.

```
SQL> select student_id
     from student;
     student_id
```

     S 10231
     S 10232
     S 10233
     S 10234
     S 10235
     S 10236
     6 rows selected.

2. To select student_id and students Last name, the select statement is :

```
SQL> select student_id, First_name
     from student;
     student_id      First_name
```

     S 10231   Sachin
     S 10232   Rahul
     S 10233   Ajay
     S 10234   Sunil
     S 10235   Kapil
     S 10236   Anil
     6 rows selected.

To select all columns in the table you can use :

```
     select  *
     from table_name;
```

Example :

```
SQL> select  *
     from student;
```

Student_id	Last_name	First_name	B_Date	State	City
S 10231	Deshpande	Sachin	12/3/78	Maharashtra	Pune
S 10232	Gandhi	Rahul	9/2/58	Delhi	Delhi
S 10233	Kapur	Ajay	7/12/62	Maharashtra	Bombay
S 10234	Kulkarni	Sunil	6/9/75	Maharashtra	Pune
S 10235	Dev	Kapil	2/3/71	Tamilnadu	Madras
S 10236	Kumar	Anil	5/9/80	Maharashtra	Bombay

DATABASE MANAGEMENT SYSTEMS (T.E. IT) — INTRODUCTION TO SQL

The results returned by every SELECT statement constitutes a temporary table. Each received record is a row in this temporary table, and each element of the select list is a column. If a query does not return any record, the temporary table can be thought of as empty.

Expressions in the Select List :

In addition to specifying columns, you also can specify expressions in the select list.

Following arithmetic operators can be used in select list :

Description	Operator
Addition	+
Subtraction	−
Multiplication	*
Division	/

For example : Consider the following queries using operators in select list :

```
SQL> Select E_name, Salary * 1000
     from Employee;
```

E_name	Salary * 1000
Sachin	1,00,00,000
Rahul	2,00,00,000
Ajay	1,00,00,000
Anil	1,00,00,000

4 rows selected.

```
SQL> Select E_name, Salary + 10000
     from Employee;
```

E_name	Salary + 10000
Sachin	20,000
Rahul	30,000
Ajay	20,000
Anil	30,000

4 rows selected.

Select Statement Using Where Clause :

select and *from* clauses provide you with either some columns and all rows or all columns and all rows. But if you want only certain rows, you need to add another clause, the **where** clause.

where clause consists of one or more conditions that must be satisfied before a row is retrieved by the query.

It searches for a condition and narrows your selection of data.

For example : Consider select statement with where clause given below :

```
SQL> Select Student_id, First_name
     from Student
     where Student_id = 'S10234';
```

Student_id	First_name
S10234	Sunil

1 row selected

```
SQL> Select E_name  Salary
     from Employee
     where Salary > 10000;
```

E_name	Salary
Rahul	20000
Anil	20000

2 row selected

where, uses the logical connectives : **and, or** and **not**.

where clause uses the comparison operators

Description	Operator
Less than	<
Less than or equal to	<=
Greater than	>
Greater than or equal to	>=
Equal to	=
Not equal to	!= or <>

```
SQL> Select E_name, Salary
     from Employee
     where Salary > 10000 and E_name = Anil
```

E_name	Salary
Anil	20000

1 row selected.

5. Views in SQL :

A view in SQL terminology is a single table that is derived from other tables. These other tables could be base tables or previously defined views. A view does not necessarily exist in physical form; it is considered a virtual table in contrast to base tables whose tuples are actually stored in the database. This limits the possible update operations that can be applied to views but does not provide any limitations on querying a view. We can think of view as a way specifying a table that we need not exist physically.

Specification of Views in SQL :

The command to specify a view is CREATE VIEW. We give the view a table name, a list of attribute names and a query to specify the contents of view. If none of the view attributes result from applying functions or arithmetic operations, we do not have to specify attribute names for the view as they will be the same as the names of the attributes of the defining tables.

Example :

Consider the following relation scheme and corresponding relation.

employee_schema (emp_name, street, city)

works_schema (emp_name, comp_name, salary

company_schema (comp_name, city)

emp_name	street	city
Sachin	XYZ	Pune
Rahul	ABC	Mumbai
Raj	ABC	Pune
Ajay	XYZ	Mumbai
Anil	XYZ	Delhi
Sunil	ABC	Mumbai

emp_name	comp_name	salary
Sachin	TCS	10000
Rahul	MBT	12000
Raj	PCS	13000
Ajay	MBT	14000
Anil	PCS	15000
Sunil	TCS	11000

comp_name	city
TCS	Delhi
MBT	Mumbai
PCS	Pune

Create view emp_detail (emp, comp, street, city)
   As select C.emp_name, C.comp_name, E.street, E.city
      from Employee E.company C
      where E.emp_name = C.emp_name;

A view is always up date; if we modify the base tables on which the view is defined, the view automatically reflects these changes. Hence, the view is not realized at the time of view definition but rather at the time we specify a query on the view. It is the responsibility of the DBMS and not the user to make sure that the view is up to date.

If we do not need a view any more, we can use the DROP VIEW command to dispose of it.
   Drop View emp_detail;

Updating of Views :

1. A view with a single defining table is up data table if the view attributes contain the primary key or some other candidate key of the base relation, because this maps each view tuple to a single base tuple.
2. Views defined on multiple tables using joins are generally not update table.
3. Views defined using grouping and aggregate functions are not update table.

Example :

Consider the view consisting of branch names and names of customers who have either an account or a loan at that branch.

   SQL> Create view all_customer as
      (select branch_name, customer_name
      from depositor, account
      where depositor·account_number=
      account·account·account_no)
      Union
      (select branch_name, customer_name
      from borrower
      where borrower·loan_number=loan·loan_number);

The attribute names of a view can be specified explicitly as follows :

   SQL> Create view branch_total_loan (branch_name,
      total_loan) as
      select branch_name, sum (amount)
      from loan
      group by branch_name;

6. Indexes in SQL :

SQL has statements to create and drop indexes on attributes of base relation. These commands are generally considered to be part of the SQL data definition language (DDL).

An index is a physical access structure that is specified on one or more attributes of the relation. The attributes on which an index is created are termed indexing attributes. An index makes accusing tuples based on conditions that involve its indexing attributes more efficient. This means that in general executing a query will take less time if some attributes involved in the query conditions were indexed than if they were not. This improvement can be dramatic for queries where large relations are involved. In general, if attributes used in selection conditions and in join conditions of a query are indexed, the execution time of the query is greatly improved.

In SQL indexed can be created and dropped dynamically. The create Index command is used to specify an index. Each index is given a name, which is used to drop the index when we do not need it any more.

Example :

```
Create Index Emp_Index
ON Employee (Emp_name);
```

In general, the index is arranged in ascending order of the indexing attribute values. If we want the values in descending order we can add the keyword DESC after the attribute name. The default in ASC for ascending. We can also create an index on a combination of attributes.

Example :

```
Create Index Emp_Index1
ON Employee (Emp_name ASC,
             Comp_name DESC);
```

There are two additional options on indexes in SQL. The first is to specify the key constraint on the indexing attribute or combination of attributes.

The keyword unique following the CREATE command is used to specify a key. The second option on index creation is to specify whether on index is clustering index. The keyword cluster is used in this case of the end of the create Index command. A base relation can have atmost one clustering index but any number of non_clustering indexes.

To drop an index, we issue the Drop Index command. The reason for dropping indexes is that they are expensive to maintain whenever the base relation is updated and they require additional storage. However, the indexes that specify a key constraint should not be dropped as long as we want the system to continue enforcing that constraint.

Example :

```
Drop Index Emp_Index;
```

5.5 DATA CONTROL LANGUAGE

The data control language commands are related to the security of database. They perform tasks of assigning privileges, so users can access certain objects in the database. This section deals with DCL commands.

1. GRANT Command :

The objects created by one user are not accessible by another user unless the owner of those objects gives such permissions to other users. These permissions can be given by using the **GRANT** statement. One user can grant permission to another user if he is the owner of the object or has the permission to grant access to other users.

The grant statement provides various types of access to database objects such as tables, views and sequences.

Syntax :

```
GRANT {object privilages}
    ON object name
    To user name
    [with GRANT OPTION]
```

Object Privilages :

Each object privilage that is granted authorizes the grantee to perform some operations on the object. The user can grant all the privileges or grant only specific object privilages.

The list of object privilages is as follows :

ALTER : Allows the grantee to change the table definition with the ALTER TABLE command.

DELETE : Allows the grantee to remove the records from the table with the DELETE command.

INDEX : Allows the grantee to create an index on table with the CREATE INDEX command.

INSERT : Allows the grantee to add records to the table with the INSERT command.

SELECT : Allows the grantee to query the tables with SELECT command.

UPDATE : Allows the grantee to modify the records in tables with UPDATE command.

With grant option : It allows the grantee to grant object privileges to other users.

Examples

1. Grant all privilages on student table to user Pradeep.

```
SQL > GRANT ALL
    ON student
    To Pradeep;
```

2. Grant select and update privilages on student table to Mita

> SQL> GRANT SELECT, UPDATE
> ON student
> To Mita;

3. Grant all privilages on student table to user Sachin with grant option.

> SQL> GRANT ALL
> ON student
> To Sachin
> WITH GRANT OPTION;

2. REVOKE Command :

The REVOKE statement is used to deny the grant given on an object.

Syntax :

> REVOKE {object privilages}
> ON object name
> FROM user name;

The list of object privilages is :

ALTER : Allows the grantee to change the table definition with the ALTER TABLE command.

DELETE : Allows the grantee to remove the records from the table with the DELETE command.

INDEX : Allows the grantee to create an index on table with the CREATE INDEX command.

INSERT : Allows the grantee to add records to the table with the INSERT command.

SELECT : Allows the grantee to query the tables with SELECT command.

UPDATE : Allows the grantee to modify the records in tables with UPDATE command.

You cannot use REVOKE command to perform following operations :

1. Revoke the object privilages that you did not grant to the revokee.
2. Revoke the object privilages granted through the operating system.

Examples

1. Revoke Delete privilege on student table from Pradeep.

> REVOKE DELETE
> ON student
> From Pradeep;

2. Revoke the remaining privilages on student that were granted to Pradeep.

> Revoke ALL
> ON student
> FROM Pradeep

3. COMMIT Command :

Commit command is used to permanently record all changes that the user has made to the database since the last commit command was issued or since the beginning of the database session.

Syntax :
   COMMIT;

Implicity COMMIT :
   The actions that will force a commit to occur even without your instructing it to are :
   - quit, exit,
   - create table or create view
   - drop table or drop view
   - grant or revoke
   - connect or disconnect
   - alter
   - audit and non-audit

Using any of these commands is just like using commit. Until you commit, only you can see how your work affects the tables. Anyone else with access to these tables will continue to get the old information.

4. ROLLBACK Command :

The ROLLBACK statement does the exact opposite of the commit statement. It ends the transaction but undoes any changes made during the transaction. ROLLBACK is useful for two reasons :

1. If you have made a mistake, such as deleting the wrong row for a table, you can use ROLLBACK to restore the original data. ROLLBACK will take you back to intermediate statement in the current transaction, which means that you do not have to erase the entire transaction.
2. ROLLBACK is useful if you have started a transaction that you cannot complete. This might occur if you have a logical problem or if there is an SQL statement that does not execute successfully. In such cases ROLLBACK allows you to return to the starting point to allow you to take corrective action and perhaps try again.

Syntax :

   ROLLBACK [WORK] [TO [SAVEPOINT] savepoint]

Where,
WORK   - is optional and is provided for ANSI compatibility,
SAVEPOINT   - is optional and is used to rollback a partial transaction, as far as the specified savepoint.

Savepoint : is a savepoint created during the current transaction.

Using rollback without savepoint clause.
   1. Ends the transaction.
   2. Undoes all the changes in the current transaction.
   3. Erases all savepoints in that transaction

4. Releases the transaction locks.

Using rollback with the to savepoint clause.
1. Rolls back just a portion of the transaction.
2. Retains the savepoint rolled back to, but losses those created after the named savepoint.
3. Releases all tables and row locks that were acquired since the savepoint was taken.

Example :
To rollback entire transaction : ROLLBACK,
To rollback to savepoint sps : ROLLBACK TO SAVEPOINT sps;

Savepoints :
Savepoints mark and save the current point in the current processing of a transaction. Used with the ROLLBACK statement, savepoints can undo part of a transaction.

By default the maximum number of savepoints per transaction is 5. An active savepoint is the one that is specified since the last commit or rollback.

Syntax : SAVEPOINT savepoint :
After a savepoint, is created, you can either continue processing, commit your work rollback the entire transaction or rollback to the savepoint.

REVIEW QUESTIONS ON INSTRUCTIONAL OBJECTIVES

1. Define following terms :
   (i) DDL   (ii) DML
2. What are the data types in SQL ?
3. Give syntax of following SQL commands :
   (i) Create   (ii) Alter
   (iii) Drop   (iv) Insert
   (v) Delete   (vi) Update
   (vii) Select
4. What are sub-divisions of SQL ?
5. What are the set operations of SQL-92 ? Explain with examples.
6. Write a note on :
   (i) Nested sub-queries   (ii) Views in SQL
   (iii) Indexes in SQL   (iv) DCL
   (v) Embedded SQL   (vi) Dynamic SQL.

UNIVERSITY QUESTIONS

1. Explain SQL commands for transaction processing.   (May 2003)
2. Explain SQL Data types.   (Nov. 04, May 06)
3. Write a note on Indexes.   (Oct. 2000, Oct. 03, May 06)
4. Explain various database languages.   (May 13)

CHAPTER 6
SQL DML QUERIES

6.1 Select Query and Clauses
6.2 Select Statement with Order By Clause
6.3 Group By Clause
6.4 Having Clause
6.5 String Operation
6.6 Distinct Rows
6.7 Rename Operation
6.8 Set Operations
6.9 Aggregate Functions
6.10 Nested Sub Queries
• Example Queries
• Review Questions on Instructional Objectives
• University Questions

6.1 SELECT QUERY AND CLAUSES

The basic structure of an SQL expression consists of three clauses :
select, from and where.

- The **Select Clause** corresponds to the projection operation of the relational algebra. It is used to list the attributes desired in the result of a query.
- The **From Clause** corresponds to the cartesian product operation of the relational algebra. It lists the relations to be scanned in the elevation of the expression.
- The **Where Clause** corresponds to the selection predicate of the relational algebra. It consists of predicate involving attributes of the relations that appear in the from clause.

Simple SQL query i.e. select statement has the form :

    select $A_1, A_2, ..., A_n$

    from $r_1, r_2, ..., r_m$

    where P is the predicate.

The variables are defined as follows :

    $A_1, A_2, ..., A_n$ represent the attributes.

    $r_1, r_2, ..., r_m$ represent the relations from which the attributes are selected.

    P - is the predicate.

This query is equivalent to the relational algebra expression

$$\pi_{A_1, A_2, \ldots, A_n} (\sigma_p (r_1 \times r_2 \times \ldots \times r_m))$$

where, clause is optional. If the where clause is omitted, the predicate P is true.

Select Clause forms the cartesian product of relations named in the *from* clause, performs a relational algebra selection using the *where,* clause and then projects the results onto the attributes of the select clause.

The purpose of select statement is to retrieve and display data from one or more database tables It is an extremely powerful statement capable of performing the equivalent relational algebra's Selection, Projection and Join operations in a single statement. Select is the most frequently used SQL command and has the following general form :

```
SELECT      DISTINCT |ALL]
FROM        Table_Name [alias][,...]
[WHERE      condition]
[GROUP BY   column_List] [HAVING condition]
[ORDER BY   column_List]
```

The sequence of processing in a select statement is :

FROM
WHERE
GROUP BY
HAVING
SELECT
ORDER BY

The order of the clauses in the select command can not be changed. The only two mandatory columns are : SELECT and FROM, the remainder are optional.

1. Expressions in the Select List :

In addition to specifying columns, you also can specify expressions in the select list.

Following arithmetic operators can be used in select list :

Description	Operator
Addition	+
Subtraction	−
Multiplication	*
Division	/

For example : consider the following queries using operators in select list :

SQL> Select E_name, Salary * 1000
     from Employee;

E_name	Salary * 1000
Sachin	1,00,00,000
Rahul	2,00,00,000
Ajay	1,00,00,000
Anil	1,00,00,000

4 rows selected.

SQL> Select E_name, Salary + 10000
from Employee;

E_name	Salary + 10000
Sachin	20,000
Rahul	30,000
Ajay	20,000
Anil	30,000

4 rows selected.

2. **Select statement using Where Clause :**

select and **from** clauses provide you with either some columns and all rows or all columns and all rows. But if you want only certain rows, you need to add another clause, the **where clause**.

where clause consists of one or more conditions that must be satisfied before a row is retrieved by the query.

It searches for a condition and narrows your selection of data.

For example : Consider select statement with where clause given below :

SQL> Select Student_id, First_Name
from Student
where Student_id = 'S10234';

Student_id	First_name
S10234	Sunil

1 row selected

SQL> Select E_name Salary
from Employee
where Salary > 10000

E_name	Salary
Rahul	20000
Anil	20000

2 row selected

where uses the logical connectives : **and**, **or** and **not**.

where clause uses the comparison operators

Description	Operator
Less than	<
Less than or equal to	<=
Greater than	>
Greater than or equal to	>=
Equal to	=
Not equal to	!= or <>

SQL> Select E_name, Salary
        from Employee
        where Salary>10000 and E_name = Anil

E_name	Salary
Anil	20000

1 row selected.

6.2 SELECT STATEMENT WITH ORDER BY CLAUSE

ORDER BY clause is similar to the GROUP BY clause. The ORDER BY clause enables you to sort your data in either ascending or descending order.

The ORDER BY clause consists of a list of column identifiers that the result is to be sorted on, separated by columns. A column identifier may be either a column name or a column number.

It is possible to include more than one element in the ORDER BY clause. The major sort key determines the overall order of the result table

If the values of the major sort key are unique, there is no need for additional keys to control the sort. However, if the values of the major sort key are not unique, there may be multiple rows in the result table with the same value for the major sort key. In this case it may be desirable to order rows with the same value for the major sort key by some additional sort key. If a second element appears in the ORDER BY clause, it is called a minor sort key.

Example : Consider the worker database :

SQL> select *
        from worker
        order By F_NAME asc 0;

F_NAME	STATUS	GENDER	BIRTHDATE
Ajay	Regular	M	05 / 03 / 69
Ashwini	Regular	F	11 / 01 / 70
Rahul	Summer	M	01 / 12 / 72
Smita	Regular	F	23 / 09 / 67

DATABASE MANAGEMENT SYSTEMS (T.E. IT)   SQL DML QUERIES

6.3 GROUP BY CLAUSE

Another helpful clause is the group by clause. A group by clause arranges your data rows into a group according to the columns you specify.

A query that includes group by clause is called a grouped query because it groups that data from the SELECT tables and generates single summary row for each group.

The columns named in the group by clause are called the grouping columns.

When GROUP BY clause is used, each item in the SELECT list must be single-valued per group.

The select clause may contain only :

- Column names
- Aggregate functions
- Constants
- An expression involving combinations of the above.

All column names in SELECT must appear in GROUP BY clause, unless the name is used only in an aggregate function. The contrary is not true; there may be column names in GROUP BY clause that do not appear in SELECT clause.

When the WHERE clause is used with GROUP BY the WHERE clause is applied first, then groups are formed from the remaining rows that satisfy the search condition.

Example :

Consider the worker table given below :

```
SQL> select *
     from worker;
```

F_NAME	STATUS	GENDER	BIRTHDATE
Ashwini	Regular	F	11 / 01 / 70
Rahul	Summer	M	01 / 12 / 72
Ajay	Regular	M	05 / 03 / 69
Smita	Regular	F	23 / 09 / 67

```
SQL> Select *
     from worker
     Group By status;
```

F_NAME	STATUS	GENDER	BIRTHDATE
Ashwini	Regular	F	11 / 01 / 70
Ajay	Regular	M	05 / 03 / 69
Smita	Regular	F	23 / 09 / 67
Rahul	Summer	M	01 / 12 / 72

(2) To group by more than one column,
SQL> select *
    from worker
    Group By status, Gender;

F_NAME	STATUS	GENDER	BIRTHDATE
Ashwini	Regular	F	11 / 01 / 70
Smita	Regular	F	23 / 09 / 67
Ajay	Regular	M	05 / 03 / 69
Rahul	Summer	M	01 / 12 / 72

6.4 HAVING CLAUSE

The Having clause is similar to the where clause. The Having clause does for aggregate data what where clause does for individual rows. The having clause is another search condition. In this case, however, the search is based on each group of grouped table.

The difference between where clause and having clause is in the way the query is processed.

In a where clause, the search condition on the row is performed before rows are grouped. In having clause, the groups are formed first and the search condition is applied to the group.

Syntax :

    select select_list
    from table_list
    [where condition [AND : OR] ...... condition]
    [group by column 1, column 2, ... column N]
    [Having condition]

Example :

SQL> select *
    from worker
    Group By status, Gender
    Having Gender = 'F';

F_NAME	STATUS	GENDER	BIRTHDATE
Ashwini	Regular	F	11 / 01 / 70
Smita	Regular	F	23 / 09 / 72

```
SQL> select *
     from worker
     where Birthdate < 11 / 01 / 70
     Group By status, Gender
     Having Gender = 'M';
```

F_NAME	STATUS	GENDER	BIRTHDATE
Ajay	Regular	M	05 / 03 / 69

6.5 STRING OPERATION

1. Searching for rows with the LIKE operator.

The most commonly used operation on strings is pattern matching using the operator like.

We describe patterns using two special characters.
- **Percent (%) :** The % character matches any substring
- **Underscore (_) :** The _ character matches any character.

Patterns are case sensitive.

To illustrate consider the following examples :

1. "con%" matches with any string beginning with 'con'.
   For example : Concurrent, Conference.
2. "% nfi %" matches any string containing "nfi" as a substring.
   For example : Confidence, Confidential, Confirm, Confine.
3. "- - -" matches any three characters.
4. "- - - %" matches any string of at least three characters.

Patterns are expressed in SQL using like operator.

Example queries :

1. Find the names of customers whose city name include "bad".

```
SQL>  select cust_name, cust_city
      from customer
      where cust_city like "%bad";
```

Cust_name	Cust_city
Sachin	Aurangabad
Rahul	Hyderabad
Ajay	Ahemadabad

2. Find the student's last name and id if the last name begins with "Desh".

SQL> select student_id, last_name
from student
where last_name like "Desh %";

student_id	last_name
101	Deshpande
102	Deshmukh

For patterns to include the special characters (i.e. % & _), SQL allows the specification of an escape character (\). The escape character is used immediately before a special character to indicate that the special pattern character is to be treated like a normal character. We define the escape character for a like comparison using the escape keyword. To illustrate, consider the following patterns, which use a backslash (\) as the escape character :

1. like 'ab\%cd' escape '\'

    matches all strings beginning with "ab%cd".

2. like 'ab\\cd' escape '\'

    matches all strings beginning with ab\cd.

3. like 'ab_cd' escape '\'

    matches all strings beginning with ab_cd.

SQL allows us to search for mismatches instead of matches by using the not like comparison operator.

6.6 DISTINCT ROWS

SELECT statement has an optional Keyword distinct. This keyword follows select and return only those rows which have distinct values for the specified columns. i.e. it eliminates duplicate values.

The keyword all allows to specify explicitly that the duplicates are not removed.

For example :

SQL> select **distinct** branch_name
from loan;

which eliminates duplicate values in the result.

SQL> select **all** branch_name
from loan;

it specifies that duplicates are not eliminated from result relation.

Since duplicate retention is by default, we will not use **all**.

6.7 RENAME OPERAITON

SQL provides a mechanism for renaming both relations and attributes. It uses as clause and the syntax is :

old_name as new_name

The as clause can appear in both the select and from clauses.

Example :

SQL> select **distinct** customer_name, borrower_loan_no.
from borrower, loan
where borrower·loan_no = loan·loan_no and branch_name
= 'ICICI';

This query can be rewritten using as clause as follows :

SQL> select customer_name, borrower_loan_no as loan_id
from borrower, loan
where borrower loan_no = loan·loan_no and
branch_name = 'ICICI';
where borrower_loan_no attribute is renamed as
loan_id.;

6.8 SET OPERATIONS

The SQL-92 operations UNION, INTERSECT and MINUS operate on relations and correspond to the relational algebra operations ∪, ∩, − .

Like the union, intersect and set difference in relational algebra, the relations participating in the operations must be compatible, i.e. they must have the same set of attributes.

There are restrictions on the tables that can be combined using the set operations, the most important one being that the two tables have to be union-compatible; that is they have the same structure. This implies that the two tables must contain the same number of columns, and that their corresponding columns have the same data types and lengths. It is the user's responsibility to ensure that data values in corresponding columns come from the same domain.

Union operator :

The syntax for this set operator is :

select_statement 1
Union
select_statement 2
[order_by_clause]

The variables are defined as :

select_statement 1 and select_statement 2 are valid select statements

order_by_clause is optional ORDER By Clause that references the columns by number rather than by name.

The UNION operator combines the rows returned by the first SELECT statement with rows returned by the second SELECT statement.

Keep following things in mind when you use the UNION operator.

1. The two SELECT statement may not contain an ORDER By clause; however, you can order the results of the union operation.
2. The number of columns retrieved by select_statement 1 must be equal to the number of columns retrieved by select_statement 2.
3. The data types of the columns retrieved by select_statement 1 must match with the data types of the columns retrieved by select_statement 2.
4. Here the optional ORDER_BY clause differs from the usual ORDER By clause in a select statement, because the columns used for ordering must be referenced by number rather than by name. The reason that columns must be referenced by number is that SQL does not require that the column names retrieved by select_statement 1 be identical to the column names retrieved by select_statement 2.

Example :

Find all customers having a loan, an account or both at the bank.

```
SQL> select customer_name
     from depositor
     union
     select customer_name
     from borrower.
```

Union operation finds all customer having an account, loan or both at bank.

Union operation eliminates duplicates.

Intersect Operator :

The Intersect operator returns the rows that are common between two sets of rows.

The syntax for using the INTERSECT operator is :

```
select_statement1
Intersect
select_statement2
[Order By Clause]
```

The variables are defined as follows :

Select_statement 1 and select_statement 2 are valid SELECT statements.

Order By clause is an optional Order By clause that references the columns by number rather than by name.

Here, are some requirements and considerations for using the INTERSECT operator.

1. The two select statement may not contain Order By clause; however, you can order the results of the entire Intersect operation.
2. The number of columns retrieved by select_statement 1 must be equal to the number of columns retrieved by select_statement 2.
3. The data types of columns retrieved by select_statement 1 must match the data types of the columns retrieved by select_statement 2.
4. The optional Order By clause differs from the usual Order By clause in the SELECT statement because the columns used for ordering must be referenced by number rather than by name. The reason that the columns in the Order By clause must be referenced by number rather than by name is that SQL does not require that the column names retrieved by select statement 1 be identical to column names retrieved by select-statement 2. Therefore, you must indicate the columns to be used in ordering results by their position in select list.

Example :

Find all customers who have both an account and loan at the bank.

```
SQL> (select customer_name
      from depositor)
      INTERSECT
      (select customer_name
      from borrower)
```

The intersect operator automatically eliminates duplicates. If we want to retain all duplicates, we must write INTERSECT all in place of INTERSECT.

The Minus Operator (Except Operator) :

The syntax for using Minus operator is :

```
        select_statement 1
        Minus
        select_statement 2
        [order by clause]
```

The variables defined are :

select_statement 1 and select_statement 2 are valid SELECT statements.

Order By clause is an ORDER By

Clause that references columns by numbers rather than by name.

The requirements and considerations for using the MINUS operator are essentially the same as those for the INTERSECT and UNION operator.

Example : Find all customers who have an account but no loan at the bank.

```
SQL> Select customer_name
     from depositor
     MINUS
     Select customer_name
     from borrower
```

6.9 AGGREGATE FUNCTIONS

Aggregate functions are the functions that take a collection of values as input and return a single value.

SQL offers five built-in aggregate functions.

1. Average   :   AVG
2. Minimum   :   MIN
3. Maximum   :   MAX
4. Total   :   SUM
5. Count   :   COUNT

These functions operate on a single column of a table and return a single value.

COUNT, MIN and MAX apply to both numeric and non-numeric fields, but SUM and AVG may be used on numeric fields only.

part from COUNT(*), each function eliminates nulls first and operates only on the remaining non-null values.

If we want to eliminate duplicates before the function is applied, we use the keyword DISTINCT before the column name in the function.

The keyword ALL can be used if we do not want to eliminate the duplicates. ALL is assumed if nothing is specified.

DISTINCT has no effect on MIN and MAX functions. It may effect on the result of SUM or AVG.

It is important to note that an aggregate function can be used only in SELECT list and in the HAVING clause. It is incorrect to use it elsewhere.

1. **avg Function :**

    avg function computes the column's average value.

    The input to *avg* must be a collection of numbers.

   Example : Find the average balance.

   ```
   SQL> select avg (balance)
        from account;
   ```

This aggregate function can also be applied to a group of set of tuples using group by clause.

Example : Find the average balance at each branch.

```
SQL> select branch_name, avg (balance)
     from account
     group by branch_name;
```

2. Min and Max Functions :

min and *max* return the minimum and maximum values for the specified column.

Example :

Find the minimum and maximum values of balance.

Select *max* (balance) *min* (balance) from account.

3. Sum Function :

sum function computes the column's total value. Input to this function must be a collection of numbers.

4. Count Function :

count function counts the number of rows. There are two forms of count.

count (*) - which counts all the rows in a table that satisfy any specified criteria.

count (column_name) - which counts all rows in a table that have a non-null value for column_name and satisfy the specified criteria.

NULL Values :

SQL allows the use of NULL values to indicate absence of information about the value of an attribute.

We can use the special keyword NULL in a predicate to test for a NULL value.

Example :

```
SQL> select loan_no
     from loan
     where amount is NULL;
```

The predicate NOT NULL tests for the absence of NULL values.

The use of a NULL value in arithmetic and comparison operations causes several complications. The result of an arithmetic expressions is NULL if any of the input values is NULL. The result of any comparison involving a NULL value can be thought of as being false.

SQL-92 treats the results of such comparisons as unknown, which is neither true nor false. It also allows us to test whether the result of a comparison is unknown.

In general, aggregate functions treat nulls using the following rule :

All aggregate functions except count (*) ignore NULL values in their input collection.

6.10 NESTED SUB QUERIES

SQL provides a mechanism for the nesting of sub queries. A sub query is a select-from-where expression that is nested within another query. A common use of sub queries is to perform tests for :

1. Set Membership
2. Set Comparison
3. Set Cardinality.

1. Set Membership : (in connective)

The **in** connective tests for the set membership, where the set is a collection of values produced by a select clause.

The **not** in connective tests for the absence of set membership.

As an illustration consider the following query :

1. "Find all customers who have both a loan and an account at the bank".

    Note : The result of this query can be obtained using INTERSECT operator.

    ```
    SQL> select customer_name
         from borrower
         where customer_name in (select customer_name from depositor);
    ```

i.e. find all customers having an account who are members of the set of borrowers from the bank.

2. Find all customers who have both an account and loan at the ICICI branch.

    ```
    SQL> select customer_name
         from borrower, loan
         where borrower.loan_no = loan.loan_no and
             branch_name = 'ICICI' and
         (branch_name, customer_name) in
         (select branch_name, customer_name
             from depositor, account
             where depositor.account_no = account.account_no);
    ```

Example query for not in connective :

1. Find all customers who do have a loan at the bank, but do not have an account at the bank.

    ```
    SQL> select customer_name
         from borrower
         where customer_name not in
             (select customer_name
             from depositor);
    ```

The **in** and **not** in operators can also be used on enumerated sets.

Example :

Find the customer names who have a loan at a bank and whose names are neither 'Sachin' nor 'Ajay'.

```
SQL> select customer_name
     from borrower
     where customer_name not in ('Sachin', 'Ajay');
```

2. Set Comparison :

SQL allows following set comparison operators :

< some	-	Less than at least one
<= some	-	Less than or equal to at least one
> some	-	Greater than at least one
>= some	-	Greater than or equal to at least one
= some	-	Equal to at least one
< > some	-	Not equal to at least one.

Example query :

"Find the names of all branches that have assets greater than those of at least one branch located in Bombay".

```
SQL> select branch_name
     from branch
     where assets > some (select assets
                          from branch
                          where branch_city = 'Bombay')
   Sub query(select assets
     from branch
     where branch_city = Bombay)
```

generates the set of all asset values for all branches in Bombay. The > some comparison in where clause of the outer select is true if the asset value of the tuple is greater than at least one member of the set of all asset values for branches in Bombay.

SQL also supports following set of comparison operators :

< all	:	Less than all
<= all	:	Less than or equal to all
> all	:	Greater than all
>= all	:	Greater than or equal to all
= all	:	Equal to all
< > all	:	Not equal to all.

Example Query :
Find the branch that has the highest average balance.

```
SQL> select branch_name
     from account
     group by branch_name
     having avg (balance) >= all (select avg (balance)
                                  from account
                                  group by branch_name);
```

Test for Empty Relations :
SQL includes a feature for testing whether a sub query has any tuples in its results.

The exists construct returns the value true if the argument query is non-empty.

Similarly, we can test the non-existence of tuples in a sub-query by using the not-exists construct.

Example Query using exists construct :
"Find all customers who have both an account and a loan at the bank".

```
SQL> select customer_name
     from borrower
     where exists (select *
              from depositor
              where depositor.customer_name =
              borrower.customer_name);
```

Example Query using Not exists construct :
Find all customers who have an account at all branches located in Bombay.

Note : For each customer we need to see whether the set of all branches at which that customer has an account contains the set of all branches in Bombay.

```
SQL> select distinct customer_name
     from depositor as S
     where not exists (select branch_name
     from branch
     where branch_city = 'Bombay')
              minus
     (select R.branch_name
     from depositor as T, account as R
     where T.account_number = R.account_number
              and
     S.customer_name = T.customer_name)
```

Where,
>   (select branch_name
>   from branch
>   where branch_city = 'Bombay')

Finds all the branches in Bombay.

The sub query,
>   (select R·branch_name
>   from depositor as T, account as R
>   where T·account_number = R·account_number
>   and S·customer_name = T·customer_name)

Finds all branches at which customer S·customer_name has an account.

Thus, the outer select takes each customer and tests whether the set of all branches at which the customer has an account contains the set of all branches located in Bombay.

Test for the Absence of Duplicate Tuples :

SQL includes a feature for testing whether a sub query has any duplicate tuples in its result.

The unique construct returns the value true if the argument sub query contains no duplicate tuples.

Example Query :

Find all customers who have only one account at ICICI branch.

```
SQL> select T·customer_name
     from depositor as T
     where unique (select R·customer_name
     from account, depositor as R
     where T·customer_name
         = R·customer_name and
     R·account_no = account·account_number
         and
     account·branch_name = 'ICICI');
```

We can test for the existence of duplicates in a sub-query by using the not unique construct.

Example Query :

Find all customers who have at least two accounts at the ICICI branch.

```
SQL> select distinct T·customer_name
     from depositor T
     where not unique (select R·customer_name
     from account, depositor as R
```

where T·customer_name = R·customer_name
and
R·account_number = account·account_number
and account·branch_name = 'ICICI');

6.11 EXAMPLE QUERIES

(I) Consider the following database :
    Employee (emp_no, name, skill, pay_rate)
    Position (posting_no, skill)
    Duty-allocation (posting_no, emp_no, day, shift)

Find SQL queries for the following :

1. Get complete details from Duty_allocation
    select *
    from Duty_allocation;

2. Get duty allocation details for Emp_no 123461 for the month of April 1986.
    select posting_no., shift, day
    from Duty_allocation
    where emp_no.=123461 and
        Day$\geq$19860401 and Day$\leq$19860430 ;

3. Find the shift details for employee 'XYZ' :
    select posting_no., shift, day
    from Duty_allocation, Employee
    where Duty allocation.emp_no.=Employee.emp_no and
        Name = 'XYZ';

4. Get employees whose rate of pay is more than or equal to the rate of pay of employee 'XYZ'
    select S.name, S.pay_rate
    from Employee as S, Employee as T
    where S.pay_rate>T.pay_rate
    and T.name='XYZ';

5. Compile all pairs of posting_nos requiring the same skill
    select S.posting_no., T.posting_no.
    from Position S, Position T
    where S.skill=T.skill
    and S.posting_no.<T.posting_no.;

6. Find the employees eligible to fill a position.
   select Employee.emp_no, position.posting_no, position.skill
   from Employee, Position
   where employee.skill = position.skill;

7. Get the names and pay rates of employees with emp_no less than 123460 whose rate of pay is more than the rate of pay of at least one employee with emp_no greater than or equal to 123460.
   select name, pay_rate
   from Employee
   where emp_no<123460 and
       pay_rate>some
       (select pay_rate
           from Employee
           where emp_no≥123460);

8. Get employees who are working either on the date 19860419 or 19860420
   select emp_no
   from Duty_allocation
   where Day in (19860419, 19860420);

   OR

   select emp_no
   from Duty_allocation
   where Day = 19860419 or Day = 19860420.

9. Find the names of all employees who are assigned to all positions that require a Chef's skill.
   select S.Name
   from Employee S
   where
   (select posting_no
   from Duty_allocation D
   where S.emp_no=D.emp_no)
   contains
   (select P.posting_no
   from position P
   where P.skill='Chef');

10. Find the employees with the lowest pay rate,

    select emp_no, Name, Pay_rate
    from Employee
    where pay_rate≤all
        (select pay_rate
        from Employee)

11. Get the names of Chef's paid at the minimum pay_rate.

    select name
    from Employee
    where skill='Chef' and
        pay_rate≤all
        (select pay_rate
        from Employee
        where skill='Chef')

12. Find the names and the rate of pay of all employees who are allocated a duty.

    select name, pay_rate
    from Employee
    where EXISTS
    (select *
    from Duty_allocation
    where Employee.emp_no=Duty_allocation.emp_no)

13. Find the names and the rate of pay of all employees who are not allocated a duty.

    select name, pay_rate
    from Employee
    where NOT EXISTS
    (select *
    from Duty_allocation
    where Employee.emp_no
        =Duty_allocation.emp_no)

14. Get employees who are waiters or work at posting-no 321.

> (select emp_no
> from Employee
> where skill='waiter')
> Union
> (select emp_no
> from Duty_allocation
> where posting_no=321)

15. Get employee numbers of persons who work at posting_no 321 but don't have the skill of waiter.

> (select emp_no
> from Duty_allocation
> where posting_no=321)
> minus
> (select emp_no
> from Employee
> where skill 'waiter')

16. Get a list of employees not assigned a duty.

> (select emp_no
> from Employee)
> minus
> (select emp_no
>   from Duty_allocation)

17. Get a list of names of employees with the skill of Chef who are assigned a duty.

> select Name
> from Employee
> where emp_no in
> ((select emp_no
> from Employee
> where skill='Chef')
> intersect
> (select emp_no
> from Duty_allocation));

18. Get a count of different employees on each shift.
    select shift, count (distinct emp_no)
    from Duty_allocation
    group by shift;
19. Get the employee numbers of all employees working on at least two dates.
    select emp_no
    from Duty_allocation
    group by emp_no
    having (count;*)>1

(II) Consider the given database :
    Project (project_id, proj_name, chief_arch)
    Employee (Emp_id, Emp_name)
    Assigned_To (Project_id, emp_id)
    Find the SQL queries for the following statements :

1. Get employee number of employees working on project C353.
    select emp_id
    from Assigned_To
    where project_id='C353';
2. Get details of employees working on project C353.
    select A.emp_id, emp_name
    from A.Assigned_To A, Employee
    where project_id='C353' ;
3. Obtain details of employees working on Database project.
    select Emp_name, A. Emp_id
    from A. Assigned_To A, Employee
    where project_id in (select P. project_id
        from P. project
        where P. project_name='Database');
4. Get details of employees working on both C353 and C354.
    (select Emp_name, A. emp_id
    from Assigned_to A, Employee
    where A.Project_id=C354)
    intersect
    (select emp_name, A.emp_id
    from A.Assigned_To A, Employee
    where project_id='C354');

5. Get employee numbers of employees who do not work on project C 453

    (select emp_id
    from Employee)
    minus
    (select emp_id
    from Assigned_to
    where project_id='C453');

6. Get the employee numbers of employees who work on all projects.

    select emp_id
    from Assigned_To
    where project_id=all
        (select project_id
        from project);

7. Get employee numbers of employees who work on at least all those projects that employee 107 works on

    ((select emp_id
        from Assigned_To
        where project_id=all
            (select project_id
            from Assigned_To
            where emp_id=107))
    minus 107);

8. Get employee numbers who work on at least one project that employee 107 works on.

    ((select emp_id
        from Assigned_To
        where project_id in
            (select project_id
            from Assigned_To
            where emp_id=107)
        minus 107);

(III) Consider the employee database :

employee (employee_name, street, city)
works (employee_name, company_name, salary)
company (company_name, city)

manages (employee_name, manager_name).

Give an expression in SQL for each of the following :

1. Find the names of all employees who work for FBC.
   ```
   select employee_name
   from works
   where company_name = 'FBC' ;
   ```

2. Find the names and cities of all employees who work for FBC.
   ```
   select employee.employee_name, city
   from works, employee
   where employee.employee_name = works.employee_name and company_name = 'FBC';
   ```

3. Find the names, street address, and cities of residence of all employees who work for FBC and earn more than $ 10,000.
   ```
   select employee.employee_name, street, city
   from works employee
   where employee.employee_name=works.employee_name and
   company_name ='FBC' and salary > 10000;
   ```

4. Find all employees in the database who live in the same cities as the companies for which they work.
   ```
   select w.employee_name
   from works  w, emple, comp c
   where e.emp_name=w.emp_name and
   C.company_name.w.company_name and e.city = city;
   ```

5. Find all employees in the database who live in the same cities and on the same street as do their managers.
   ```
   select E.employee_name
   from employee E.employee T, manages
   where E.employee_name=manages.employee_name
   and E.street=T.street and E.city=T.city and
   T.employee_name=manages.manager_name;
   ```

6. Find all employees in the database who do not work for FBC.
   ```
   (select employee_name
   from employee)
   minus
   (select employee_name
   from works
   where company_name='FBC');
   ```

7. Find all employees in the database who earn more than every employee of small bank corporation.

    select employee_name
    from works
    where salary>(select max (salary)
    from works
    where company_name='FBC');

8. Find all employees who earn more than the average salary of all employees of their company.

    select T.employee_name
    from works T.
    where salary>(select avg (S.salary)
    from works S.
    where T.company_name=S.company_name);

9. Find the company that has the smallest payroll.

    SQL> create view payroll (compname, smallpay)
    as
    select company_name, min (salary)
    from works
    group by company_name;

    SQL> select company_name
    from payroll
    where small_pay=(select min (small_pay) from payroll);

10. Find those companies whose employees earn a higher salary, on average than the average salary at FBC

    SQL> create view avg_salary (comp_name, av_sal)
    as
    select companyname, avg (salary)
    from works
    group by company_name

    SQL> select T.comp_name
    from avg_salary T. avg_salary S.
    where S.company_name='FBC'
    and T.av_sal>S.av_sal;

11. Find the company that has must employees.

    SQL> create view no_emp (compname, no_employee)

    as

    select company_name, count (employee_name)

    from works

    group by company_name;

    SQL> select company_name

    from no_emp

    where no_employee=(select max no_emplyee)

    from no_emp)

REVIEW QUESTIONS ON INSTRUCTIONAL OBJECTIVES

1. Explain various types of clauses.
2. Write short note on :
   (i) Group by clause,
   (ii) Having clause.
3. Explain string operation.
4. Explain aggregate function with example.

UNIVERSITY QUESTIONS

1. Consider the insurance database : **(Dec. 2004)**

   Person(driver_id, name, address)

   Car(license, model, year)

   Accident(report_no, data, location)

   Owns(driver_id, license)

Participated(driver_id, report_no, damage_amount)

Give an expression in SQL for each of the following :

(i) Find the total number of people who owned cars that were involved in accident in 1989.

(ii) Find the total number of accidents in which car belonging to John Smith is evolved.

(iii) Add a new accident to the database

(iv) Delete the Mazda belonging to John Smith.

2. Consider the schema for Presidential database, **(May 2004)**

   President (pres_id, last_name, first_name, political_party, state_from)

   Administration (start_data, pre_id, end_data, VP_last_name, VP_first_name)

   State (state_name, data_admitted, area, population, capital_city)

   Write SQL queries.

3. Considre the relation schemas : **(May 2003)**

   Customer (customer_name, customer_street, customer_city) account (branch_name, account_no, balance)

   Depositor(customer_name, account_no)

   Give an expression in SQL for following query:

   Find the average balance for each customer who lives in Harison and has at least three accounts.

4. Consider the following database : **(May 2001)**

   Frequents (visitor, stall)

   Servers (stall, icecream)

   Likes (visitor, icecream)

   Write the following queries in SQL :

   (i) Print the stalls that serve the ice cream that visitor john likes.

   (ii) Print the visitors that frequently visit at least one stall that serves the ice cream they like.

5. Write a note of Aggregate Function. **(Nov. 04)**

6. Explain in Detail Nested subqueries. **(May 05)**
7. What are the views ? Explain.
   (T.E. (Comp.) Oct. 00, T.E.(I.T.), Oct. 02, May 06, May 07)
8. Write a note modification of the database. **(April 04, May 06)**
9. Write a short note on :
   (i) Outer Join **(April 04)**
   (ii) Functions **(April 01)**
10. What is the stored procedures ? **(April 03, April 04, Dec. 05)**
11. What are the Triggers ?
    (Oct. 03, April 01, April 03, Dec. 05, Dec. 06, May 07)

CHAPTER 7
ADVANCED SQL PROGRAMMING

7.1 Embedded SQL
7.2 Dynamic SQL
7.3 Programming in MySQL
7.4 NOSQL (Not Only SQL)
    7.4.1   NOSQL Databases
    7.4.2   Important Terms used in NOSQL Databases
    7.4.3   Advantages of NOSQL Database System
    7.4.4   Drawbacks of NOSQL Database System
    7.4.5   Major DBMS Products under NOSQL
    7.4.6   Programming in NOSQL with MongoDB
    7.4.7   Query Optimization with NOSQL Databases
- Review Questions on Instructional Objectives
- University Questions

7.1 EMBEDDED SQL

Need of Embedded SQL : SQL provides a powerful declarative query language. Writing queries in SQL is typically much easier than is coding the same queries in a general-purpose programming language. However, access to a database from a general purpose language is required for at least two reasons :

1. Not all queries can be expressed in SQL since, SQL does not provide the full expressive power of a general purpose language. That is there exist queries that can be expressed in a language such as Pascal, C, Cobol, or Fortran that cannot be expressed in SQL. To write such queries, we can embed SQL within a more powerful language.

SQL is designed such that queries written in it can be optimized automatically and executed efficiently and providing the full power of a programming language makes automatic optimization exceedingly difficult.

2. Non-declarative actions such as printing a report, interacting with a user or sending the results of a query to a graphical user interface, cannot be done from within SQL. Applications typically have several components and querying or updating data is only one component, other components are written in general purpose programming languages. For an integrated application, the programs written in the programming language must be able to access the database.

The SQL standard defines embedding of SQL in a variety of programming languages, such as Pascal, PL/I, C and Control.

A language in which SQL queries are embedded is referred to as a host language, and the SQL structures permitted in the host language constitute embedded SQL.

Programs written in host language can use the embedded SQL syntax to access and update data stored in a database. This form of SQL extends the programmer's ability to manipulate the database even further.

Working of Embedded SQL :

In embedded SQL all query processing is performed by the database system. The result of query is then made available to the program one tuple at a time. An embedded SQL program must be processed by a special preprocessor prior to compilation. Embedded SQL requests are replaced with host language declarations and procedure calls that allow run-time execution of the database accesses. Then the resulting program is compiled by the host language compiler.

Syntax of Embedded SQL :

To identify embedded SQL request to the preprocessor we use EXEC SQL statement. The format is :

EXEC SQL < embedded SQL statement > END EXEC.

The exact syntax for embedded SQL requests depends on the language in which SQL is embedded.

For example : A semi-colon is used instead of END-EXEC when SQL is embedded in C or Pascal.

We place the statement SQL INCLUDE in the program to identify the place where preprocessor should insert the special variables used for communication between the program and database system.

Variables of the host language can be used within embedded SQL statements, but they must be preceded by a colon (:) to distinguish them from SQL variables.

To write a query, we use *declare cursor* statement.

Example :

Consider the banking schema, we have host language and variable *amount*. The query is to find the names and cities of residence of customers who have more than amount dollars in any account.

```
EXEC SQL
declare c cursor for
select customer_name, customer_city
from depositor, customer
where depositor.customer_name = customer.customer_name
    and
    depositor.balance > : amount
END EXEC.
```

The variable c in the example is called cursor for the query. This variable is used to identify the query in open and fetch statements.

Open Statement : Open statement causes the query to be evaluated.

The open statement for the above given query is :

    EXEC SQL open c END-EXEC

It causes the database system to evaluate the query and stores results within a temporary relation. If SQL query results in an error, the database system stores an error diagnostic in the SQL communication area (SQLCA) variables, whose declarations are inserted by SQL INCLUDE statement.

Fetch Statement : A fetch statement causes the values of one tuple be placed in host language variables. A series of fetch statements is executed to make the results available to program. The fetch statement requires one host-language variable for each attribute of the result relation.

For example : Consider that customer_name is stored in cn and customer city in cc.

    EXEC SQL fetch c into : cn : cc END EXEC :

One fetch statement return only one tuple. To obtain all tuples of the result, the program must contain a loop to iterate overall tuples. Embedded SQL assists the programmer in managing this iteration. In a relation, tuples of the result of a query are in some fixed physical order. When an open statement is executed, the cursor is set to point to the first tuple of result. When fetch is executed, the cursor is updated to point to the next tuple of the result. A variable in SQLCA is set to indicate that no further tuples remain to be processed. Thus we can use while loop to process each of the tuples.

Close Statement : A close statement must be used to tell the database system to delete the temporary relation that held the result of the query.

For example : The close statement is,

  EXEC SQL close c END EXEC

  Embedded SQL expression for database modification can be given as :

  EXEC SQL < any valid update, insert

       or delete > END EXEC

Host language variables, preceded by a colon, may appear in SQL database modification expression. If an error arises in the execution of the statement, a diagnostic is set in the SQLCA.

7.2 DYNAMIC SQL

Dynamic SQL component of SQL-92 allows programs to construct and submit SQL queries at run-time. Using dynamic SQL programs can create SQL queries as string s at run time and can execute them immediately or prepare them for subsequent use.

Preparing a dynamic SQL statement compiles it, and subsequent uses of the prepared statement use the compiled version.

Example :

    char * sqlprog = "Update account set
        balance = balance * 1.05
        where account_no = ?"
    EXEC SQL prepare dynprog from : sqlprog;
    char account -[10] = "A = 101";
    EXEC SQL execute dynprog using : account;

The dynamic SQL program contains a ? which is a place holder for a value that is provided when the SQL program is executed.

7.3 PROGRAMMING IN MYSQL

MySQL is the most popular Open Source Relational SQL database management system. MySQL is a fast, easy-to-use RDBMS being used for many small and big business applications. Being an open source DBMS, most of the organizations prefer use of it. It is flexible with JAVA and .NET platforms. It can be installed on either Windows or any open source OS like Ubuntu etc.

Features of MySQL:
- It is released under open source so easily and freely available.(One can try to change its binary too if required!)
- It handles a large subset of the functionality of the most expensive and powerful database packages.
- It makes use of standard form of the well-known SQL data language.
- It works on many operating systems and with many languages including PHP, PERL, C, C++, JAVA, etc.
- MySQL works very quickly and works well even with large data sets and with PHP.
- It supports large databases, up to 50 million rows or more in a table.
- The default file size limit for a table is 4GB, but it can be extended to a theoretical limit of 8 million terabytes (TB) depending upon OS support.
- Each MySQL server can host many databases. A web application may use its own proprietary database or a standard database like MySQL.

MySQL Commands:
- Most MySQL commands end with a semicolon (;)
- MySQL returns the total number of rows found, and the total time to execute the query after successful execution of any command..
- Commands may be entered in any letter case i.e uppercase or lowercase.

The following commands are equivalent.
   mysql>select current_date();
   mysql>select CURRENT_DATE();

Most of the MySQL commands are similar to normal SQL commands executed on Oracle with slight variation in data types.

Table 7.1 MySQL Commands

Command	Parameter	Meaning
Quit	-------------------------	Exit the command-line utility/MySQL Prompt
Use	Database name	Use a specific database
show	tables or databases	Show lists such as tables or databases available
describe	Table name	Describe a table's columns
status	-------------------------	Display database version and status
source	Filename	Execute commands from a file as a script
current_date()	-------------------------	Displays the current date of the system
version()	-------------------------	Displays the current MySQL version number installed

MySQL Data Types:

MySQL uses many different data types broken into three main categories as follows:
   (1) Numeric
   (2) Date and Time
   (3) String

Table 7.2 Data Types in MySQL

Category	Data type	Purpose
Numeric	INT	A normal signed/unsigned integer whose limit is up to 11 digits.
	TINYINT	A very small signed/unsigned integer whose limit is up to 4 digits
	SMALLINT	A small signed/unsigned integer whose limit is up to 5 digits
	MEDIUMINT	A medium sized signed/unsigned integer whose limit is up to 9 digits
	BIGINT	A large integer which can be signed/unsigned whose limit is up to 20 digits
	FLOAT(M,D)	A floating-point number that cannot be

		unsigned. Where one can define the display length (M) and the
	DOUBLE(M,D)	A double precision floating-point number that cannot be unsigned. You
	DECIMAL(M,D)	An unpacked floating-point number that cannot be unsigned. Each decimal corresponds to one byte.
Date & Time	DATE	A date in YYYY-MM-DD format, between 1000-01-01 and 9999-12-31. For instance, 09 June 1989 would be stored as 1989-06-09.
	DATETIME	A date and time combination in YYYY-MM-DD HH:MM:SS format,
	TIME	Stores the time in HH:MM:SS format.
	YEAR(M)	Stores a year in 2-digit or 4-digit format. For instance, year(2) stores year 89 for 1989 while year(4) stores 1989 actually.
String	CHAR(size)	A fixed-length string between 1 and 255 characters in length (Ex: Defining a size is optional which considers the default size as 1.
	VARCHAR (size)	A variable length string between 1 and 255 characters in length. It is similar to varchar2(size) of oracle.
	LOB Or TEXT	A field with a maximum length of 65535 characters. BLOBs are "Binary Large Objects" and it is used to store huge amount of binary data such as images. TEXT is used alternatively with BLOB to store large data with a single difference that sorts and comparisons on stored data are case sensitive on BLOBs and are not case sensitive in TEXT fields.
	ENUM	A list of items can be created from which a value is to be chosen.

Sample Table Creation in MySQL

```
mysql> create table student
    > ( rollno int,
    > sname varchar(10),
    > class  varchar(10),
    > admission_date  date
    > );
```

Different SQL commands which we have seen earlier can be easily executed on MySQL prompt.

7.4 NOSQL (NOT ONLY SQL)

NOSQL is new type of non relational database which stores data in the form of key /value store (similar to JSON in JavaScript) and many other such formats like BSON. Each NOSQL database has its own syntax of interacting with the database. NOSQL database are becoming famous because of their scalability and ability to support huge amount of data (BIG DATA).

Each database has its own advantages and user background. For example, Redis is used as caching server, Mongodb can be used in place of MySql depending upon the specific user community. They are fast, scalable, open source, support feature like Auto sharding, Replication, Dynamic schema, etc. One can't simply replace Relational database with NOSQL database because still transaction isn't supported natively in most of the NOSQL databases.

7.4.1 NOSQL Databases:

NOSQL databases can be divided into following categories:

1. Column Oriented Databases

This category involves most popular databases like **Hadoop/Hbase, Cloudera, and Amazon SimpleDB.**

A column oriented database stores data tables as sections of columns of data instead of rows of data.

E.g. a column oriented database may store data like

01: Sahil, 9922137422 ; 02: Raj, 21258962;

Here data are stored in the form of columns. 01: 02: indicate beginning of new record while 01, 02 being the unique id and colon (:) marks the beginning of new record, column data are separated by comma(,) while two record are separated by   semicolon (;). There are many advantage s of column oriented database like faster retrieval of records and compression ratio is about 1:10 (which is 1:3 in case of RDBMS).

2. Document Databases:

This category consists of one of the most popular databases nowadays in industry such as **MongoDB, CouchDB, Cloudbase Server** etc.

As the name suggests these type of database stores data in the form of documents. A document can be in a JSON, BSON, XML, YAML, etc format. Documents are retrieved from the database using unique key that represents that document. This key may be a simple string, URI, or a path.

3. Key Value Databases:

In key-value database each item in the database is stored as an attribute name (or "key"), together with its value.

DynamoDB, Redis, Azure Table storage are some of the databases from this category.

4. Graph Databases:

This category of database uses graph structures with nodes, edges, and properties to represent and store data in database. A graph databases is faster for associative data sets and hence it's gaining popularity these days. Example databases include **OrientDB, Neo4J, and InfinityGraph.**

7.4.2 Important Terms used in NOSQL Databases

1. **Horizontal Scaling**: To scale horizontally means to add more nodes to a system, such as adding a new computer to a distributed software application.
2. **Key/Value**: A key–value pair is a fundamental data representation in computing systems and applications. Associative array, JSON, etc. are popular key-value examples.
3. **Indexing**: Indexing is a way of sorting on multiple fields. Creating an index on a field in a table creates another data structure which holds the field value, and pointer to the record it relates to. This index structure is then sorted, allowing Binary Searches to be performed on it.
4. **Replication**: Replication means sharing information between systems so as to ensure consistency between redundant resources. It is used in case of failure of node for error recovery.
5. **JSON**: JavaScript object notation is universal data exchange format. It is used to exchange data between client and server (for E.g. .during an Ajax request).
6. **BSON**: BSON (Binary JSON) is a binary encoded serialization of JSON. Like JSON, BSON supports the embedding of documents and arrays within other documents and arrays. BSON also contains extensions that allow representation of data types that are not part of the JSON spec. It allows programmer to store binary data.

7. **In Memory and On Disc Database Systems**: In memory means storing data in the RAM so that it can be accessed faster, as RAM are must faster than secondary storage devices like HARD drive. Redis, Memcache is best example of in memory database management system. Data that are stored on HARD Drive are called as on disc database system. MYSQL is classic example.

7.4.3 Advantages of NOSQL Database Systems

1. Scalability :

NOSQL database can be scaled up easily and with minimum effort and hence it's well suited for today's ever increasing database need (big data).

NOSQL database have scalable architecture, so it can efficiently manage data and can scale up to many machines instead of costly machines that are required while scaling using of SQL DBMS.

2. Dynamic Schemas :

SQL DBMS require one to define the structure of the data (table and its relationship) before adding actual data so for e.g. If we want to store a student data we need to create a table with the id, name, etc column with the data type like int, varchar, etc. But NOSQL databases are having dynamic schema. This means that, in future if we want to change the length of column, or add new column we don't need to change whole table data instead the new data will be stored with the new structure without affecting the previous data /structure. In NoSQL databases we can insert new data without a predefined schema. That helps us to make significant application changes in real-time, without worrying about interruption of service and hence development is faster, code integration is more reliable, and less database administrator time is needed.

3. Auto-Sharding :

This is one of the most important advantages of NOSQL database. A SQL database usually scales vertically which means a single server host the entire database to serve the application. This becomes highly expensive and unmanageable. Many NOSQL database support auto-sharding feature so that we can scale horizontally; Horizontal scaling simply means adding more server instead of storing data in single server. In auto-sharding data are spread across different server and inter server communication is managed by NOSQL database.

4. Replication :

Most NoSQL databases also support automatic replication feature, which simply means we can get high availability and disaster recovery without a separate application to manage these tasks.

5. Integrated Caching :
Caching is one of the important factors in any application; data which is requested repeatedly can be cached so that data can be served rapidly. Many NoSQL database have integrated caching mechanism, hence frequently used data are stored in system memory as much as possible and discarding the need for a separate caching layer.

7.4.4 Drawbacks of NOSQL Database Systems

1. Maturity :
Currently, NOSQL database are new and emerging technologies. Since its under heavy development there are chances of new bugs/errors.

2. Enterprise Support :
If system fails company must be able to get timely support. In case of NOSQL, there are very few companies which know the technology and hence can be a crucial factor before using NOSQL.

3. Transaction Support :
NOSQL doesn't support SQL transaction features and hence for financial applications SQL is still one of the best in industry.

4. Expertise (Highly Skilled Programmers) :
There are millions of people around the world who knows RDBMS while very few people are aware of such technology hence getting a NOSQL programmer is a challenge.

7.4.5 Major DBMS Products under NOSQL

1. MongoDB :
MongoDB is a cross-platform document-oriented database management system. It is "NoSQL" database which stores data in the form of BSON (Binary JSON) documents with dynamic schemas, making the integration of data in certain types of applications easy and fast. It is one the most discussed NoSQL technology in today's world because of the features like auto sharding, replication, schema less design, scalability, etc. It is emerging technology and is in high development.

2. CouchDB :
A CouchDB is NOSQL DBMS developed by Apache software foundation. It stores data in the form of collection of document. Each document is a bunch of "keys" and corresponding "values" (A value can be numbers, strings, lists, etc).CouchDB support indices, queries, views, etc. It is a NoSQL database that uses JSON to store data, JavaScript as its query language using MapReduce and HTTP for the API.

3. Redis :
Redis is an in-memory, key-value data store. It is mostly used as a caching mechanism in most of the application because it stores data in RAM which makes its blazing fast during retrieving data. It is a data structure server and not a replacement to traditional

database. Redis is used in combination with database like MySql to deliver high performance when data are need to be delivered rapidly and frequently.

4. Hadoop :

Apache Hadoop is an open-source software framework written in java that supports data-intensive distributed applications. It supports applications running on large clusters of computers and allows us to analyze data stores in many different computers. It is one of the Big Data technologies in demand today. It is reliable, scalable and supports distributed computing and data storage. The Apache Hadoop software library is used as a framework which allows distributed processing of large data sets across clusters of computers using simple programming models.

7.4.6 Programming in NOSQL with MongoDB

As explained in earlier section, MongoDB is a NOSQL database which is not having a predefined structure as opposed with traditional relational DBMS. This means one can create a table (referred as collection in "MongoDB") without need of data type specification. MongoDB creates records based on attribute/value pairs.

MongoDB consists of following important members:

- A *document* is the basic unit of data for MongoDB and is roughly equivalent to a row in a relational database management system.
- Similarly, a *collection* can be thought of as a table with a dynamic schema.
- A single instance of MongoDB can host multiple independent *databases*, each of which can have its own collections.
- Every document has a special key, "_id", that is unique within a collection.
- MongoDB comes with a simple but powerful JavaScript *shell*, which is useful for the administration of MongoDB instances and data manipulation.

Table 7.3 Comparison in SQL and MongoDB

SQL	MONGODB
Table	It is replaced with new term called collection.
Row	BSON document/general document
Unique key	In MongoDB, _id is created automatically for each document which could be treated as primary key
Aggregation	It makes use of aggregation pipeline
Operators like 'or', 'and' etc. Special symbols >,< ,!=can be used easily while retrieval of data or while updation of existing data.	All operators must use "$" as a prefix before any operator and/or special symbol.

Programming in MongoDB:

MongoDB will create a collection implicitly upon its first use. There is no need of creating a collection before inserting actual data. Furthermore, because MongoDB uses dynamic schemas, there lies no need of specifying the structure of documents before inserting them into the collection.

1. From the mongo shell, switch to any existing database. For instance "mydb" (This is nothing but a private workspace that stores different collections).

use mydb

2. Create two documents named d1 and d2 by using the following sequence of JavaScript operations:

d1 = {name : "Sahil"}
d2 = {city:"Pune" }

3. Insert the d1 and d2 documents into the "info" collection with the following sequence of operations:

db.info.insert(d1)
db.info.insert(d2)

When you insert the first document, the mongod will create both the mydb database and the "info" collection.

Alternatively, one may create a "info" collection using

db.createCollection("info")

4. One may confirm that the "info" collection exists using following operation:

show collections

The mongo shell will return the list of the collections in the current (i.e. mydb) database. At this point, the only collection is "Info". All mongod databases also have a system.indexes collection by default.

5. One can easily obtain list of records present in a given collection using find() operation as follows:

db.info.find()

This operation returns the following results. It works on similar fashion of select statement in SQL. The ObjectId values will be unique:

{ "_id" : ObjectId("4c2209f9f3924d31102bd84a"), "name" : "Sahil"}
{ "_id" : ObjectId("4c2209fef3924d31102bd84b"), "city" : "Pune" }

All MongoDB documents must have an _id field with a unique value. These operations do not explicitly specify a value for the _id field, so mongo creates a unique ObjectId value for the field before inserting it into the collection.

Selection with condition:

db.student.find({rollno:101})

This operation retrieves the record of student whose roll no is 101 assuming that student collection exists with a field rollno.

db.emp.find({salary:{$gt:10000}})

This operation retrieves all employees whose salary is greater than 10000 assuming that employee collection exists with a field salary.

Update Operation:

*db.emp.update({salary:{$gt:10000}},{$set:{salary=1.1*salary}}, {multi:true})*

This operation increases the salary values of all employees whose salary is greater than 1000 by 10%.

Delete Operation:

db.emp.remove({})

db.emp.remove({eid:101})

The first command deletes all records from emp collection while second command is used to delete a specific record of employee with eid 101.

Alter Operation:

At the document level, update() operation can be used to add new field or column to the existing collection.

db.emp.update({},{$set:{city},{multi:true})

The above command adds a new field "city" to existing collection "emp".

7.4.7 Query Optimization with NOSQL Databases

NOSQL database are not a replacement to SQL. They don't support transaction (yet) and hence cannot be used in any financial application. But NOSQL has its specific use in many case where speed, flexibility, scalability is required like searching thousand of document using SQL DBMS would be tedious and slow while fast in NOSQL. NOSQL are in heavy development and can be a database of choice in future replacing SQL.

Considering query optimization, as there is no restriction in query specification, NOSQL databases perform well as compared to SQL databases in case of big data retrieval.

REVIEW QUESTIONS ON INSTRUCTIONAL OBJECTIVES

1. Explain various types of databases supported by NOSQL
2. Write short note on :
   (i) MongoDB
   (ii) Hadoop
3. Explain major database products which makes use of NOSQL.
4. Explain advantages and drawbacks of NOSQL.

5. Write short note on :
   (i) Embedded SQL,
   (ii) Dynamic SQL.

UNIVERSITY QUESTIONS

1. What is Query Language? **(May 06)**
2. Explain embedded SQL. **(Oct. 2000, April 01, 03, Oct. 02, 03, April 04, May 05, Dec. 05, Dec. 06, May 07)**
3. What is dynamic SQL ? **(Oct. 03, Dec. 05, 06, May 07)**
4. What is open database connectivity ? **(Oct. 02, Oct. 03, April 04)**

Unit - III

CHAPTER 8
TRANSACTION MANAGEMENT

- 8.1 Introduction
- 8.2 Basic Concepts of Transaction
    - 8.2.1 Transaction
    - 8.2.2 Properties of Transaction
    - 8.2.3 Significance of ACID Properties
    - 8.2.4 Transaction Model
    - 8.2.5 Schedule
    - 8.2.6 Serializability
    - 8.2.7 Testing for Serializability
    - 8.2.8 Recoverable and Non-Recoverable Schedule
    - 8.2.9 Cascadeless Schedule
- 8.3 Concurrency Control
    - 8.3.1 Lock-Based Protocol
    - 8.3.2 Time Stamp Based Protocol
    - 8.3.3 Validation Based Protocol
    - 8.3.4 Multiple Granularity
    - 8.3.5 Multiversion Scheme
    - 8.3.6 Optimistic Technique
- 8.4 Deadlock Handling
    - 8.4.1 Deadlock Prevention
    - 8.4.2 Timeout Based Schemes
    - 8.4.3 Deadlock Detection and Recovery
- 8.5 Recovery System
    - 8.5.1 Failures and Errors
    - 8.5.2 Recovery Algorithms
- Review Questions on Instructional Objectives
- University Questions

8.1 INTRODUCTION

Collection of operations that forms a single logical unit of work is called **transaction**. A transaction accesses and possibly updates various data items. After every transaction, the database should be in a consistent state.

Usually a transaction is the result of execution of a user program, written in a high-level data manipulation language or programming language. Every transaction is delimited by statements or function calls of the form begin transaction and end transaction.

A computer system is an electro-chemical device and it is subject to failures of various types. During the execution of a transaction if some failure occurs, the transaction may result in some inconsistent state of database. Hence, the reliability of DBMS is linked to the reliability of computer system, and some solution must be there to deal with such computer system failures. Recovery system, the main component of Transaction management/Processing unit, deals with such failures. It makes the database fault tolerant.

Number of transactions can be executed at the same time and they may be accessing the same database. Such concurrent access to the database, may result in some inconsistent state of database. Concurrency control/management unit of transaction management preserves the consistency of database in case of concurrent accesses.

This chapter deals with the following topics :
1. Basic concepts of transaction
2. Concurrency control
3. Recovery system.

8.2 BASIC CONCEPTS OF TRANSACTION

8.2.1 Transaction

A transaction is a program unit whose execution accesses and possibly updates the contents of a database. If the database was in consistent state before a transaction, then on execution of transaction, the database will be in a consistent state.

8.2.2 PROPERTIES OF TRANSACTION

To ensure the integrity of data, database system maintains following properties of transaction.

1. Atomicity : Atomicity property ensures that at the end of the transaction, either no changes have occurred to the database or the database has been changed in a consistent manner. At the end of a transaction, the updates made by the transaction will be accessible to other transactions and processes outside the transaction.

2. Consistency : Consistency property of transaction implies that if the database was in consistent state before the start of a transaction, then on termination of a transaction, the database will also be in a consistent state.

3. Isolation : Isolation property of transaction indicates that action performed by a transaction will be hidden from outside the transaction until the transaction terminates. Thus, each transaction is unaware of other transactions executing concurrently in the system.

4. Durability : Durability property of a transaction ensures that once a transaction completes successfully (commits), the changes it has made to the database persist, even if there are system failures.

These four properties are often called ACID (Atomicity, Consistency, Isolation, Durability) properties of transaction.

8.2.3 SIGNIFICANCE OF ACID PROPERTIES

Consider a banking system consisting of several accounts and a set of transactions that accesses and updates those accounts. Here consider that the database resides on disk, but some portion of database is temporarily stored in main memory.

Following are the functions to access the database.

read (X) : Which transfers the data item X from the database to a local buffer, belonging to the transaction that executed the read operation.

write (X) : Which transfers the data item X from the local buffer of the transaction that executed the write back to the database.

Let T_i be a transaction that transfers Rs. 50 from account A to account B. This transaction can be defined as :

T_i :   Read (A);
           A := A – 50;
           write (A);
           Read (B);
           B := B + 50;
           write (B).

Let us now consider the significance of ACID properties.

Consistency : Here, consistency requirement is that the sum of accounts A and B must be unchanged. It can be easily verified that if database is consistent before an execution of transaction and the database remains consistent after the execution of transaction. This task may be fascilitated by atomic testing of integrity constraints.

Atomicity : Suppose that just prior to the execution of transaction T_1, the values of account A and B are Rs. 80 and Rs. 200 respectively. If a failure has occurred during the execution of transaction T_i and that prevented T_i from completing its execution successfully. Suppose that failure happened after the write (A) operation was executed but before the write (B) operation was executed. In this case, the values of accounts A and B reflected in database are Rs. 50 and Rs. 200. But now A + B is no longer preserved and the database is in inconsistent state.

But if the atomicity property is provided, all actions of the transaction are reflected in the database or none are reflected i.e. the database contents are Rs. 80 and Rs. 200 or Rs. 50 and Rs. 250.

Durability : The durability guarantees that once transaction completes successfully, all updates that it carried out on the database persist even if there is a system failure. We can guarantee durability by ensuring that either :

1. The updates carried out by a transaction have been written to disk before the transaction completes.
2. Information about updates carried out by the transaction and written to disk is sufficient to enable the database to reconstruct the updates when the database system is restarted after failure.

Isolation : Even if the consistency and atomicity properties are ensured for each transaction, if several transactions are executed concurrently, their operations may interleave in some undesirable way. The isolation property ensures that the concurrent execution of transactions results in system state that is equivalent to a state that could have been obtained by execution of one transaction at a time.

Each of these properties are ensured by components of transaction management unit.

8.2.4 TRANSACTION MODEL

Following are the possible states of a transaction during its execution.

Active : Transaction is active when it is executing. This is the initial state of transaction.

Partially committed : When a transaction completes its final statement, it enters in partially committed state.

Failed : If the system decides that the normal execution of the transaction can no longer proceed, then transaction is termed as failed.

Committed : When the transaction completes its execution successfully it enters committed state from partially committed state.

Aborted : To ensure the atomicity property, changes made by failed transaction are undone i.e. the transaction is rolled back. After rollback, that transaction enters in aborted state.

A state is said to be terminated if it is committed or aborted.

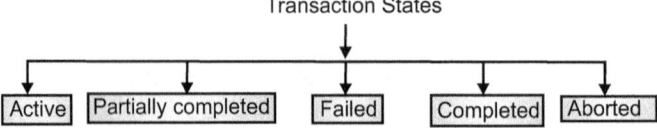

The state diagram corresponding to transaction states is :

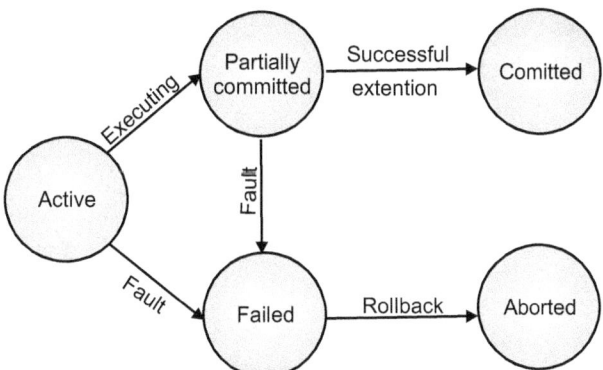

Fig. 8.1 : State Diagram of Transaction

A transaction always starts with active state. It remains in active state till all commands of that transaction are executed. When it completes executing the last command of that transaction, it enters partially committed state and when the transaction execution is successfully completed, it enters committed state. But, if some failure occurs in active state or partially committed state transaction enters failed state. When the transaction is in failed state, it rollsback that transaction and enters aborted state.

When the transaction is in aborted state, the system has two options :

1. If the transaction was aborted as a result of some hardware or software error (software error which is not created because of some internal logic of transaction), then such transaction can be restarted. A restarted transaction is considered to be a new transaction.
2. If the transaction was aborted because of some internal logical error which can be corrected only by rewriting of the application program or because the input was bad or because the desired data were not found in the database, then system can kill such transactions.

8.2.5 SCHEDULE

Schedule represent the chronological order in which instructions are executed in the system. Two schedule types are serial schedule and concurrent schedule.

1. Serial Schedule : It consists of a sequence of instructions from various transactions where the instructions belonging to one single transaction appear together in that schedule. Thus for a set of n transactions, there exist n ! different valid serial schedules.

2. Concurrent Schedule : When several transactions are executed concurrently, the corresponding schedule is called concurrent schedule. Several execution sequences are possible since the various instructions from both transactions may now be interleaved. In general it is not possible to predict exactly how many instructions of a transaction will be executed before CPU switches to other transaction. Thus the number of possible schedules for a set of n transactions is much larger than n !

Examples of schedules :

Consider the banking system of several accounts and a set of transactions that accesses and updates those accounts. Let T_1 and T_2 be two transactions.

T_1 : Transfers Rs. 50 from account A to account B.

T_1 : read (A);
A = A − 50;
write (A);
read (B);
B = B + 50;
write (B).

T_2 : Transfers 8% of balance from account A to B.

T_2 : read (A);
temp : = A * 0.1;
A := A − temp;
write (A);
read (B);
B := B + temp;
write (B).

For T_1 and T_2, two serial transactions are possible :

1. **<T_1, T_2> Serial Schedule** : It will execute transaction T_1 first and then T_2.

After executing both transactions, account balance of A is Rs. 855 and account balance of B is Rs. 2145. i.e. <T_1 T_2> preserves A + B i.e. the database is consistent.

Table 8.1 : Schedule 1

T_1	T_2
read (A)	
A := A − 50	
write (A)	
read (B)	
B := B + 50	
Write (B)	
	read (A)
	temp := A * 0.1
	A := A − temp
	write (A)
	read (B)
	B := B + temp
	write (B)

2. **<T_2, T_1> Serial Schedule :** It executes T_2 first and then T_1.

Table 8.2 : Schedule 2

T_1	T_2
	read (A)
	temp := A * 0.1
	A := A – temp
	write (A)
	read (B)
	B := B + temp
	write (B)
read (A)	
A := A – 50	
write (A)	
read (B)	
B := B + 50	
write (B)	

Here, after executing both the transactions, values of A and B are Rs. 850 and Rs. 2150 respectively. In this case also A + B is constant and it preserves the consistency.

For T_1 and T_2, number of concurrent schedules are possible. But, not all the transactions are consistency preserving.

A concurrent schedule for T_1 and T_2 is given in Table 8.3.

3. **Consistent concurrent schedule for T_1 and T_2 :**

This concurrent schedule preserves the consistency of database and A + B is constant.

Table 8.3 : Schedule 3

T_1	T_2
read (A)	
A := A – 50	
write (A)	
	read (A)
	temp := A * 0.1
	A := A – temp
	write (A)
read (B)	
B := B + 50	
write (B)	
	read (B)
	B := B + temp
	write (B)

4. **Inconsistent concurrent schedule for T_1 and T_2.**

Table 8.4 : Schedule 4 (concurrent schedule)

T_1	T_2
read (A)	
A := A − 50	
	read (A)
	temp := A * 0.1
	A := A − temp
	write (A)
	write (B)
write (A)	
read (B)	
B := B + 50	
write (B)	
	B := B + temp
	write (B)

8.2.6 Serializability

For a transaction always a serial schedule results in a consistent database and not every concurrent schedule can result in consistent database.

But a concurrent schedule results in a consistent state if its result is equivalent to a serial schedule of that transaction. Such concurrent schedule is known as 'serializable'.

A **serializable schedule** is defined as :

Given (an interleaved execution) a concurrent schedule for n transactions; the following conditions hold for each transaction in the set.

1. All transactions are correct i.e. if any one of the transactions is executed on a consistent database, the resulting database is also consistent.
2. Any serial execution of the transactions is also correct and preserves the consistency of the database.

The given concurrent schedule is said to be serializable if it produces the same result as some serial schedule of the transaction.

There are two forms of serializability

    (i) Conflict serializability

    (ii) View serializability

1. Conflict Serializability :

Consider that T_1 and T_2 are two transactions and S is a schedule for T_1 and T_2. I_i and I_j are two instructions.

If I_i and I_j refer to different data items, then I_i and I_j can be executed in any sequence.

But, if I_i and I_j refer to same data items then the order of two instructions may matter. Here, I_i and I_j can be a read or write operation only. Hence, following 4 conditions are possible.

(i) I_i = read (A)
I_j = read (A)

The order of I_i and I_j does not matter because both are reading the data.

(ii) I_i = read (A) I_j = write (A)
I_i = write (A) I_j = read (A)

Here, if read (A) is executed before write (A) then it will read the original value of A otherwise it will read that value of A which is written by write (A). Hence, the order of I_i and I_j matters.

(iii) I_i = write (A) I_j = write (A)

Here order of I_i and I_j does not affect either T_i or T_j. But the database is changed, and it makes difference for next read.

We say that I_i and I_j conflict if they are operated by different transactions on the same data item and at least one of them is write operation. i.e. only in case 1, I_i and I_j do not conflict.

Consider an example of concurrent schedule 5.

Table 8.5 : Concurrent schedule 5

T_1	T_2
read (A)	
write (A)	
	read (A)
	write (A)
read (B)	
write (B)	
	read (B)
	write (B)

Here write (A) of T_1 conflicts with read (A) of T_2, similarly write (B) of T_1 conflicts with read (B) of T_2. But write (A) of T_2 does not conflict with read (B) of T_1 because both are accessing different data items.

If I_i and I_j are two consecutive instructions of schedule S and if they do not conflict, then we can swap the order of I_i and I_j, to produce new schedule S'. We say that S and S' are equivalent since all instructions appear in the same order except for I_i and I_j whose order does not matter.

Equivalent schedule for a schedule given in Table 8.5 can be obtained by following swap.

Swap write (A) of T_2 with read (B) of T_1.

Table 8.6 : Schedule 6 (Schedule after swapping instructions)

T_1	T_2
Read (A)	
write (A)	
	read (A)
read (B)	
	write (A)
write (B)	
	read (B)
	write (B)

Similarly swap the following in schedule given in Table 8.6.
1. read (B) instruction and read (A) instruction of T_1 and T_2 respectively.
2. write (B) instruction and write (A) instruction of T_1 and T_2 respectively.
3. write (B) instruction and read (A) instruction of T_1 and T_2 respectively.

The final schedule S' after these swapping is given below :

Table 8.7 : Schedule 7

T_1	T_2
read (A)	
write (A)	
read (B)	
write (B)	
	read (A)
	write (A)
	read (B)
	write (B)

Which is a serial schedule of T_1 and T_2. Thus, concurrent schedule S is transferred to serial schedule S' by a series of swaps of non-conflicting instructions and schedules S and S' are conflict equivalent. We say that a schedule S is conflict serializable, if it is conflict equivalent to a serial schedule. Consider the schedule shown in Table 8.8.

Table 8.8 : Schedule 8

T_1	T_2
read (Q)	
	write (Q)
read (Q)	

This schedule is not conflict serializable, since it is not conflict equivalent to any serial schedule $<T_3\ T_4>$ or $<T_4\ T_3>$.

There may be any two schedules which are not conflict equivalent but produce same outcome. Schedule given in Table 8.9 is not conflict serializable.

Table 8.9 : Schedule 9 (Concurrent schedule)

T_1	T_5
read (A)	
A := A − 50	
write (A)	
	read (B)
	B := B − 8
	write (B)
read (B)	
B := B + 50	
write (B)	
	read (A)
	A := A + 8
	write (A)

Result of above schedule is same as serial schedule $<T_1, T_5>$, but this is not conflict serializable, since, in above schedule write (B) of T_5 conflicts with read (B) of T_1. Thus we cannot move all instructions of T_1 before those of T_5 by swapping consecutive non-conflicting instructions.

2. View Serializability :

Consider two schedules S and S', where same set of transactions participate in both schedules. The schedules S and S' are said to be view equivalent if the following three conditions are satisfied :

1. For each data item Q if transaction T_i reads the initial value of Q in schedule S, then transaction T_i in schedule S' must also read the initial value of Q.

2. For each data item Q if transaction T_i executes read (Q) in schedule S, and that value was produced by transaction T_j (if any), then transaction T_i in schedule S', must also read the value of Q that was produced by T_j transaction.

3. For each data item Q, the transaction that performs the final write (Q) operation in schedule S must perform the final write (Q) operation in schedule S'.

A schedule S is view serializable if it is view equivalent to a serial schedule.

Example of view equivalence :

Schedule 1 is not view equivalent to schedule 2 since, in schedule 1 the value of account A read by transaction T_2 was produced by T_i, whereas this is not the case in schedule 2.

Schedule 1 is view equivalent to schedule 3, because values of account A and B read by transaction T_2 were produced by T_1 in both schedules.

Example of view serializable schedule :

A schedule given in Table 8.8 is view serializable schedule.

Table 8.8 : Schedule 8

T_3	T_4	T_6
read (A)		
	write (A)	
write (A)		
		write (A)

This schedule is view equivalent to serial schedule $<T_3, T_4, T_6>$.

Note : Transactions T_4 and T_6 perform write (A) operations without having performed a read (A) operation. Writes of this form are called blind writes.

Every conflict serializable schedule is view serializable, but there are view serializable schedules that are not conflict serializable. A view serializable schedule in which blind write appear is not a conflict serializable.

Schedule 8 is view serializable but it is not conflict serializable.

8.2.7 Testing for Serializability

A serializability schedule gives same result as some serial schedule.

A serial schedule always gives correct result.

i.e. a schedule that is serializable schedule is always correct.

Hence, we must show that schedules generated by concurrency control scheme are serializable. This section deals with methods for determining conflict and view serializability.

1. Conflict serializability :

There is an algorithm to establish the serializability of a given schedule for a set of transactions.

This algorithm uses a directed graph called precedence graph, constructed from given schedule.

Precedence graph : It consists of a pair $G = (V_1 E)$ where,

    V – set of vertices.

The set of vertices consists of all transactions participating in the schedule.

    E – the set of edges.

The set of edges consists of all edges $T_i \rightarrow T_j$ for which one of the following three conditions hold :

1. T_i executes write (Q) before   : T_j executes read (Q)
2. T_i executes read (Q) before   : T_j executes write (Q)
3. T_i executes write (Q) before   : T_j executes write (Q)

A precedence graph is said to be acyclic if there are no cycles in the graph otherwise it is a cyclic graph.

Algorithm : Conflict serializability

    Step 1   :   Construct a precedence graph G for given schedule S.

    Step 2   :   If the graph G has a cycle, schedule S is not conflict serializable.

If the graph is acyclic, then find, using the topological sort given below, a linear ordering of transactions, so that if there is arc from T_i to T_j in G, T_i precedes T_j. Find a serial schedule as follows :

(i) Initialize the serial schedule as empty.

(ii) Find a transaction T_i, such that there are no arcs entering T_i, T_i is the next transaction in the serial schedule.

(iii) Remove T_i and all edges emitting from T_i. If the remaining set is non-empty, return to (ii), otherwise the serial schedule is complete.

Examples :

1. Given schedule is :

Table 8.11

T_{11}	T_{12}	T_{13}
Read (A)		
	Read (B)	
$A := f_1(A)$		
		Read (C)
	$B := f_2(B)$	
	write (B)	
		$C := f_3(C)$
		write (C)
write (A)		
	Read (A)	
	$A := f_4(A)$	
Read (C)		
	Write (A)	
$C := f_5(C)$		
Write (A)		
		$B := f_6(B)$
		write (B)

Precedence graph for the schedule is :

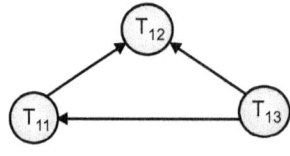

Fig. 8.2

This graph contains cycle. Hence, the schedule is not conflict serializable.

2. The given schedule is :

Table 8.12

T_{14}	T_{15}	T_{16}
Read (A)		
A := f_1 (A)		
Read (C)		
write (A)		
A := f_2 (C)		
	Read (B)	
write (C)		
	Read (A)	
		Read (C)
	B := f_3 (B)	
	write (B)	
		C := f_4 (C)
		Read (B)
		write (C)
	A := f_5 (A)	
	write (A)	
		B := f_6 (B)
		write (B)

The precedence graph for the given schedule is :

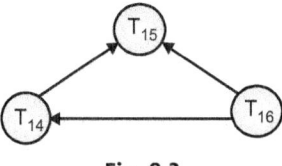

Fig. 8.3

The graph is acyclic. The conflict equivalent serial schedule for given schedule can be obtained using step 2 of algorithm.

T_{14} is the transaction with no arcs entering in T_{14}. Hence T_{14} is the first transaction in serial schedule. Remove T_{14} and all edges emitting from T_{14}.

T_{15} is the next schedule, since it has no incoming edges. Remove T_{15} and edges emitting from T_{15}.

T_{16} is the last schedule. Hence the serial schedule which is conflict equivalent to given schedule is :

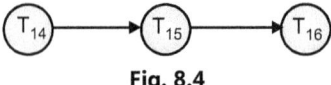

Fig. 8.4

Hence, the schedule is conflict serializable.

3. Consider schedule 3, the precedence graph for it is given as :

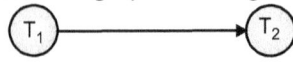

Fig. 8.5

Since, T_1 executes write (A) and write (B) before T_2 executes read (A) and read (B).

This graph is acyclic and the conflict equivalent serial schedule is $T_1 \rightarrow T_2$. Hence, schedule 3 is conflict serializable.

4. Consider schedule 4, the precedence graph for it is :

Fig. 8.6

which is a cyclic graph and hence it is not conflict serializable.

5. Consider the precedence graph given in Fig. 8.7.

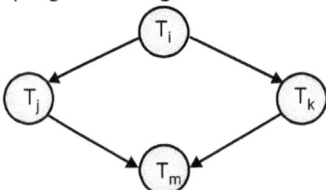

Fig. 8.7

The graph is acyclic. The conflict equivalent serial schedules equivalent to this are :

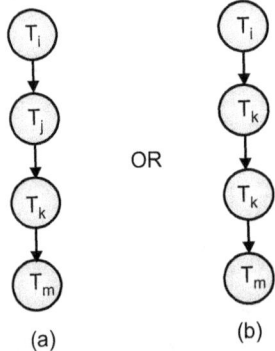

Fig. 8.8

Hence the schedule corresponding to precedence graph in Fig. 8.8 is conflict serializable.

6. Consider the precedence graph in Fig. 8.9.

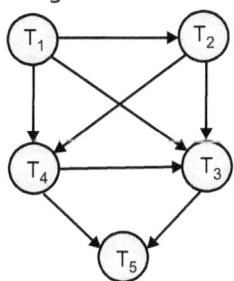

Fig. 8.9

The graph is acyclic. The serial schedules that are conflict equivalent to given schedule are :

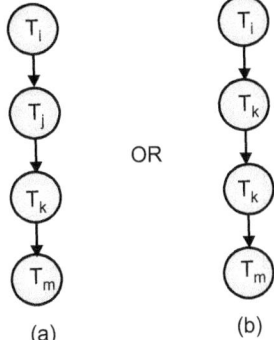

Fig. 8.10

Hence the schedule corresponding to given precedence graph is conflict serializable.

2. View serializability :

Testing for view serializability is complicated. It has been shown that testing for view serializability is itself NP-complete. Thus there exists no algorithm to test for view serializability. However concurrency control schemes can still use sufficient conditions for view serializability. That is if sufficient conditions are satisfied, the schedule is view serializable schedule. But there may be view serializable schedules that do not satisfy the sufficient conditions.

8.2.8 RECOVERABLE AND NON-RECOVERABLE SCHEDULE

A recoverable schedule is one where for each pair of transactions T_i and T_j such that T_j reads a data item previously written by T_i, the commit operation of T_i appears before the commit operation of T_j. Otherwise the schedule is non-recoverable.

Consider the schedule given in Table 8.13. Transaction T_9 reads the data written by T_8. commit of transaction T_8 occurs after commit of transaction T_9. Hence it is a non-recoverable schedule.

Table 8.13

T_8	T_9
Read(A)	
Write(A)	Read(A)
Read(B)	

8.2.9 CASCADELESS SCHEDULES

Even if a schedule is recoverable, to recover correctly from the failure of a transaction T_i, we may have to rollback the transaction.

Consider the partial schedule shown below :

T_8	T_{11}	T_{12}
Read(A)		
Read(B)		
Write(A)		
	Read(A)	Read(A)
	Write(A)	

Transaction T_8 writes a value of A that is read by transaction T_{11}. Transaction T_{11} writes a value of A that is read by transaction T_{12}. Suppose that at a point transaction T_8 fails. T_8 must be rolled back. Since T_{11} is dependent on T_8, T_{11} must be rolled back. Since T_{12} is dependent on T_{11}, T_{12} must be rolled back.

This phenomenon, in which a single transaction failure leads to a series of transaction rollbacks, is called **cascading rollback.**

A **cascadeless schedule** is one where, for each pair of transactions T_i and T_j such that T_j reads a data item previously written by T_i, the commit operation of T_i appears before commit operation of T_j.

8.3 CONCURRENCY CONTROL PROTOCOLS

If all schedules in a concurrent environment are restricted to serializable schedule, the result will be consistent with some serial execution of transactions and will be considered correct. But there are some disadvantages of serializability.

- It limits the degree of concurrency.
- Testing for serializability of a scheme is computationally expensive.
- Testing for serializability of a scheme is an after-the-fact technique and it is impractical.

  This section deals with some concurrency control schemes. These schemes ensure that the schedules produced by concurrent transaction are serializable.

Following are the concurrency control schemes :
- Lock-based protocol
- Time-stamp based protocol
- Validation based protocol
- Multiple granularity
- Multiversion schemes.

8.3.1 LOCK-BASED PROTOCOL

Serializability can easily be ensured if access to database is done in mutually exclusive manner i.e. if one transaction is accessing a data item, no other transaction can modify that data item. The most common method to implement mutual exclusion is to use locks.

1. Lock :

Consider that database is made up of data-items.

A lock is a variable associated with each data item.

Manipulating the value of lock is called locking.

The value of lock is used in locking schemes to control the concurrent access and to manipulate the associated data items.

Following are the two types or modes of locks.

(i) Shared : If a transaction T_i has obtained a shared mode lock (denoted by S) on item A, then T_i can read but it cannot write A.

(ii) Exclusive : If a transaction T_i, has obtained an exclusive mode lock (denoted by X) on item A, then T_i can both read and write A.

Depending on the type of the operation, the transaction requests a lock in an appropriate mode on data item. The request is made to the concurrency-control manager, and the transaction can proceed with operation only after the concurrency-control manager grants the lock to that transaction.

2. Compatibility Function :

Given a set of lock modes, the compatibility function can be defined as :

Let A and B represent arbitrary lock modes. Suppose that a transaction T_i requests a lock of mode A on item Q on which transaction T_j currently holds a lock of mode B. If transaction T_i can be granted a lock on Q immediately, in spite of presence of the lock of mode B, then we say that mode A is compatible with B.

Such a function can be represented conveniently by a matrix.

Compatibility of two modes of lock is given in matrix comp.

	S	X
S	true	false
X	false	false

Comp lock-compatibility matrix

If comp (A, B) is true it to means that A is compatible with B. Notice that shared mode (S) is compatible with shared mode (S).

At any time, several shared-mode locks can be held simultaneously on a particular data item.

A transaction requests a shared lock on data item Q by executing the lock - S (Q) instruction and an exclusive lock is requested through lock-X (Q) instruction.

A data item Q can be unlocked via the unlock (Q) instruction.

Transaction T_i can unlock the data item Q by executing unlock (C) instruction. But transaction must hold a lock on a data item, as long as it accesses the data item.

Locking protocols indicate when a transaction may lock and unlock each of the data items. Each transaction must follow the set of rules specified by locking protocols. Locking protocols restrict the number of possible serializable schedules. This section deals with only those locking protocols which allow conflict serializable schedules.

3. Conflict Serializability :

Let $\{T_0, T_1, ..., T_n\}$ be a set of transactions participating in a schedule S. We say that T_i precedes T_j in S, written $T_i \rightarrow T_j$ if there exists a data item Q such that T_i has held lock mode A on Q and T_j has held lock mode B on Q later and comp (A, B) = false. If $T_i \rightarrow T_j$, then that precedence implies that in any equivalent serial schedule, T_i must appear before T_j. This graph is similar to the precedence graph. Conflicts between instructions correspond to non-compatibility of lock modes.

We say that a schedule S is legal under a given locking protocol if S is possible schedule for a set of transactions following the rules of locking protocol.

We say that a locking protocol ensures conflict serializability if and only if for all legal schedules the associated → relation is acyclic.

4. Starvation of Locks :

Suppose that transaction :

T_2 - has a shared mode lock on data item, and

T_1 - requests an exclusive mode lock on same data item.

Clearly T_1 has to wait for T_2 to release the shared mode lock.

Meanwhile, suppose that

T_3 - request a shared mode lock on same data item.

This lock request is compatible with the lock granted to T_2, so T_3 may be granted the shared mode lock.

At this point, T_2 may release the lock but still T_1 has to wait for T_3. But again there may be a new transaction T_4 requesting a shared mode lock on the same data-item. It is possible that there is a sequence of transactions that each requests a shared mode lock on same data item and T_1 never gets the exclusive mode lock on the data item. The transaction T_1 may never make progress and is said to be starved.

Starvation of transactions can be avoided by granting locks as follows. When a transaction T_i requests a lock on a data item Q in a particular mode M, the lock is granted provided that :

1. There is no other transaction holding a lock on Q in a mode that conflicts with M.
2. There is no other transaction that is waiting for a lock on Q and that made its lock request before T_i.

5. Locking protocols :

Now we shall study the locking protocols.

1. The two-phase locking protocol
2. Graph-based protocols

1. Two Phase Locking Protocol :

This protocol requires that each transaction issue a lock and unlock requests in two phases :

(i) Growing phase : A transaction may obtain locks, but may not release any lock.

(ii) Shrinking phase : A transaction may release locks, but may not obtain any new locks. Initially the transaction is in growing phase. In this it acquires locks as needed. Once the transaction releases a lock, it enters the shrinking phase and it can issue no more lock requests.

The point in the schedule where the transaction has obtained its final lock (the end of its growing phase) is called the lock point of the transaction. The transactions can be ordered according to lock points. This ordering gives the serializability ordering for transaction. This serial schedule is conflict equivalent i.e. the two-phase locking protocol ensures conflict serializability.

Example :

Following two transactions are two phase transactions.

T_3: lock - X (B);
read (B);
B : = B – 50;
write (B);
lock – X(A);
read (A);
A : = A + 50;
write (A);
Unlock (B);
Unlock (A).

T_4 :   lock-S (A);
         read (A);
         locks (B);
         read (B);
display (A + B);
         Unlock (A);
         Unlock (B).

The unlock instructions do not need to appear at the end of the transaction.

Two phase locking does not ensure freedom from deadlock. Transactions T_3 and T_4 are two phases, but they are deadlocked in the schedule.

Table 8.14

T_3	T_4
Lock-X (B)	
read (B)	
B := B – 50	
write (B)	
	lock- S (A)
	read (A)
	lock-S (B)
Lock-X (A)	
read (A)	
A := A + 50	
write (A)	
unlock (B)	
unlock (A)	
	read (B);
	display (A + B);
	unlock (A);
	unlock (B)

Cascading rollback may occur under two phase locking.

Variations on two-phase locking :

1. Strict Two Phase Locking Protocol :

Cascading rollbacks can be avoided by a modification of two phase locking called strict two phase locking protocol.

It requires that in addition to locking being two-phase, all exclusive-mode locks taken by a transaction must be held until that transaction commits.

This requirement ensures that any data written by an uncommitted transaction are locked in exclusive mode until the transaction commits, preventing any other transaction from reading the data.

2. Rigorous Two Phase Locking Protocol :

It requires that all locks to be held until the transaction commits.

With rigorous two-phase locking, transactions can be serialized in the order in which they commit. Most database system implement strict or rigorous two-phase locking.

3. Two Phase Locking with Lock Conversion :

Basic two phase locking is modified and lock conversions are allowed. We shall provide a mechanism for upgrading a shared lock to an exclusive lock and downgrading an exclusive lock to shared lock.

Upgrade (Q) : Convert shared lock lock-S (Q) to exclusive lock lock-X (Q).

Downgrade (Q) : Convert exclusive lock lock-X (Q) to shared lock lock-S (Q).

Lock conversion can not be allowed to occur arbitrarily. Upgrading can take place in growing phase and downgrading can take place in only the shrinking phase.

Two phase locking with lock conversion generates conflict serializable schedule.

Example :

Consider the following two transactions with only read and write operations :

T_8 : read (a_1);
    read (a_2);
    read (a_3);
    read (a_4);
    read (a_5);
    write (a_1)

T_9 : read (a_1)
    read (a_2)
    display ($a_1 + a_2$)

If we employ two phase locking with lock conversion, the schedule can be given as :

Automatic generation of appropriate lock and unlock instructions for a transaction is also possible.

When a transaction issues a read (a) operation, the system issues lock-S (a) instruction followed by read (a) operation.

When a transaction T_i issues a write (Q) operation, the system checks to see whether T_i already holds a shared lock on Q. If it does then the system issues an upgrade (Q) instruction, followed by the write (Q) instruction.

Otherwise the system issues lock-X (Q) instruction followed by write (Q) operation.

Table 8.15

T_8	T_9
lock-S (a_1)	
read (a_1)	
	lock-S (a_1)
	read (a_1)
lock-S (a_2)	
read (a_2)	
	lock-S (a_2)
	read (a_2)
lock-S (a_3)	
lock-S (a_4)	
	display ($a_1 + a_2$)
	unlock (a_1)
	unlock (a_2)
lock-S (a_5)	
upgrade (a_1)	
write (a_1)	

Graph - Based Protocols :

Graph-based protocol is not a two phase locking protocol and it requires prior knowledge of how each transaction will access the database.

To acquire such prior knowledge it uses data graph.

Let D = {$d_1, d_2, ..., d_n$} is the set of all data items. If $d_i \rightarrow d_j$, then any transaction accessing both d_i and d_j must access d_i before accessing d_j. This partial ordering may be a result of either the logical or physical organization of data or it may be imposed solely for the purpose of concurrency control.

The partial ordering implies that the set D may be viewed as a directed acyclic graph, called database graph. For simplicity we shall consider only those graphs which are rooted trees.

A simple protocol called tree-protocol, which is restricted to exclusive locks is stated here.

Each transaction T_i can lock (lock-X (Q)) a data item at most once and observe the following rules.

1. The first lock by T_i may be on any data item.
2. Subsequently, a data item Q can be locked by T_i only if the parent of Q is currently locked by T_i.
3. Data item may be unlocked at any time.

DATABASE MANAGEMENT SYSTEMS (T.E. IT)   TRANSACTION MANAGEMENT

4. A data item that has been locked and unlocked by T_i cannot subsequently be relocked by T_j.

All schedules that are legal under the tree protocol are conflict serializable.

Example :

Consider the database graph in Fig. 8.11. The following four transactions follow the tree protocol on this graph.

T_8 :   lock-X (B);
         lock-X (E);
         lock-X (D);
         unlock (B);
         unlock (E);
         lock-X (G);
         unlock (D);
         unlock (G).

T_{11} : lock-X (D);
         lock-X (H);
         unlock (D);
         unlock (H).

T_{12} : lock-X (B);
         lock-X (E);
         unlock (E);
         unlock (B).

T_{13} : lock-X (D);
         lock-X (H);
         unlock (D);
         unlock (H).

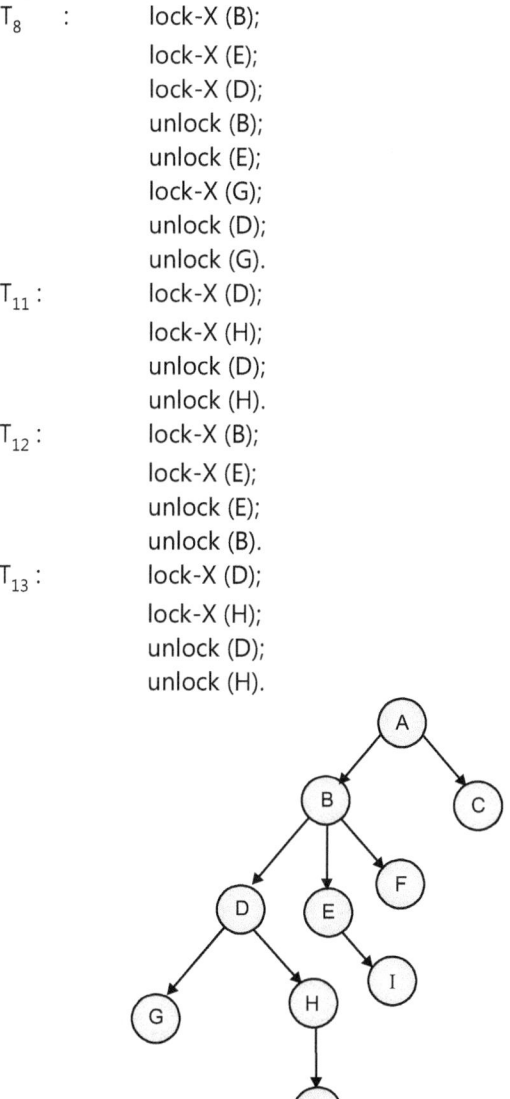

Fig. 8.11 : Database Graph

The schedule following tree protocol is given below :

Table 8.16

T_8	T_{11}	T_{12}	T_{13}
lock-X (B)			
	lock-X (D)		
	lock-X (H)		
	unlock (D)		
lock-X (E)			
lock-X (D)			
unlock (B)			
unlock (E)			
		lock-X (B)	
		lock-X (E)	
	unlock (H)		
lock-X (G)			
unlock (D)			
			lock-X (D)
			lock-X (H)
			unlock (D)
			unlock (H)
		unlock (E)	
		unlock (B)	
unlock (G)			

This schedule is conflict serializable.

Tree protocol ensures conflict serializability and it is free from deadlocks.

Advantages :

Tree locking protocol has an advantage over two phase locking protocol :

1. Unlocking may occur earlier. Earlier unlocking may lead to shorter waiting times and to an increase in concurrency.
2. It is deadlock free and hence no rollbacks are required.

Disadvantages :

But it has one disadvantage that in some cases, a transaction may have to lock data items that it does not access.

Example :

A transaction that needs to access data items A and J in the database graph given in Fig. 8.11 must lock not only A and J but also data items B, D and H.

This additional locking results in increased locking overhead, the possibility of additional waiting time and potential decrease in concurrency.

Further, without prior knowledge of what data item will need to be locked, transactions will have to lock the root of tree and that can reduce the concurrency greatly.

8.3.2 Timestamp Based Protocol

This protocol decides the ordering of transactions in advance to determine the serializability order. For this it uses time-stamp ordering scheme.

Timestamp :

With each transaction T_i in the system, a fixed value called timestamp is associated, denoted by $T_s(T_i)$.

This timestamp is assigned by database system before T_i starts execution.

If transaction T_i is assigned a timestamp $T_s(T_i)$ and a new transaction T_j enters the system, then $T_s(T_i) < T_s(T_j)$. There are two simple methods for implementing timestamp scheme.

(i) Use the value of system clock as the timestamp i.e. a transaction's timestamp is equal to the value of system clock, when the transaction enters the system.

(ii) Use a logical counter that is incremented after a new timestamp has been assigned. i.e. a transaction's timestamp is equal to the value of the counter when the transaction enters the system.

Timestamp of transaction determines the serializability order. If $T_s(T_i) < T_s(T_j)$ then the system must ensure that the produced schedule is equivalent to serial schedule in which T_i appears before T_j.

To implement this scheme, two timestamp values are associated with each data item Q.

W-Timestamp (Q) : It denotes the largest timestamp of any transaction that executed write (Q) successfully.

R-Timestamp (Q) : It denotes the largest timestamp of any transaction that executed read (Q) successfully.

These timestamps are updated whenever, a new read (Q) or write (Q) instruction is executed.

Timestamp - Ordering Protocol :

Timestamp ordering protocol ensures that any conflicting read and write operations are executed in timestamp order. This protocol operates as follows :

1. **Suppose that transaction T_i issues read (Q).**
    (a) If $T_s(T_i) <$ W-Timestamp (Q), then T_i needs to read a value of Q that was already overwritten. Hence, the read operation is rejected, and T_i is rolledback.
    (b) If $T_s(T_i) \geq$ W-Timestamp (Q), then the read operation is executed, and R-Timestamp (Q) is set to maximum of R-Timestamp (Q) and $T_s(T_i)$.

2. **Suppose that T_i issues write (Q).**
    (a) If $T_s(T_i) <$ R-Timestamp (Q) then the value of Q that T_i is producing was needed previously and the system assumed that value would never be produced. Hence, the write operation is rejected, and T_i is rolled back.

(b) If $T_s(T_i)$ < W-timestamp (Q), then T_i is attempting to write an obsolete value of Q. Hence, this write operation is rejected, T_i is rolled back.

(c) Otherwise the write operation is executed and W-timestamp is set to $T_s(T_i)$.

A transaction T_i, that is rolled back by the concurrency control scheme as a result of either a read or write operation being issued, is assigned a new timestamp and is restarted.

Example :

Consider the given transactions T_{14} and T_{15}.

T_{14} : read (B);
read (A);
display (A + B)

T_{15} : read (B);
B := B – 50;
write (B);
read (A);
A := A + 50;
write (A);
display (A + B).

Concurrent schedule for the two transactions is given below.

Here we consider that $T_s(T_{14}) < T_s(T_{15})$. The schedule given in figure is possible under the timestamp protocol.

Table 8.17

T_{14}	T_{15}
read (B)	
	read (B)
	B : = B – 50
	write (B)
read (A)	
	read (A)
display (A + B)	
	A : = A + 50
	write (A)
	display (A + B)

1. read (B) of T_{14} is executed because $T_s(T_{14}) \geq$ W-timestamp (B) and it sets R-Timestamp (B) = $T_s(T_{14})$

2. read (B) of T_{15} is executed because $T_s(T_{15}) \geq$ W-timestamp (B) and it sets R-Timestamp (B) = $T_s(T_{15})$.
3. write (B) of T_{15} is executed because $T_s(T_{15})$ = R-Timestamp (B)

Similarly, read (A) of T_{14} and write (A) of T_{15} are executed.

Thomas write rule :

Consider the schedule given in Table 8.18.

Table 8.18

T_{16}	T_{17}
read (Q)	
	write (Q)
write (Q)	

Apply Timestamp-ordering protocol to given schedule.

Since T_{16} starts before T_{17}, $T_j(T_{16}) < T_i(T_{17})$, read (Q) of T_{16} and write (Q) operations succeed. When T_{16} attempts its write (Q) operation, $T_s(T_{16})$ < W-Timestamp (Q) since W-Timestamp = T_{17}. According to 2b of Timestamp protocol, write (Q) must be rejected, T_{16} will be rolled back.

Timestamp ordering protocol rolls back the transaction T_{16}, but the value of write (Q) operation of T_{16} is already written by write (Q) of T_{17}, and the value that write (Q) of T_{16} is attempting to write will never be read. i.e. we can ignore the write (Q) of T_{16}.

This leads to a modification of Timestamp-ordering protocol. This modified protocol operates as follows :

1. **Suppose that transaction T_i issues read (Q)**

(a) If $T_s(T_i)$ < W-Timestamp (Q), then T_i needs to read a value of Q that was already over written. Hence, the read operation is rejected, and T_i is rolled back.

(b) If $T_s(T_i) \geq$ W-timestamp (Q), then read operation is executed, and R-timestamp (Q) is set to the maximum of R-timestamp (Q) and $T_s(T_i)$.

2. **Suppose that transaction T_i issues write (Q).**

(a) If $T_s(T_i)$ < R-Timestamp (Q) then the value of Q that T_i is producing was previously needed, and it was assumed that the value would never be produced. Hence, the write operation is rejected, and T_i is rolled back.

(b) If $T_s(T_i)$ < W-timestamp (Q), then T_i is attempting write an obsolete value of Q. Hence, the write operation can be ignored.

(c) Otherwise, the write operation is executed, and W-timestamp (Q) is set to $T_s(T_i)$.

i.e. here if $T_s(T_i)$ < W-Timestamp (Q), then we ignore the obsolute write operation. This modification to timestamp ordering protocol is called Thomas write rule.

Thomas write rule for schedule 8 given in table results in a serial schedule < T_{16}, T_{17} > which is view equivalent to given schedule.

8.3.3 Validation Based Protocol

We assume that each transaction T_i executes in two or three phases depending on read only operation or an update operation.

Following are the three phases of execution.

1. **Read phase :** During this phase, the execution of transaction T_i takes place. The values of various data item are read and stored in variable local to T_i. All write operations are performed on local variables, without updates of actual database.

2. **Validation phase :** It performs a validation test to determine whether it can copy the results of write operations stored in temporary local variables to database without causing violation of serializability.

3. **Write phase :** If transaction T_i succeeds in validation phase, then write phase, actually updates the database, otherwise T_i is rolled back. Each transaction must go through the three phases in the order shown. The three phases of concurrently executing transaction can be interleaved.

Three different timestamps are associated with transaction T_i to determine when the various phases of transaction T_i take place.

Start (T_i) : The time when T_i started its execution.

Validation (T_i) : The time when T_i finished its read phase and started its validation phase.

Finish (T_i) : The time when T_i finished its write phase.

Timestamp of transaction T_i is $T_s(T_i)$ = validation (T_i)

If $T_s(T_j) < T_s(T_k)$ then any produced schedule must be equivalent to a serial schedule in which transaction T_j appears before transaction T_k.

The validation test of validation phase for transaction T_f requires that, for all transactions T_s with $T_i(T_i) < T_s(T_j)$, one of the following two conditions must hold.

1. Finish (T_i) < Start (T_j), since if T_i completes its execution before T_j started, then the serializability order is maintained.

2. The set of data items written by T_i does not intersect with the set of data items read by T_j, and T_i completes its write phase before T_j starts its validation phase i.e.

   Start (T_j) < Finish (T_i) < Validation (T_j)

   This condition ensures that writes of T_i and T_j do not overlap.

Since the write of T_i does not affect read of T_j and since, T_j cannot affect the read of T_i, the serializability order is maintained.

Example :

Consider again the transactions T_{14} and T_{15}. A schedule produced using validation is given in Table 8.19.

Table 8.19

T_{14}	T_{15}
read (B)	
	read (B)
	B := B − 50
	read (A)
	A := A + 50
read (A)	
<Validate>	
display (A + B)	
	<Validate>
	write (B)
	write (A)

8.3.4 Multiple Granularity

In the concurrency control schemes described so far, we have used each individual data item as the unit on which synchronization is performed.

But in some cases it would be advantageous to group several data items, and to treat them as one individual synchronization unit.

For example : If a transaction T_i needs to access the entire database, and locking protocol is used, then it must lock each data item in the database. It would be better if T_i could issue a single lock request to lock the entire database. Similarly, if transaction T_i needs to access only one record in the database, it should not be required to lock the entire database.

i.e. we need a mechanism to allow the system to define multiple levels of granularity.

We can make one by allowing data items to be of various sizes and defining a hierarchy of data granularities where the small granularities are nested within larger ones. Such a hierarchy can be represented by tree.

As an illustration consider the tree of Fig. 8.12.

DATABASE MANAGEMENT SYSTEMS (T.E. IT) — TRANSACTION MANAGEMENT

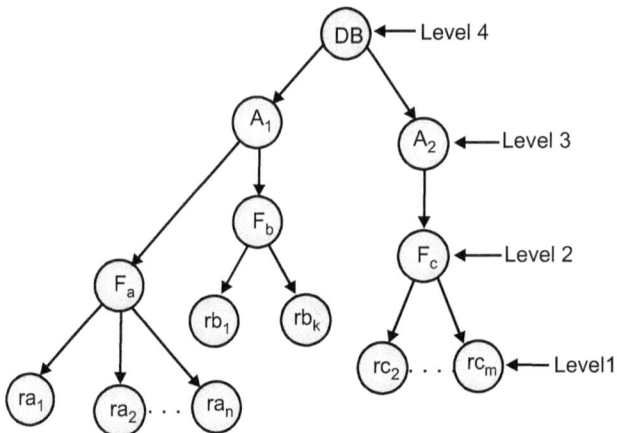

Fig. 8.12 : Hierarchy which is represented by Tree

- The highest level represents the entire database.
- Below that are nodes of type area.
- Each area in turn has nodes of type file as its children. Each area contains exactly those files that are its child nodes. No file is in more than one area.
- Each file has nodes of type record. The file consists of those exactly records that are its child nodes and no record can be present in more than one file.

Each node in the tree can be locked individually.

Following are modes of lock used in multiple granularity scheme.

1. Shared mode lock (S)
2. Exclusive mode lock (X)
3. Intension-shared mode lock (IS)
4. Intension-exclusive mode lock (IX)
5. Shared and Intension-exclusive mode lock (SIX).

When transaction locks a node in shared or exclusive mode, the transaction also has locked all the descendents of that node in the same lock mode.

If a node is locked in intension-shared mode, then explicit locking is being done at lower level of the tree, but with only shared mode locks.

If a node is locked in intension-exclusive mode, then explicit locking is being done at a lower level, with exclusive-mode or shared mode locks.

If a node is locked in shared and intension-exclusive mode, the subtree rooted by that node is locked explicitly in shared mode and that explicit locking is being done at a lower level with exclusive-mode locks.

The compatibility matrix is given :

Table 8.20 : Compatibility matrix

	IS	IX	S	SIX	X
IS	true	true	true	true	false
IX	true	true	false	false	false
S	true	false	true	false	false
SIX	true	false	false	false	false
X	false	false	false	false	false

Multiple granularity locking protocol that follows ensures serializability.

Each transaction T_i can lock a node Q, using the following rules :

1. The lock compatibility function given in Table 8.20 must be observed.
2. The root of the tree must be locked first, and can be locked in any mode.
3. A node Q can be locked by T_i in S or IS mode only if the parent Q is currently locked by T_i in either IX or IS mode.
4. A node Q can be locked by T_i in X, SIX or IX mode only if the parent of Q is currently locked by T_i in either IX or SIX mode.
5. T_i can lock a node only if it has not previously unlocked any node.
6. T_i can unlock a node Q only if none of the children of Q are currently locked by T_i.

Example :

Consider the tree given in Fig. 8.12 and following transactions.

1. Suppose that transaction T_{18} reads record r_{a2} in file F_a.

   Then T_{18} needs to lock, the database area A_1 and file F_a in IS mode and to lock r_{a2} in S mode.

2. Suppose that transaction T_{19} modifies record r_{a9} in file F_a.

   Then T_{19} needs to lock the database area A_1 and file F_a in IX mode and finally to lock r_{a9} in X mode.

3. Suppose that transaction T_{20} reads all records in file F_a.

   Then T_{20} needs to lock the database area A_1 in IS mode and finally to lock file F_a in S mode.

4. Suppose that transaction T_{21} reads the entire database. It can do so after locking the database in S mode.

Advantages and Disadvantages :

1. This protocol ensures concurrency and reduces lock overhead.
2. It is particularly useful in applications that include a mix of :

- Short transactions that access only a few data items
- Long transactions that produce reports from an entire file or set of files.

3. Deadlock is possible in this protocol.

   But there are techniques to reduce deadlock frequency to eliminate deadlock entirely.

8.3.5 Multiversion Schemes

The concurrency control schemes discussed so far ensure serializability by either delaying an operation or aborting the transaction that issued the operation. A read operation may be delayed because appropriate value has not been written yet or it may be rejected because the value that it was supposed to read has already been overwritten.

These difficulties can be avoided by if old copies of data item were kept in system.

In multiversion database systems, each write (Q) operation creates a new version of Q. When a read (Q) operation is issued, the system selects one of the versions of Q to be read.

Concurrency control scheme ensures that selection of version to be read is done in a manner that ensure serializability.

Following are the two schemes to ensure serializability in multiversion database systems.

Multiversion Time Stamp Ordering :

In this scheme with each transaction a unique static timestamp denoted by $T_s(T_i)$ is associated.

With each data item Q, a sequence of versions $<Q_1, Q_2, ... Q_m>$ is associated. Each version Q_k contains three fields :

1. **Content :** The value of version Q_k.
2. **R-Timestamp (Q_k) :** The largest timestamp of any transaction that successfully read version Q_k.
3. **W-Timestamp (Q_k) :** The timestamp of transaction that created version Q_k.

A new version Q_k of data item Q is created by a transaction by issuing write (Q) operation.
- The content field holds the value written by T_i.
- The W-timestamp and R-Timestamp are initialized to $T_s(T_i)$.
- The R-Timestamp is updated wherever a transaction T_j reads the contents of Q_k and R-Timestamp (Q_k) $<T_s(T_j)$.

Multiversion Timestamp scheme operates as follows :

Suppose that transaction T_i issues a read (Q) or write (Q) operation.

Let Q_k denote the version of Q whose write timestamp is the largest write timestamp less than or equal to $T_s(T_i)$.

1. If transaction T_i issues a read (Q), then the value returned is the content of version Q_k.
2. If transaction T_i issues a write (Q), and if $T_s(T_i)$ < R-Timestamp (Q_k), then transaction T_i is rolled back. Otherwise if $T_s(T_i)$ = W-Timestamp (Q_k), the contents of Q_k are overwritten, otherwise a new version of Q is created.

Rule 1 : It is if transaction reads the most recent version that comes before in time.

Rule 2 : It is if T_i attempts to write a version that some other transaction would have read then we cannot allow that write to succeed. Versions of Q_k that are no longer needed are removed based on the following rule :

Suppose that there are two versions Q_k and Q_j of a data item and that both versions have a W-Timestamp less than the timestamp of the oldest transaction T_i in the system. Then the older of the two versions Q_k and Q_j will not be used again and can be deleted.

Advantages and Disadvantages :
1. In multiversion timestamp ordering scheme, a read request never fails and is never made to wait.
2. Reading of a data item requires updating of R-timestamp field, resulting in two potential disk accesses.
3. Conflicts between transactions are resolved through rollbacks, rather than through waits.

Multiversion Two-Phase Locking :

Multiversion two-phase locking scheme combines the advantages of multiversion concurrency control with two phase locking.

This protocol differentiates between read-only transactions and update transactions.

Update transactions perform rigorous two-phase locking i.e. they hold all locks upto the end of the transaction. Thus they can be serialized according to their commit order. Each data item has a single timestamp. The timestamp in this case is not a real clock based timestamp. But rather it is counter, which is called ts-counter. It is incremented during commit processing.

Read-only transactions follow the multiversion timestamp ordering scheme. Timestamp is assigned to read-only transactions by reading the current value of ts-counter before they start execution. Thus when a read-only transaction issues a read (Q) request, the value read is the content of the version whose timestamp is the largest timestamp less than $T_s(T_i)$.

Update transactions :
1. When an update transaction reads an item, it gets a shared lock on the item, and reads the largest version of that item.
2. When an update transaction wants to write a item, it first gets exclusive lock on the items and then creates a new version of the data item. The timestamp of the new version is initially set to a value $\cdot$, which value is greater than that of any possible timestamp.
3. When update transaction T_i completes its actions, it carries out commit processing :

First T_i sets the timestamp on every version it has created to 1 more the value of ts-counter; then T_i increments ts-counter by 1. Only one update transaction is allowed to perform commit processing at a time.

Read-only transactions :

1. Read-only transactions that start after T_i increments ts-counter, can see the values updated by T_j.
2. Read-only transactions that start before T_i increments ts-counter, can see the values before updated by T_j.

Versions are deleted in a manner similar to that of multiversion timestamp ordering.

8.3.6 Optimistic Technique

Optimistic techniques are based on the assumption that conflict is rare and that is more efficient to allow transactions to proceed without imposing delays to ensure serializability. When a transaction wishes to commit a check is performed to determine whether conflict has occurred. If their has been a conflict the transaction must be rolled back and restarted.

There are two or three phases to an optimistic concurrency control protocol, depending on whether it is a read only or an update transaction :

Read Phase : This extends from the start of the transaction until immediately before the commit. The transaction reads the values of all data items it needs from the database and stores them in local variables. Updates are applied to a local copy of data, not to the database itself.

Validation Phase : This follows the read phase. Checks are performed to ensure that the serializability is not violated if the transaction updates are applied to the database.

For a read only transaction this consists of checking that the data values read are still current values for the corresponding data item. If no interference occurred then the transaction is committed otherwise it is aborted.

For a transaction that updates, validation consists of determining whether the current transaction leaves the database in a consistent state, with serializability maintained. If not, then the transaction is aborted and restarted.

Write Phase : This follows the successful validation phase for update transaction. During this phase, the updates made to the local copy are applied to the database.

The validation phase examines the reads and writes of transactions that may cause interference. Each transaction T is assigned a timestamp at the start of its execution, start(t), one at the start of the validation phase validation(t), and one at its finish time finish(t).

To pass the validation test, one of the following must be true :

1. All transactions S with earlier timestamps must have finished before transaction T started; that is finish(S) < start(T)
2. If transaction T starts before an earlier one S finishes

(i) The set of data items written by the earlier transaction are not the ones read by the current transaction.

(ii) The earlier transaction completes its write phase before the current transaction enters its validation phase, that is start(T) < finish(TS) < validation(T)

8.4 DEADLOCK HANDLING

A system is in deadlock state if there exist a set of transactions such that every transaction in the set is waiting for another transaction in the set.

If $\{T_0, T_1, ..., T_n\}$ is the set of transactions such that T_0 is waiting for a data item that is held by T_1 and T_1 is waiting for a data item that is held by T_2 ... and T_{n-1} is waiting for a data item that is held by T_n. T_n is waiting for a data item that is held by T_0. Hence, none of the transactions can make progress in such situation. That is the system is in deadlock state.

There are three methods for dealing with deadlock problems:
1. Deadlock prevention.
2. Time-out based schemes.
3. Deadlock detection and deadlock recovery.

8.4.1 Deadlock Prevention

There are two approaches to deadlock prevention.
1. It ensures that no cyclic waits can occur by ordering the requests for locks or requiring all locks to be acquired together.
2. It performs transaction rollbacks instead of waiting for a lock, whenever the wait could potentially result in a deadlock.

Following are the schemes under first approach:

Lock all the data items before a transaction begins its execution. But there are two main disadvantages of using this protocol.
1. It is often hard to predict, before the transaction, what data items need to be locked.
2. Data item utilization may be very low since many of the data items may be locked but unused for a long time.

Another scheme is to impose a partial ordering of all at data items, and transaction can lock the data items only in that order. Using tree protocol, this scheme can be implemented.

Following are the schemes for second approach:

The second approach uses preemption and transaction rollbacks.

When a transaction T_2 requests a lock that is held by a transaction T_1, the lock granted to T_1, may be preempted by rolling back of T_1 and granting of lock to T_2.

To control the preemption, we assign a unique timestamp to each transaction. These timestamps will be used to decide whether the transaction should wait or rollback. Locking is used for concurrency control. If a transaction is rolledback, it retains the old timestamp when restarted.

Two different deadlock prevention schemes using timestamps under the second approach are :

1. **Wait-Die :** Scheme is based on non-preemptive technique.

When a transaction T_i requests a lock on a data item currently held by T_j, T_i is allowed to wait only if it has a timestamp smaller than that of T_j. Otherwise T_i is rolled back (die).

Example : $T_s(T_i) = 5$
$T_s(T_j) = 8$
$T_s(T_k) = 15$

If T_i requests a lock on a data item held by T_j then T_i will wait since $T_s(T_i) < T_s(T_j)$.

If T_k requests a lock on a data item held by T_j, then T_k will be rolled back since $T_s(T_k) > T_s(T_j)$.

2. **Wound-wait :** This scheme is based on preemptive technique.

When a transaction T_i requests a lock on a data item, currently held by T_j, T_i is allowed to wait only if it has a timestamp larger than that of T_j. Otherwise T_j is rolled back (T_j is wounded by T_i).

Example :

Consider the timestamps given in previous example for T_i, T_j and T_k transactions.

If T_i requests a lock on data item held by T_j, then T_j will be rolled back.

$T_s(T_i) < T_s(T_j)$

If T_k requests a lock on a data item held by T_j, then T_k will wait since

$T_s(T_k) > T_s(T_j)$

Comparison of wait-die and wait-wound schemes :

1. Both the wait-die and wait-wound schemes avoid starvation.
2. In wait-die scheme, an older transaction must wait for younger one to release the data item. Whereas in wait-wound scheme the older transaction never waits for a younger transaction.
3. Number of rollbacks in wait-wound scheme are fewer as compared to wait-die scheme.
4. Major problem in both the schemes is unnecessary rollbacks.

8.4.2 Time out Based Schemes

In this approach deadlock handling is based on lock time-outs. A transmission that has requested a lock, waits for at most a specified amount of time. If the lock has not been granted within that time, the transaction is said to time out and it rolls back itself back and restarts.

If there was a deadlock, one or more transactions involved in deadlock will time-out and rollback allowing others to proceed.

Advantages and Disadvantages :
1. It is easy to implement.
2. It works well if transactions are short and if long waits are likely to be due to deadlocks.
3. It is difficult to decide how long a transaction must wait before time-out.
   Too long wait results in unnecessary delays once a deadlock has occurred.
   Too short wait results in transaction rollbacks even when there is no deadlock, leading to wasted resources.
4. Starvation is the possibility with this scheme.

8.4.3 Deadlock Detection and Recovery

This is one method for dealing with deadlock. It allows the system to enter a deadlock state, and then try to recover using deadlock detection and dead-lock recovery scheme. If the probability that system enters deadlock state is relatively low, this method is efficient.

An algorithm that examines the state of the system is invoked periodically to determine whether a deadlock has occurred. If it has occurred then the system must attempt to recover from the deadlock. Following are the requirements for deadlock detection and recovery :

1. Maintain information about the current allocation of data items to transactions, as well as any outstanding data item requests.
2. Provide an algorithm that uses this information to determine whether the system has entered a deadlock state.
3. Recover from the deadlock when detection algorithm determines that a deadlock exists.

Deadlock Detection :

Deadlocks can be detected using a directed graph called wait for graph.

The wait for graph consists of a pair $G = (V, E)$ where V is a set of vertices and E is a set of edges. The set of vertices consists of all transactions in the system. Each element in the set E of edges is an ordered pair $T_i \rightarrow T_j$.

A directed edge $T_i \rightarrow T_j$ in graph imply that T_i is waiting for transaction T_j to release the data item.

The edge $T_i \rightarrow T_j$ is removed when T_j is no longer holding a data item needed by transaction T_i.

A deadlock exist in the system if the wait for graph for that system contain a cycle.

Consider the wait graph given in Fig. 8.13.

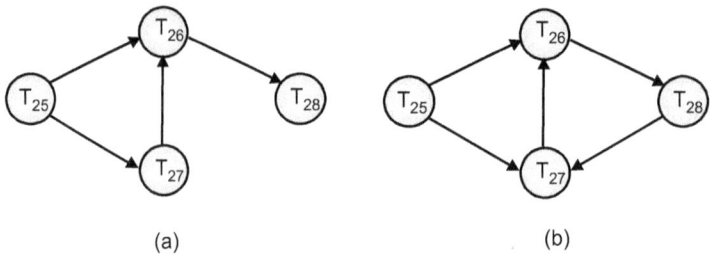

Fig. 8.13 : Wait Graph

Transaction T_{25} is waiting for T_{26} and T_{27}.

Transaction T_{26} is waiting for T_{28}.

Transaction T_{27} is waiting for T_{26}.

The graph contains no cycle. Hence, the system is not in deadlock state.

But now consider the Fig. 8.13 (b). It contains a cycle

$$T_{26} \to T_{28} \to T_{27}$$

Hence, the system is in deadlock state. In this way using this algorithm deadlocks can be detected. Depending on the frequency of deadlock occurrence, the deadlock detection algorithm should be invoked.

Recovery from deadlock :

The most common solution to recover from deadlock is to rollback one or more transactions to break the deadlock. A transaction can be recovered using following three actions.

1. Selection of victim :

Determine which transaction to rollback.

Those transactions that will incur the minimum cost will be rolled back.

The cost of rollback can be decided by following factors.

(i) How long the transaction has computed and how much longer the transaction will compute before it completes the designated task ?

(ii) How many data items it has use ?

(iii) How many more data items it needs to complete ?

(iv) How many transactions will be involved in the rollback ?

2. Rollback :

One method to rollback a transaction is to abort transaction and restart it.

The other more effective method is to rollback the transaction only as far as necessary to break the deadlock. But this require additional information about all the running transactions.

3. Starvation :

It may happen that the same transaction is always selected as victim. This results in starvation. The most common solution is to include the number of rollbacks in the cost factor.

8.5 RECOVERY SYSTEM

A computer system is subject to failure of various types. If some failure occurs during the execution of a transaction, it results in inconsistent database. Recovery system is an integral part of database system. It is responsible for restoration of the database to a consistent state that existed prior to the occurrence of the failure.

In this section we shall study the various failure types and recovery schemes.

8.5.1 Failures and Errors

A system is reliable if it works as per its specifications and produces correct set of output values for a given set of input values.

The failure of a system occurs when the system does not work according to its specifications and fails to deliver the service for which it was intended.

An error in the system occurs when a component of a system assumes a state that is not desirable.

A fault is detected either when an error is propagated from one component to another or the failure of the component is observed.

There are two types of failures :

1. Failure that results in loss of information.
2. Failure that does not results in loss of information. In this section we will study following types of failures :

1. Transaction failure :

There are two types of errors that may cause a transaction to fail.

1. Logical error : Logical error occurs because of following conditions :

- Bad input
- Data not found
- Overflow
- Resource limit exceeded.

2. System error : A system error occurs.

When a system enters an undesirable state such as deadlock, and transaction cannot continue with its normal execution.

2. System crash :

System crash occurs in following condition :

When there is a hardware malfunction or a bug in the database or the operating system, it cause loss of content of volatile storage and brings transaction processing to a halt.

3. Disk failure :

A disk failure occurs when a disk loses its contents as a result of either a head crash or failure during a data transfer operation.

Note :

1. Transaction failure doesn't result in loss of information.
2. System crash loses the contents of volatile storage but it doesn't corrupt the non-volatile storage contents. (This is known as fail-stop assumption).
3. Disk failure loses the data stored on disk. Copies of data on other disks or archival backups on tertiary media such as tapes, are used to recover from the failure.

8.5.2 Recovery Algorithms

The algorithms which ensure database consistency and transaction atomicity despite failures are known as recovery algorithms and they have two parts :

1. Actions taken during normal transaction processing to ensure that enough information exists to allow recovery from failures.
2. Actions taken following a failure to recover the database contents to a state that ensures database consistency, transaction atomicity and durability.

Recoverable Schedule :

A recoverable schedule is defined as a schedule where for each pair of transactions T_i and T_j such that T_j reads a data item previously written by T_i, the commit operation of T_i appears before the commit operation of T_j.

If some failure occurs during the execution of a transaction and database is in some inconsistent state following are two simple recovery procedures.

1. Reexecute : Execute the same transaction. But because of previous incomplete execution of that transaction, the database is already in an inconsistent state. Hence it results in an inconsistent database.

2. Do not reexecute : If we do not reexecute the transaction, the database will remain in same inconsistent state.

The atomicity property (perform either all or no database modifications) is not achieved.

DATABASE MANAGEMENT SYSTEMS (T.E. IT) — TRANSACTION MANAGEMENT

To achieve the goal of atomicity, information about modifications must be stored to stable storage before modifying the database. In this procedure, if some failures occurs and modification information is complete then system can reexecute the transaction. Otherwise system will not reexecute the transaction.

Following are the two schemes to achieve the recovery from transaction failures :

1. Log-based recovery
2. Shadow paging.

(1) Log-based recovery :

It assumes that transactions are executed serially. i.e. only one transaction is active at a time. It uses a structure called log to store the database modifications. There are two techniques for using log to achieve the recovery and ensure atomicity in case of failures.

1. Deferred database modification
2. Immediate database modification.

Deferred modification technique ensures transaction atomicity by recording all database modifications in the log, but deferring the execution of all write operations of transaction until the transaction partially commits.

The immediate update technique allows database modifications to be output to the database while the transaction is still in the active state. Data modifications written by active transactions are called uncommitted modifications. If a failure occurs during execution, the system must use the old value field of log records.

Log :

Log is a structure used to store the database modifications. It is a sequence of log records and maintains a record of all the update activities in the database.

There are several types of log records to record significant events during transaction processing.

1. **Start of transaction :**

    denoted as $<T_i \text{ start}>$

2. **Update log :**

    It describes a single database write and it is denoted as :

    $<T_i, X_j, V_1, V_2>$

    where,

    $T_i \rightarrow$ Transaction identifier

    $X_j \rightarrow$ Data item identifier

    $V_1 \rightarrow$ Old value of X_j

    $V_2 \rightarrow$ New value of X_j after the write operation.

3. **Transaction commits :**
    denoted as : <T_i commit>
4. **Transaction abort :**
    denoted as : <T_i abort>

Log resides in stable storage.

a. Deferred database modification :

Deferred database modification technique stores the database modifications in the log.

Execution of write operation is done when transaction is in partially committed state.

According to transaction state diagram, a transaction is in partially committed state when transaction completes executing the last instruction.

Execution of transaction T_i proceed as follows :

Before T_i starts its execution record, a record <T_i start> is written to log.

Write (X) operation of T_i results in writing a new record <T_i, X, V_2> to the log.

Note : It doesn't write V_1 - old value of X.

When T_i partially commits a record <T_i commit> is written to log.

When T_i partially commits, the records associated with it in the log are used in executing the deferred writes.

If system crashes before the transaction completes its execution or if the transaction aborts, then the information on the log is ignored.

If some failure occurs while updating the database using log records, the log record is written in some stable storage, hence, the transaction can resume its database modification.

Using log the system can handle any failure that results in loss of information on volatile storage.

The recovery scheme uses the following recovery procedure.

redo (T_i) : It sets the value of all data items updated by transaction T_i to the new values. The set of data items and their respective new values can be found in the log.

The redo operation must be idempotent i.e. executing it several times must be equivalent to executing it once.

A transaction can execute redo (T_i) if the log contains both the record <T_i start> and the record <T_i commit>.

Example :

Consider the transaction T_i, it transfers Rs. 50 from account A to account B. Original values of account A and B are Rs. 800 and Rs. 2000 respectively. This transaction is defined as :

DATABASE MANAGEMENT SYSTEMS (T.E. IT)   TRANSACTION MANAGEMENT

T_0 : read (A);
     A := A - 50;
     write (A);
     read (B);
     B := B + 50;
     write (B).

Consider the second transaction T_i that withdraws Rs. 80 from amount C. This transaction is defined as :

T_1 : read (C);
     C := C - 80;
     write (C).

These two transactions are executed serially $<T_0, T_1>$.

The log containing relevant information on these two transactions is given below :

<T_0 start>
<T_0, A, 950>
<T_0, B, 2050>
<T_0 commit>
<T_1 start>
<T_1, C, 600>
<T_1 commit>

It shows the log that result from the complete execution of T_0 and T_1.

The actual output can take place to database system in various orders. One such order is given below :

log	Database
<T_0 start>	
<T_0, A, 950>	
<T_0, B, 2050>	
<T_0 commit>	
	A = 900
	B = 2050
<T_1 start>	
<T_1, C, 600>	
<T_1 commit>	C = 600

If system crashes before the completion of transactions :

Case 1 : Crash occurs just after the log record for write (B) operation.

Log contents after the crash are :

Ch. 8 | 8.45

DATABASE MANAGEMENT SYSTEMS (T.E. IT) — TRANSACTION MANAGEMENT

$<T_0$ start$>$
$<T_0, A, 950>$
$<T_0, B, 2050>$

$<T_0$ commit$>$ is not written, hence no redo operation is possible. The values of amount remain unchanged i.e. amount A is Rs. 800 and B is Rs. 2000.

Case 2 : Crash occurs just after log record for write (C) operation.

The log contents after the crash are :

$<T_0$ start$>$
$<T_0, A, 950>$
$<T_0, B, 2050>$
$<T_0$ commit$>$
$<T_1,$ start$>$
$<T_1, C, 600>$

When the system comes back it finds $<T_0$ start$>$ and $<T_0$ commit$>$. But there is no $<T_1$ commit$>$ for $<T_0$ start$>$. Hence, system can execute redo (T_0) but not redo $<T_1>$. Hence, the value of account C remains unchanged.

Case 3 : Crash occurs just after the log record $<T_1$ commit$>$.

The log contents after the crash are :

$<T_0$ start$>$
$<T_0, A, 950>$
$<T_0, B, 2050>$
$<T_0,$ commit$>$
$<T_1$ start$>$
$<T, C, 600>$
$<T_1$ commit$>$

When system comes back it can execute both redo (T_0) and redo (T_1) operations.

For each commit record, the redo (T_i) operation is performed. redo (T_i) writes the values to the database independent of the values currently in the database. Hence, the redo (T_i) is idempotent.

b. Immediate database modification :

It allows the database modifications to be output to the database while transaction is still in active state.

Database modifications written by active transactions are called **uncommitted modifications**.

Execution of transaction proceeds as follows :

- Before T_i starts its execution, the record $<T_i$ start$>$ is written to the log.
- Before executing any write (X) i.e. before modifying the database for write operation, it writes an update record $<T_i, X, V_1, V_2>$ to the log.
- When T_i partially commits, the record $<T_i$ commit$>$ is written to log.

As an illustration consider the same example of bank accounts and transactions T_0 and T_1.

Transactions T_0 and T_1 are executed serially. The log corresponding to this execution is given below :

$<T_0$ start$>$
$<T_0, A, 800, 950>$
$<T_0, B, 2000, 2050>$
$<T_0$ commit$>$
$<T_1$ start$>$
$<T_1, C, 700, 600>$
$<T_1$ commit$>$

The order in which output took place to both database system and log as a result of execution of T_0 and T_1 is :

Data	Database
$<T_0$ start$>$	
$<T_0, A, 800, 950>$	
$<T_0, B, 2000, 2050>$	
$<T_0$ commit$>$	A = 950 B = 2050
$<T_1$ start$>$	
$<T_1, C, 700, 600>$	C = 600
$<T_1$ commit $>$	

Using the log, the system can handle any failure. Two recovery procedures are there to recover :

DATABASE MANAGEMENT SYSTEMS (T.E. IT)   TRANSACTION MANAGEMENT

1. **Undo (T_i)** : It restores the value of all data items updated by transaction T_i to the old values.
2. **Redo (T_i)** : It sets the value of all data items updated by transaction T_i to the new values.

The undo (T_i) and redo (T_i) operations must be idempotent.

Depending on the log, the recovery scheme determine which transaction need to be redone and which need to be undone.

If the log record contains the record <T_i start> but does not contain the record <T_i commit> then T_i needs to be undone.

If the log record contains both the records <T_i start> and <T_i commit> then T_i needs to be redone i.e. If a failure occurs before <T_i commit> the database modifications are rolled back by undo (T_i) operation. If a failure occurs after <T_i commit> then the transaction is reexecuted by redo (T_i) operation.

Consider the following conditions of failure for transactions T_0 and T_1.

Case 1 : Failure occurs just after the log record for write (B) operation.

Log contents and database are :

Log	Database
<T_0 start>	
<T_0 A, 800, 950>	
<T_0, B, 2000, 2050>	
	A = 950
	B = 2050

Log contains <T_0 start> but does not contain <T_0, commit>. Hence T_0 must be undone hence undo (T_0) is executed, the values of account A and B are restored to 800 and 2000 respectively.

Case 2 : If some failure occurs just after log record for write (C) T_i has written to log.

The log and database contents are :

Log	Database
<T_0 start>	
<T_0 A, 800, 950>	
<T_0 B, 2000, 2050>	
database	A = 950
	B = 2050
<T_0 commit>	
<T_1 start>	
<T_1 C, 700, 600>	C = 600

Ch. 8 | 8.48

Log contains <T_0 start> and <T_0 commit>. Hence, the redo (T_0) is executed and values of accounts A and B are restored to the same (or new values) 950 and 2050 respectively. But the log doesn't contain <T_1 commit> for <T_1 start>. Hence, the value of account C is restored to old value by undo (T_1) operation. Hence, value of C is Rs. 700.

Case 3 : If system crashes just after the log record <T_1 commit> has been written to log.

The log and database contents are :

```
Log                                    Database
<T0 start>
<T0 A, 800, 950>
<T0 B, 2000, 2050>
                      database ----> A = 950
                                     B = 2050
<T0 commit>
<T1 start>
<T1 C, 700, 600>
                      database ----> C = 600
<T1 commit>
```

Log contains <T_0 start>, <T_0 commit> and <T_1 start> <T_1 commit> operations. Hence, recovery system executes redo (T_0) and redo (T_1) operations. The values of accounts A, B and C are Rs. 950, Rs. 2050 and Rs. 600 respectively.

Checkpoints :

When a system failure occurs, some transactions need to be redone and some need to be undone.

Log record can determine this. But for that we need to search the entire log. There are two major difficulties with this approach.

1. The search process is time consuming.
2. Most of the transactions that will be redone have already written their updates into the database. Hence, it is better to avoid such redo operations.

To reduce these types of overhead, checkpoints are introduced.

During the execution the system maintains log using immediate database modification technique or deferred database modification technique. In addition, the system periodically performs checkpoints, which require following sequence of operations :

1. Output onto stable storage all log records currently residing in main memory.
2. Output to the disk all modified buffer blocks.
3. Output onto stable storage a log record <checkpoint>.

Transactions are not allowed to perform any update actions, such as writing to a buffer block or writing a log record, while a checkpoint is in progress.

The presence of <checkpoint> record in log allows the system to streamline its recovery procedure.

After the failure has occurred, the recovery system examines the log to determine the most recent transaction T_i that started execution before the most recent checkpoint took place. It can find such a transaction by searching the log backward from the end of the log until it finds the first <checkpoint> record, then it continues the search backward until it finds the next <T_i start> record. This record identifies a transaction T_j. Once the transaction is identified, redo or undo operation can be applied to transaction T_i and all the transactions T executing after T_j. The earlier part of transaction can be ignored. The recovery can be done by using immediate database modification or deferred database modification technique.

2. Shadow Paging :

Shadow paging is an alternative to log-based crash recovery technique. This is one possible form of indirect page allocation.

Paging : Paging scheme is used in operating system for virtual memory management.

The memory that is addressed by a process is called **virtual memory**.

It is divided into pages, that are assumed to be of a certain size (1 KB or 4 KB). The virtual or logical pages are mapped onto physical memory blocks of same size. The mapping of pages is provided by means of table called as page table.

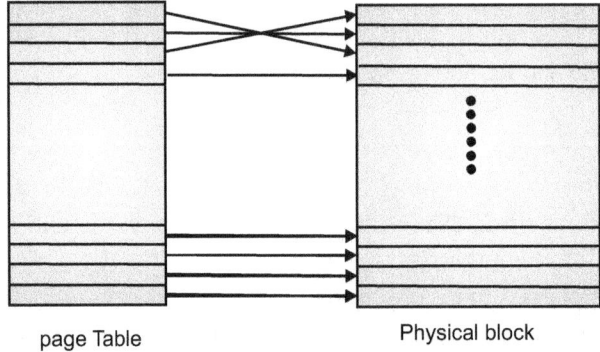

page Table   Physical block

Fig. 8.14 : Page Table

Page table contains one entry for each logical page of the processes virtual address space. Page table is shown in the Fig. 8.14.

In the shadow page scheme, the database is considered to be made up of logical units of storage called pages. The pages are mapped into physical blocks of storage by means of a page table with one entry for each logical page. This entry contains the block number of physical storage where this page is stored.

The shadow page scheme uses two page tables.
1. Current page table.
2. Shadow page table.

Transaction addresses the database using current page table. It may change the current page table entries. The changes are made whenever the transaction executes write operation. To modify a page, it copies that page to new blocks of physical storage. The page table entry corresponding to that page is made to point to new block of storage.

The shadow page table is the original page table. It contains the entries that existed prior to the start of transaction. It remains unaltered by the transaction and it is used for undoing the transaction.

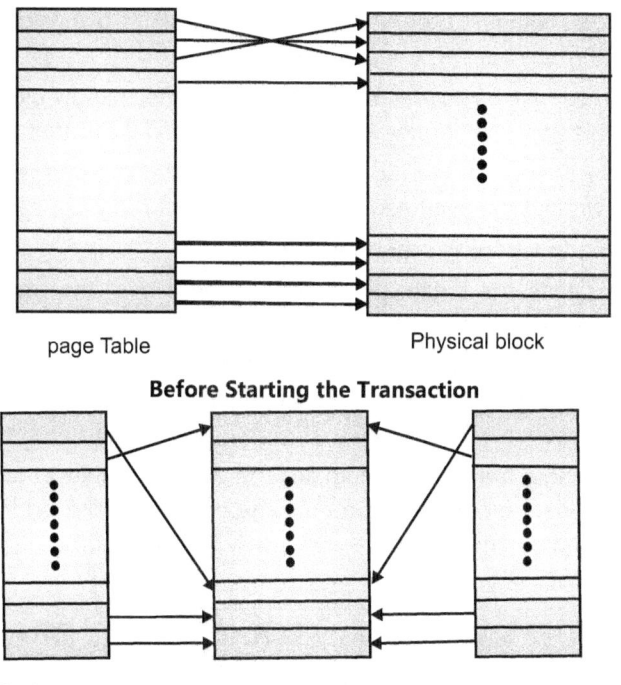

page Table   Physical block

Before Starting the Transaction

Shadow page   Physical Blocs   Current page Table

Fig. 8.15 : After Executing Write Operation

Now, let us see how the transaction accesses data.

The transaction uses the current page table to access the database blocks. The shadow paging scheme handles a write operation of transaction as follows :

1. A free block of non-volatile storage is located from the pool of free blocks accessible by the database system.

2. The block to be modified is copied onto this block.
3. The original entry in the current page table is changed to point to this new block.
4. The updates are propagated to the block pointed to by the current page table which in this case would be newly created block.

Any changes made to the database are propagated to the blocks pointed to by the current page table.

Once a transaction commits, all modifications made by the transaction and still in buffers are propagated to physical database. It causes the current page table to be written to non-volatile storage.

In case of system crash before the transaction commits, the shadow page table and the corresponding blocks containing the old database will continue to be accessible. The old database is made accessible just by modifying a single pointer from shadow page table to current page table.

Once the transaction completes its execution successfully, the shadow block can be returned to the pool of available non-volatile storage blocks to be used for further transactions.

Advantage of shadow paging scheme is : Recovery from system crash is relatively inexpensive and this is achieved without the overhead of logging.

Disadvantages of shadow paging scheme are :

1. Over a period of time the database will be scattered over the physical memory and related records may require a very long access time.
2. When the transaction completed its execution, shadow blocks have to be returned to the pool of free blocks. If this is not done successfully, when a transaction commits, such blocks become inaccessible. This is called as **garbage collection operation**.
3. The commit of a single transaction using shadow paging requires multiple blocks to be output (the actual data blocks, the current page table, and disk address of the current page table log based schemes need to output only the log records.

REVIEW QUESTIONS ON INSTRUCTIONAL OBJECTIVES

1. Specify what is meant by "Transaction". Explain abstract transaction model using state diagram.
2. Differentiate between Serial schedule and serializable schedule.
3. Explain two-phase lock protocol with example.
4. Explain timestamp-based and lock-based protocols.
5. Define stable storage.

6. When do deadlocks happen, how to prevent them, and how to recover if deadlock takes place ?
7. State the rules for a timestamp based concurrency control protocol and demonstrate its working.
8. How does the recovery take place in case of log file based deferred database modification scheme ? What is the log file structure used ?
9. Give two examples of transactions after defining the concept of transaction.
8. Briefly define any one locking protocol.
11. Briefly define any one time stamping protocol.
12. Give a clear example of a view serializable schedule which is not conflict serializable.
13. What are the checkpoints, how are they useful ?
14. How do log files assist in database recovery ?
15. Show how shadow paging works.
16. A transaction is characterized by four properties atomicity, consistency, isolation and durability. How are these properties supported by DBMS system ? Just identify the modules/ components responsible for each property. What happens if each of this property is not ensured or not maintained. Give clear examples for consequences of not supporting a properly.
17. Illustrate difference between conflict serializable schedule and view serializable schedule by an appropriate example.
18. Explain the purpose of checkpoints ? How often should a database system do a checkpoint.
19. Explain shadow paging recovery scheme.
20. What do you understand by serializable and non-serializable schedule ? How would you test whether the given schedule S is conflict serializable schedule.
21. Show that the two phase locking protocol ensures conflict serializability.
22. Write a note on :
    (i) Timestamp Based Protocol.
    (ii) Deadlock Handling.
23. Discuss the problems with concurrency. Describe any two methods based on locks to control concurrency.
24. Discuss the concept of transaction in terms of the properties atomicity, durability, isolation and consistency. How is the concept of serializability relevant in context of transactions. Give examples.
25. What measures are required for recovery of a database using log based recovery methods ?

DATABASE MANAGEMENT SYSTEMS (T.E. IT)   TRANSACTION MANAGEMENT

26. What do you understand by conflict serializable schedule ? Discuss methods for determining conflict serializability.
27. Draw the state diagram representing various transaction states.
28. What are the various concurrency control schemes ?
29. Explain multiple granularity.
30. State advantages and disadvantages of using multiple granularity.
31. Explain multiversion timestamp ordering and multiversion two phase locking.

UNIVERSITY QUESTIONS

1. List and explain ACID properties. **(Dec. 2004)**
2. Differentiate between serial and serializable schedule. **(Dec. 2004)**
3. Consider the following two transactions :

   T1 :   read(A)
           read(B)
           if A = 0 then B := B + 1
           write(B)

   T2 :   read(B)
           read(A)
           if b = 0 then A := A + 1
           write(A)

   Let the consistency requirement be A = 0 VB = 0, with A = B = 0.

   Show that every serial execution involving these two transactions preserve the consistency of the database.

   Show a concurrent execution of T_1 and T_2 that produces a nonserializable schedule.

   (Dec. 2004)

4. Explain two phase locking protocol. **(Dec. 2004)**
5. Why concurrent execution of transactions is desirable ? Support your answer with example. **(May 2004)**
6. Explain how database system supports atomicity and durability of transactions. **(May 2004)**
7. Consider the following transactions : **(Dec. 2003)**

   T_1 :   read (A)
           Read (B)

```
       if A = 0 then B := B+1
       write (B)
   T₂: read (B)
       read (A)
       if b=0 then A := A+1
       write (A)
```

    Add lock and unlock instructions to above transactions so that they observe two phase locking protocol. Can execution of these transactions results in deadlock. **(Dec. 2003)**

8. Explain recoverable and Cascadeless schedules. **(Dec. 2003)**
9. What is concurrency control ? Explain timestamp based protocol.

    Compare the deferred and immediate versions of the log based recovery scheme in terms of ease of implementation and overhead cost. **(Dec. 2003)**

8. Explain following states of transaction : Partially committed, failed, Aborted, Active. **(May 2003)**
11. What is the need for concurrent execution of transactions ? **(May 2003)**
12. Explain when schedule is conflict serializable when it is view serializable ? Test if the given schedule is view serializable.

T_3	T_4	T_5
read(Q)		
	write(Q)	
write(Q)		
		write(Q)

    (May 2003)

13. Explain state diagram of transaction. **(Dec. 2002)**
14. Differentiate between serial and serializable schedule. **(Dec. 2002)**
15. Define : Transaction. **(Oct. 2000, April 01, Oct. 03, May 06)**
16. What is transaction concept ? **(Oct. 2000, April 01, Oct. 03)**
17. Give the properties of transaction. **(T.E. (Comp.) April 01, Oct. 03, April 04) (T.E. (I.T.) Oct. 02, Dec. 05, May 07)**
18. Write a note : 1) Atomiticy   2) Durability **(April 04)**
19. What is concurrent executions ? **(April 03, April 04)**
20. What is Transaction State ? **(T.E. (Comp.) Oct. 2000, April 03, T.E. (I.T.), Oct. 03, May 05, 06)**

21. Explain : View serializability. **(May 05)**
22. What is the test for conflict serializability ? **(T.E. Comp. April 04)**
   (T.E.(I.T.) Oct. 02, Dec. 04, May 06, May 07)
23. What is the test view serializability ? **(April 01, 03)**
24. What is recoverable schedule ? Why it is desirable ? **(Dec. 05)**
25. What is lock based protocols ? **(Oct. 03, May 06)**

Unit - IV

CHAPTER 9
DATABASE SYSTEMS ARCHITECTURE & MONGODB

9.1 Introduction

9.2 Centralized System

9.3 Client-Server System

9.4 2-Tier Architecture

9.5 3-Tier Architecture

9.6 Parallel System

9.7 Distributed System

9.8 Web-Enabled Database System

9.9 MongoDB and its Connectivity with Java

- Review Questions on Instructional Objectives
- University Questions

9.1 INTRODUCTION

Architecture of database system is greatly influenced by the architecture of computer system. This chapter deals with the following types of architecture of a database systems.
1. Centralized System
2. Client-server System
3. Parallel System
4. Distributed System
5. Web-enabled System.

Each architecture reflects following aspects of computer architecture
- Networking: It is in terms of how different nodes are connected with each other and how they communicate with each other with respect to databases.
- Parallelism: It involves execution of several transactions/execution of same transaction on several nodes concurrently to optimize the overall performance.
- Distribution: It refers to division of total workload (query execution) amongst different nodes in a network.

9.2 CENTRALIZED SYSTEM

Centralized systems run on a single computer system and do not interact with other computer systems.

It is a single user database system which can be used on personal computer and also on the mainframe system.

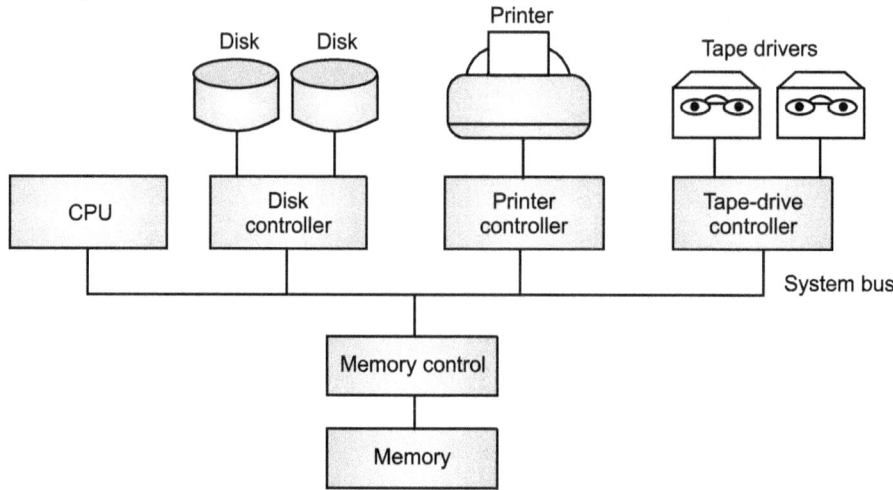

Fig. 9.1 : Centralized Computer System

A centralized computer system shown in Fig.9.1 consists of one to a few CPUS and a number of device controllers, that are connected through a common bus that provides access to stored memory. The CPU and device controllers can execute concurrently competing for memory access. The CPU have local cache memory that stores local copies of parts of memory to speed up access to data and to reduce the number of times that the CPU needs to access the shared memory.

A single user system is a desktop unit used by a single person. It has only one CPU and one or two hard-disks. It has an operating system that may support only one user.

Database system designed for a single user system does not provide many of the facilities that a multiuser database system provides. Such types of systems are intended for a specific work goal and are capable of operating on their own without any need of communication with other nodes.

Advantages:

Increased Throughput: Number of queries executed per unit of time can be increased with more than one processor.

High Execution Speed: Query execution speed is high as there is no intercommunication delay involved.

Disadvantages:
No Support for Failure Recovery:
As there is only one node, if it fails/crashes whole system will crash and there is no means or very few chances of recovery after failure. Thus, operating node itself becomes a major bottleneck.

No support for concurrency control and SQL
Many such systems do not support concurrency control and querying using SQL. Rather such systems provide simpler query languages, such as a variant of Query by Example (QBE).

9.3 CLIENT-SERVER SYSTEM

Client-server architecture is a system consisting of more than one nodes/machines. Generally, these types of systems consist of one node capable of executing all user applications and performing database related operations. The second node will operate as a database server where actual database/data resides. It is a high end machine capable of operating numerous database related operations.

Example: Students appearing for online exam attempt the exam from client end and their answers will get saved on the server side.

Generally, there will be only one server capable of handling multiple clients concurrently.
A typical architecture of a client-server system is shown in Fig. 9.2.

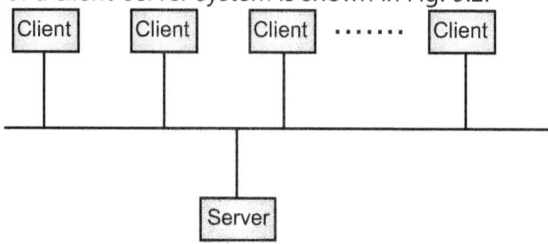

Fig. 9.2: Typical Client-Server System

Client-server relationship can be further categorized as:
1. Several clients might be able to share the same server. This relationship is shown in Fig. 9.2.
2. Client might be able to access several servers as shown in Fig. 9.3. In this relationship, again two possibilities are there:

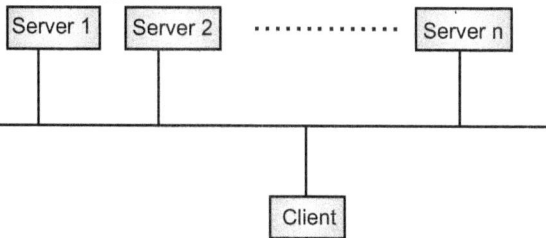

Fig. 9.3 : Accessing Several Servers

(i) The client is limited to access just one server at a time. i.e. each individual request must be directed to just one server. A single request cannot combine data from two or more different servers. The user has to know which particular server stores which piece of data. According to that request can be directed.

(ii) The client can access many servers simultaneously. i.e. a single database request can combine data from several servers, which means that user does not have to know which server store which pieces of data.

Database functionality can be broadly divided into two parts:

- Front-end
- Back-end.

As shown in Fig. 9.4.

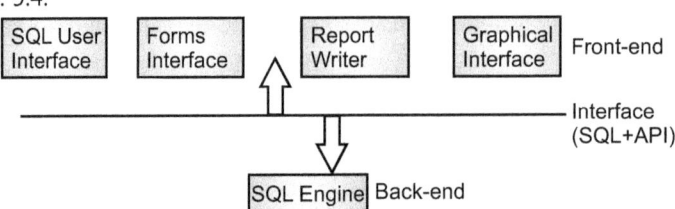

Fig. 9.4: Front-End and Back-End Functionality

The front-end of a database application consists of tools such as:

- Forms
- Report writer
- Graphical interface
- SQL user interface.

The back-end manages:

- Access structures.
- Query evaluation and Optimization.
- Concurrency control.
- Recovery.

The interface between the front-end and the back-end is through SQL or through an application program interface (JDBC/ODBC etc)

Server systems are broadly categorized as:

1. Transaction Server/Query Server
2. Data Server.

1. Transaction Server:

Transaction server systems, also called query server system provide an interface to which clients can send requests to perform an action in response to which they execute the action and send back results to the client.

Users may specify requests in SQL or through an application program interface, using a remote-procedure-call mechanism.

In the client-server system, the transaction server support functional division between back-end and front-end.

Front-end functionality is supported on personal computers which act as clients of server system which support back-end functionality.

Clients ship transactions to the server system where those transactions are executed and results are shipped back to clients that are in charge of displaying the data.

Standards such as : Open Database Connectivity (ODBC) are used for interfacing of clients with servers. ODBC is an application program interface that allows clients to generate SQL statements that are sent to server where the statements are executed. Any client that uses ODBC interface can connect to any server that provides interface.

Client-server interfaces other than ODBC are defined by an application program interface, using which clients make transactional remote procedure calls on the server.

These calls appear like ordinary procedure calls to the programmer. But all the remote procedure calls from a client are enclosed in a transaction at the server end.

Advantages of using transaction server are :
1. Better functionality for the cost.
2. More flexibility in locating resources and expanding facilities.
3. Better user interfaces.
4. Easier maintenance.

2. Data Server:

Data server systems allow clients to interact with the servers by making requests to read or update data, in units such as files or pages.

Data servers are used in local area networks where:
- There is high speed connection between the clients and server.
- The client machines are having comparatively more processing power.
- Tasks to be executed are computing intensive.

In such an environment, server machine sends data to the client machines to perform all processing at the client machine and then client sends that data back to the server machine.

This architecture requires full back-end functionality at the client side. Data server architecture is mainly useful in object oriented database systems.

The time cost of communication between the client and the server is high compared to that local memory reference.

Following issues decide the time cost of communication between client and server.

- **Data Shipping :** Units of communication for data are page or an item (tuple or an object). Data can be fetched by fetching the page or single item (tuple or object).

- **Locks :** Locks are usually granted by the server for data item/page that it ships to the client machine.

Disadvantage of page shipping is that locks on a page implicitly locks all items contained in the page. Other client machines that require lock on those data items may be blocked unnecessarily.

- **Data Caching:** Data that are shipped to a client on behalf of a transaction can be cached at the client. Successive transactions at the same client may be able to make use of the cached data. But it must ensure that those data are up to date, since they may have been updated by different client after they were cached. Thus, the client must communicate with the server to check the validity of the data and to acquire a lock on the data.

- **Lock Caching:** If the use of data is mostly partitioned among the clients with clients rarely requesting data that are also requested by other clients, then locks can also be cached at the client machine.

9.4 2-TIER CLIENT-SERVER ARCHITECTURE

Generally any business application requiring data consist of four major pillars viz. the actual database, the transaction logic, the application logic and user interface. To support ever increasing customer need, decentralization of above tasks is proposed. This decentralization leads to division of work amongst different nodes (a.k.a tiers). The client (tier1) is dedicated for presentation of data to the user in most flexible and suitable format. These services handle user interface actions and main business application logic. The server (tier 2) is meant for providing data services to the client. It involves providing access to requested data, independent of its location along with data validation. Fig.9.5 gives a general schematic of this type of architecture.

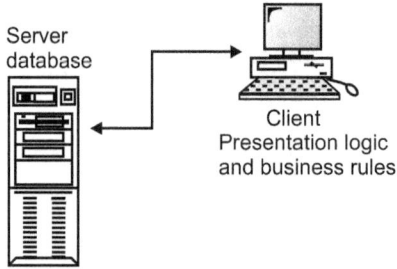

Fig. 9.5 : 2 Tier Architecture

However, such systems suffer from following cons:

1. Client requires more resources (processor, memory, disk requirements are high) as it is running user interface as well as business application logic. In today's generation there lies a need to have light weight clients performing only interaction with servers.
2. It causes a significant overhead on client side administration and maintenance.

To deal with such major drawbacks there lies a need of separation between client end and business logic processing. This separation is achieved in 3-tier architecture.

9.5 3-TIER CLIENT-SERVER ARCHITECTURE

As the need for enterprise scalability is increasing, it challenged the traditional 2 tier architecture. In 1995, a new variant of 2 tier architecture came into existence where there was reduction in client-side headache. Such systems comprised of following three levels/tiers:

1. User Interface Layer: This layer/tier comprised of functionality for simple GUI required for communication with database server and it runs on end-users computer. It sometimes performs a role of validating the input at users' side.

2. Business Logic & Data Processing Layer: It acts as a middleware which runs on separate machine and whose responsibility is to handle business and application logic. Sometimes it is also known as "Application Server".

3. Database Server: It stores the data required by middle layer. This layer may run on separate server known as database server whose primary job is to handle all database related requests from client side or through middle layer.

As there is clear separation between business logic and user interface, client will require very few resources. So it is known as "Thin Client". Fig.9.6 shows the architecture of 3-tier systems.

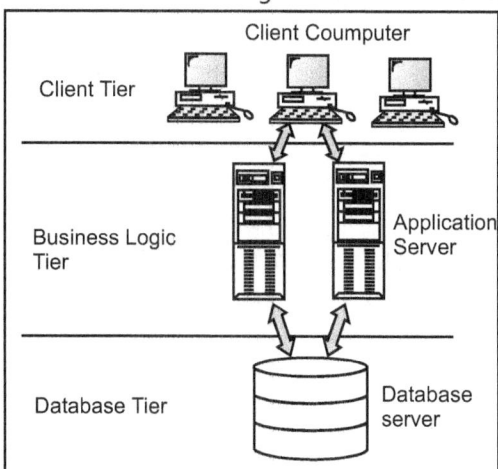

Fig. 9.6 : 3-tier architecture

Advantages of 3-Tier Architecture:

- It is less expensive as client requires very limited amount of resources like hardware, memory etc.
- Application maintenance is centralized with transfer of business logic for many clients into single application server.

- The added modularity makes it convenient for modification or replacement of any one of the tier without affecting others.
- Load balancing is easier with separation of core business logic from database functions.

This architecture easily maps to web environment with a web browser acting as "Thin Client" and web server acting as application server. This architecture can be easily extended to n-tiers which will provide more flexibility and modularity.

9.6 PARALLEL SYSTEM

Parallel systems improve processing and I/O speeds by using multiple CPUs and disks in parallel. Many operations are executed simultaneously.

There are two types of parallel machines :

1. A Coarse-grain Parallel Machine : Which consists of a small number of powerful processors.

2. A Massively Parallel or Fine-grain Machine : Which uses thousands of smaller processors.

Massively parallel computers are distinguished from the coarse-grain parallel machines by the degree of parallelism that they support.

Most high-end machines today offer some degree of course-grain parallelism. Two or four processor machines are common. Parallel computers with hundreds of CPUS are also available.

There are two main measures of performance of the database system.

1. Throughput :

The number of tasks/queries executed per unit amount of time leads to throughput. According to parallel system design point of view, throughput is always high.

2. Response Time :

Amount of time it takes to complete a single task from the time when it is submitted. This time should be minimal and its achievable if one uses parallel systems.

A system that processes large number of small transactions can improve throughput by processing many transactions in parallel.

A system that processes large transactions can improve response time as well as throughput by performing subtasks of each transaction in parallel.

The two important issues in studying the parallelism are :
1. Speed-up
2. Scale-up.

1. Speed-up :

Speed-up refers to handling large number of tasks by increasing the degree of parallelism.

Consider a database application running on a parallel system with certain number of processors and disks.

Suppose that we increase the size of the system by increasing the number of processors, disks and other components of the system.

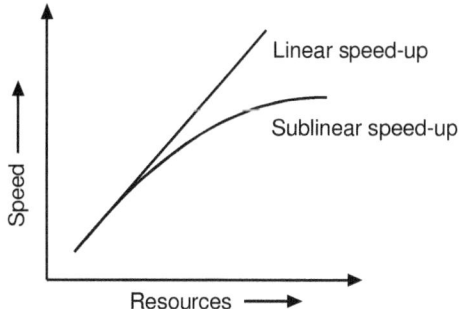

Fig. 9.7 : Speed-up with Increasing Resources

Let the execution time of a task on the large machine is T_L and that the execution time of the same task on the smaller machine is T_S.

The speed-up due to parallelism is defined as T_S/T_L.

The parallel system demonstrate linear speed-up if the speed-up is N when the larger system has N times the resources of smaller system.

If the speed-up is less than N, system is said to demonstrate **sublinear speed-up**.

Scale-up :

The scale-up refers to handling larger tasks by increasing the degree of parallelism.

Let Q be a task and let Q_N be a task that is N times larger than Q.

Suppose that execution time of Q on a given machine M_S is T_S and the execution time of task Q_N on a parallel machine M_L which is N times larger than M_S is T_L.

The scale-up is defined as T_S/T_L.

Parallel system demonstrate-**linear scale-up** on task Q if $T_L = T_S$.

If $T_L > T_S$, the system is said to demonstrate **sublinear scale-up**.

Fig. 9.8 illustrates the linear and sublinear scale-up.

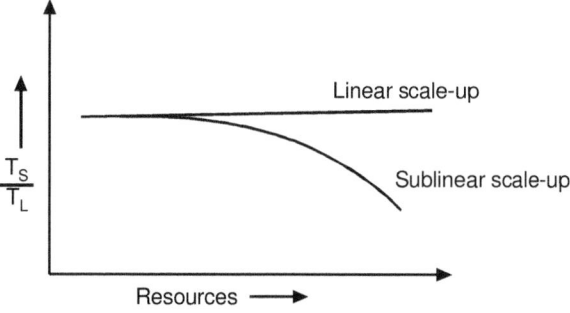

Fig. 9.8 : Scale-up with Increasing Problem Size

There are two kinds of scale-up depending on how the size of the task is measured.
  (i) Batch Scale-up
  (ii) Transaction Scale-up.

Scale-up is a more important metric for measuring the efficiency of parallel database system. Following are the factors which work against efficient parallel operation and diminish both speed-up and scale-up.

1. Startup Costs : There is a start-up cost associated with initiating a single process. In parallel operation consisting of thousands of processes, the start-up time may overshadow the actual processing time, affecting speed-up adversely.

2. Interference : Since processes executing in a parallel system often access shared resources, a slowdown may result from the interference of each new process, as it competes with existing processes for commonly held resources such as a system bus or shared disks or locks. Both speed-up and scale-up are affected by this phenomenon.

3. Skew : By breaking down a single task into a number of parallel steps, we can reduce the size of the average step. The service time for the single slowest step will determine the service time for the task as a whole. It is difficult to divide a task into exactly equal sized parts and the way that the sizes are distributed is therefore skewed.

For example : If the task size is 100 and it is divided into 10 parts. If the division is skewed there may be some tasks of size less than 10 and some tasks of size more than 10. If even one task happens to be of size 20, the speed-up obtained by running tasks in parallel is only five, instead of ten.

Interconnection Network :

Parallel system consists of components (processors, memory and disks) that can communicate with each other via a connection network.

Interconnection network include :

BUS : All the system components can send data on and receive data from a single communication bus. The bus could be an ethernet or parallel interconnect.

Bus architectures work well for small number of processors, since it can handle communication from only one component at a time.

Mesh : The components are arranged in a grid and each component is connected to all its adjacent nodes.

In a two-dimensional mesh, each node is connected to four adjacent nodes. In a three-dimensional mesh each node is connected to six adjacent nodes.

Nodes that are not directly connected can communicate with one another by routing messages via a sequence of intermediate nodes that are directly connected to one another.

The number of communication links as the number of components grows and the communication capacity of mesh therefore scales better with increasing parallelism.

Hypercube : The components are numbered in binary and a component is connected to another, if the binary representations of their numbers differ exactly by one bit.

This each of the n components is connected to log (n) of other components.

In a hypercube interconnection, a message from a component can reach any other component by going via. at most log (n) links (in mesh it is $\sqrt{n} - 1$ links).

Thus communication delays in hypercube interconnection network are significantly lower than in a mesh.

Parallel Database Architectures :

(1) Shared Memory :

In this model, all the processors share a common memory. The model is depicted in Fig. 9.9.

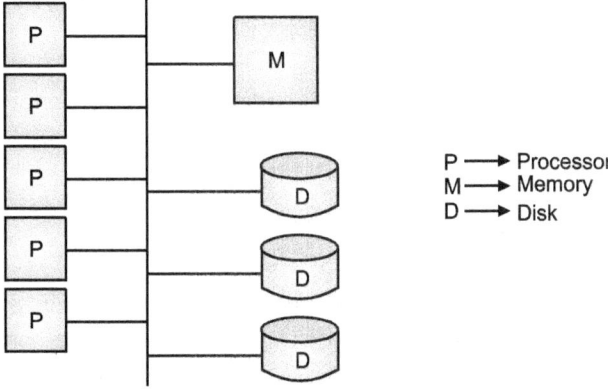

Fig. 9.9: Shared Memory

In shared memory parallel databases, communication between components is through interconnection network.

Shared memory results in extremely efficient communication between processors.

Data in shared memory can be accessed by any processor without being moved with software.

A processor can send messages to other processors using memory writes.

But the shared memory machine is not scalable beyond 32 or 64 processors since the interconnection network becomes bottle neck.

(2) Shared Disk:

In this model, all processors share a common disk. Shared disk models are sometimes called as clusters.

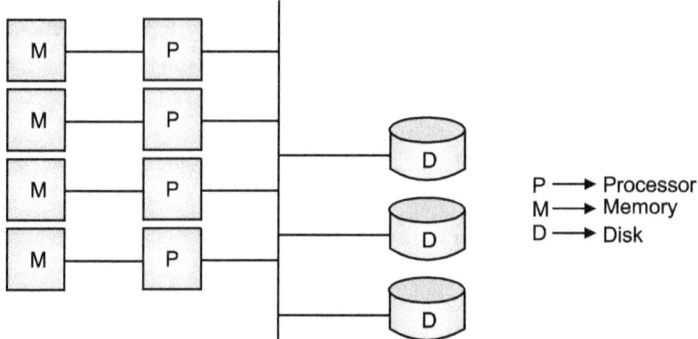

Fig. 9.10 : Shared-Disk System

Fig. 9.10 shows shared disk system model..

In this model, all processors can access all disks directly via. an interconnection network. All the processors are having their private memories.

Advantages of Shared-disk :
1. Each processor has its own memory hence, the memory bus is not the bottleneck.
2. This architecture offers a cheap way to provide a degree of fault tolerance. If a processor (or its memory) fails, other processors can take over its tasks, since the database is resident on disks that are accessible from any processor.

Disadvantage of Shared-disk :

The interconnection to disk sub-system is the bottleneck. It affects the scalability as the number of processors increases. But as compared to shared memory system, shared disk systems can scale to a somewhat large number of processors but the communication across processors is slower.

(3) Shared Nothing :

In this model, processors share neither a common memory nor common disk.
The model is depicted in Fig. 9.11.

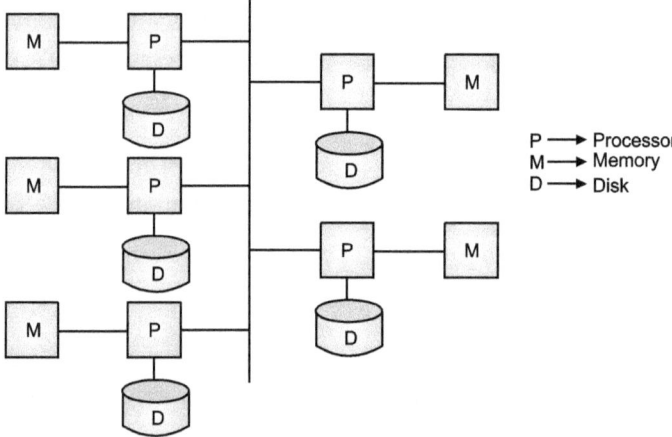

Fig. 9.11 : Shared Nothing

In this model, each node of the machine consists of a processor, memory and one or more disks.

The processor at one node may communicate with processor at another node using a high-speed interconnection network.

Shared-nothing architecture is more scalable and can easily support a large number of processors.

The main drawback of shared nothing model is the cost of communication and of non-local disk access, which are higher than in shared-memory and shared-disk architecture.

(4) Hierarchical :

It is a hybrid of preceding architectures. This model is depicted in Fig. 9.09.

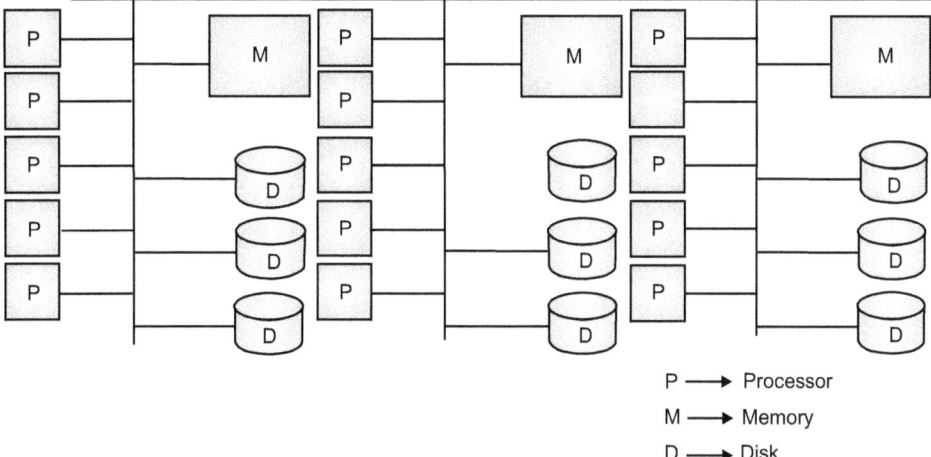

P ⟶ Processor
M ⟶ Memory
D ⟶ Disk

Fig. 9.12 : Hierarchical Parallel System

It combines the characteristics of shared-memory, shared-disk and shared-nothing architectures.

The top level is a shared-nothing architecture. Each node of the system could actually be a shared-memory system with a few processor. Alternatively, each node could be a shared disk system.

9.7 DISTRIBUTED SYSTEM

In distributed database system, the database is shared on several computers. The computers in a distributed system communicate with one another through various communication media, such as high-speed networks or telephone lines. They do not share main memory or disks.

The computers in distributed system may vary in size and function, ranging from workstations up to mainframe systems.

The computers in distributed system are referred to by a number of different names, such as sites or nodes depending on the context in which they are mentioned.

A distributed database system consists of single logical database which is split into different fragments. Each fragment is stored on one or more computers under the control of separate DBMS with computers connected by communication network. Each site is capable of independently processing user requests that require access to local data and is also capable of performing processing on remote machines in the network.

Characteristics of Distributed System:
- Data set can be splitted in to fragments and can be distributed across different nodes within network.
- Individual data fragments can be replicated and allocated across different nodes.
- Data at each site is under control of a DBMS.
- DBMS at each site can handle local applications autonomously.
- Each DBMS site will participate in at least one global application.

The typical structure of distributed system is shown in Fig. 9.13.

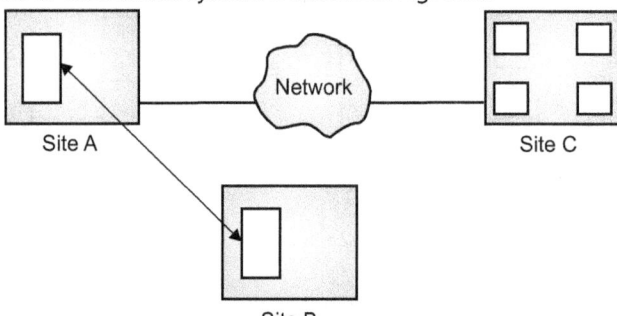

Fig. 9.13 : General Structure of Distribution System

Differences between shared nothing Parallel System and Distributed system are :
1. In distributed system, databases are geographically separated, they are administered separately and have slower interconnection.
2. In distributed systems, we differentiate between local and global transactions. Local transaction is one that accesses data in the single site at that the transaction was initiated. Global transaction is one which either accesses data in a site different from the one at which the transaction was initiated or accesses data in several different sites.

Advantages of Distributed System :

(1) Sharing Data : There is a provision in the environment where user at one site may be able to access the data residing at other sites.

(2) Autonomy : Because of sharing data by means of data distribution each site is able to retain a degree of control over data that are stored locally.

In distributed system there is a global database administrator responsible for the entire system. A part of global data base administrator responsibilities is delegated to local database administrator for each site. Depending upon the design of distributed database system, each local database administrator may have different degree of local autonomy.

(3) Availability : If one site fails in a distributed system, the remaining sites may be able to continue operating. Thus a failure of a site doesn't necessarily imply the shutdown of the system.

Disadvantages of Distributed Systems :

The added complexity required to ensure proper co-ordination among the sites, is the major disadvantage. This increased complexity takes various forms :

1. **Software Development Cost :** It is more difficult to implement a distributed database system; thus it is more costly.
2. **Greater Potential for Bugs :** Since the sites that constitute the distributed database system operate parallel, it is harder to ensure the correctness of algorithms, especially operation during failures of part of the system, and recovery from failures. The potential exists for extremely subtle bugs.
3. **Increased Processing Overhead :** The exchange of information and additional computation required to achieve intersite co-ordination are a form of overhead that does not arise in centralized system.

9.8 WEB-ENABLED DATABASE SYSTEM

There are lots and lots of data on the web; some of them stored in files and some in databases. This data has to be managed efficiently.

Web is a distributed information system based on hypertext. Web pages are designed using HTML. HTML generates only static pages. An interface of database to web must be established for two reasons : with the growth of electronic commerce on the web, databases used for transaction processing must be linked with the web.

The HTML form interface is convenient for transaction processing. The user can fill in details in an order form and can click the submit button to send a message to the server containing information that he has filled in. The second reason for interfacing the databases to web is that fixed HTML sources for display to users have limitations.

1. The use of fixed web document does not allow the display to be tailored to the user.
2. When data are updated, web documents become outdated if they are not updated simultaneously.

We can fix these problems by generating web documents dynamically. When a document is requested, a program can be executed at the server site, which runs queries on the database and generates a document based on the query results. Web document can also be tailored to the user based on user information stored in the database. Data in web documents can also be defined by queries on a database so that, whenever relevant data in the database are updated, the web documents will be up to date.

The most popular language for the web is Java. SQL calls are embedded into Java program. Java softs Java database connectivity (JDBC) is used to connect to the database through Java programs. Clients as well as database servers build interfaces compliant with JDBC.

Another popular standard for web data management is XML (Extensible markup language) with XML, one can eliminate the gateway.

Every major database system vendor including Oracle, Sybase, Informix have designed their product in such a way that they have web interfaces.

Oracle corporation's recent web database system product called oracle 8i and Oracle Web DB Oracle 8i combines internet database capabilities with traditional warehousing and transaction processing capabilities.

The internet file system feature of Oracle 8i enables users to move their data into Oracle's database. Oracle 8i integrates the Java Virtual Machine into the server and this way can deploy Java program at various tiers (such as client and middle tiers).

In additions to supporting web data management, Oracle 8i also support various database management functions. It has enhanced features for transaction processing and warehouse management, database administration, indexing, parallel server management, replication, caching, fine-grained access control as well as support for objects. Oracle Web DB is essentially a web browser that builds web pages from various types of data in Oracle database. Oracle 8i supports management of multimedia databases.

Oracle 11g, Oracle Web DB and many other tools that are emerging makes web data management a reality.

9.9 MONGO DB AND ITS CONNECTIVITY WITH JAVA

MongoDB is a powerful, flexible, and scalable general-purpose database. It combines the ability to scale out with features such as secondary indexes, range queries, sorting, aggregations, and geospatial indexes.

It is a document-oriented database, not a relational one. The primary reason for moving away from the relational model is to make it support more scalability.

A document-oriented database replaces the concept of a "row" with a more flexible model called the "document." By allowing embedded documents and arrays, the document oriented approach makes it possible to represent complex hierarchical relationships with a single record. This fits naturally into the way developers in modern object-oriented languages think about their data.

There are also no predefined schemas: a document's keys and values are not of fixed types or sizes. Without a fixed schema, adding or removing fields as needed becomes easier. Generally, this makes development faster as developers can quickly iterate. It is also easier to experiment. Developers can try various combinations of models for the data and then choose the best one to pursue.

Important Features of MongoDB

- **Indexing**

It supports generic secondary indexes, allowing a variety of fast queries and provides unique, compound, geospatial, and full-text indexing capabilities.

- **Aggregation**

It supports an "aggregation pipeline" that allows you to build complex aggregations from simple pieces and allow the database to optimize it.

- **Special collection types**

It provides a support for time-to-live collections for data that should expire at a certain time, such as sessions. It also supports fixed-size collections, which are useful for holding recent data, such as logs.

- **File storage**

It supports an easy-to-use protocol for storing large files and file metadata

MongoDB consists of following important members:

- A document is the basic unit of data for MongoDB and is roughly equivalent to a row in a relational database management system.
- Similarly, a collection can be thought of as a table with a dynamic schema.
- A single instance of MongoDB can host multiple independent databases, each of which can have its own collections.
- Every document has a special key, "_id", that is unique within a collection.
- MongoDB comes with a simple but powerful JavaScript shell, which is useful for the administration of MongoDB instances and data manipulation.

A Simple MongoDB document:

```
{"greeting": "Hello, Baramati!", "Name": "Sahil"}
```

The above example shows a simple MongoDB document consist of two attributes with values like "Hello, Baramati" and "Sahil".

Connectivity of MongoDB with JAVA

Steps for connection from Java program to MongoDB can be listed as follows:

1. **Get MongoDB Driver:** Download the mongo-java driver from authenticated websites like github.
2. **MongoDB Connection:**

Use following code for connecting to mongo version >2.10

```
// Old version, uses Mongo
Mongo mongo = new Mongo("localhost", 27017);

// Since 2.10.0, uses MongoClient
MongoClient mongo = new MongoClient( "localhost" , 27017 );
```

3. Get Mongo Database:
If database exists, it will be made available otherwise a new database will get created.
DB db = mongo.getDB("database name");

4. Get Mongo Collection/Table:
Get the collection or information about existing tables and retrieve the values inside it.
DB db = mongo.getDB("testdb");
DBCollection table = db.getCollection("user");

A sample Java & MongoDB connectivity example:

```java
import java.net.UnknownHostException;
import java.util.Date;
import com.mongodb.BasicDBObject;
import com.mongodb.DB;
import com.mongodb.DBCollection;
import com.mongodb.DBCursor;
import com.mongodb.MongoClient;
import com.mongodb.MongoException;
public class Sample {
 public static void main(String[] args) {

 try {

    /**** Connect to MongoDB ****/
    // Since 2.10.0, uses MongoClient
    MongoClient mongo = new MongoClient("localhost", 27017);
    /**** Get database ****/
    // if database doesn't exists, MongoDB will create it for you
    DB db = mongo.getDB("testdb");
    /**** Get collection / table from 'testdb' ****/
    // if collection doesn't exists, MongoDB will create it for you
    DBCollection table = db.getCollection("user");
    /**** Insert ****/
    // create a document to store key and value
    BasicDBObject document = new BasicDBObject();
    document.put("name", "sahil");
    document.put("age", 24);
    document.put("createdDate", new Date());
    table.insert(document);
    /**** Find and display ****/
    BasicDBObject searchQuery = new BasicDBObject();
```

```java
        searchQuery.put("name", "sahil");
        DBCursor cursor = table.find(searchQuery);

        while (cursor.hasNext()) {
            System.out.println(cursor.next());
        }

        /**** Update ****/
        // search document where name="sahil" and update it with new values
        BasicDBObject query = new BasicDBObject();
        query.put("name", "sahil");

        BasicDBObject newDocument = new BasicDBObject();
        newDocument.put("name", "ajay");

        BasicDBObject updateObj = new BasicDBObject();
        updateObj.put("$set", newDocument);

        table.update(query, updateObj);

        /**** Find and display ****/
        BasicDBObject searchQuery2
            = new BasicDBObject().append("name", "ajay");

        DBCursor cursor2 = table.find(searchQuery2);

        while (cursor2.hasNext()) {
            System.out.println(cursor2.next());
        }
        /**** Done ****/
        System.out.println("Done");

    } catch (UnknownHostException e) {
        e.printStackTrace();
    } catch (MongoException e) {
        e.printStackTrace();
    }
  }
}
```

REVIEW QUESTIONS ON INSTRUCTIONAL OBJECTIVES

1. Define following terms :
   (i) Throughput
   (ii) Response time
   (iii) Speed-up
   (iv) Scale-up
2. Write a note on :
   (i) Centralized system
   (ii) Client-server system
   (iii) Parallel database architectures
   (iv) Distributed system
   (v) Web Enabled systems
   (vi) Speed-up and scale-up
3. State advantages of using transaction server.
4. What are the various issues that decide the time cost of communication between client and server ?
5. What are the two measure of performance of the database system ?
6. Differentiate between a coarse-grain parallel machine and fine-grain parallel machine.
7. Which factors affect the efficiency of parallel operations ? Explain.
8. Specify advantages and disadvantages of all the parallel database architecture.
9. Specify advantages and disadvantages of distributed system.
10. Explain MongoDB with one sample example.
11. Enlist the different connectivity steps related to connection of MongoDB with JAVA.
12. Distinguish in between:2-tier architecture & 3-tier architecture.
13. What are the various characteristics associated with distributed databases?

UNIVERSITY QUESTIONS

1. What are the advantages and disadvantages of Distributed database system ?
   (May 2003)
2. Compare : Centralized vs. Client server architecture.
   (Dec. 05, April 01, 03, May 05, 06, 07)
3. Explain centralized system. **(Nov. 04, May 06, Dec. 05, May 07)**
4. What is distributed systems ? **(April 03, May 06, May 07)**
5. What is data replication ? **(April 03)**
6. What are the advantages and disadvantages of distributed database system architecture?
   (Dec. 05)

Unit - V

CHAPTER 10
XML AND JSON

10.1   Introduction

10.2   XML Data Model

10.3   Well Formed XML

10.4   XML Document Schema

      10.4.1   Document Type Definition (DTD)

10.5   Querying XML Document

      10.5.1   XPath

      10.5.2   XQuery

10.6   Application Program Interfaces to XML

      10.6.1   Document Object Model (DOM)

      10.6.2   Simple API for XML (SAX)

10.7   Java Script Object Notation (JSON)

      10.7.1   Uses of JSON

      10.7.2   Characteristics of JSON

      10.7.3   JSON Syntax

      10.7.4   Data types supported by JSON

      10.7.5   Object Creation in JSON

      10.7.6   JSON Schema

10.8   JSON With JAVA

10.9   JSON with PHP

10.10   JSON with Python

10.11   JSON with Ruby

- Review Questions on Instructional Objectives

10.1 INTRODUCTION

XML: XML (eXtensible Markup Language) is a growing technology in the internet era. This technology has been proposed by World Wide Web consortium (W3C).

Nowadays, many web pages are designed using Standard Generalized Markup Languages (SGML) like HTML and XML.

HTML: one of the pioneers in web technologies suffers to store information i.e. it only facilitates displaying of data without any information. (Users can create different web pages and display different data using various formats (markup)). Furthermore, it doesn't provide a facility of data interchange over the internet.It is only intended for displaying documents in a browser. The tags it makes available do not provide any information about the content they enclose (tags will only instruct browser about how to display the data). For instance, one could create an HTML document that displays information about a student XYZ. But, one couldn't write a program to identify from that document which part of information relates to the student's first name, last name, college etc. This is for the reason that HTML doesn't have any facilities to describe any kind of specialized information. For the family of markup languages that includes HTML, SGML, and XML, the markup takes the form of tags enclosed in angle brackets, <>. Tags are used in pairs, with <tag> and </tag> delimiting the beginning and the end of the portion of the document to which the tag refers. Unlike HTML, XML does not prescribe the set of tags allowed, and the set may be chosen as needed by each application. This feature is the key to XML's major role in data representation and exchange, whereas HTML is used primarily for document formatting.

XML is a subset of SGML, with the same goals (markup of any type of data), but with as much of the complexity eliminated as possible. XML describes a syntax that one can use to create his/her own language. Coming back to earlier example, suppose we are having data about a student names, and we want to be able to share this information with others as well as use the same in a computer program. Table shows sample representation of simple text/html and xml files.

Table 10.1 Example table showing different ways of representation

A Simple Text File (*.txt)	HTML Representation (*.htm)	XML Representation (*.xml)
Name: Paras Shah	\<html\> \<head\> \<title\>Name\</title\> \</head\> 　\<body\> 　\<p\>Paras Shah\</p\> 　\</body\> 　\</html\>	\<Name\> \<first\>Paras\</first\> \<last\>Shah\</last\> \</Name\>

Looking at above example table, with XML one can easily tell that this is information about a student name <stud_name>. It is easier to define user defined tags which are meaningful. (This is not possible in HTML)

10.2 XML DATA MODEL

The data model for XML is very simple or very abstract, depending on one's point of view. XML provides no more than a baseline on which more complex models can be built. Generally, XML document structure is tree like but there lies a way to make connections between arbitrary nodes in a tree. For instance, in following XML document there is root node with two children.

```
<stud_name>
<first>Paras</first>
<last>Shah</last>
</stud_name>
```

Graphically, same model can be interpreted as shown in figure.

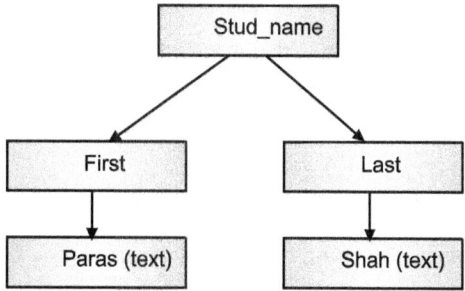

Fig. 10.1 : XML Data Model

The tree that an XML document represents has a number of different types of nodes:
- Element
- Document
- Comment
- Data

Element Nodes :

Elements typically make up the majority of the content of an XML document. Every XML document has exactly one top-level element, known as the document element. Elements have a name and may also have children. They can be annotated with attributes. Users can define any element names. However, element names are case-sensitive and these must begin with either a letter or underscore (_).

Example:
```
<Student>
<roll_no> 101511 </roll_no>
<name> xyz </name>
<class> TE </class>
</Student>
```

Attributes:

Elements can be annotated with attributes. Attributes can be used to encode

actual data or to provide metadata about an element i.e. provide extra information about the content of the element on which they appear. Attributes

appear as name-value pairs separated by an equal sign (name = 'value'). An element may have any number of attributes, but they must all have different names.

Example:
```
<Person name='Martin' age='33'>
</Person>
```

Document Node:

It is a specialized kind of element node without any attribute.

`<!DOCTYPE book [list of elements and respective data types]>`

It confirms that xml document follows document type declaration (DTD's).

Comments:

Comments always begin with <!- - and end with -->. Whatever written inside these will be ignored by the XML processor. However, comments cannot come before the XML declaration and cannot appear inside an element tag.

Example:
```
<Student>
<! -- This is data about student information-->
<roll_no> 101511 </roll_no>
<name> xyz </name>
<class> TE </class>
</Student>
```

Data:

Whatever comes in between pair of element tags is treated as data.

Example:
```
<name> xyz </name>
```

In this example xyz is the data.

Sample XML Document:

```
<?xml version="1.0" encoding="UTF-8"?>
<!DOCTYPE UOP:Student SYSTEM "sample.dtd">
<!-- Here begins the XML data for Pune University Students -->
<UOP:Student xmlns:UOP=http://www.unipune.ac.in>
<UOP:Student_name>Varun Jain</UOP:Student_name>
<UOP:College>VPCOE</UOP:College>
</UOP:Student>
```

In the first line, the code between the <?xml and the ?> is called an **XML declaration.** This declaration contains special information for the XML processor (the program reading the XML), indicating that this document conforms to Version 1.0 of the XML standard and uses UTF-8 (Unicode optimized for ASCII) encoding. The second line points to the root element declaration followed by name of DTD (sample.dtd) which will be used to validate this xml document. In above example UOP:Student is the root element. Third line represents the general comment describing about theme of xml document. Line 4 introduces a new concept called as **namespaces.**

Namespaces:

These are created to ensure uniqueness amongst the various user defined xml elements. Same element name may have different meaning in different organizations. Hence to avoid ambiguity, namespace usage is preferred. In above example, we scoped each tag with the UOP namespace. Namespaces are declared using the xmlns: something attribute, where something defines the prefix of the namespace. The attribute value is a unique identifier that differentiates this namespace from all other namespaces; the use of a URI is recommended. In this case, we use the Pune University URI http://www.unipune.ac.in as the default namespace, which should guarantee uniqueness. This declaration avoids ambiguity between student information of Pune University as compared with other universities.

Advantages of XML

- Presence of user defined tags makes the XML a self-describing document. The user defined tags are easier to understand.
- The format of XML document is not rigid meaning one can easily add or remove the tags in XML.
- XML allows nested structures. Sub elements can be properly nested inside elements and so on. Such representation helps to built concept of relational schema.
- As XML format is widely accepted, variety of tools are available for its processing including programming language API's to create and read XML data and various database tools.

10.3 WELL-FORMED XML

These are the rules for a well-formed XML document:
- All element attribute values must be in quotation marks.
- An element must have both an opening and a closing tag, unless it is an empty element.
- If a tag is a standalone empty element, it must contain a closing slash (/) before the end of the tag.
- All opening and closing element tags must be nested properly.

10.4 XML DOCUMENT SCHEMA

Normally, various databases have schemas that validate the actual contents stored inside the database. For instance, a student database having an attribute roll number may have a data type number/integer which will be used for actual data validation. In contrast, XML documents may be created without any schemas (or more generally without any constraints). However, there lies a need of proper data type validation when large amount of data is to be formatted in XML. Here, we describe the first schema-definition language included as part of the XML standard, the Document Type Definition

10.4.1 Document Type Definition (DTD)

The main purpose of a DTD is much like that of a schema: to constrain and type the information present in the document. However, the DTD does not in fact constrain types in the sense of basic types like integer or string. Instead, it restricts only the appearance of sub elements and attributes within an element. The DTD is primarily a list of rules for what pattern of sub elements may appear within an element.

```
<!DOCTYPE Student
[
<!ELEMENT Student((rollno|name|college)+)>
<!ELEMENT name(fname,mname,lname)>
<!ELEMENT rollno(#PCDATA)>
<!ELEMENT fname(#PCDATA)>
<!ELEMENT mname(#PCDATA)>
<!ELEMENT lname(#PCDATA)>
<!ELEMENT college(#PCDATA)>
]>
```

Each declaration is in the form of a regular expression for the sub elements of an element. Thus, in the DTD in Figure, a Student element consists of one or more rollno, name, or college elements; the | operator specifies "or" i.e. XML document may involve information about multiple students. The '+' operator specifies one or more occurrences. Further name element consist of three sub elements viz fname, mname and lname. Finally, the elements rollno, fname, mname, lname and college are all declared to be of type #PCDATA. The keyword #PCDATA indicates text data; it derives its name, historically, from "parsed character data." The allowable attributes for each element are also declared in the DTD. Unlike sub elements, no order is imposed on attributes. Attributes may be specified to be of type CDATA, ID, IDREF, or IDREFS; the type CDATA simply says that the attribute contains character data. Attributes of type ID can be used to uniquely identify an element within an XML document. Once you have uniquely identified the element, you can later use an IDREF to refer to that element.

10.5 QUERYING XML DATA:

As there is tremendous growth of XML applications and corresponding XML documents, there arises a need to have querying tools for XML documents which will retrieve XML documents. In this section, we study XPath and XQuery languages:

10.5.1 XPath:

XPath is a language for path expressions and is actually a building block for XQuery. It addresses parts of an XML document by means of path expressions. This language can be viewed as an extension of the simple path expressions in object oriented and object-relational databases. The current version of the XPath standard is XPath 2.0.

A **path expression** in XPath is a sequence of location steps separated by "/". The result of a path expression is a set of nodes. For instance, on following XML document,

```
<Student>
<! -- This is data about student information-->
<roll_no> 101511 </roll_no>
<name> xyz </name>
<class> TE </class>

<roll_no> 101514 </roll_no>
<name> abc </name>
<class> TE </class>
</Student>
```

the XPath expression: /Student/name returns following elements:

`<name>xyz </name>`

`<name> abc </name>`

While, the expression /Student/name/text() returns xyz, abc without any enclosing tags.

10.5.2 XQuery:

XQuery is the standard language for querying XML data. It is modelled after SQL but is significantly different, since it has to deal with nested XML data. XQuery also incorporates XPath expressions. These are modelled in to five sections viz **For, Let, Where, Order by and Return** which are referred as **"FLWOR"** (pronounced as "flower") expressions.

```
for $x in /Student
return <roll_no> {$x/@roll_no} </roll_no>
```

The for clause is like the from clause of SQL, and specifies variables that range over the results of XPath expressions. When more than one variable is specified, the results include the Cartesian product of the possible values the variables can take, just like the SQL from clause.

The let clause simply allows the results of XPath expressions to be assigned to variable names for simplicity of representation. The where clause, like the SQL where clause, performs additional tests (condition checking) on the joined tuples from the for clause. The order by clause, like the SQL order by clause, allows sorting of the output. Finally, the return clause allows the construction of results in XML.

A FLWOR query need not contain all the clauses; for example a query may contain just the for and return clauses, and omit the let, where, and order by clauses as shown in above example.

Note the use of curly brackets ("{ }") in the return clause. When XQuery finds an element such as <roll_no> starting an expression, it treats its contents as regular XML text, except for portions enclosed within curly brackets, which are evaluated as expressions. Thus, if we omitted the curly brackets in the above return clause, the result would contain several copies of the string "$x/@roll_no" each enclosed in a roll_no tag.

10.6 APPLICATION PROGRAMMING INTERFACES TO XML:

With recent advancements in data interchange over web, various software tools are available for manipulation of XML data. There are two standard models for programmatic manipulation of XML data viz. Document Object Model (DOM) and Simple API for XML(SAX). Both these APIs can be used to parse an XML document and create an in-memory representation of the document. These are compatible with most of the popular programming languages.

10.6.1 Document Object Model (DOM)

This API treats whole XML document as a tree where every element in XML document corresponds to a node in a tree. Programs may access elements of XML document in navigational pattern. DOM libraries are available for most of the programming languages. Some of the interfaces in the JAVA API for DOM are listed below:

- The Java DOM API provides an interface called **Node**, and interfaces **Element** and **Attribute**, which inherit from the Node interface.
- The Node interface provides methods such as **getParentNode()**, **getFirstChild()**,and **getNextSibling()**, to navigate the DOM tree, starting with the root node.
- Attribute values of an element can be accessed by name, using the method **getAttribute(name).**

DOM also provides a variety of functions for updating the document by adding and deleting attribute and element children of a node, setting node values, and so on.

10.6.2 Simple API for XML (SAX)

It provides a common interface between parsers and applications. This API is built on concept of event handing which consists of user-specified functions with parsing events. Parsing events correspond to the recognition of parts of a document; for example, an event is generated when the start-tag is found for an element, and another event is generated when the end-tag is found.

The SAX application developer creates handler functions for each event, and registers them. When a document is read in by the SAX parser, as each event occurs, the handler function is called with corresponding parameters describing the event (such as element tag or text contents). The handler functions then carry out their task. For instance, to construct a tree representing the XML data, the handler functions for an attribute or element start event could add a node (or nodes) to a partially constructed tree. SAX generally requires more programming effort than DOM, but it helps avoid the burden of generating a DOM tree in circumstances where the application needs to generate its own data representation.

10.7 JAVA SCRIPT OBJECT NOTATION (JSON)

It is a lightweight text-based open standard designed for human readable
data interchange.

- It was specified by Douglas Crockford.
- This was designed for human-readable data interchange
- JSON has been extended from the JavaScript scripting language.
- JSON filename extension is **.json**
- JSON Internet Media type is **application/json**
- The Uniform Type Identifier is public.json

10.7.1 Uses of JSON

- It is used when writing JavaScript based application which includes browser extension and websites.
- JSON format is used for serializing and transmitting structured data over network connection.
- JSON is primarily used to transmit data between server and web application.
- Web Services and API's use JSON format to provide public data.
- JSON can be used with modern programming languages.

10.7.2 Characteristics of JSON

1. It is easy to read and write JSON.
2. JSON is lightweight text based interchange format
3. JSON is language independent.

JSON Example

```
{
"book": [
{
"id":"01",
"language": "Java",
"edition": "third",
"author": "Herbert Schildt"
},
{
"id":"04",
"language": "C++",
"edition": "second"
"author": "E.Balagurusamy"
}]
}
```

Above example shows information about books. There are two book records separated by ",". The object "book" is a JSON format.

JSON objects can be used with Java script as follows:

```
<head>
<title>JSON example with JSP</title>
<script language="javascript" >
var object1 = { "language" : "Java", "author" : "Herbert Schildt" };
document.write("<h1>JSON with JavaScript example</h1>");
document.write("<br>");
document.write("<h3>Language = " + object1.language+"</h3>");
document.write("<h3>Author = " + object1.author+"</h3>");
</script>
</head>
<body>
</body>
</html>
```

In above HTML code, object1 is object of JSON format and the code displays following output in browser:

JSON with JavaScript example
Language = Java
Author = Herbert Schildt

10.7.3 JSON Syntax:

The JSON syntax is considered as subset of java script syntax which includes

- Data is included in name/value pairs.
- Curly braces hold objects and each name is followed by ':'(colon), the name/value pairs are separated by ',' (comma).
- Square brackets hold arrays and values are separated by "," (comma).

JSON supports following two data structures:

- **Collection of name/value pairs:** This Data Structure is supported by different programming language.
- **Ordered list of values:** It includes array, list, vector or sequence etc.

10.7.4 Data Types Supported by JSON

Table 10.2 Data Types supported by JSON

Data Type	Description
Number	Double precision floating point format in java script.
String	Double quoted Unicode with backslash escaping
Boolean	True or false
Array	Ordered sequence of values
Value	Can be anything a string, number etc.
Object	an unordered collection of attribute value pairs
Whitespace	Can be used between any pair of tokens
Null	Empty

10.7.5 JSON Object Creation:

Creation of an empty object:

var emptytjsonob = { };

Creation of object with attribute/value pair:

var JSONObj = { "bookname ":"VB BLACK BOOK", "price":500 };

10.7.6 JSON Schema

JSON Schema is a specification for JSON based format for defining structure of JSON data. JSON Schema has following properties:

- It describes your existing data format.
- It is clear and has human and machine readable documentation.
- It supports complete structural validation, useful for automated testing and validation of client-submitted data on server side.

There are several validators currently available for different programming languages. Currently the most complete and compliant JSON Schema validator available is JSV

Example

{
"$schema": "http://json-schema.org/draft-04/schema#",
"title": "Book",
"description": "A book from central library",
"type": "object",

```
"properties": {
"id": {
"description": "The unique identifier for a book",
"type": "integer"
},
"name": {
"description": "Name of the book",
"type": "string"
},
"price": {
"type": "number",
"minimum": 0,
"exclusiveMinimum": true
}
},
"required": ["id", "name", "price"]
}
```

The various keywords used in JSON schema are as follows:

- $schema : This keyword specifies that this schema is written according to draft 04 specification.
- Title: it is a general title used to describe the JSON schema.
- Description: It's a general description of schema.
- Type : It's a first constraint on JSON data. (Must be a JSON object).
- Properties: Defines various keys and their value types, minimum and maximum values to be used in JSON file.
- Required: It keeps a list of required properties.
- Minimum: represents minimum acceptable value.
- Exclusiveminimum: If "exclusiveMinimum" is present and has boolean value true, the instance is valid if it is strictly greater than the value of "minimum".

10.8 JSON WITH JAVA

Encoding: It is the method of conversion of JAVA object to JSON object.

Decoding: It is the reverse of encoding i.e. it converts JSON object back to JAVA object.

Environment

Before starting with encoding and decoding JSON using Java, there lies a need to install any of the JSON modules available. For instance, JSON.simple and (**json-simple-1.1.1.jar**)

Mapping between JAVA and JSON entities

JSON.simple maps entities from the left side to the right side while decoding or parsing, and maps entities from the right to the left while encoding.

Table 10.3 Mapping between JAVA and JSON entities

JSON	JAVA
String	java.lanag.String
Number	java.lang.Number
True|false	java.lang.Boolean
Null	Null
Array	java.util.List
Object	java.util.Map

Encoding JSON in JAVA

The following JAVA code

```
import org.json.simple.JSONObject;
class JsonEncodeDemo
{
public static void main(String[] args)
{
JSONObject obj = new JSONObject();
obj.put("name", "foo");
obj.put("num", new Integer(100));
obj.put("balance", new Double(1000.21));
obj.put("is_vip", new Boolean(true));
System.out.print(obj);
}
}
```

is encoded to following JSON object

`{"balance": 1000.21, "num":100, "is_vip":true, "name":"foo"}`

Decoding JSON in JAVA

```
import org.json.simple.JSONObject;
import org.json.simple.JSONArray;
import org.json.simple.parser.ParseException;
import org.json.simple.parser.JSONParser;
```

```
class JsonDecodeDemo
{
public static void main(String[] args)
{
JSONParser parser=new JSONParser();
String s = "[0,{\"1\":{\"2\":{\"3\":{\"4\":[5,{\"6\":7}]}}}}]";
try{
Object obj = parser.parse(s);
JSONArray array = (JSONArray)obj;
System.out.println("The 2nd element of array");
System.out.println(array.get(1));
System.out.println();
}
}
```

It produces following output:

The 2nd element of array

{"1":{"2":{"3":{"4":[5,{"6":7}]}}}}

10.9 JSON WITH PHP

JSON extension is bundled with PHP by default from version 5.2.0 so there is no need of any special environment.

JSON Functions:
1. json_encode: It returns the JSON representation of a value.
2. json_decode: It decodes a JSON string.
3. json_last_error: It returns the last error occurred.

Encoding:

json_encode () function is used for encoding which returns JSON representation of a value.
Syntax:

`string json_encode ( $value [, $options = 0 ] )`

The value parameter specifies value being specified. It works only with UTF-8 encoded data. The options parameter specifies the a bitmask consisting of JSON_HEX_QUOT, JSON_HEX_TAG, JSON_HEX_AMP, JSON_HEX_APOS, JSON_NUMERIC_CHECK, JSON_PRETTY_PRINT, JSON_UNESCAPED_SLASHES, JSON_FORCE_OBJECT.

Example:

The following PHP code

```php
<?php
class Emp {
public $name = "";
public $hobbies = "";
public $birthdate = "";
}
$e = new Emp();
$e->name = "sachin";
$e->hobbies = "sports";
$e->birthdate = date('m/d/Y h:i:s a', strtotime("8/5/1974 11:20:03"));
echo json_encode($e);?>
```

can be encoded to JSON object

`{"name":"sachin","hobbies":"sports","birthdate":"08/05/1974 11:20:03 pm"}`

Decoding:

json_decode () function is used for decoding JSON object in to PHP.

Syntax:

`json_decode ($json [,$assoc = false [, $depth = 511 [, $options = 0 ]]])`

Parameters:

- **json_string** : It is encoded string which must be UTF-8 encoded data.
- **assoc** : It is a boolean type parameter, when set to TRUE, returned objects will be converted into associative arrays.
- **depth:** It is an integer type parameter which specifies recursion depth
- **options:** It is an integer type bitmask of JSON decode. It supports JSON_BIGINT _AS_STRING

Example:

The following JSON object

```php
<?php
$json = '{"a":1,"b":2,"c":3,"d":4,"e":5}';
var_dump(json_decode($json));
var_dump(json_decode($json, true));
?>
```

can be decoded into

object(stdClass)#1 (5) {

["a"] => int(1)

["b"] => int(2)

["c"] => int(3)

["d"] => int(4)

["e"] => int(5)

}

array(5) {

["a"] => int(1)

["b"] => int(2)

["c"] => int(3)

["d"] => int(4)

["e"] => int(5)

}

10.10 JSON WITH PYTHON

Encoding JSON in Python (encode)

Python encode() function encodes the Python object into a JSON string representation.

Syntax:

demjson.encode(self, obj, nest_level=0)

Example

The following example shows arrays under JSON with Python

#!/usr/bin/python

import demjson

data = [{ 'a' : 1, 'b' : 2, 'c' : 3, 'd' : 4, 'e' : 5 }]

json = demjson.encode(data)

print json

While executing , this will produce following result:

[{"a":1,"b":2,"c":3,"d":4,"e":5}]

Decoding JSON in Python (decode)

Python uses demjson.decode() function for decoding JSON. This function returns the value decoded from JSON to appropriate Python type.

Syntax:

demjson.decode(self, txt)

Example

Following example shows how Python can be used to decode JSON objects.

```
#!/usr/bin/python
import demjson
json = '{"a":1,"b":2,"c":3,"d":4,"e":5}';
text = demjson.decode(json)
print text
```

While executing, it will produce following result:

{u'a': 1, u'c': 3, u'b': 2, u'e': 5, u'd': 4}

10.11 JSON WITH RUBY

Parsing JSON using Ruby

The following example shows that the first 2 keys hold string values and the last 3 keys hold arrays of strings.

Let's define an input JSON file as ip1.json represented below:

```
{
"President": "Alan Isaac",
"CEO": "David Richardson",
"India": [
"Sachin Tendulkar",
"Virat Kohli",
"Gautam Gambhir",
],
"Srilanka": [
```

"Lasith Malinga",
"Angelo Mathews",
"Kumar Sangakkara"
],
"England": [
"Alastair Cook",
"James Anderson",
"Kevin Petersen"
]
}

The following is ruby program which will be used to parse above mentioned JSON document:

```ruby
#!/usr/bin/ruby
require 'rubygems'
require 'json'
require 'pp'
json = File.read('input.json')
obj = JSON.parse(json)
pp obj
```

While executing, this will produce following result:

{"President"=>"Alan Isaac",
"CEO"=>"David Richardson",
"India"=>
["Sachin Tendulkar", "Virat Kohli", "Gautam Gambhir"],
"Srilanka"=>
["Lasith Malinga ", "Angelo Mathews", "Kumar Sangakkara"],
"England"=>
["Alastair Cook", "James Anderson", "Kevin Petersen"]
}

REVIEW QUESTIONS ON INSTRUCTIONAL OBJECTIVES

1. Explain the following terms:
   (a) XML Namespace
   (b) XML Data Model
   (c) XML DTD
2. What is XML and how does XML compare to SGML and HTML?
3. What is well-formed XML document?
4. Describe the difference between Document Type Definition (DTD) and the XML Schema.
5. Write a note on:
   (a) XQuery
   (b) Document Object Model (DOM)
6. Discuss the API's provided by XML.
7. Explain how encoding and decoding of JSON objects in Java with proper example.
8. Define the terms encoding and decoding with respect to JSON.
9. Explain the mapping of JSON and JAVA entities.

CHAPTER 11
HADOOP

11.1 Introduction to Big Data
11.2 Introduction to Hadoop
11.3 Building blocks of Hadoop
11.4 Hadoop components
11.5 Hadoop DataBase (HBase)
    11.5.1 Features of HBase
    11.5.2 HBase Architecture
11.6 HBase Data Model
    11.6.1 Important Terms used in HBase
11.7 Hive
- Review Questions on Instructional Objectives

11.1 INTRODUCTION TO BIG DATA

Big data is a new term used for any large collection of data sets which are complex and difficult to process. Such data sets are difficult to process using traditional data processing applications.

The challenges to process such large data include acquisition, storage, search and analysis, visualization of such huge collection of data. In 2012, analysis shows it is difficult to manage with huge collection of data (millions of terabytes of data) for finding out any sort of correlation amongst them. Many times, there lies a need to find correlation between large data sets to know the trends associated with various business products, commercial softwares for example. Big data is difficult to work with using most relational database management systems and desktop statistics and visualization packages, requiring instead "massively parallel software running on tens, hundreds, or even thousands of servers". What is considered "big data" varies depending on the capabilities of the organization managing the set, and on the capabilities of the applications that are traditionally used to process and analyze the data set in its domain. "For some organizations, facing hundreds of gigabytes of data for the first time may trigger a need to reconsider data management options. For others, it may take tens or hundreds of terabytes before data size becomes a significant consideration."

Big data differs from business intelligence as Business Intelligence uses descriptive statistics with data with high information density to measure things, detect trends etc. while Big data uses inductive statistics and concepts from nonlinear system identification to infer laws (regressions, nonlinear relationships, and causal effects) from large data sets to reveal relationships, dependencies and perform predictions of outcomes and behaviors.

Major Big Data Softwares:
- HADOOP
- ASTER
- HP VERTICA
- SPARK
- INFOSPHERE BIGINSIGHTS

11.2 INTRODUCTION TO HADOOP

Apache Hadoop is an open source JAVA framework for processing and querying large bundled data on clusters of commodity hardware. It is a top level Apache project initiated by Yahoo and Doug cutting.

Nowadays, Hadoop is most popular in Big Data processing and used by most of the industries. It enables scalable, cost-effective, flexible and fault tolerant solutions. It has two main features viz. Hadoop Distributed File System (HDFS) and MapReduce layer which are covered in detail in further sections.

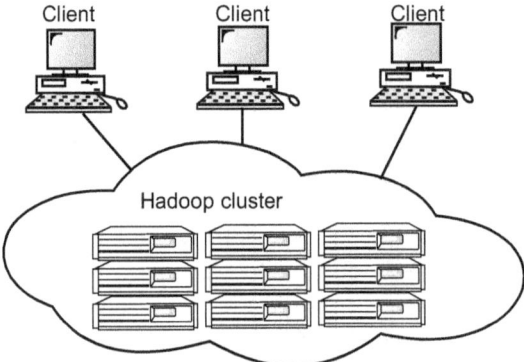

Fig. 11.1: A Typical Hadoop Cluster having many parallel machines for storage and processing of Big data.

11.3 BUILDING BLOCKS OF HADOOP

Hadoop works on distributed computation idea. On a fully configured cluster, "running Hadoop" means running a set of daemons, or resident programs, on the different servers in a network. These daemons (blocks) have specific roles; some exist only on one server, some exist across multiple servers. The daemons are as follows:

- NameNode
- DataNode
- Secondary NameNode
- JobTracker
- TaskTracker

An HDFS cluster is comprised of a single NameNode which manages the cluster metadata and DataNodes that store the data. Files and directories are represented on the NameNode by inodes. Inodes record attributes like permissions, modification and access times, or namespace and disk space quotas. The file content is split into large blocks (typically 118 megabytes), and each block of the file is independently replicated at multiple DataNodes. The blocks are stored on the local file system on the DataNodes. The NameNode actively monitors the number of replicas of a block. When a replica of a block is lost due to a DataNode failure or disk failure, the NameNode creates another replica of the block. The NameNode maintains the namespace tree and the mapping of blocks to DataNodes, holding the entire namespace image in RAM. Fig.11.2 shows typical master/slave architecture of HDFS comprising of one NameNode and several DataNodes. The various building blocks are explained below.

1. NameNode:

This is the most important daemon/building block of Hadoop. Hadoop implements master/slave architecture for both distributed storage and distributed computation. The distributed storage system is called the Hadoop File System (HDFS). The NameNode is the master of HDFS that directs the slave DataNode daemons to perform the low-level I/O tasks. The NameNode is the accountant of HDFS i.e. it keeps track of how various files are broken down into file blocks, which nodes store and monitor those blocks, and the overall health of the distributed file system.

The major drawback associated with this is failure to NameNode is the major bottleneck. (i.e. Failure will directly lead to whole system/Hadoop cluster failure)

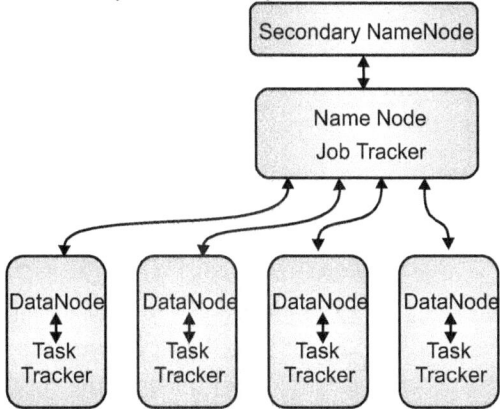

Fig 11.2: Building blocks of Hadoop cluster: Master/Slave Architecture (HDFS)

2. DataNode:

Each slave machine in a Hadoop cluster will host a DataNode daemon to perform the work of the distributed file system viz reading and writing HDFS blocks to actual files on the local file system. When one want to read or write a HDFS file, the file is broken into blocks and the NameNode will tell client machine that in which DataNode each block resides in so that client machine can directly communicate with the DataNode daemons to process the local files corresponding to the blocks. Furthermore, a DataNode may communicate with other DataNodes to replicate its data blocks for redundancy.

DataNodes are constantly reporting to the NameNode. Upon initialization, each of the DataNodes informs the NameNode of the blocks it's currently storing. After this mapping is complete, the DataNodes continually poll the NameNode to provide information regarding local changes as well as receive instructions to create, move, or delete blocks from the local disk.

3. Secondary NameNode(SNN):

It is an assistant daemon for monitoring the state of the cluster HDFS. Like the NameNode, each cluster has one SNN. It differs from the NameNode in that this process doesn't receive or record any real-time changes to HDFS. Instead, it communicates with the NameNode to take snapshots of the HDFS metadata at intervals defined by the cluster configuration. These snapshots are used in the process of recovery after failure of NameNode.

4. JobTracker

This daemon is responsible for determining the execution plan by determining which files to process, assigns nodes to different tasks, and monitors all tasks as they're running. When a particular task fails to execute, JobTracker will automatically relaunch that task until it gets successfully executed.There is only one JobTracker daemon per Hadoop cluster. It's typically run on a server as a master node of the cluster.

5. TaskTracker

JobTracker is responsible for controlling overall execution of a MapReduce job (resides on master) and the TaskTracker daemon is responsible to manage individual task execution on each slave/data node.

Each TaskTracker is responsible for executing the individual tasks that the JobTracker assigns. Although there is a single TaskTracker per slave node, each TaskTracker can spawn multiple JVMs to handle many map or reduce tasks in parallel. Additionally TaskTracker is responsible to constantly communicate with the JobTracker. If the JobTracker fails to receive a reply from a TaskTracker within a specified amount of time, it will assume the TaskTracker has crashed and will resubmit the corresponding tasks to other nodes in the cluster.

11.4 HADOOP COMPONENTS

Hadoop includes series of various products that operate on HDFS and MapReduce layer to support different operations on the platform.

The main components of Hadoop are as follows:

- **Mahout:**

It is a library of machine learning algorithms. The various machine learning techniques can be applied on Big Data with the aid of this.

- **Pig:**

Pig is a high-level language (such as PERL) to analyse large datasets with its own language syntax.

- **Hive:**

Hive is a data warehouse system for Hadoop that facilitates easy data
summarization, ad hoc queries, and the analysis of large datasets stored in HDFS. It has its own SQL-like query language called Hive Query Language (HQL), which is used to issue query commands to Hadoop.

- **Hadoop DataBase (HBase):**

It is a distributed, column-oriented database which uses HDFS for the underlying storage. It supports both batch style computations using MapReduce and atomic queries (random reads).

- **Sqoop:**

Apache Sqoop is a tool designed for efficiently transferring bulk data between Hadoop and Structured Relational Databases. Sqoop is an abbreviation for (SQ)L to Had(oop).

- **ZooKeper:**

It is a centralized service to maintain configuration information, naming, providing distributed synchronization, and group services, which are very useful for a variety of distributed systems.

- **Ambari:**

It's a web-based tool for providing, handling, and monitoring Apache Hadoop clusters, which includes support for Hadoop HDFS, Hadoop MapReduce along with various building blocks of Hadoop. In addition, Ambari is able to install security based on the Kerberos authentication protocol over the Hadoop cluster. Also, it provides role-based user authentication, authorization, and auditing functions for users to manage integrated LDAP and Active Directory.

11.5 HBASE (HADOOP DATABASE):

It is a distributed big data store for Hadoop. This is designed as a column-oriented database innovated after inspiration from Google Big table. it provides a fault-tolerant way of storing large quantities of sparse data (small amounts of information caught within a large collection of empty or unimportant data, such as finding the 50 largest items in a group of 2 billion records, or finding the non-zero items representing less than 0.1% of a huge collection). Tables in HBase can serve as the input and output for MapReduce jobs run in Hadoop, and may be accessed through the Java API but also through REST, Avro or Thrift gateway APIs.

It uses Log Structured Merge trees (LSM trees) to store and query the data. It supports compression, in-memory caching, bloom filters, and very fast scans. HBase tables can serve as both the input and output for MapReduce jobs

11.5.1 Features of HBase:

- It provides RESTful web service with XML
- It provides Linear and modular scalability
- It provides Strict consistent reads and writes
- It supports Extensible shell
- It supports in memory caching via block cache and bloom filters for real time queries.
- It supports easy integration with Hadoop MapReduce for data processing
- It provides web-based UIs for management of both the master and region servers.
- It supports replication across data centers.

Basically, HBase is a column oriented database whose functioning varies with respect to traditional row oriented databases. As shown in following figure, in a row-oriented data store, a row is a unit of data that is read or written together while in a column-oriented data store, the data in a column is stored together and hence quickly retrieved. Following table gives comparison between row oriented and column oriented databases/data stores.

Table 11.1 Comparison between Row Oriented and Column Oriented Data Store

Row oriented data store	Column oriented data store
Data is stored and retrieved one row at a time and hence could read unnecessary data if only some of the data in a row is required	Data is stored and retrieved in columns and hence can read only relevant data if only some data is required
It is easier to read and write records.	Read and write are slower as compared to row oriented databases.
It is well suited for OLTP systems.	It is well suited for OLAP systems.
Not efficient in performing operations applicable to the entire dataset and hence aggregation is an expensive operation	Can efficiently perform operations applicable to the entire dataset and hence enables aggregation over many rows and columns
Compression results are less efficient.	Permits high compression rates due to few distinct values in columns

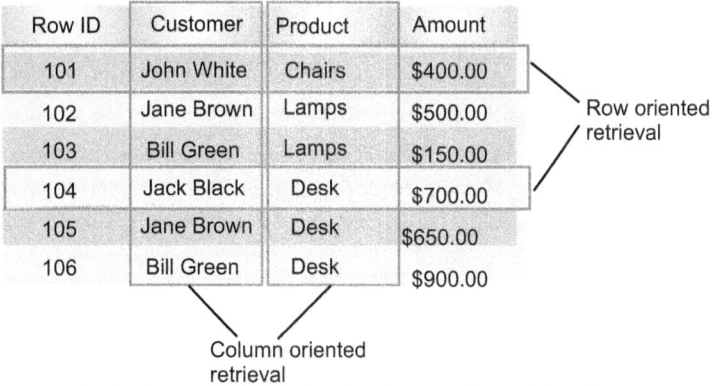

Fig 11.3: Row oriented and column oriented databases

11.5.2 HBase Architecture:

The HBase Physical Architecture consists of servers in a Master-Slave relationship as shown in fig. below. Typically, the HBase cluster has one Master node, called HMaster and multiple Region Servers called HRegionServer. Each Region Server contains multiple Regions – HRegions.

Just like in a Relational Database, data in HBase is stored in Tables and these Tables are stored in Regions. When a Table becomes too big, the Table is partitioned into multiple Regions. These Regions are assigned to Region Servers across the cluster. Each Region Server hosts roughly the same number of Regions. Fig 11.4 shows typical HBase architecture.

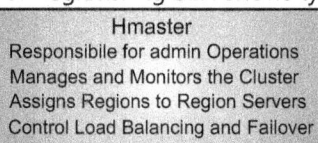

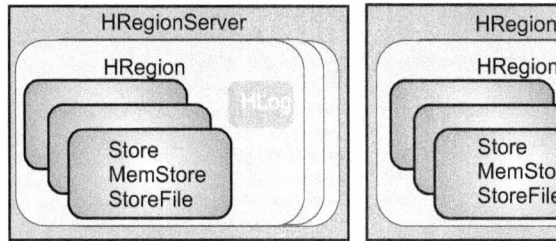

Fig 11.4: HBase Architecture

The HMaster in the HBase is responsible for
- Performing Administration
- Managing and Monitoring the Cluster
- Assigning Regions to the Region Servers
- Controlling the Load Balancing and Failover

On the other hand, the HRegionServer perform the following work

- Hosting and managing Regions
- Splitting the Regions automatically
- Handling the read/write requests
- Communicating with the Clients directly

Each Region Server contains a Write-Ahead Log (called HLog) and multiple Regions. Each Region in turn is made up of a MemStore and multiple StoreFiles (HFile). The data lives in these StoreFiles in the form of Column Families (explained below). The MemStore holds in-memory modifications to the Store (data).

The mapping of Regions to Region Server is kept in a system table called .META. When trying to read or write data from HBase, the clients read the required Region information from the .META table and directly communicate with the appropriate Region Server. Each Region is identified by the start key (inclusive) and the end key (exclusive).

11.6 HBASE DATA MODEL

Several applications store data into an HBase table. Tables are made of rows and columns. All columns in HBase belong to a particular column family. A cell's content is an uninterpreted array of bytes. Rows in HBase tables are sorted by row key. The sort is byte-ordered. All table accesses are via the table row key which is its primary key.

The Data Model in HBase is designed to accommodate semi-structured data that could vary in field size, data type and columns. Additionally, the layout of the data model makes it easier to partition the data and distribute it across the cluster. The Data Model in HBase is made of different logical components such as Tables, Rows, Column Families, Columns, Cells and Versions. Fig. shows example column families for a sample table.

Row Key	Customer		Sales	
Customer Id	Name	City	Product	Amount
101	John White	Los Angeles, CA	Chairs	$400.00
102	Jane Brown	Atlanta, GA	Lamps	$200.00
103	Bill Green	Pittsburgh, PA	Desk	$500.00
104	Jack Black	St. Louis, MO	Bed	$1600.00

Column Families

Fig 11.5: HBase Column Families

11.6.1 Important Terminology used in HBase Data Model

- **Tables**

The HBase Tables are more like logical collection of rows stored in separate partitions called Regions. As shown above, every Region is then served by exactly one Region Server. The figure above shows a representation of a Table.

- **Rows**

A row is one instance of data in a table and is identified by a *rowkey*. Rowkeys are unique in a Table and are always treated as a byte[].

- **Column Families**

Data in a row are grouped together as Column Families. Each Column Family has one more Columns and these Columns in a family are stored together in a low level storage file known as HFile. Column Families form the basic unit of physical storage to which certain HBase features like compression are applied. Hence it's important that proper care be taken when designing Column Families in table. The table above shows Customer and Sales Column Families. The Customer Column Family is made up 2 columns – Name and City, whereas the Sales Column Families is made up to 2 columns – Product and Amount.

- **Columns**

A Column Family is made of one or more columns. A Column is identified by a Column Qualifier that consists of the Column Family name concatenated with the Column name using a colon – example: columnfamily:columnname. There can be multiple Columns within a Column Family and Rows within a table can have varied number of Columns.

- **Cell**

A Cell stores data and is essentially a unique combination of *rowkey*, Column Family and the Column (Column Qualifier). The data stored in a Cell is called its value and the data type is always treated as byte[].

- **Version**

The data stored in a cell is versioned and versions of data are identified by the timestamp. The number of versions of data retained in a column family is configurable and this value by default is 3.

11.7 HIVE

Hive is a Hadoop-based data warehousing-like framework developed for facebook data processing. It allows users to fire queries in SQL, with languages like HiveQL, which are highly abstracted to Hadoop MapReduce. This allows SQL programmers with no MapReduce experience to use the warehouse and makes it easier to integrate with business intelligence and visualization tools for real-time query processing.

Its target users remain data analysts who are comfortable with SQL and who need to do ad hoc queries, summarization, and data analysis on Hadoop-scale data/big data.

For Example, a query to get all active users from a user table looks like

Select user.* from user where user.active=1;
Here, we assume if user is active status is 1 otherwise 0.

Hive's design reflects its use as a system for managing and querying structured data. By focusing on structured data, Hive can add certain optimization and usability features that MapReduce, being more general, doesn't have. Hive's SQL-inspired language separates the user from the complexity of MapReduce programming. It reuses familiar concepts from the relational database world, such as tables, rows, columns, and schema, to simplify learning. In addition, Hive can use directory structures to "partition" data to improve performance on certain queries which is not possible in Hadoop(it works on flat files). To support such additional features, a new and important component of Hive known as a metastore is introduced which stores schema information. This metastore typically resides in a relational database.

One can interact with Hive using several methods, including a Web GUI and Java Database Connectivity (JDBC) interface. However, most of the interactions take place over a command line interface (CLI). Fig 11.6 represents a high-level architecture diagram of Hive.

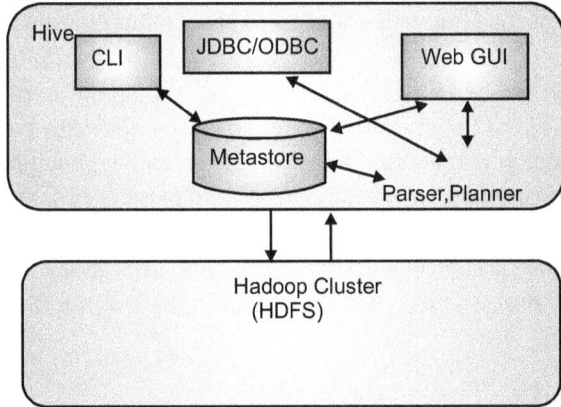

Fig 11.6 Hive Architecture

REVIEW QUESTIONS ON INSTRUCTIONAL OBJECTIVES

1. Write a note on :
   (i) HBase Data Model
   (ii) Hive Architecture
   (iii) Hadoop
2. State advantages of using HBase over Hadoop.
3. Distinguish between Row oriented and column oriented databases.
4. Explain the main components of Hadoop.
5. Explain HDFS with neat diagram.
6. What is the use of secondary name node in HDFS?
7. What are the building blocks of Hadoop architecture?
9. Explain Hive Architecture and its use in detail.

Unit - VI

CHAPTER 12
DATA WAREHOUSING AND DATA MINING

12.1	Introduction	
12.2	Teradata RDBMS	
12.3	Need for Data Analysis	
12.4	Decision Support System	
12.5	Data Warehousing	
12.6	Data Mining	
12.7	Business Intelligence	
12.8	Business Analytics	
•	Review Questions on Instructional Objectives	
•	University Questions	

12.1 INTRODUCTION

This chapter deals with the major pillars in databases viz. data warehousing and data mining that are used in data analysis by most of the organizations.

Today, there are number of applications of relational database in commercial world. It is used in :
- Transaction processing for banks,
- Stock exchanges,
- Sales,
- Reservations for a verity of business,
- Inventory and payroll for all companies.

In this chapter we study following points:
1. Teradata RDBMS
2. Decision support system
3. Data ware housing
4. Data mining
5. Business intelligence
6. Business Analytics in detail.

12.2 TERADATA RDBMS

Teradata RDBMS is a complete relational database management system. The system is based on Symmetric Multiprocessing (SMP) technology combined with a communication network connecting the SMP systems to form a Massively Parallel Processing (MMP) system. BYNET is a hardware inter-processor network to link SMP nodes. All processors in a same SMP node are connected by a virtual BYNET. Fig. 12.1 shows how Teradata RDBMS is related with each other and how this work together.

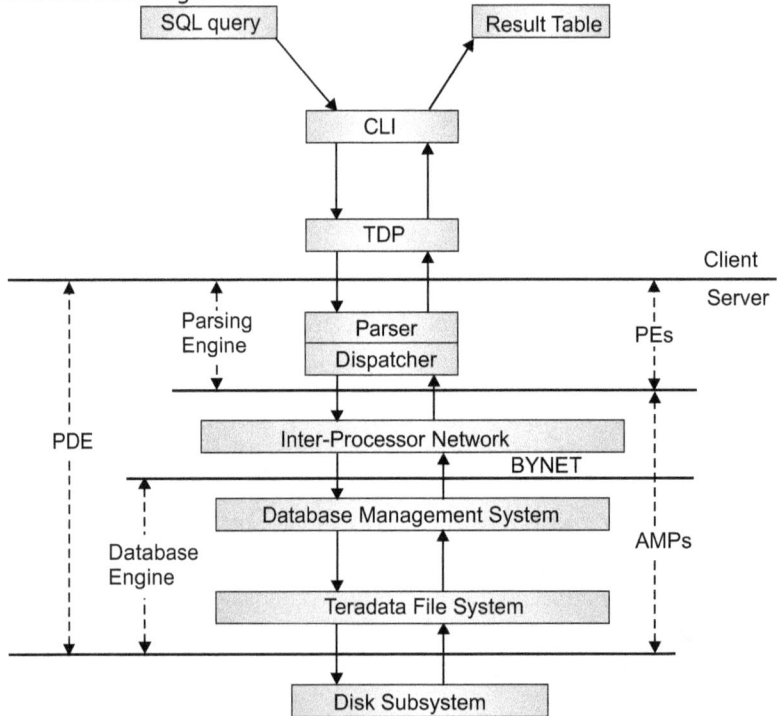

Fig.12.1: Teradata RDBMS Technology

The different components are explained as follows:

PDE (Parallel Database Extensions):

This component is an interface layer on the top of operating system. Its functions include: executing vprocs (virtual processors), providing a parallel environment, scheduling sessions, debugging, etc.

Teradata File System:

It allows Teradata RDBMS to store and retrieve data regardless of low-level operating system interface.

PE (Parsing Engine):
- It communicates with client
- It supports managing different sessions

- It supports parsing of SQL statements
- It provides support to communicate with AMPs
- It returns result to the client

AMP (Access Module Processor):
- It provides BYNET interface
- Supports database management.
- Provides an interface to disk subsystem

CLI (Call Level Interface):
A SQL query is submitted and transferred in CLI packet format

TDP (Teradata Director Program):
It routes the packets to the specified Teradata RDBMS server.

Teradata RDBMS has the following components that support all data communication management:

1. Call Level Interface (CLI)
2. WinCLI & ODBC
3. Teradata Director Program (TDP for channel attached client)
4. Micro TDP (TDP for network attached client)

It supports connectivity with application programs using ODBC.

12.3 NEED FOR DATA ANALYSIS

Data stored in database are usually in large volume. Users need that data to be summarized in some fashion. The database should support simple commonly used forms of data analysis.

SQL aggregate functions are commonly used for extracting the information. But the SQL aggregation functionality is limited, so several extensions have been implemented by different database.

Histograms are frequently used in data analysis. A histogram partitions the valves taken by an attribute into ranges, and computes an aggregate, such as sum, over valves in each range:

For example: A histogram on salaries values counts the number of people whose salaries fall in each of the ranges :

    0 to 20000, 20001 to 40000, 40001 to 60,000 and above 60000.

Using SQL to construct such a histogram efficiently would be cumbersome. Extensions to *SQL syntax that allow functions to be used in the* **group by** *clause have been proposed to* simplify the task. But that is not an efficient method, it results in duplicate values.

Data analysis often requires aggregation on multiple attributes.

For example:

Consider the sales relation with relation schema.

       Sales – Schema   =   (color, size, number)

It is to be analyzed by color (light versus dark) and size (small, medium, large).

The sales relation should be displayed as follows :

Table 12.1

	Small	Medium	Large	Total
Light	8	35	10	53
Dark	20	10	5	35
Total	28	45	15	88

This table is an example of cross-tabulation (cross-tab). In this case data are two dimensional, since they are based on two attributes, size and color. In general data can be represented as a multidimensional array with a value for each element of the array. Such data are called multidimensional data.

The data in cross-tabulation cannot be generated using a single SQL query.

Moreover, we can easily see that a cross-tabulation is not the same as relational table. This data can be represented in relational form by introducing a special value *all* to represent subtotals, as shown in Table 12.2.

Table 12.2

Color	Size	Number
Light	Small	8
Light	Medium	35
Light	Large	10
Light	All	53
Dark	Small	20
Dark	Medium	10
Dark	Large	5
Dark	All	35
All	Small	28
All	Medium	45
All	Large	15
All	All	88

Moving from a finer granularity data to a coarser granularity by means of aggregation is called doing a *rollup*. In the previous attribute, size attribute is rolled up.

The opposite operation is moving from coarser-granularity data to finer granularity data is called *drill down*.

A finer granularity data cannot be generated from coarser granularity data, they must be generated either from the original data or from yet more fine granularity summary data.

Although the tables such as shown in Table 12.2 can be generated using SQL, but doing so is cumbersome.

12.4 DECISION SUPPORT SYSTEM

Database applications are broadly classified into two categories :
1. Transaction processing
2. Decision support.

Transaction processing systems are widely used today. Companies have accumulated a vast amount of information generated by these systems.

Company databases often contain enormous quantities of information about customers and transactions. The size of the information storage required may range into gigabytes or even terabytes for large retail chains.

Transaction information for a retailer may include the name or identifier of customer, the items purchased, the price paid and the dates on which the purchases were made.

Information about items purchased may include the type of item, the manufacturer, the model number, the color and the size.

Customer information may include credit history, annual income, residence, age.

With such a large database it becomes difficult to make business decisions, such as what items to stock or what discounts to offer.

Decision support system can make such decision for the company or the user.

Storage and retrieval of data for decisions support system raises several issues.

- We can extract much information for decision support system by using simple SQL queries. But some queries cannot be expressed in SQL. Several SQL extensions have therefore been proposed.
- Database query languages are not suited to the performance of *detailed statistical analysis* of data. Hence, packages such as S++ which help in statistical analysis have been interfaced with databases to allow large amounts of data to be stored in the database and retrieved efficiently for analysis.
- Knowledge-discovery techniques, developed by the artificial intelligence community attempt to discover automatically statistical rules and patterns from data. Data mining combines ideas about knowledge discovery with efficient implementation techniques that enable them to be used on extremely large databases.

- Large companies have diverse sources of data that they need to be used for making business decisions. The sources may store data under different schemes. For performance reasons and organization control the data sources will not permit other parts of the company to retrieve data on demand.

So there lies a need of techniques to deal with these issues efficiently.

12.5 DATA WAREHOUSING

Data warehouse is a subject oriented, integrated, non-volatile, time-variant collection of data in support of management's decision.

It provides access to data for complex analysis, knowledge discovery and decision-making.

It supports several types of applications such as:
- On-line analytical processing,
- Decision support system,
- Data mining.

Architecture of typical data warehouse is illustrated in Fig. 12.2 given below:

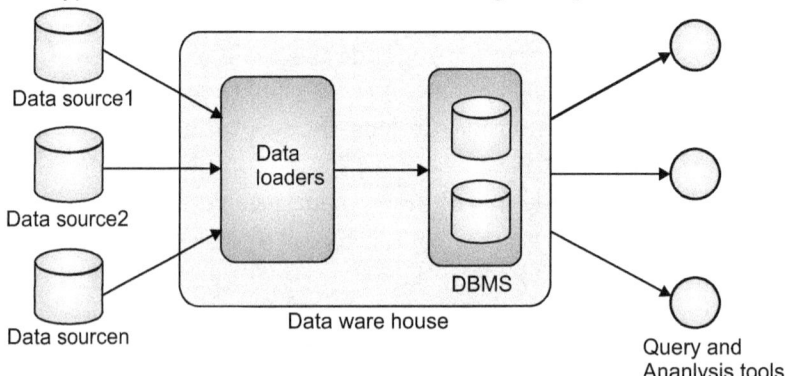

Fig. 12.2: Data Warehouse

The four keywords used in definition are used to characterize data warehouse from other relational databases and other repositories.

Subject-Oriented: A data warehouse is organized around major subjects, such as customer, supplier, product, and sales. Rather than concentrating on the day-to-day operations and transaction processing of an organization, a data warehouse focuses on the modelling and analysis of data for decision makers. Hence, data warehouses typically provide a simple and specific view around particular subject issues by excluding data that are not useful in the decision support process.

Integrated: A data warehouse is usually constructed by integrating multiple heterogeneous sources, such as relational databases, flat files, and on-line transaction records. Data cleaning and data integration techniques are applied to ensure consistency in naming conventions, encoding structures, attribute measures etc.

Time-Variant: Data are stored to provide information from a historical perspective (e.g., the past 5–10 years). Every key structure in the data warehouse contains, either implicitly or explicitly, an element of time.

Non-Volatile: A data warehouse is always a physically separate store of data transformed from the application data found in the operational environment. Due to this separation, a data warehouse does not require transaction processing, recovery, and concurrency control mechanisms. It usually requires only two operations in data accessing: *initial loading of data* and *access of data*.

In short a data warehouse is a semantically consistent data store that serves as a physical implementation of a decision support data model and stores the information on which an enterprise needs to make strategic decisions.

Data warehousing provides an alternative to the traditional approach of heterogeneous database integration described above. Rather than using a query-driven approach, it employs an update-driven approach in which information from multiple, heterogeneous sources is integrated in advance and stored in a warehouse for direct querying and analysis.

Characteristics of Data Warehousing:

Data warehouses have the following distinctive characteristics:
1. Multidimensional conceptual view.
2. Unlimited cross-dimensional operations.
3. Client-server handling.
4. Multi-user support.
5. Accessibility
6. Transparency
7. Institutive data manipulation
8. Consistent report performance
9. Flexible reporting.

In constructing or building a data warehouse, builders should take a broad view of anticipated use of warehouse. The design should support, ad-hoc querying that is accessing data with any meaningful combination of values for the attributes in the dimension or fact tables. Acquisition of data for the warehouse involves the following steps :

1. Data must be extracted from multiple, heterogeneous sources.
2. Data must be formatted for consistency within the warehouse.
3. The data must be cleaned to ensure validity.

Data cleaning is the most complex process in constructing data warehouse. It involves various operations such as :
- Checking the validity and quality of data.
- Recognizing erroneous and incomplete data.

4. Data must be fitted into the data model of the warehouse.
5. Data must be loaded into the warehouse.

Data storage involves following processes :
- Storing the data according to the data model.
- Creating and maintaining required data structures.
- Creating and maintaining appropriate access paths.
- Providing for time-variant data as new data are added.
- Supporting the updating of warehouse data.
- Refreshing the data.
- Purging data.

Main Components of Data Warehouse:

Fig. 12.3 gives a schematic representation of main components of typical data warehouse system.

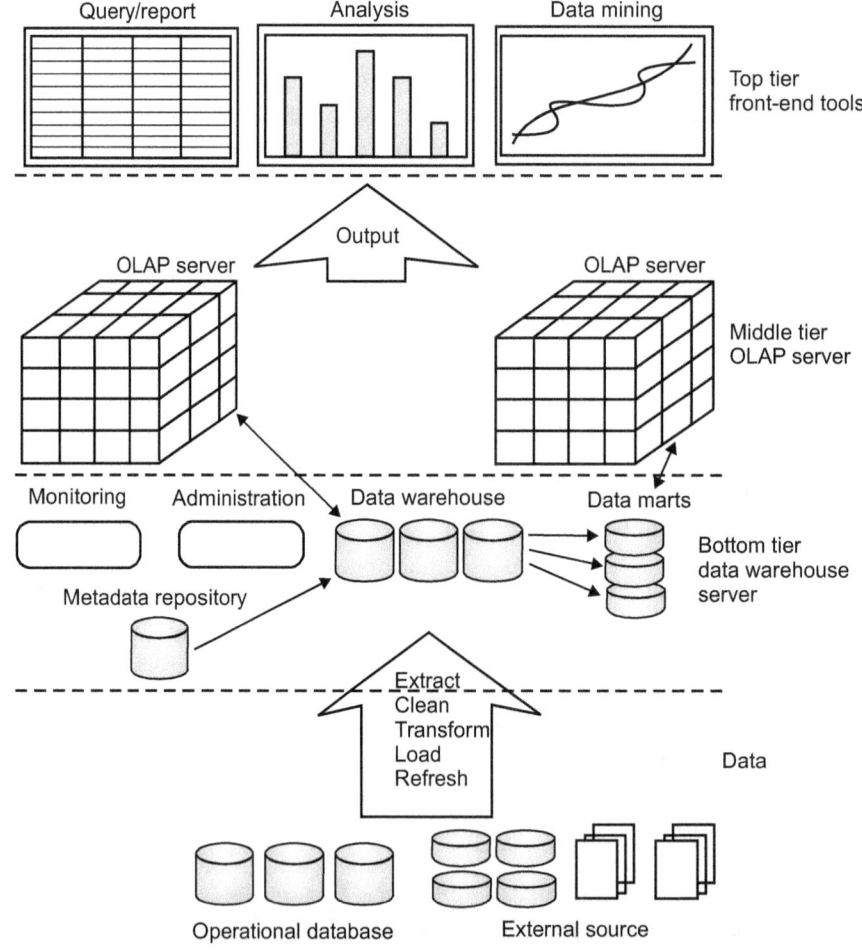

Fig.12.3 Main Components of Data warehouse

It operates in three tiers as follows:

1. Data Warehouse Server:

This is bottom tier that makes use of various back-end tools and utilities to feed data from operational databases or other external sources (such as customer profiles, information provided by external advisors). These tools and utilities perform data extraction, cleaning, and transformation (e.g., to merge similar data from different sources in to one unified or homogeneous format). The data are extracted using application programs known as gateway(one could have OLEDB connectivity using this).

2. On-line Analytical Processing (OLAP) Server:

This tier is implemented using

(1) A relational OLAP (ROLAP) model, that is, an extended relational DBMS that maps operations on multidimensional data to standard relational operations; or

(2) A multidimensional OLAP (MOLAP) model, that is, a special-purpose server that directly implements multidimensional data and operations.

Normally, there can be two kinds of processing related with databases viz. OLAP & OLTP which are described below:

On-line Analytical Processing (OLAP): Data warehouse systems serve users or knowledge workers in the role of data analysis and decision making. Such systems can organize and present data in various formats in order to accommodate the diverse needs of the different users.

These systems are market-oriented and mostly used by knowledge workers, managers, analysts for data analysis.

Basically, these systems deal with huge data analysis and mostly used by most of the commercial organizations for learning the different trends in market. For instance, changing customer needs, interest of particular community could be easily learned by analyzing tons of heterogeneous databases.

On-line transaction processing (OLTP): On-line transaction processing applications are the mission critical applications that handle day-to-day transactions such as order processing, receivables, collections etc.

It was traditionally implemented using mainframe computers with hard core transaction monitors such as IBM's, CICS etc.

Basically, OLTP means business on the internet. Big companies make their own web sites. Customers can visit these websites and can get list of product with all details. The transaction can take place on the web itself.

3. Front-end tier:

This is a client tier which is responsible for providing query and report-generation tools (eg. sql editor, graph generator etc) along with data analysis tools/mining tools like trend analyzer, predictor and so on.

From the architecture point of view, there are three data warehouse models viz. *enterprise warehouse*, *data mart*, and *virtual warehouse*.

Enterprise warehouse: An enterprise warehouse collects all of the information about subjects spanning the entire organization. It provides corporate-wide data integration, usually from one or more operational systems or external information providers, and is cross-functional in scope. It typically contains detailed data as well as summarized data, and can range in size from a few gigabytes to hundreds of gigabytes, terabytes, or beyond.

It may be implemented on traditional mainframes, computer super servers, or parallel architecture platforms.

Data mart: A data mart contains a subset of corporate-wide data that is of value to a specific group of users. The scope is confined to specific selected subjects.

For example, a marketing data mart may confine its subjects to customer, product and sales. The data contained in data marts tend to be summarized.

Data marts are usually implemented on low-cost departmental servers that are

UNIX/LINUX- or Windows-based.

Depending on the source of data, data marts can be categorized as independent or dependent.

Independent data marts are sourced from data captured from one or more operational systems or external information providers, or from data generated locally within a particular department or geographic area.

Dependent data marts are sourced directly from enterprise data warehouses.

Virtual Warehouse: A virtual warehouse is a set of views over operational databases. For efficient query processing, only some of the possible summary views may be materialized.

It is easy to build but requires excess capacity on operational database servers.

Limitations of Data Ware Housing

- ➤ The top-down approach suffers from cons like it is very expensive and it takes a long time for complete development. Moreover, it lacks flexibility due to the difficulty in achieving consistency for a common data model for the entire organization.
- ➤ The bottom-up approach leads to problems when integrating various disparate data marts into a consistent enterprise data warehouse.

12.6 DATA MINING

Data mining refers to the mining or discovery of new information in terms of patterns or rules from vast amounts of data.

Like knowledge discovery in artificial intelligence, data mining attempts to discover statistical rules and patterns automatically from data.

However, data mining differs from machine learning in that it deals with large volumes of data, stored primarily on disk.

Knowledge discovered from a database can be represented by a set of rules.

We can discover rules from database using one of two models :
1. In the first model, the user is involved directly in the process of knowledge discovery.
2. In the second model, the system is responsible for automatically discovering knowledge from the database, by detecting patterns and correlations in the data.

Knowledge discovery systems may have elements of both models, with the system discovering some rules automatically and the user guiding the process of rule discovery.

Knowledge Representation Using Rules:

Rules provide a common framework in which to express various types of knowledge.

A general form for rules is given as:

$$\forall \overline{X} \text{ antecedent} \Rightarrow \text{Consequent}$$

Where, $\overline{X}$ is a list of one or more variables with associated ranges.

Let the database contain a relation *buys*, that specifies what was bought in each transaction. The following is an example of a role :

$\forall$ transactions T, buys (T, bread) $\Rightarrow$ buys (T, milk).

Here, T is a variable whose range is the set of all transactions.

The rule says that : if there is a tuple (ti, bread) in the relation buys, there must be a tuple (ti, milk) in the relation buys.

The range of variables defines a set of values that the variable can take. The cross-product of the ranges of the ranges of the variables in the roles forms the **population**. Many data-mining systems restrict a role to have a single variable.

Rules have an associated support, as well as an associated confidence.

Support : It is a measure of what fraction of population satisfies the both the antecedent and the consequent of the rule.

Examples :
1. If 0.001 percent of all transactions include the purchase of milk and bread, the support for the rule.

    $\forall$ transaction T, buys (T, bread) $\Rightarrow$ buys (T, milk) is low.

On the other hand if 50 percent of all transactions involve the purchase of milk and bread, then the support is relatively high and the rule is worth attention.

Confidence : It is a measure of how often the consequent is true when the antecedent is true.

2. Consider the rule,

    $\forall$ transactions T, buys (T, bread) $\Rightarrow$ buys (T, milk).

This rule, has a confidence of 80 percent if 80 percent of transactions that include the purchase of bread also include the purchase of milk.

A rule with low confidence is not meaningful.

In business applications, rules usually have confidences significantly less than 100 percent, whereas in other domains, such as physics, rules may have high confidences.

Classes of Data-mining Problems :

Two important classes of problems in data mining are :
1. Classification rule and
2. Association rule.

1. Classification: It involves finding rules that partition the given data into disjoint groups.

Example:

Suppose that a credit card company wants to decide whether or not to give a credit card to an applicant.

The company has a varity of information about the person, such as

- age
- educational background
- annual income
- current debts and
- housing location.

which it can use for making decision. Some of this information could be relevant to the credit worthiness of the applicant, whereas, some may not be.

To make decisions, the company assigns a credit worthiness level of

- excellent
- good
- average or
- bad to each of a sample set of current customers.

The assignment of credit worthiness is based on customer's payment history.

Then the company attempts to find rules that classify its current customers into excellent, good, average or bad, based on the information about the person, other than the actual payment history.

Let us consider just two attributes :

- education level (highest degree earned)
- income

The rules may be of the following form :

$\forall$ person P, P·degree = Masters and P·income > 75000 $\Rightarrow$ P·credit = excellent $\forall$ person P, P·degree = Bachelors or (P·income > 25000 and P·income < 75000) $\Rightarrow$ P·credit = good

Similar rules would also be present for the other credit worthiness levels.

Other important uses of classification include, making loan approvals, setting insurance premiums, deciding whether or not to stock a particular item in a shop based on statistical information about customers and so on.

2. Association :

Association rules specify the association between different items.

Example :

Someone who buys bread is quite likely also to buy milk.

The association between bread and milk can be represented by the rule.

$\forall$ transactions T, buys (T, bread) $\Rightarrow$ buys (T, milk).

Association information can be used in several ways.

- A shop may decide to place bread close to milk.
- Or shop may place them at opposite ends of a row and place other associated items in between them to tempt people to buy those items.
- A shop that offers discounts on one associated item may not offer a discount on other.

User - Guided Data Mining :

In user guided model for data mining, the user has primary responsibility for discovering rules and the database system plays a supporting rule. The user makes up a hypothesis, and runs tests on the database to verify that hypothesis.

Examples:

1. A user may have a hypothesis that people who hold master's degree are most likely to have an excellent credit rating, and may use the database to verify this hypothesis.

The data may indicate that people who hold master's degrees are most likely than others to have an excellent credit rating.

The users may then come up with a new hypothesis, or may refine the existing hypothesis, and may verify it against the database. Thus, there may be several iterations, involving successive refinement of the hypothesis.

2. With number of iterations, the user comes up with a hypothesis that customers who hold master's degree and who earn 75,000 or more per year are likely to have an excellent credit rating.

The confidence and support for the rule can be derived from the database.

If the confidence is high (close to 1) the user may stop at this point with the rule.

$\forall \cdot$ people P, P·degree = Masters and P·income $\geq$ 75000 $\Rightarrow$ P·credit = excellent.

Data visualization systems help users to examine large volumes of data, and to detect patterns visually. Visual displays of data such as maps, charts, and other graphical representations allow data to be presented compactly to the user. A single graphical screen can encode as much information as can a far larger number of text screens.

Automatic Discovery of Rules :

The manner in which rules are discovered depends on the class of data-mining application. Hence, the automatic rule discovery can be illustrated using two application classes :
1. Classification
2. Association

Discovery of Classification Rules :

The process of discovery of classification rules starts from a sample of data, called **'training set'**.

For each tuple in the training set, the grouping is already known.

For example :

The training set for a credit-card application may be the existing customers, with their credit worthiness determined from their payment history.

The actual data may consist of all people, including those who are not existing customers.

Process of discovery of classification Rule : Consider the example of finding which class of people have excellent credit rating.

- The data-mining system starts with antecedents consisting of only a simple condition on a single attribute.

For example : The possible conditions on the degree attribute are :

P·degree = None
P·degree = Bachelors
P·degree = Masters
P·degree = Doctorate

- For attributes whose value is numeric, the data-mining system divides up the possible values into intervals.

For example : The salary value could be divided into intervals

0 to 25,000
25,000 to 50,000
50,000 to 75,000 and
over 75,000.

Thus, if we consider any attribute, the conditions based on that attribute partition the set of tuples into disjoint groups.

- If for any attribute, all or most of the tuples in each group have the same classification value, a set of rules based on that attribute can be output and the data mining stops.

Example: Consider that degree is chosen as attribute on which to partition the data. The data are divided into groups based on the conditions on this attribute and then classification is done separately based on other attributes for each group.

Degree attribute partitions the data into four groups with four types of degrees (none, bachelors, masters, doctorate).

Consider the partition corresponding to Masters. This group can be further divided using the attribute income.

The rules in the group for Masters would have a condition of the form -

degree = Masters, in addition to the condition on income.

This method generates a classification tree from top to bottom.

The classification tree for our problem is given in Fig. 12.4.

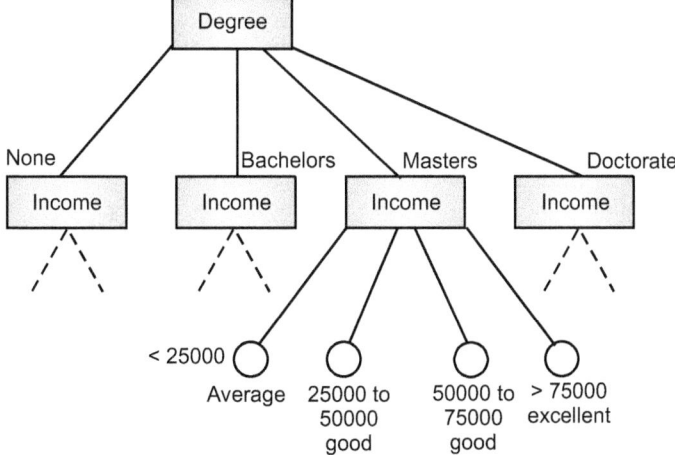

Fig. 12.4 : Classification Tree

Discovery of Association Rules:

Consider the earlier example of an association rule.

∀ transaction T, buys (T, bread) ⇒ buys (T, milk)

We can derive such rules efficiently by associating a bitmap with each transaction, with one bit per item of interest in the shop.

This approach is reasonable if the number of items of interest is not large.

To discover association rules of the form

∀ transactions T, buys (T, i_1) and ...... and buys (T, i_n) ⇒ buys (T, i_0)

We must consider all subsets of the set of all relevant items and for each set must check whether there is a sufficient number of transactions in which all the items in the set are purchased.

If the number of such sets is small, a single pass over the transactions is sufficient to detect the level of support.

But if the number of sets is high, the cost of processing each transaction becomes correspondingly high.

Applications of Data Mining :

Data mining technology can be applied to a large variety of decision- making contexts in business. Following are the significant areas of applications.

1. **Marketing:** Application includes:
   - Analysis of consumer behavior based on buying patterns.
   - Determination of marketing strategies including advertising, store locations and targeted mailing.
   - Segmentation of customers, stores, or products.
   - Design of catalogs, store layouts and advertising campaigns.

2. **Finance:** Applications include:
   - Analysis of credit worthiness clients.
   - Segmentation of account receivables, performance analysis of finance in investments like stocks, bonds and mutual funds.
   - Evaluation of financing options.
   - Fraud detection.

3. **Manufacturing:** Applications involve:
   - Optimization of resources like machines, manpower and materials
   - Optimal design of manufacturing processes, shop - floor layouts, and product design, such as automobiles based on customer requirements.

4. **Health care:** Applications include
   - Fraud detection.
   - Analysis of effectiveness of certain treatments.
   - Optimization of processes within a hospital.
   - Relating patients' wellness data with doctor qualifications.
   - Analyzing side effects of drugs.

12.7 BUSINESS INTELLIEGNCE

Business intelligence (BI) (term introduced by Richard Miller Devens' in 1865) is a set of theories, methodologies, architectures, and technologies that transform raw data into meaningful and useful information for business analysis purposes.

It can handle enormous amounts of unstructured data to help identify, develop and create new strategic business opportunities if required. It allows for the easy interpretation of volumes of data. Identifying new opportunities and implementing an effective strategy can provide a competitive market advantage and long-term stability.

BI technologies provide historical, current and predictive views of business operations.

Important Functions of Business Intelligence Technologies are :

- Reporting
- Online analytical processing and analytics
- Data mining
- Process mining
- Complex event processing
- Business performance management
- Benchmarking
- Text mining etc.

Basically business intelligence is comprised of various components like multidimensional aggregation, denormalization, real time reporting with analytical alert, provides a method of interface to deal with unstructured data.

Business intelligence as it is referenced today is said to have evolved from the decision support systems (DSS) that began in the 1960s and developed throughout the mid-1980s. DSS originated in the computer-aided models created to assist with decision making and planning. From DSS, data warehouses, Executive Information Systems, OLAP and business intelligence came into focus beginning in the late 80's. Fig.12.5 gives a brief overview about various business intelligence functionalities.

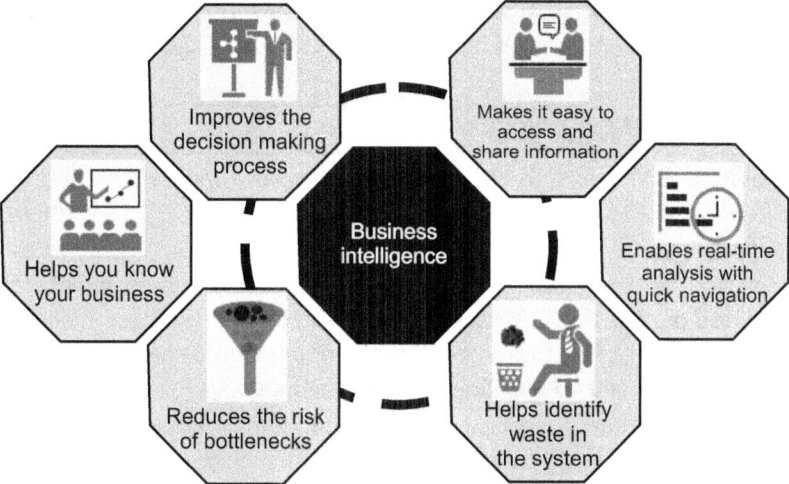

Fig.12.5 : Functionalities of Business Intelligence

Applications of Business Intelligence:

BI can be easily applied to following business purposes and on application of which, business value will surely increase.

1. **Measurement** – program that creates a hierarchy of performance metrics and benchmarking that informs business leaders about progress towards business goals.
2. **Analytics** – program that builds quantitative processes for a business to arrive at optimal decisions and to perform business knowledge discovery. It involves all the common functionalities provided by BI.
3. **Reporting/Enterprise Reporting** – program that builds infrastructure for strategic reporting to serve the strategic management of a business, not operational reporting. It involves data visualization, executive information system and OLAP.
4. **Collaboration/Collaboration Platform** – program that gets different areas (both inside and outside the business) to work together through data sharing and electronic data interchange (emails).
5. **Knowledge Management** – program to make the company data driven through strategies and practices to identify, create, represent, distribute, and enable adoption of insights and experiences that are true business knowledge.

In addition to the above, business intelligence can provide a down to business approach, such as alert functionality that immediately notifies the end-user if certain conditions are met.

For example, if some business metric exceeds a pre-defined threshold, the metric will be highlighted in standard reports, and the business analyst may be alerted via email or another monitoring service.

Generally, various BI portals (simplified web browsers) are used which provides simplified access to various data warehouse and business intelligence applications.

12.8 BUSINESS ANALYTICS

Business analytics (**BA**) refers to the skills, technologies, applications and practices for continuous iterative investigation of past business performance to gain insight and drive business planning.

It mainly focuses on developing new approaches and understanding of business performance based on data and statistical methods. In contrast, business intelligence focuses on using a consistent set of metrics to both measure past performance and guide business planning, which is also based on data and statistical methods.

It makes extensive use of data, statistical and quantitative analysis, explanatory and predictive modelling and fact-based management to impel decision making.

Business analytics can answer questions like why is this happening, what if these trends continue, what will happen next (that is, predict future), what is the best that can happen (that is, optimize).

Example:

Various banks in country use data analysis to differentiate amongst customers while sanctioning a particular loan. For instance they may categorize customers based on credit, customer royalty, and property/belongings with customer etc.

Types of Analytics:
- **Decisive Analytics:** supports human decisions with visual analytics the user models to reflect reasoning.
- **Descriptive Analytics:** Gain insight from historical data with reporting, scorecards, clustering etc.
- **Predictive Analytics** (predictive modelling using statistical and machine learning techniques)
- **Prescriptive Analytics** recommend decisions using optimization, simulation etc.

However, Business analytics depends on sufficient volumes of high quality data. The difficulty in ensuring data quality is integrating and reconciling data across different systems and then deciding what subsets of data to make available.

REVIEW QUESTIONS ON INSTRUCTIONAL OBJECTIVES

1. Write a note on :
   (i) Business Intelligence
   (ii) Data Mining and Data ware housing
   (iii) Teradata RDBMS
   (iv) Online analytical processing
   (v) Decision support system.
2. What is the concept of Data mining ? Why it is required ?
3. What is the need for Data analysis ?
4. Define, 'support' and 'confidence' of knowledge representation rule.
5. What are the two classes of Data mining problems ? Explain with example.
6. What are the two models to discover the rules from database ? Explain.
7. What are the applications of data mining ?
8. What are the three spatial index structures ? Explain each in detail.
9. What are the applications of business intelligence ?
10. Explain main components of data warehouse design.

11. Compare & contrast:
    i. OLAP vs. OLTP
    ii. Business Intelligence & Business Analytics

UNIVERSITY QUESTIONS

1. Write short note on : Data mining. **(May 2003)**
2. Distinguish between OLAP & OLTP.
3. Write a note on Data warehouse manager. **(Dec 2012)**

CHAPTER 13
EMERGING DATABASE TECHNOLOGIES

13.1 Introduction
13.2 Cloud computing and Data Management
13.3 Mobile Databases
    13.3.1 Client-Server Mobile Databases
    13.3.2 Peer-Peer (P2P) Mobile Databases
13.4 Massive data sets Map Reduce and Hadoop
13.5 Introduction to SQlite Databases
13.6 XML Databases
- Review Questions on Instructional Objectives

13.1 INTRODUCTION

This chapter deals with the various current and emerging techniques in databases.

In today's era there lies a need to deal with huge amount of data (big data) for various applications and commercial organizations. Dealing with such tremendous data requires performing following operations on it:

- Data Storage and Management
- Efficient and correct data retrieval
- Dealing with heterogeneous data
- Providing flexible access to data at any place (what we call "mobile databases)
- Analyze the big data to predict future trends in market. For example, social networking site like Facebook makes use of big data analysis to learn user trends in fashion of his/her likes, interests etc.

In this chapter we study following technologies that deal with such big data:

1. Cloud Computing and Data Management
2. Mobile Databases
3. MapReduce and Hadoop
4. SQLite Databases
5. XML databases

13.2 CLOUD COMPUTING AND DATA MANAGEMENT

Data stored in database are usually in large volume. Users need that data to be summarized in some fashion. Currently, database management in Big Data is becoming complex as one need to deal with semi-structured and/or unstructured data.

The biggest source of this hard-to-analyze information is the mobile web. The flow of data just doesn't slow down as more and more people around the world access the Internet and use social media on mobile devices. And most organizations struggle to collect, organize, store and analyze all of it on their own. To cope with this issue, cloud computing can be used in following directions:

Enter the Cloud: Cloud is a viable option for companies that don't have a lot of money for capital investments in equipment or the budget to maintain an IT department of the size needed to manage Big Data in house. It can be used for storage of such Big Data.

A variety of cloud database management systems are available to store and analyze both relational (SQL) and non-relational (NoSQL) types of data. A list of some of the leading service providers and their solutions for data management using cloud computing is given below:

Cloud Database Management Options

- **Microsoft Azure/SQL Database:**

Its a "full featured relational database-as-a-service," with "Tables" that offer NoSQL capabilities for storing large amounts of unstructured data, and "Blobs" (Binary Large Objects) for storing large amounts of unstructured text, video, audio and images.

- **Amazon Web Services/DynamoDB/Relational Database Service**

It includes NoSQL, MySQL, Oracle and MS SQL Server solutions. SimpleDB is Amazon's "highly available and flexible non-relational data store that [takes on] the work of database administration."

- **Xeround**

It is a fully managed MySQL Data Base As –a –Service (DBAAS) that the vendor calls a "drop-in solution" because it "automates all configuration and ongoing DB operations."

- **Google Cloud SQL/Google App Engine Datastore**

It's a platform provided by Google for storing structured and unstructured data.

- **ClearDB**

This MySQL DBAAS provides 24*7 support due to its "multi-regional read/write mirroring."

- **Database.Com**

It is a native cloud database service developed in house at Salesforce.com that is built with the needs of a social and mobile world at its core.

The unique features of cloud databases (namely the ability to distribute data across wide geographical areas and among different servers in one physical data center) are based on cloud computing technology made possible by virtualization. This is mostly not compatible with traditional RDBMS.

To get around this limitation, leading DBAAS companies including Microsoft and Amazon offer their own RDBMS applications or software optimized for the cloud computing environment.

Moving from RDBMS to Cloud

Moving to the Cloud can be straightforward or quite complex process, depending on the application.

NoSQL is a non-relational database management system. NoSQL was designed specifically to handle storing and retrieving large quantities of data without defined relationships (i.e., Big Data). But, data stored in a NoSQL database can be structured.

"DataStax" one of the leading provider of enterprise-level cloud database products says moving data to the Cloud requires more consideration than one might think because an RDBMS is not designed to run on a virtualized platform. It further deduces that moving an existing RDBMS from an on-premise server to a cloud platform "in no way maximizes the capabilities of a cloud computing environment."

If any organization is thinking of moving its data to the Cloud, there are **eight defining characteristics of NoSQL cloud databases** that one should be aware of, according to DataStax:

1. **Elasticity**

It is the ability to "add and subtract nodes (defined as actual physical machines or virtual machines) when the underlying application and business demands it." The adding and subtracting of nodes in response to demand happens on the fly so that no failure occurs.

2. **Scalability**

Elasticity makes it possible to scale out in a linear fashion so that database performance increases when necessary.

For example, "if two nodes are able to handle the throughput of 200,000 transactions, then four nodes should be able to manage 400,000" if there is increase in demand.

The ability to scale out also means that large volumes of data are processed in the same amount of time that small volumes of data are.

3. **High availability**

High availability or "uptime" is critical to businesses that can lose tens of thousands or even millions of dollars per minute of downtime, depending on the industry and its product/service.

Cloud databases claim high availability because they "piggyback off of a cloud provider's infrastructure" which is designed to provide easy data distribution and redundancy.

4. Easy data distribution
Because cloud providers have the ability to "distribute resources(computing like CPU, storage space etc.) and data across different geographies or 'zones', the underlying database of a cloud application can read and write from any node that makes up the cloud database.

5. Redundancy
Redundant copies of data are important so if "the primary copy is destroyed, another copy is available for use." Redundant copies can be stored over a wide geographic area or within the same data center on different physical server racks. These redundant copies ensure high availability.

6. Support for all data types
Cloud-based NoSQL databases "offer flexible and dynamic schema that accepts all key data formats" including structured, semi-structured, and unstructured on the other hand traditional RDBMS can only handle structured data.

7. Easier manageability
Tools or sets of tools for carrying out "routine administrative operations" are provided by the vendor. Usually these tools are accessed via a web browser.

8. Lower cost
The elasticity and scalability of cloud databases is what makes them less costly because the pricing model for cloud computing is pay-as-you-go.

These eight characteristics of NoSQL cloud databases are helpful background information that IT managers can use when moving an organizations data to a cloud platform.

13.3 MOBILE DATABASES

Now-a-days most of the people around the world use mobile/smart phones to access data from the internet. Mobile data-driven applications enable us to access any data from any corner of the world leading to "Ubiquitous computing".

For example, doctors' can retrieve patients information from anywhere or news reporters can update news from any corner of the world using mobile databases. Mobile DBMSs are needed to support these applications data processing capabilities

Mobile Database is a database that can be connected to by a mobile computing device over a wireless mobile network.

Generally, Mobile Databases:
- Physically separate from the central database server.
- Resided on mobile devices.
- Capable of communicating with a central database server or other mobile clients from remote sites.
- Handle local queries without connectivity.

Mobile Databases are categorized into following types:
1. Client-Server Mobile Databases
2. Peer-Peer Mobile Databases

13.3.1 Client-Server Mobile Databases

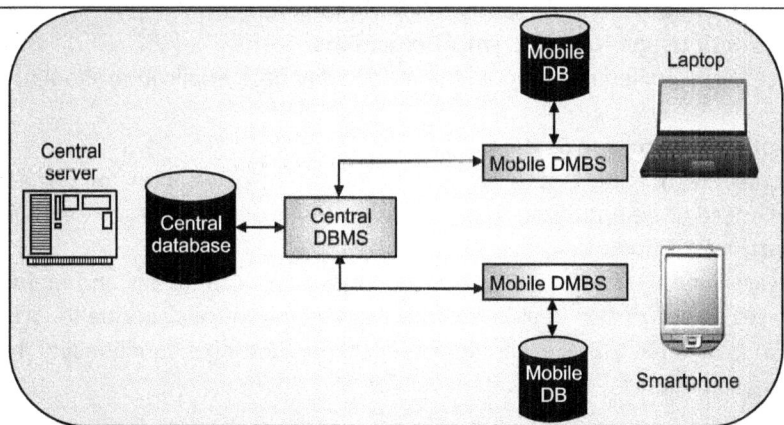

Fig.13.1 Client-Server Mobile Databases

Fig.13.1 shows traditional and mostly used client-server databases. In this type of mobile database, there will be a single server to which multiple clients may communicate to satisfy their data access needs. One central DBMS will manage all database related operations like storage, updation etc. Clients can communicate using a wireless network for data access with very limited functionality. Clients are provided with local mobile databases with limited storage space. Server plays the important role.

As there is only a centralized server, it becomes the bottleneck. Failure of server will crash whole system.

13.3.2 Peer-Peer (P2P) Mobile Databases

In P2P mobile databases, the database maintenance activities are
distributed amongst clients. Every process plays part of the role of the server, besides its client role. A client that wants to access a piece of data, sends a request to other peer clients and they forward the request until the data is found.Fig.13.2 shows a typical P2P mobile database.

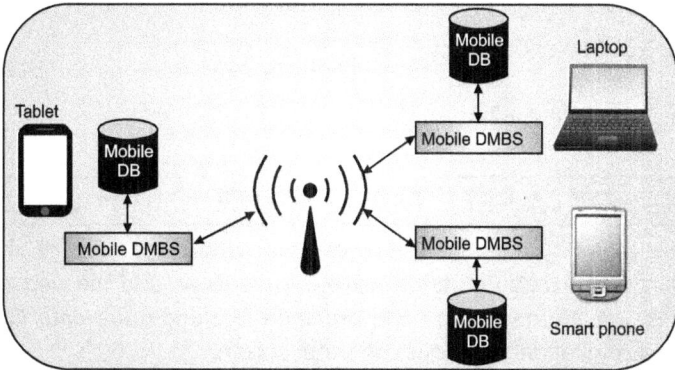

Fig.13.2 Typical Peer-Peer Mobile Database

However, the major problem in this model is ensuring the availability of data.
Basically, mobile databases should satisfy following requirements:

1. Small Memory Usage for Different Applications:
Mobile devices have limited memory, so the mobile database application should have a small footprint.

2. Flash-Optimized Storage System:
Flash memories are dominant storage devices in current generation for portable devices. Mobile DBMS need to be optimized to exploit advantages of flash storage devices.

3. Data Synchronization:
Portable devices cannot stay connected all the time. Users can access and manipulate data on their devices. They are also unable to store a large amount of data due to lack of storage capacity. Thus, mobile DBMSs should have the synchronize functionality to integrate different versions of data into a consistent version.

4. Security:
Security is very important for data-centric mobile applications. It is more important when the application works with critical data that its disclosure results in potential loss or damage. Data that are transmitted over a wireless network are more prone to security issues. To cope with these issues, Mobile DBMSs should implement a complete end-to-end security to ensure the secure transfer of data.

5. Low Power Consumption:
Processor, display and network connectivity are the main power consumers in a mobile device. Mobile DBMSs need to be optimized for efficient power consumption.

6. Embeddable in Existing Applications:
Administrators do not have direct access to mobile devices. Mobile DBMSs should be an integral part of the application that can be delivered as a part of the applications. The database must be embeddable as a DLL file in the applications. It must be also possible to deploy the database as a stand-alone DBMS with support of multiple transactions.

Existing Mobile Databases:
1. Sybase SQL Anywhere
2. Oracle Lite
3. Microsoft SQL Server Compact
4. SQLite
5. IBM DB2 Everyplace (DB2e)

13.4 MASSIVE DATA SETS: MAP REDUCE AND HADOOP

Today, we're surrounded by data. People upload videos, take pictures on their cell phones, text friends, update their Facebook status, leave comments around the web, click on ads, and so forth. Machines, too, are generating and keeping more and more data. One may even be reading this book as digital data on your computer screen.

The exponential growth of data first presented challenges to cutting-edge businesses such as Google, Yahoo, Amazon, and Microsoft. They needed to go through terabytes and petabytes of data to figure out which websites were popular, what books were in demand, and what kinds of ads liked by people. Existing tools were becoming inadequate to process such large data sets. Google was the first to launch MapReduce a system they had used to scale their data processing needs.

MapReduce:

This system is used to handle massively large dat. It aroused a lot of interest because many other businesses were facing similar scaling challenges, and it wasn't feasible for everyone to reinvent their own proprietary tool and this MapReduce was Google's proprietary and one need licence to use it.

To deal with this issue, Doug Cutting developed an open source version of this MapReduce system called Hadoop. Soon after, Yahoo and others provided a support to this effort. Today, Hadoop is a core part of the computing infrastructure for many web companies, such as Yahoo, Facebook, LinkedIn, and Twitter. Many more traditional businesses, such as media and telecom, are beginning to adopt this system too.

Hadoop:

Apache Hadoop is an open source JAVA framework for processing and querying large bundled data on clusters of commodity hardware. It is a top level Apache project initiated by Yahoo and Doug cutting.

Nowadays, Hadoop is most popular in Big Data processing and used by most of the industries. It enables scalable, cost-effective, flexible and fault tolerant solutions. It has two main features viz. Hadoop Distributed File System (HDFS) and MapReduce layer which are covered in detail in unit 5.

13.5 INTRODUCTION TO SQLITE DATABASES

SQLite is a relational database management system contained in a C programming library. In contrast to other database management systems, SQLite is not a separate process that is accessed from the client application, but an integral part of it. It was designed by D. Richard Hipp in 2000.

SQLite is compliant with ACID properties and implements most of the SQL standard, using a dynamically and weakly typed SQL syntax that does not guarantee the domain integrity.

It is a popular choice as embedded database for local/client storage in application software such as web browsers. It is the most widely deployed database engine, as it is used today by several popular browsers, operating systems, and embedded systems. The source code for SQLite is available freely in the public domain (i.e. it's an open source).

Design of SQLite Databases:

Unlike client–server database management systems, the SQLite engine has no standalone processes with which the application program communicates. Instead, the SQLite library is linked in and thus becomes an integral part of the application program.

The application program uses SQLite's functionality through simple function calls, which reduce latency in database access: function calls within a single process are more efficient than inter-process communication. SQLite stores the entire database (definitions, tables, indices, and the data itself) as a single cross-platform file on a host machine. It implements this simple design by locking the entire database file during writing. SQLite read operations can be multitasked i.e. many clients can access same data concurrently. However, writes can only be performed sequentially.

Features of SQLite:

- SQLite implements most of the SQL-92 standard for SQL but it lacks some features. For example it has partial support for triggers, and it can't write to views (however it supports INSTEAD OF triggers that provide this functionality).
- While it supports complex queries, it still has limited ALTER TABLE support, as it can't modify or delete columns.
- SQLite uses an unusual type system for an SQL-compatible DBMS; instead of assigning a type to a column as in most SQL database systems, types are assigned to individual values; in language terms it is *dynamically typed*.
- Several computer processes or threads may access the same database concurrently. Several read accesses can be satisfied in parallel. A write access can only be satisfied if no other accesses are currently being serviced.
- A standalone program called sqlite3 is provided that can be used to create a database, define tables within it, insert and change rows, run queries and manage an SQLite database file. This program is a single executable file on the host machine. It also serves as an example for writing applications that use the SQLite library.
- SQLite full Unicode support is optional.
- As of version 3.8.2 it's possible to create tables without rowid.

13.6 XML DATABASES

An XML database is a data persistence software system that allows data to be stored in XML format. These data can then be queried, exported and serialized into the desired format. XML databases are usually associated with document-oriented databases.

Two major classes of XML database exist as follows:

1. **XML-enabled**:

These type may either map XML to traditional database structures (such as a relational database), accepting XML as input and rendering XML as output, or more recently support native XML types within the traditional database.

This term implies that the database processes the XML itself (as opposed to relying on middleware).

XML enabled databases typically offer one or more of the following approaches to storing XML within the traditional relational structure:

1. XML is stored into a CLOB (Character large object block)
2. XML is `shredded` into a series of Tables based on a Schema.
3. XML is stored into a native XML Type as defined by the ISO.

These kinds of databases are best suited for data of non-xml kind.

2. Native XML (NXD):

The internal model of such databases depends on XML and uses XML documents as the fundamental unit of storage, which are however not necessarily stored in the form of text files.

The formal definition from the XML: DB initiative states that a native XML database defines a (logical) model for an XML document as opposed to the data in that document and stores and retrieves documents according to that model. At a minimum, the model must include elements, attributes, PCDATA, and document order.

Examples of such models include the XPath data model, the XML Infoset, and the models implied by the DOM and the events in SAX 1.0.

NXDs can use relational, hierarchical, or object-oriented database structures, or use a proprietary storage format (such as indexed, compressed files).

Additionally, many XML databases provide a logical model of grouping documents, called "collections". Databases can set up and manage many collections at one time. In some implementations, a hierarchy of collections can exist, much in the same way that an operating system's directory-structure works.

All XML databases now support at least one form of querying syntax. Minimally, just about all of them support XPath for performing queries against documents or collections of documents. XPath provides a simple pathing system that allows users to identify nodes that match a particular set of criteria.

In addition to XPath, many XML databases support XSLT as a method of transforming documents or query-results retrieved from the database. XSLT provides a declarative language written using an XML grammar. It aims to define a set of XPath filters that can transform documents (in part or in whole) into other formats including plain text, XML, or HTML.

Many XML databases also support XQuery to perform querying. XQuery includes XPath as a node-selection method, but extends XPath to provide transformational capabilities. Users sometimes refer to its syntax as "FLWOR" (pronounced 'Flower') because the query may include the following clauses: 'for', 'let', 'where', 'order by' and 'return'. Traditional RDBMS vendors are now shipping with hybrid SQL and XQuery engines.

Hybrid SQL/XQuery engines help to query XML data alongside the relational data, in the same query expression. This approach helps in combining relational and XML data.

Most XML Databases support a common vendor neutral API called the XQuery API for Java (XQJ). The XQJ API was developed as a standard interface to an XML/XQuery data source, enabling a Java developer to submit queries conforming to the World Wide Web Consortium (W3C) XQuery 1.0 specification and to process the results of such queries. Ultimately the XQJ API is to XML Databases and XQuery as the JDBC API is to Relational Databases and SQL. More details on XML can be found in Unit 05.

REVIEW QUESTIONS ON INSTRUCTIONAL OBJECTIVES

1. Write a note on :
   (i) Mobile databases (ii) XML Databases (iii) SQLite databases
2. What are the major requirements as per as mobile databases are concerned?
3. Why there lies a need of moving traditional RDBMS to clouds?
4. Explain the use of cloud computing in database management.
5. How MapReduce and Hadoop can be used to deal with massive data?
6. Explain the major types of mobile databases.
7. What are the applications of mobile databases?
8. What are the major categories of XML databases?

PROFICIENCY EXAMINATION

TYPE - I : DRAW E-R DIAGRAM

(1) Consider a university database for the scheduling of classrooms for final exams. This database could be modeled as the single entity set exam. with attributes course_name, section_no. and time. Alternatively, one or more additional entity sets could be defined, along with relationship sets to replace some of the attributes of the exam entity sets as :
- Course with attributes name, department and c_no.
- Section with attributes s_no and enrollment and dependent as a weak entity set on course.
- Room with attributes number, capacity and building.

Draw an E-R diagram illustrating the use of all three additional entity sets listed.

(2) Construct E-R diagram for the following database schema :
Person (s_id, name, address)
Car (license, year, model)
accident (date, driver, damage_amt)
Owns (s_id, license)
log (license, date, driver)
Primary keys are underlined)

(3) An insurance agent sells insurance policies to clients, policies can be of different types such as vehicle insurance, life insurance, accident insurance etc. The agent collects monthly premiums on the policies in the form of cheques of local banks. Appropriate attributes must be assumed for various entities such as agent, vehicle policy.
Draw - an E-R model for above system.

TYPE - II : RELATIONAL ALGEBRA AND RELATIONAL CALCULUS QUERIES

(1) Consider the following database :
project (project_id, project_name, architect)
emp (emp_id, emp_name)
assign to (project_id, emp_id)

Represent the following queries in relational algebra :
1. Get employee details working on project 'C300'.
2. Obtain details of employees working on the project DBMS Design.
3. Get employee numbers of employees who work on all projects.

4. List the employee numbers of employees other than emp. 107 who work on at least one project that emp. 107 works on.

(2) Let the following relation schemes be given :
R = (A, B, C) and S = (D, E, F). Let relations r (R) and s (S) be given. Give an expression in the tuple relational calculus that is equivalent to each of the following :
(i) π_A (r1)   (ii) r × s

(3) Let R = (A, B, C) and let r1 and r2 both be relations on scheme R. Give an expression in the domain relational calculus that is equivalent to
(i) π_A (r1)   (ii) r1 ∪ r2

(4) Consider schema,
Gives (Student, Seminar, Marks)
Seminar (Seminar, Guide)
Guide (Guide, Department)
Give relational algebra queries for the following :
(i) List students, their seminar names for those students who have scored above 60 marks.
(ii) List all students with their guide names and department to which guides belong.
(iii) List of students guided by say computer department.
(iv) Pairs of students (A, B) sharing the seminar topic (at most two can share a topic).

(5) Consider supplier_part database with the following relational scheme.
supplier (s_id, supplier_name, s_city, phone, status)
part (p_id, p_name, color, weight, unit)
supp_part (s_id, p_id, qty)
Write an efficient relational algebra expression that is equivalent to the following SQL query. Justify your choice.
```
select      supplier_name
from        supplier, part, supp_part
where       supp_part·p_id = part·p_id and
            supp_part·s_id = supplier·s_id and
            part·color = "Red" and
            supplier·city = 'Pune'
```

(6) Consider the supplier_parts_project database with following relational scheme.
supplier (s_no, s_name, city)
part (p_no, color, weight, p_city)

project (pr_no, pr_name, pr_city)
spj (s_no, p_no, pr_no, quantity)

(i) Write an efficient relational algebra expression that is equivalent to the following SQL query. Justify your choice.

select project, pr_no
from supplier, project, SPJ
where supplier s_no = SPJ·s_no
and SPJ.pr_no = project.pr_no
and supplier.city = project.pr_city

(ii) Give an expression for each of the following queries in relational algebra and tuple calculus.

(a) Get project name for projects supplied supplier 'sg'.
(b) Get s_no values for suppliers who supply the same part to all projects.

(7) Let the following relation schemas be given,

$$R = (A, B, C)$$
$$S = (D, E, F)$$

Let relations r (R) and s (S) be given. Give expressions in the tuple-relational calculus and domain relational calculus that are equivalent to each of the following :

1. $\sigma_{B = 17} (r)$
2. $\pi_{A, F} (\sigma_{C = D} (r \times s))$

(8) Consider the database schema :

Emp	=	(e_name, set of (children set of (skills)))
children	=	(name, Birthday)
Birthday	=	(day, month, year)
Skills	=	(type, set of (Exams))
Exams	=	(year, city)

Write the following queries for the relation emp (Emp)

1. Find the names of all employees who have a child who has a birthday in march.
2. Find those employees who took an examination for the skill type "typing" in the city "Dayton".

(9) Given the relation schemas,

Enroll (s_id, c_id, section)
Teach (prof, c_id, section)
Advice (prof, s_id)
Pre-req (c_id, pre-c_id)

DATABASE MANAGEMENT SYSTEMS (T.E. IT)   PROFICIENCY EXAMINATION

Grades (s_id, c_id, Grade, year)
Student (s_id, sname)

Give queries expressed in relational algebra, tuple calculus and domain calculus for the following queries :

(i) List all students taking courses with Smith or Jones.
(ii) List all students taking at least one course that their advisor teaches.
(iii) List those professors who teach more than one section of the same course.
(iv) List the courses that student "John Doe" can enroll in i.e. has passed the necessary prerequisite courses but not the course itself.

(10) Consider the following relations concerning a driving school. The primary key of each relation is in boldface.

Student (**St_name**, class_id, Th_mark, Dr_mark)
Student_Driving_Teacher (**St_name**, Dr_T_name)
Teacher_Theory_class (**Class_id**, Th_T_Name)
Teacher_Vehicle (**Dr_T_Name**, Licence_id)
Vehicle (**Licence_id**, Make, Model, Year)

A student takes one theory class as well as driving lessons and at the end of the session receives marks for theory and driving. A teacher may teach theory, driving or both. Write the following queries in relational algebra, domain calculus, and tuple calculus.

(i) Find the list of teachers who teach theory and give driving lessons on all the vehicles.
(ii) Find the list of students who are taught neither theory lessons nor driving lessons by Johnson (teacher).
(iii) Find the list of students who have better marks than John in both theory and driving.
(iv) Find the list of students who have more marks than the average theory marks of class 8.
(v) Find the list of teachers who can drive all the vehicles.

TYPE - III : SQL QUERIES

(1) Following relations are given :
Project (**project_id**, project_name, chief_architect)
employee (**emp_no**, emp_name)
assigned_to (**project_id, emp_no**)
The primary keys are underlined.
Express the following queries in SQL

DATABASE MANAGEMENT SYSTEMS (T.E. IT) PROFICIENCY EXAMINATION

1. Get details of employees working on both P$_1$ and P$_2$ projects.
2. Get employee numbers of employees who work on at least all those projects that employee abc works on.
3. Get names of all employees who are assigned to projects designed by the chief_architect XYZ.

(2) Consider the following database scheme :
emp (emp_name, street, city)
works (emp_name, company_name, salary)
company (company_name, city)
manager (emp_name, manager_name)
Write SQL queries for the following, by considering above database schemes.
   (i) Find employees whose names having second character e.
   (ii) Find all employees in the same cities as the companies for which they work.
   (iii) Find all employees who earn more than every employee of UCO bank.
   (iv) Find all companies located in every city in which SBI is located.

(3) Give SQL DDL definition of the database scheme of above question. Identify referential integrity constraints that should hold and include them in the DDL definition.

(4) The schema describes a production system,
part (part_no, name, description, stock)
part assembly (super_part_no, sub_part_no, quantity)
production - plan (part_no, quantity)
Show SQL queries for following :
   (i) Display description of all sub parts of part number 555.
   (ii) Display part numbers whose plan quantity exceeds stock.
   (iii) Display part number having maximum number of sub parts.
   (iv) Part assembly table constraints that quantity for a sub part should not be zero.

(5) Consider the schema,
employee (name, id, project_id)
Project 1 (name, project_id, customer)
Project 2 (project_id, budget, cost)
Project 3 (project_id, project_incharge_id)
Give SQL queries for :
   (i) All employees who work for projects of customer 'Amar'
   (ii) Customers whose project costs have exceeded budget.
   (iii) Project_incharge (names) whose project budget is light.
   (iv) All project_incharge employees who for some other project work as ordinary team members.

DATABASE MANAGEMENT SYSTEMS (T.E. IT)   PROFICIENCY EXAMINATION

(6)   Give syntax for SQL commands for
      (i) Table creation
      (ii) View creation

(7)   Consider the following relation :
      CUST (cust_id, i_name, fname, area, phone_no)
      MOVIE (mv_no, title, type, star, price)
      INVOICE (Inv_no, mv_no, cust_id, issue_date, return_date)
      Write SQL queries for following :
      (i)   List the customer names who have issued comedy type movies before August 97.
      (ii) Select the title, cust_id, mv_no for all movies that are issued.
      (iii) List all customers who have returned the movies between Jan 98 to today.

(8)   Consider schema :
      Gives (student, seminar, Marks)
      Seminar (Seminar, Guide)
      Guide (Guide, Department)
      Give SQL queries for :
      (i) List all students guided by say computer department.
      (ii) Pairs of students (A, B) sharing the seminar topic. (at most two can share a topic)

(9)   Consider the following relations :
      Person (Id_no, Name, Street, City, Blood_group, Rh)
      Donated (Id_no, Quantity, Donate Date)
      Write SQL statements for following queries :
      (i) List the names and addresses of persons donated maximum quantity of blood in year 1996, for every blood category.
           Note : Blood category is given by combination of blood group and Rh-factor.
      (ii) Find names and addresses of persons with blood-group AB Rh'   –Ve' who have not donated blood in year 1996.

(10) Consider the following relational database :
      Lives (person_name, street, city)
      Works (person_name, company_name, salary)
      Located in (company_name, city)
      Manages (person_name, manager_name)
      Give an expression for each of the following queries in SQL.
      (i)   Find all amployees who earn more than the average salary of employee in their company.
      (ii) Give all the persons in company 'ABC consultancy' a 10% raise.
      (iii) Find the company with least number of employees.

DATABASE MANAGEMENT SYSTEMS (T.E. IT)   PROFICIENCY EXAMINATION

(11) Consider supplier (s), parts (p), Project (J) database suppliers, parts and projects are uniquely identified by supplier number (s #), part number (p #) and project number (J #) respectively. The significance of an SPJ record is that the specified supplier, supplies the specified part to the specified project in the specified quantity and combination s#, p#, J# uniquely identifies a record.

    S (s#, supp_name, city)

    P (p#, part_name, color, weight, city)

    J (J#, proj_name, city)

    SPJ (s#, p#, J#, qty)

Write SQL statements for the following queries :

    (i) Get J# values for projects using at least one part available from supplier S_1.

    (ii) Get names of the supplier who supply the same part to all projects.

    (iii) Change color of all blue parts to white.

    (iv) Get total quantity of part P_1 supplied by supplier S_2.

(12) Consider the following relations :

Person (Id_no, Name, street, city, blood_group Rh)

donated (Id_no, donate_date)

Write SQL statements for following queries :

    (i) Get names and address of person with blood group B Rh '–Ve' who have donated blood more than once.

    (ii) Get number of persons with blood group AB Rh '+Ve'.

(13) Consider the following relational scheme for order-entry system.

order_in (order_no, cust_id, order date)

order_item (order_no, item_name, quantity)

customer (cust_id, cust_name, street, city, balance)

Give an expression for each of the following in SQL :

    (i) The maximum amount of any item ordered in a single order.

    (ii) List of customers who live in Bombay and have never ordered item Bag.

    (iii) List of order_no, for the customer 'XYZ'.

(14) An orchestra database consists of the following relations :

Conducts (conductor, composition)

Requires (composition, instrument)

Plays (player, instrument)

LIKES (player, composition)

DATABASE MANAGEMENT SYSTEMS (T.E. IT)   PROFICIENCY EXAMINATION

Give SQL queries for the following :
  (i) List all players and their instruments who can be part of orchestra when 'XYZ' conducts.
  (ii) From the above list of players, identify those who would like the composition they are to play.

TYPE - IV : NORMALIZATION

(1) You are given the universal schema of sales order system describing the despatch schedule for items in the order

(order_no, date, cust_name, cust_telno, item_id, item_qty, Item_desc, Item_desp_qty, Item_desp_ord, order_remarks)

  (i) Normalize the above system to 3NF showing functional dependencies, tables before and after each normalization step.
  (ii) What is the need to denormalize tubles (controlled) at times ? Give specific examples.

(2) Consider the universal relation student (roll_no, name, class, class_teacher, project_no, project_name, guide, guide_dept, dept_strength, project_student).

  (i) Show all functional dependencies, primary key in the universal table.
  (ii) Normalize above table to 3NF showing tables before and after each normalization step.

(3) The universal relation given below describes an inventory database for cars (Relation R). R (vehicle_no, description, model, year_of_model, colour, basic_price, distributor, distributor_location (city), discount_offered_by_distributor, customer, phone_no_of_customer).

Give all normalized table schemes in 3NF.

(4) Following information is maintained manually in a library :

Books (Accession_no, name, authors, price, book_type, publisher)

Borrowers (membership_no, name, address, category, max_no_of_books that can be issued).

The following constraints are observed,
  (i) Each book has unique accession_no.
  (ii) A book may have more than one author.
  (iii) There may be more than one copy of a book.
  (iv) The category of borrower determines the maximum number of books that may be issued to borrower.

Identify the entities. Normalize the entities. Give the definition of each normal form.

DATABASE MANAGEMENT SYSTEMS (T.E. IT)   PROFICIENCY EXAMINATION

(5) An institute runs various part time and full time courses. The duration of each course ranges from 6 months to 4 years. A student can undergo atmost one course at a time. The institute has four departments and a course is run by only one department. It is required to maintain complete data of courses, students and departments in database. Give the attributes, functional dependencies and the corresponding relational model. Specify the highest normal form of each relation in your data model. Assume suitable data, if necessary.

(6) It is required to set-up medical record database system, given in the following data :
- Patient's identification_no, name, address, date_of_birth, blood_group.
- Physician – identification_no, name, address and their specialities.
- Data about patients visit to physician like date_of_visit, the medicine prescribed, the dose of each medicine, tests ordered at the visit, result of those tests, temperature, blood pressure, etc.

Give functional dependencies and corresponding relational model. Specify highest - normal form of each relation in your model.

(7) Consider the relation scheme :
R (course, teacher, hour, room, student, grade).
Assume the following FD
(i) Each course has one teacher.
(ii) Only one course can meet in a room at one time.
(iii) A teacher can be in only one room at a time.
(iv) Each student has one grade in each course.
(v) A student can be in only one room at one time.

Decompose this relation scheme into Boyce-Codd normal form. Explain each step in detail.

(8) A movie studio wishes to institute a database to manage their files of movies, actors and directors. The following facts are relevant.
Each actor has appeared in many movies.
Each movie has one director and one or more actors.
Each actor and director may have several addresses and telephone number normalize the entities.

(9) Show that it is possible to ensure that a decomposition into 3NF is a loss-less-join decomposition by guarantering that at least one schema contains candidate key for the schema being decomposed.

(10) List the three design goals for relational databases. Explain why each is desirable.

(11) In designing a relational database, why might we choose a non-BCNF design ?

(12) Show that, if a relation schema is in BCNF, then it is also in 3 NF.

(13) Consider R (A, B, C, D, E, F, G) with the set D of FDs and MVDs given by,
D { A →→ B, B →→ G, B →→ EG, CD →→ E}
Decompose R into 4NF. Show that the decomposition is not dependency prescribing.

(14) Consider the relation scheme R (ABCDE) and the FDs {A → B, C → D, A → E}. Is the decomposition of R into (ABC) (BCD), (CDE) loss-less ?

(15) Find a 3NF decomposition of the following relation scheme :
(Faculty, Dean, Department, Chairperson, Professor, Rank, Student). The relation satisfies the following functional dependencies :

Faculty	→	Dean
Dean	→	Faculty
Department	→	Chairperson
Professor	→	Rank chairperson
Department	→	Faculty
Student	→	Department faculty dean
Professor Rank	→	Department-Faculty

(16) Determine if the decomposition of :
Student_Advisor (Name, Department, Advisor)
with functional dependencies F {Name · Department,
Name · Advisor, Advisor · Department }
into Advisor - student (Name, Advisor)
Student-Department (Name, Department) and
Advisor - Department (Advisor, Department) is loss-less.

(17) Consider the relation R (A, B, C, D) where A is a candidate key with no information about the FDs involved, can you determine its normal form ? Justify your answer.

(18) Give a loss-less join decomposition of schema R into 4NF.
$$R = (A, B, C, D, E)$$
Set of multivalued dependencies,
A → BC
B → CD
E → AD

(19) Determine if the relation student (s_id, Name, Phone_no, Major) is in BCNF. The functional dependencies are :

S_id	→	Major
Name	→	Major
Phone no.	→	Major
S_id	→	Name

S_id → Phone_no.
Name → S_id
Name → Phone_no.
Phone_no → S_id
Phone_no → Name.

Where S_id is unique student identification number and where name and phone_no are assumed to be unique.

(20) List all functional dependencies satisfied by following relation.

A	B	C
a1	b1	c1
a1	b1	c2
a2	b1	c1
a2	b1	c3

(21) Make a universal relation from this document and convert it into the relations in the 3NF format. State the functional dependencies used in the normalization process.

M/s Zen Asia Ltd.   Packing Slip   Slip No. : 123
                                                       Date   : 9 - 7 - 98

Material code : OP – 54   Oil Paint : 54

Production Lot No. : 12 - 53 - 03   Dated : 6 - 7 - 98

Pacing Details

Sr. No.	Container no.	Container size	Total containers	Quantity Packed
1.	176	5 litres	2	10 litres
2.	845	10 litres	6	60 litres
...	...	...	...	...
			Total Quantity = 230 litres	

TYPE V : TRANSACTIONS

(1) Consider the transaction :
    (S1)   START TRANSACTION
    (S2)   READ X
    (S3)   X = X + L
    (S4)   WRITE X
    (S5)   READ Y
    (S6)   Y = Y + L
    (S7)   WRITE Y
    (S8)   END TRANSACTION T_1
    (S9)   START TRANSACTION T_2

Assume that immediate database modification scheme is used. Show the log file contents for successful completion of statment (S9).

Describe the recovery results if system crashed :

(i) after executing statement six (S6)

(ii) after executing statement (S9) the system crashed.

(2) How are concurrency problems in database system different from concurrency problem in operating system ?

(3) Explain the recovery procedure that needs to take place after a disk crash.

(4) Define recovery algorithm.

(5) State advantages and disadvantages of shadow paging scheme.

(6) What are the variants of two phase locking protocol ?

(7) Define "Starvation of locks". Explain how starvation of locks can be avoided.

(8) With an example and explain tree-protocol. Specify advantages and disadvantages of tree protocol.

(9) What is Thoma's write rule ?

(10) With an example, explain validation based protocol.

Compare data server architecture and transaction server architecture.

(11) Define forest protocol.

(12) What is the use of wait-for graph ? With an example explain.

(13) Explain two different deadlock prevention schemes using timestamps. Give an example.

(14) Compare wait-die and wait-wound schemes.

(15) What is Timeout based scheme ? Specify advantages and disadvantages of Timeout based scheme.

(16) What are the modes of lock used in multiple granularity scheme ? Give compatibility matrix for them.

(17) Write an algorithm to find a cycle in a precedence graph.

(18) What benefit is provided by strict-two phase locking ?

(19) Consider the following two transactions

T_1 : read (A);
read (B);
if A = 0 then B := B + 1;
write (B);

T_2 : read (B);
read (A);
if B = 0 then A := A + 1;
write (A);

(a) Let the consistency requirement be,
A = 0, V B = 0, with A = B = 0 the initial values.

(i) Show that every serial execution involving these two transactions preserves the consistency of the database.

(ii) Show a concurrent execution of T_1 and T_2 that produces a non-serializable schedule.

(iii) Is there a concurrent schedule of T_1 and T_2 that produces a serializable schedule ?

(b) Add lock and unlock instructions to transactions T_1 and T_2, so that they observe the two phase locking protocol. Can the execution of these transactions result in a deadlock ?

(20) Consider a database system that includes an atomic 'increment' operation in addition to the 'read' and 'write' operations'. Let V be the value of data item X. The operation increment (X) by C sets the value of X to V + C in an atomic step. The value of X is not available to the transaction unless the latter executes a read (X).

Fig. 1 shows a lock compatibility matrix for three lock modes : Share mode, exclusive mode and increment mode.

(i) Show that if all transactions lock the data that they access in the corresponding mode, then two-phase locking ensures serializability.

(ii) Show that the inclusion of increment mode lock allows for increased concurrency

	S	X	T
S	T	F	F
X	F	F	F
T	F	F	T

Fig. 1

T → True, F → False, S → Shared mode, I → Increment mode, X → Exclusive mode

GLOSSARY

INTRODUCTION : BASIC CONCEPTS

1. **Database :** Database is a collection of data.
2. **Database Management System :** Database management system is collection of interrelated data and a set of programs to access the data.
3. **Data Independence :** Data independence is the ability to modify a schema definition in one level without affecting a schema definition in the next higher level.
4. **Data Model :** Data model is collection of conceptual tools for describing data, data schema and consistency constraints.
5. **Data Definition Language :** Database schema is specified by a set of definitions expressed by a special language called Data Definition Language.
6. **Data Storage and Definition Language :** This is the special type of Data Definition Language. The storage structure and access methods used by database system are specified by a set of definitions in data storage and definition language.
7. **Data Manipulation Language :** It enables users to access or manipulate data as organised by the appropriate data model.
8. **Database Manager or Storage Manager :** Database manager is a program module which provides the interface between low level data stored in the database and the application programs and queries submitted to the system.
9. **Database Administrator :** Database administrator is the person having central control over the system.

E-R MODEL

1. **Entity :** Entity is an object in the real world that is distinguishable from all other objects.
2. **Entity Set :** Entity set is a set of the same type that share the same properties or attributes.
3. **Simple or Composite Attribute :** The attribute which cannot be divided into subparts is called simple attribute, on the other hand, composite attributes can be divided into subports.
4. **Single-valued and Multi-valued Attribute :** Single-valued attribute has a single value for a particular attribute. Multi-valued attribute has a set of values for a specific attribute.
5. **Null Attribute :** An attribute which is having no value is called null attribute. Null value is used to represent the null attribute.

6. **Derived Attribute :** The value for this type of attribute is derived from the values of other related attributes or entities.
7. **Relationship :** Relationship is an association among several entities.
8. **Relationship Set :** It is the set of relationships of the same type. Formally, it is mathematical relation on $n \geq 2$ (possibly non-distinct) entity sets. If $E_1, E_2, E_3, \ldots E_n$ are entity sets, then a relationship set R is a subset of $\{(e_1, e_2, \ldots e_n) \in e_1 \in E_1, e_2 \in E_2, e_3 \in E_3, \ldots e_n \in E_n\}$

   where, $(e_1, e_2, \ldots e_n)$ is a relationship.
9. **Super Key :** Super key is a set of one or more attributes that are taken collectively to allow us to identify uniquely an entity in the entity set.
10. **Candidate Key :** Candidate key is a minimal super key. No proper subset of candidate key is super key.
11. **Primary Key :** Primary key is the candidate key chosen by the database designer as a principal means of identifying entities within an entity set.
12. **Weak Entity Set :** An entity set which does not have sufficient attributes to form a primary key is called weak entity set.
13. **Strong Entity Set :** An entity set which has a primary key is called as strong entity set.
14. **Subordinate Entity :** Member of weak entity set is called as subordinate entity.
15. **Dominant Entity :** Member of strong entity set is called as dominant entity.
16. **Specialization :** Specialization is the process of designating sub groupings within an entity set.
17. **Generalization :** It is a containment relationship that exist between a higher level entity set and one or more lower level entity sets.
18. **Aggregation :** Aggregation is an abstraction through which relationships are treated as higher level entities. It helps to express relationship among relationships.

RELATIONAL MODEL

1. **Domain :** Domain D is the set of values of same type. Domain of an attribute is defined as the set of allowable values for the attribute.
2. **Tuple :** Tuple is an ordered set of attributes. It is comparable to a record in a conventional file processing system and an entity in ER model.
3. **Procedural Query Language :** In procedural query language, the user instructs the system to perform a sequence of operations on the database to compute the desired result, i.e. how to retrieve the data. Relational algebra is procedural query language.
4. **Non-procedural Query Language :** In non-procedural query language, the user describes the information desired without giving a specific procedure for obtaining that

information. Tuple relational calculus and Domain relational calculus are the Non-procedural query languages.

5. **Extension :** Extension of a relation is the set of tuples appearing in that relation at any given instant. Extension varies with time.

6. **Intension :** Intension of a given relation is independent of time. Basically, it is the permanent part of the relation. It corresponds to what is specified in relation schema. More precisely the intension is combination of two things; a naming structure and a set of integrity constraints :
   - The naming structure consists of the relation name plus the names of attributes.
   - The integrity constraints can be subdivided into key constraints, referential constraints and other constraints.

7. **Key Constraints :** Key constraints are constraints implied by the existence of candidate keys.

8. **Referential Constraints :** Referential constraints are the constraints implied by the existence of foreign keys.

9. **Assertions :** An assertion is a predicate expressing a condition that we wish the database always to satisfy. Domain constraints and referential-integrity constraints are special forms of assertions.

   An assertion in SQL-92 takes the form :

   Create assertion <assertion_name> **check** <predicate>

   Example :

   The sum of loan amounts for each branch must be less than the sum of all account balances at the branch.

   Create assertion sum-constraint **check**.
   (not exists (select* from branch
       where (select sum (amount) from loan
       where loan branch_name = branch·branch_name)
       > = (select sum (amount) from account
       where loan·branch_name = branch·branch_name)))

   When an assertion is created, the system tests it for validity. If the assertion is valid then any future modification to the database is allowed only if it does not cause that assertion to be violated.

10. **Trigger :** A trigger is a statement that is executed automatically by the system as a side effect of a modification to the database. To design a trigger mechanism, we must meet two requirements :
    (i) Specify the conditions under which the trigger is to be executed.
    (ii) Specify the actions to be taken when the trigger executes.

The SQL-92 standard does not include trigger. The original system R proposal included a limited trigger feature.

SQL

SQL Commands :

1. CREATE Table Command :

Format :

```
CREATE TABLE table
({column data type [DEFAULT expr]
                [column_constraint] ||
        table constraint}
[, { column data type [DEFAULT expr]
                [column_constraint] || table_constraint } ]
            ..........) ;
```

Description :

CREATE TABLE command creates the database table with specified list of attributes.

  table - table name

  column - name of the column (attribute)

  data type - is the SQL data type

DEFAULT - specifies the value to be assigned to the column if a row is inserted without a value for this column.

Column-constraints define the restrictions placed on this column and consists of following :

```
[CONSTRAINT constraint]
[ [NOT] NULL] :
[ { UNIQUE : PRIMARY KEY} ]
[REFERENCES table [(column)] ]
[CHECK (condition)]
```

Constraint is an optional name assigned to this constraint.

NULL permits NULL values.

NOT NULL specifies that every row must have a non-NULL value for this column.

UNIQUE forces column values to be unique.

If a column is UNIQUE it cannot be declared the PRIMARY KEY.

REFERENCES identifies this column as a foreign key from table [column].

CHECK assures that the value for this column satisfies a condition. Condition may be any valid expression that tests TRUE or false.

Table Constraint : Table constraint is identical to column-constraint except that it can reference multiple columns with a single constraint. The format of table constraint is :

```
[CONSTRAINT constraint]
    [ [NOT] NULL] |
    [UNIQUE | PRIMARY (column [, column] ) ]
    [FOREIGN KEY (column [, column] )
    REFERENCES table [column [, column] ]
    [CHECK (condition) ]
```

2. **DROP Table Command :**
   Format :
   ```
   DROP TABLE table;
   ```
   Description : DROP TABLE drops the table and commits pending changes to the database.

   To drop a table you must either own the table or have DROP ANY TABLE system privilege. Droping a table also drops indexes and grants associated with it.

3. **ALTER Table Command :**
   Format :
   ```
   ALTER TABLE table
       [ADD ({column_element | table constraint}
           [, column_element | table constraint}] ...... )]
       [MODIFY (column_element [, column_element] ...... )]
       [DROP drop];
   ```
   Description :
   ADD allows you to add a new column to the end of an existing table or add a constraint to the table's definition. These follow the same format used in CREATE TABLE.

   MODIFY changes an existing column, with some restrictions :
   - You may change the type of column or decrease its size if every row for the column is NULL.
   - A NOT NULL column may be added only to a table with no rows.
   - An existing column can be modified to NOT NULL only if it has a non-NULL value in every row.
   - Increasing the length of a NOT NULL column without specifying NULL will leave it NOT NULL.
   - Views that reference a table with select from will not work after a column has been added to the table unless they are dropped and recreated.

4. INSERT :

Format :

> INSERT INTO table [(column [, column] ...)]
> { VALUES (expression [, expression] ...) : query } ;

Description :

INSERT adds one or more new rows to the table or view. The user must have the insert authority. Table is the table into which rows are to be inserted.

If a list of columns is given an expression must be matched for each of those columns. Any columns not in the list receive the value NULL, and none of them can be defined NOT NULL or INSERT will fail. If a list of columns is not given, values must be given for all columns.

INSERT with a query adds as many rows as the query returns, with each query column being matched, with columns in the column list. If no column list is given, the tables must have the same number and type of columns.

5. UPDATE :

Format :

> UPDATE table
> SET {column = expression [, column = expression] ...... :
> (column [, column] ....) = (subquery)}
> [WHERE condition];

Description :

UPDATE updates (changes) the values in the listed columns in the specified table.

Without where clause, all rows will be updated. With a where clause, only those rows it selects will be updated.

The expressions are evaluated as the command is executed, and their results replace the current values for the columns in the row(s).

6. DELETE :

Format :

> DELETE FROM table
> [WHERE condition];

Description :

DELETE deletes all rows that satisfy condition from table. The condition may include a correlated query. If where condition is not specified, it will delete all rows in the table.

7. SELECT :

Format :

```
SELECT [ALL : DISTINCT
        { * : { column [, column] ...... }}]
FROM {table [, table] ...... }
[WHERE condition]
[GROUP By expression [, expression] ...... ] [HAVING condition]
[{UNION [ALL] : INTERSECT : MINUS } SELECT ...... ]
[ORDER BY {expression : position} [ASC : DESC]
        ...... {expression : position} [ASC : DESC] ..........
```

Description :

SELECT retrieves rows from one or more tables. All means that all rows satisfying the conditions will be returned.

DISTINCT means that only rows that are unique will be returned, any duplicates will be removed.

An * (asterisk) represent that all columns from all tables in the from clause will be displayed.

If the list of columns is given, select will select only those columns from the tables. The rows in the table which satisfy the where condition will be selected.

8. ROLLBACK :

Format :

```
ROLLBACK [WORK] { [TO [SAVE POINT] savepoint]
                : [FORCE text] }
```

Description :

ROLLBACK reverses all changes made to tables in the database since changes were last committed or rolled back and releases any locks on the table.

It discards part or all of the work you have done in the current transaction, since the last COMMIT or SAVEPOINT.

9. COMMIT :

Format :

```
COMMIT
```

Description :

To commit means to make changes to data permanent. COMMIT commits any changes made to the database since the last COMMIT was executed implicitly or explicitly.

10. DESCRIBE :
Format :

> DESC [RIBE] table

Description :
DESCRIBE displays a specified table's definition. The definition includes the table and its columns, with each column's name, NULL or NOT NULL status, data type and width or precision.

11. TRUNCATE :
Format :

> TRUNCATE TABLE table

Description :
TRUNCATE removes all the rows from a table. It deletes rows much faster than the DELETE statement does. TRUNCATE is not a DML statement. Therefore if you issue a TRUNCATE TABLE statement, you cannot perform roll back to recover the lost rows.

NORMALIZATION

1. **Decomposition :** The decomposition of a relation schema
   $R = [A_1, A_2, A_3, ... A_n]$ is its replacement by a set of relation schemas, $\{R_1, R_2 ... R_n\}$ such that,
   $R_i \subseteq R$ for $1 \leq i \leq n$ and
   $R_1 \cup R_2 ... \cup R_n = R$

2. **Loss-Less-Join Decomposition :** Let R be a relation schema and let F be a set of functional dependencies on R. Let R_1 and R_2 form a decomposition of R. This decomposition is a loss-less-join decomposition of R if at least one of the following functional dependencies are in F^+.
   - $R_1 \cap R_2 \rightarrow R_2$
   - $R_1 \cap R_2 \rightarrow R_1$

   Loss-less-join decomposition can also be defined as :
   A decomposition of a relation schema R into the relation schemas R_i ($1 \leq i \leq n$) is said to be a loss-less join decomposition if
   $r = \pi_{R1}(x) \bowtie \pi_{R2}(r) \bowtie ---- \bowtie \pi_{Rn}(r)$
   where r is relation on relation schema R.

3. **Functional Dependency :** A functional dependency can be defined as follows :
   Let $\alpha \subseteq R$ and $\beta \subseteq R$. The functional dependency $\alpha \rightarrow \beta$ holds on R if in any legal relation r (R), for all pairs of tuples t_1 and t_2 in r such that $t_1[\alpha] = t_2[\alpha]$ it is also the case that $t_1[\beta] = t_2[\beta]$.

4. **Canonical Cover :** A set of functional dependencies F_c is a canonical cover if every FD in F_c satisfies the following :
   (i) Each FD in F_c is simple. In a simple FD, the right - hand side has a single attribute. i.e. each FD is of the form $X \to A$.
   (ii) For no FD $X \to A$ with $Z \subset X$ is $\{(F_c - (X \to A)) \approx (Z \to A)\} \not\models F_c$.
   In other words, the left-hand side of each FD doesn't have any extraneous attributes or the FDs in F_c are left reduced.
   (iii) No FD $X \to A$ is redundant i.e.
   $\{F_c - (X \to A)\}$ does not logically imply F_c. A canonical cover is sometimes called minimal.

5. **Full Functional Dependency :** Given a relation schema R and an FD $X \to Y$, Y is fully functionally dependent on X if there is no Z, where Z is a proper subset of X, such that $Z \to Y$. The dependency $X \to Y$ is left reduced, there being no extraneous attributes in the left hand side of the dependency.

6. **Partial Dependency :** Given a relation schema R with the functional dependencies F defined on the attributes of R and K as candidate key, if X is a proper subset of K and if $F \models X \to A$, then A is said to be partially dependent on K.

7. **Transitive Dependency :** Given a relation schema R with the functional dependencies F defined on the attributes of R, let X and Y be subsets of R and let A be an attribute of R such that $X \not\subset Y$, $A \not\subset XY$. If the set of functional dependencies $\{X \to Y, Y \to A\}$ is implied by F (i.e. $F \models X \to Y \to A$ and $F \not\models Y \to X$) then A is transitively dependent on X.

8. **Prime and Non-prime Attribute :** An attribute A in a relation schema R is a prime attribute or simply prime if A is a part of any candidate key of the relation.
   If A is not a part of any candidate key of R, A is called a Non-prime attribute or Simply non-prime.

9. **Unnormalized Relation :** An unnormalized relation contain non-atomic values.

10. **First Normal Form (1NF) :** A relation schema is said to be in First Normal Form (1NF) if the values in the domain of each attribute of the relation are atomic.

11. **Second Normal Form :** A relation schema R (S, F) is in second normal form (2NF) if it is in the 1NF and if all non-prime attributes are fully functionally dependent on the relation keys. A database schema is in second normal form if every relation schema included in the database schema is in second normal form.

OR

Second Normal Form (2NF) : A relation schema R is in second normal form (2NF) if each attribute A in R meets one of the following criteria :
- It appears in a candidate key
- It is not partially dependent on a candidate key

12. **Boyce Codd Normal Form (BCNF) :** A relation schema R is in BCNF with respect to a set F of functional dependencies if for all functional dependencies in F^+ of the form $\alpha \rightarrow \beta$ where $\alpha \subseteq R$ and $\beta \subseteq R$ at least one of the following holds.
    - $\alpha \rightarrow \beta$ is a trival functional dependency.
    - α is a super key for schema R.

    A database design is in BCNF if each member of the set of relation schemas that constitute the database design is in BCNF.

13. **Third Normal Form (3NF) :** A relation schema is in 3NF with respect to a set F of functional dependencies if for all functional dependencies in F^+ of the form $\alpha \rightarrow \beta$ where $\alpha \subseteq R$ and $\beta \subseteq R$ at least one of the following holds :
    - $\alpha \rightarrow \beta$ is trival functional dependency.
    - α is a superkey for R.
    - Each attribute A in $\beta - \alpha$ is contained in a candidate key for R.

    OR

    Third Normal Form (3NF) : A relation schema R is in 3NF with respect to a set F of functional dependencies if there are no non-prime attributes A in R for which A is transitively dependent on a key of R.

14. **Fourth Normal Form (4NF) :** A relation schema is in fourth Normal form (4NF) with respect to a set D of functional and multivalued dependencies if, for all multivalued dependencies in D^+ of the form $\alpha \rightarrow\rightarrow \beta$ where $\alpha \subseteq R$ and $\beta \subseteq R$ at least one of the following holds :
    - $\alpha \rightarrow\rightarrow \beta$ is a trival multivalued dependency.
    - α is a super key for schema R.

    A database design is in 4NF if each member of the set of relation schema that constitutes the design is in 4NF.

15. **Project Join Normal Form (PJNF/5NF) :** A relation schema is in PJNF with respect to a set D of functional, multivalued and join dependencies if, for all join dependencies in D^+ of the form * $(R_1, R_2, ... R_n)$
    where each $R_i \subseteq R$ and $R = R_1 \cup R_2 \cup ... \cup R_n$ at least one of the following holds.
    - * $(R_1 R_2 ... R_n)$ is a trival join dependency.
    - Every R_i is a super key for R.

    A database design is in PJNF if each member of the set of relation schemas that constitutes the design is in PJNF.

16. **Armstrong's Axioms :**
    Reflexivity rule : If α is a set of attributes and $\beta \subseteq \alpha$, then $\alpha \rightarrow \beta$ holds.
    Augmentation rule : If $\alpha \rightarrow \beta$ holds and γ is a set of attributes then $\gamma\alpha \rightarrow \gamma\beta$ holds.

Transitivity rule : If $\alpha \to \beta$ holds and $\beta \to \gamma$ holds, then $\alpha \to \gamma$ holds.

This collection of rules is called Armstrong's axioms.

These rules are sound because they do not generate any incorrect functional dependencies.

These rules are complete because, for a given set F of functional dependencies, they allow us to generate all F^+.

List of Relational Algebra Operations :

	Operation	Operator	Syntax
1.	Select	σ	σ_{cond} (rel)
2.	Project	π	$\pi_{arg\text{-}list}$ (rel)
3.	Rename	ρ	ρ_x (rel)
4.	Cartesian-product	$\times$	$rel_1 \times rel_2$
5.	Union	$\cup$	$rel_1 \cup rel_2$
6.	Set difference	$-$	$rel_1 - rel_2$
7.	Intersection	$\cap$	$rel_1 \cap rel_2$
8.	Join	$\bowtie$	$rel_1 \bowtie rel_2$
9.	Division	$\div$	$rel_1 \div rel_2$
10.	Assignment	$\leftarrow$	$R \leftarrow rel_1$

Note : rel, rel_1, rel_2 represent relation names, R is a variable

cond - condition or predicate

x - new name for relation.

TRANSACTION MANAGEMENT

1. **Transaction :** A transaction is a program unit whose execution accesses and possibly updates the contents of database.
2. **Schedule :** Represent the chronological order in which instructions are executed in the system. Two types of schedule are : Serial schedule and Concurrent schedule.
3. **Serial Schedule :** It consists of a sequence of instructions from various transactions where the instructions belonging to one single transaction appear together in that schedule.
4. **Concurrent Schedule :** When several transactions are executed concurrently, the corresponding schedule is called Concurrent schedule.

5. **Serializability :** A concurrent schedule is said to be serializable if it produces the same result as some serial schedule of the transaction. There are two forms of serializability :
   (i) Conflict serializability
   (ii) View serializability.
6. **Lock :** Lock is a variable associated with each data item.
   Manipulating the value of lock is called locking.
   There are two types or modes of locks.
   (i) Shared mode
   (ii) Exclusive mode
7. **Shared Mode Lock :** If a transaction T_i has obtained a shared-mode lock on item A, then T_i can read A but cannot write A.
8. **Exclusive Mode Lock :** If a transaction T_i has obtained a shared-mode lock on item A then T_i can both read and write A.
9. **Starvation of Locks :** Suppose that transaction
   T_2 - Has a shared mode lock on data item and
   T_1 - Requests an exclusive-mode lock on same data item.
10. Hence, T_1 has to wait for T_2 to release lock on same data item.

    Mean while suppose that T_3 requests a shared mode lock on same data item. This lock request is compatible with lock granted to T_2. Hence, T_3 gets the lock.

    At this point T_2 may release the lock but still T_1 has to wait for T_3. But again there may be a new transaction T_4 requesting a shared mode lock on the same data item. It is possible that there is a sequence of transactions that each requests a shared mode lock on same data item and T_1 never gets the exclusive mode lock on the data item. The transaction T_1 may never make progress and is said to be starved.
11. **Cascading Rollback :** The phenomenon in which a single transaction failure leads to a series of transaction rollbacks is called cascading rollback.
12. **Deadlock :** A system is in deadlock state if there exist a set of transactions such that every transaction in the set is waiting for data item held by some other transaction in the set.

    If $\{T_0, T_1, ... T_n\}$ is the set of transactions such that T_0 is waiting for a data item that is held by T_1, T_1 is waiting for a data item that is held by T_2 ... and T_{n-1} is waiting for a data item held by T_n and T_n is waiting for a data item that is held by T_0.
13. **Failure :** The failure of a system occurs when the system does not work according to its specifications and fails to deliver the service for which it was intended.
14. **Error :** An error in the system occurs when a component of a system assumes a state that is not desirable.

15. **Fault :** A fault is detected either when an error is propagated from one component to another or the failure of the component is observed.
16. **Recoverable Schedule :** A recoverable schedule is defined as a schedule where for each pair of transactions T_i and T_j such that T_j reads a data item previously written by T_i, the commit operation of T_i appears before the commit operation of T_j.
17. **Log :** Log is a structure used to store database modifications. It is a sequence of log records and maintains a record of all the update activities in the database. Following are the types of log records to record significant events during transaction processing :

    (i) **Start :** Start of transaction denoted as :

    $<T_i\ start>$

    (ii) **Update log :** It describes a single database write and it is denoted as :

    $<T_i,\ X_j,\ V_1,\ V_2>$

    (iii) **Transaction commit :** Denoted as :

    $<\ T_i\ commit\ >$

    (iv) **Transaction abort :** Denoted as

    $<\ T_1\ abort\ >$

18. **Forest Protocol :** Is a variant of tree protocol. The database is organized as a forest of rooted trees. Each transaction T_i must follow the following rules :

    (i) The first lock in each tree may be on any data item.

    (ii) The second and all subsequent, locks in a tree may be requested only if the parent of the requested mode is currently locked.

    (iii) Data items may be unlocked at any time.

    (iv) A data item may not be relocked by T_i after.

    It has been unlocked by T_i.

    The forest protocol does not ensure serializability.

19. **Lock Modes :**

    Shared Mode (S) : The node and all its descedents are locked in the shared model. All these nodes, locked explicitly or implicitly, are accessible for read-only access. No transaction can update the node or any of its descedents when the node is locked in the shared mode.

    Exclusive Mode Lock (X) : The node and implicitly all its descedents are exclusively locked by a single transaction. No other transaction can access these nodes. The nodes locked in exclusive mode are accessible for read and update operations.

    Intension Share Mode (IS) : The node is locked in intension shared mode, which means that its descedents cannot be locked exclusively. The descedents of the node may be individually locked in shared or intension shared mode. The descedents of node that is locked in IS mode are not locked implicitly.

Intension Exclusive Mode (IX) : The node is locked in intension exclusive mode, which means that the node itself cannot be exclusively locked. However, any of the descedants, if not already locked can be locked in any of the locking modes. The descedents of the node that is locked in the IX mode are not locked immediately.

Shared and Intension Exclusive Mode (SIX) : The node is locked in the shared and intension exclusive mode and all the descedants are implicitly locked in the shared mode. However, any of the descedents can be explicitly locked in the exclusive, intension exclusive, or shared and intension exclusive mode.

Relative privilege of the various locking modes : The relative privilege of the various modes of locking can be given as follows :

- Exclusive mode has the highest privilege.
- The intension share mode has lowest privilege.
- The share mode is not comparable with the intension exclusive mode.

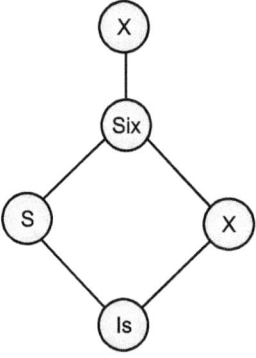

Fig. 1 : Relative Privilege of the Locking Modes

20. **Compatibility Matrix :** Compatibility between the current mode of locking and a request of another transaction for locking the node in a given mode is given in compatibility matrix. The entry TRUE represent that the request will be granted and transaction can continue. The entry FALSE indicates that the request cannot be granted and the requesting transaction will have to wait.

	IS	IX	S	SIX	X
IS	TRUE	TRUE	TRUE	TRUE	FALSE
IX	TRUE	TRUE	FALSE	FALSE	FALSE
S	TRUE	FALSE	TRUE	FALSE	FALSE
SIX	TRUE	FALSE	FALSE	FALSE	FALSE
X	FALSE	FALSE	FALSE	FALSE	FALSE
UNLOCK	TRUE	TRUE	TRUE	TRUE	TRUE

Storage Types : To ensure atomicity and durability properties of a transaction, we must gain a better understanding of these storage media and their access methods. There are the types of storage media. They are distinguished by their relative speed, capacity and resilience to failure :

1. **Volatile Storage :** Information residing in volatile storage does not usually survive system crashes. Access to volatile storage is extremely fast, both because of the speed of memory access itself and because it is possible to access any data item in volatile storage directly. Examples of such storage are main memory and cache memory.

2. **Non-volatile Storage :** Information residing in non-volatile storage survieves system crash. Non-volatile storage is slower than volatile storage by several order of magnitude. Examples of such storage are disk and magnetic tapes. Disks are used for online storage, whereas tuples are used for archival storage. Both however are subject to failure, which may result in loss of information.

Stable Storage : Information residing in stable storage is never lost. Although stable storage is theoretically impossible to obtain, it can be closely approximated by techniques that make data loss extremely unlikely.

OBJECT ORIENTED DBMS

1. **Inheritance :** Inheritance is the process by which objects of one class acquire the properties of another class.
2. **Multiple Inheritance :** Multiple inheritance occurs when a certain subclass is a subclass of two or more classes and hence inherits the functions of all super classes.
3. **Selective Inheritance :** Selective inheritance occurs when a subclass inherits only some of the functions of super class. Other functions are not in inherited. In this case, EXCEPT clause may be used to list the functions in a super class that are not inherited by the subclass.

DATABASE SYSTEM ARCHITECTURE

1. **Throughput :** Throughput is the number of tasks that can be completed in a given time interval.
2. **Response Time :** Response time is the amount of time it takes to complete a single task from the time it is submitted.
3. **Speed-up :** Speed-up refers to handling large number of tasks by increasing the degree of parallelism. It is defined as follows : If the execution time of a task on a large machine (with more number of processors, disks and other components) is T_L and execution time of same task on smaller machine is T_s then the speed-up due to parallelism is defined as T_s/T_L.

4. **Scale-up :** Scale-up refers to handling larger tasks by increasing the degree of parallelism. It is defined as follows : Let Q be a task and Q_N be a task that is N times larger than Q. Suppose that execution time of Q on a given machine M_S is T_S and the execution time of task Q_N on a parallel machine M_L which is N times larger than M_S is T_L.

Then the scale-up is defined as T_S/T_L.

NEW APPLICATION

1. **Roll-up :** Moving from a finer granularity data to a coarser granularity data by means of aggregation is called doing a rollup.
2. **Drill-down :** Drill down is the opposite operation of rollup i.e. moving from coarser-granularity to finer granularity data is called drill down.
3. **Support :** Support is a measure of what fraction of population satisfies the both the antecedent and consequent of knowledge representation rule.
4. **Confidence :** Confidence is a measure of how often the consequent is true when the antecedent is true.

◊ ◊ ◊

STRUCTURED QUERY LANGUAGE
QUESTIONS AND QUERIES WITH ANSWERS

1. What makes SQL a non-procedural language ?

Ans. : SQL determines what should be done, not how it should be done. The database must implement the SQL request. This feature is a big plus in cross-platform, cross-language development.

2. How can you tell whether a database is truly relational ?

Ans. : Apply Dr. Codd's 12 (we know there are 13) rules.

3. What can you do with SQL ?

Ans. : SQL enables you to select, insert, modify, and delete the information in a database; perform system security functions and set user permissions on tables and databases; handle online transaction processing within an application; create stored procedures and triggers to reduce application coding; and transfer data between different databases.

4. Name the process that separates data into distinct, unique sets.

Ans. : Normalization reduces the amount of repetition and complexity of the structure of the previous level.

5. Do the following statements return the same or different output :

SELECT * FROM CHECKS;

select * from checks; ?

Ans. : The only difference between the two statements is that one statement is in lowercase and the other uppercase. Case sensitivity is not normally a factor in the syntax of SQL. However, be aware of capitalization when dealing with data.

6. None of the following queries work. Why not ?

Ans. :

a. Select *

The **FROM** clause is missing. The two mandatory components of a **SELECT** statement are the **SELECT** and **FROM**.

b. Select * from checks

The semicolon, which identifies the end of a SQL statement, is missing.

c. Select amount name payee FROM checks;

You need a comma between each column name :

Select amount, name, payee
FROM checks;

DATABASE MANAGEMENT SYSTEMS (T.E. IT)   SQL

7. Which of the following SQL statements will work ?
   a. select *
      from checks;
   b. select * from checks;
   c. select * from checks

Ans.: All the above work.

8. Using the **CHECKS** table, write a query to return just the check numbers and the remarks.
   SELECT CHECK#, REMARKS FROM CHECKS;

9. **Rewrite the query from exercise 1 so that the remarks will appear as the first column in your query results.**
   SELECT REMARKS, CHECK# FROM CHECKS;

10. Using the **CHECKS** table, write a query to return all the unique remarks.
    SELECT DISTINCT REMARKS FROM CHECKS;

Use the **FRIENDS** table to answer the following questions.

LASTNAME	FIRSTNAME	AREACODE	PHONE	ST	ZIP
BUNDY	AL	100	555-1111	IL	22333
MEZA	AL	200	555-2222	UK	
MERRICK	BUD	300	555-6666	CO	80212
MAST	JD	381	555-6767	LA	23456
BULHER	FERRIS	345	555-3223	IL	23332
PERKINS	ALTON	911	555-3116	CA	95633
BOSS	SIR	204	555-2345	CT	95633

11. Write a query that returns everyone in the database whoe last name begins with **M**.
    Ans. : SELECT * FROM FRIENDS WHERE LASTNAME LIKE 'M%';

12. Write a query that returns everyone who lives in Illinois with a first_name of **AL**.
    Ans. : SELECT * FROM FRIENDS
    WHERE STATE = 'IL'
    AND FIRST_NAME = 'AL';

13. Given two tables (**PART1** and **PART2**) containing columns named **PARTNO**, how would you find out which part numbers are in both tables ? Write the query. Use the **INTERSECT**. Remember that **INTERSECT** returns rows common to both queries.
    Ans. : SELECT PART_NO FROM PART1
    INTERSECT
    SELECT PART_NO FROM PART2;

SQL | 2

14. What shorthand could you use instead of **WHERE a>=10 AND a<=30** ?
Ans. : WHERE a BETWEEN 10 AND 30;

15. What will this query return ?
Ans. : SELECT FIRSTNAME
FROM FRIENDS
WHERE FIRSTNAME = 'AL'
AND LASTNAME = 'BULHER';

Ans. : Nothing will be returned, as both conditions are not true.

16. Using the **FRIENDS** table, write a query that returns the following :

NAME ST

AL FROM IL

Ans. :
SQL > SELECT (FIRSTNAME || 'FROM') NAME, STATE
2 FROM FRIENDS
3 WHERE STATE = 'IL'
4 AND
5 LASTNAME = 'BUNDY';

17. Using the **FRIENDS** table, write a query that returns the following :

NAME PHONE
-------------------------- ------------
MERRICK, BUD 300-555-6666
MAST, JD 381-555-6767
BULHER, FERRIS 345-555-3223

Ans. :
SQL>SELECT LASTNAME || ',' || FIRSTNAME NAME,
2 AREACODE || '-' || PHONE PHONE
3 FROM FRIENDS
4 WHERE AREACODE BETWEEN 300 AND 400;

18. Which function capitalizes the first letter of a character string and makes the rest lowercase ?
Ans. : INITCAP

19. Which functions are also known by the name ?
Ans. : Group functions and aggregate functions are the same thing.

20. Will this query work ?
SQL> SELECT COUNT(LASTNAME) FROM CHARACTERS;
Ans. : Yes, it will return the total of rows.

21. How about this one ?
sql> SELECT SUM(LASTNAME) FROM CHARACTERS
Ans. : No, the query won't work because LASTNAME is a character field.

22. Assuming that they are separate columns, which function(s) would splice together FIRSTNAME and LASTNAME ?
Ans. : The CONCAT function and the || symbol.

23. What does the answer 6 mean from the following SELECT ?
INPUT :
SQL> SELECT COUNT(*) FROM TEAMSTATS;
OUTPUT :
COUNT(*)
Ans. : 6 is the number of records in the table.

24. Will the following statement work ?
SQL> SELECT SUBSTR LASTNAME, 1, 5 FROM NAME_TBL;
Ans. : No, missing () around lastname, 1, 5. Also, a better plan is to give the column an alias. The statement should look like this :
SQL> SELECT SUBSTR(LASTNAME,1,5) NAME FROM NAME_TBL;

25. Using TEAMSTATS table, write a query to determine who is batting under .25. (For the baseball-challenged reader, batting average is hits/ab.)
Ans. : SQL> SELECT NAME FROM TEAMSTATS
2 WHERE (HITS/AB) < .25;
OUTPUT :
NAME

HAMHOCKER
CASEY

26. Using today's CHARACTERS table, write a query that will return the following :
OUTPUT :
INITIALS_____CODE
K.A.P. 32
1 row selected.

Ans. : SQL> select substr(firstname,1,1)||'.'||
       substr(middlename,1,1)||'.'||
       substr(lastname,1,1)||'.' INITIALS, code
       from characters
       where code = 32;

27. Which clause works just like **LIKE(<exp>%)** ?

Ans. : STARTING WITH

28. What is the function of the **GROUP BY** clause, and what other clause does it acts like ?

Ans. : The **GROUP BY** clause groups data result sets that have been manipulated by various functions. The **GROUP BY** clause acts like the **ORDER BY** clause in that it orders the results of the query in the order the columns are listed in the **GROUP BY**.

29. Will this **SELECT** work ?

```
SQL> SELECT NAME, AVG(SALARY), DEPARTMENT
FROM PAY_TBL
WHERE DEPARTMENT = 'ACCOUNTING'
ORDER BY NAME
GROUP BY DEPARTMENT, SALARY;
```

Ans. : No, the syntax is incorrect. The GROUP BY must come before the **ORDER BY**. Also, all the selected columns must be listed in the **GROUP BY**.

30. When using the **HAVING** clause, do you always have to use a **GROUP BY** also ?

Ans. : Yes.

31. Can you use **ORDER BY** on a column that is not one of the columns in the **SELECT** statement ?

Ans. : Yes, it is not necessary to use the **SELECT** statement on a column that you put in the **ORDER BY** clause.

32. Using the **ORGCHART** table from the preceding examples, find out how many people on each team have **30** or more days of sick leave. Here is your baseline that shows how many folks are on each team.

```
SELECT TEAM, COUNT(TEAM)
FROM ORGCHART
GROUP BY TEAM;
OUTPUT :
TEAM        COUNT
===============  ===========
```

```
COLLECTIONS 2
MARKETING 3
PR 1
RESEARCH 2
```
Compare it to the query that solves the question :

Ans. :
```
INPUT :
SELECT TEAM, COUNT(TEAM)
FROM ORGCHART
WHERE SICKLEAVE>=30
GROUP BY TEAM;
OUTPUT :
TEAM              COUNT
=============== ===========
COLLECTIONS       1
MARKETING         1
RESEARCH          1
```
The output shows the number of people on each **team** with a **SICKLEAVE** balance of **30** days or more.

33. Using the **CHECKS** table, write a **SELECT** that will return the following :

OUTPUT :

CHECK#	PAYEE	AMOUNT
1	MA BELL	150

Ans. :
```
SQL> SELECT CHECK#, PAYEE, AMOUNT
     FROM CHECKS
     WHERE CHECK# = 1;
```

34. How many rows would a two-table join produce if one table had 50,000 rows and the other had 100,000 ?

Ans. : 5,000,000,000 rows.

35. What type of join appears in the following select statement ?
```
select e.name, e.employee_id, ep.salary
from employee_tbl e,
employee_pay_tbl ep
where e.employee_id = ep.employee_id;
```

Ans. : The preceding join is an equi-join. You are matching all the **employee_id**s in the two tables.

36. Will the following **SELECT** statements work ?

```
select name, employee_id, salary
```
from employee_tbl e,
employee_pay_tbl ep
where employee_id = employee_id
and name like '%MITH';

Ans. : No. The columns and tables are not properly named. Remember column and table aliases.

select e.name, e.employee_id, ep.salary
from employee_tbl e,
employee_pay_tbl ep
where name like '%MITH';

Ans. : No. The **join** command is missing in the **where** clause.

select e.name, e.employee_id, ep.salary
from employee_tbl e,
employee_pay_tbl ep
where e.employee_id = ep.employee_id
and e.name like '%MITH';

Ans. : Yes. The syntax is correct.

37. In the **WHERE** clause, when joining the tables, should you do the join first or the conditions ?

Ans. : The joins should go before the conditions.

38. In joining tables are you limited to one-column joins, or can you join on more than one column ?

Ans. : You can join on more than one column. You may be forced to join on multiple columns depending on what makes a row of data unique or the specific conditions you want to place on the data to be retrieved.

39. Rewrite the following query to make it more readable and shorter.

INPUT :

select orders.orderedon, orders.name, part.partnum,
part.price, part.description from orders, part
where orders.partnum = part.partnum and
orders.orderedon

```
between '1-SEP-96' and '30-SEP-96'
order by part.partnum;
```

Ans.:

```
SQL> select o.orderedon ORDER_DATE, o.name NAME, p.partnum PART#,
p.price PRICE, p.description DESCRIPTION
from orders o, part p
where o.partnum = p.partnum
and o.orderedon like '%SEP%'
order by ORDER_DATE;
```

40. From the **PART** table and the **ORDERS** table, make up a query that will return the following:

```
OUTPUT :
ORDEREDON NAME PARTNUM QUANTITY
================= ================= ======= ========
2-SEP-96 TRUE WHEEL 10 1
```

Ans.:

```
select o.orderedon ORDEREDON, o.name NAME, p.partnum PARTNUM,
o.quanity QUANITY
from orders o,
part p
where o.partnum = p.partnum
and o.orderedon like '%SEP%';
```

41. Are the following statements true or false?

The aggregate functions **SUM**, **COUNT**, **MIN**, **MAX**, and **AVG** all return multiple values.

Ans.: False.

They all return a single value.

The maximum number of subqueries that can be nested is two.

Ans.: False.

The limit is a function of your implementation.

Correlated subqueries are completely self-contained.

Ans.: False.

Correlated subqueries enable you to use an outside reference.

42. Will the following subqueries work using the **ORDERS** table and the **PART** table ?
INPUT/OUTPUT :

```
SQL> SELECT *
FROM PART;
PARTNUM  DESCRIPTION    PRICE
54       PEDALS         54.25
42       SEATS          24.50
46       TIRES          15.25
23       MOUNTAIN BIKE  350.45
76       ROAD BIKE      530.00
10       TANDEM         1200.00
6 rows selected.
```

INPUT/OUTPUT :

```
SQL> SELECT *
FROM ORDERS;
ORDEREDON   NAME        PARTNUM   QUANITY  REMARKS
15-MAY-96   TRUE WHEEL  23        6        PAID
19-MAY-96   TRUE WHEEL  76        3        PAID
2-SEP-96    TRUE WHEEL  10        1        PAID
30-JUN-96   BIKE SPEC   54        10       PAID
30-MAY-96   BIKE SPEC   10        2        PAID
30-MAY-96   BIKE SPEC   23        8        PAID
17-JAN-96   BIKE SPEC   76        11       PAID
17-JAN-96   LE SHOPPE   76        5        PAID
1-JUN-96    LE SHOPPE   10        3        PAID
1-JUN-96    AAA BIKE    10        1        PAID
1-JUN-96    AAA BIKE    76        4        PAID
1-JUN-96    AAA BIKE    46        14       PAID
11-JUL-96   JACKS BIKE  76        14       PAID
13 rows selected.
```

a. SQL> SELECT * FROM ORDERS
WHERE PARTNUM =
SELECT PARTNUM FROM PART
WHERE DESCRIPTION = 'TRUE WHEEL';

Ans. : No. Missing the parenthesis around the subquery.

b. SQL> SELECT PARTNUM
FROM ORDERS
WHERE PARTNUM =
(SELECT * FROM PART
WHERE DESCRIPTION = 'LE SHOPPE');

Ans. : No. The SQL engine cannot correlate all the columns in the **part** table with the operator =.

c. SQL> SELECT NAME, PARTNUM
FROM ORDERS
WHERE EXISTS
(SELECT * FROM ORDERS
WHERE NAME = 'TRUE WHEEL');

Ans. : Yes. This subquery is correct.

43. What is wrong with the following statement ?
DELETE COLLECTION;

Ans. : If you want to delete all records from the **COLLECTION** table, you must use the following syntax:

DELETE FROM COLLECTION;

Keep in mind that this statement will delete all records. You can qualify which records you want to delete by using the following syntax:

DELETE FROM COLLECTION
WHERE VALUE = 125

This statement would delete all records with a value of **125**.

44. What is wrong with the following statement ?
INSERT INTO COLLECTION SELECT * FROM TABLE_2

Ans. : This statement was designed to insert all the records from **TABLE_2** into the **COLLECTION** table. The main problem here is using the **INTO** keyword with the **INSERT** statement. When copying data from one table into another table, you must use the following syntax :

INSERT COLLECTION
SELECT * FROM TABLE_2;

Also, remember that the data types of the fields selected from **TABLE_2** must exactly match the data types and order of the fields within the **COLLECTION** table.

DATABASE MANAGEMENT SYSTEMS (T.E. IT)   SQL

45.   What is wrong with the following statement ?
          UPDATE COLLECTION ("HONUS WAGNER CARD", 25000, "FOUND IT");
Ans. : This statement confuses the **UPDATE** function with the **INSERT** function. To **UPDATE** values into the **COLLECTIONS** table, use the following syntax :
          UPDATE COLLECTIONS
          SET NAME = "HONUS WAGNER CARD",
          VALUE = 25000,
          REMARKS = "FOUND IT";
46.   What would happen if you issued the following statement ?
          SQL> DELETE * FROM COLLECTION;
Ans. : Nothing would be deleted because of incorrect syntax. The * is not required here.
47.   What would happen if you issued the following statement ?
          SQL> DELETE FROM COLLECTION;
Ans. : All rows in the **COLLECTION** table will be deleted.
48.   What would happen if you issued the following statement ?
          SQL> UPDATE COLLECTION
          SET WORTH = 555
          SET REMARKS = 'UP FROM 525';
Ans. : All values in the **COLLECTION** table for the worth column are now **555**, and all remarks in the **COLLECTION** table now say **UP FROM 525**. Probably not a good thing !
49.   Will the following SQL statement work ?
          SQL> INSERT INTO COLLECTION
          SET VALUES = 900
          WHERE ITEM = 'STRING';
Ans. : No. The syntax is not correct. The **INSERT** and the **SET** do not go together.
50.   Will the following SQL statement work ?
          SQL> UPDATE COLLECTION
          SET VALUES = 900
          WHERE ITEM = 'STRING';
Ans. : Yes. This syntax is correct.
51.   What is wrong with the following statement ?
          CREATE TABLE new_table (
          ID NUMBER,
          FIELD1 char(40),
          FIELD2 char(80),
          ID char(40));

Ans. : This statement has two problems. The first problem is that the name **ID** is repeated within the table. Even though the data types are different, reusing a field name within a table is illegal. The second problem is that the closing parentheses are missing from the end of the statement. It should look like this :

CREATE TABLE new_table (
ID NUMBER,
FIELD1 char(40),
FIELD2 char(80));

52. What is wrong with the following statement ?

ALTER DATABASE BILLS (
COMPANY char(80));

Ans. : The command to modify a field's data type or length is the **ALTER TABLE** command, not the **ALTER DATABASE** command.

53. When a table is created, who is the owner ?

Ans. : The owner of the new table would be whoever created the table. If you signed on as your ID, then your ID would be the owner. If you signed on as SYSTEM, then SYSTEM would be the owner.

54. Can you have duplicate table names ?

Ans. : Yes. Just as long as the owner or schema is not the same.

55. When nesting transactions, does issuing a **ROLLBACK TRANSACTION** command cancel the current transaction and roll back the batch of statements into the upper-level transaction ? Why or why not ?

Ans. : No. When nesting transactions, any rollback of a transaction cancels all the transactions currently in progress. The effect of all the transactions will not truly be saved until the outer transaction has been committed.

56. Can savepoints be used to "save off" portions of a transaction ? Why or why not ?

Ans. : Yes. Savepoints allow the programmer to save off statements within a transaction. If desired, the transaction can then be rolled back to this savepoint instead of to the beginning of the transaction.

57. Can a **COMMIT** command be used by itself or must it be embedded ?

Ans. : A **COMMIT** command can be issued by itself or in the transaction.

58. If you issue the **COMMIT** command and then discover a mistake, can you still use the **ROLLBACK** command ?

Ans. : Yes and No. You can issue the command, but it will not roll back the changes.

59. Will using a savepoint in the middle of a transaction save all that happened before it automatically ?

Ans. : No. A savepoint comes into play only if a **ROLLBACK** command is issued--and then only the changes made after the savepoint will be rolled back.

60. What is wrong with the following statement ?

SQL> GRANT CONNECTION TO DAVID;

Ans. : There is no **CONNECTION** role. The proper syntax is

SQL> GRANT CONNECT TO DAVID;

61. True or False (and why) : Dropping a user will cause all objects owned by that user to be dropped as well.

Ans. : This statement is true only if the

DROP USER user name **CASCADE**

statement is executed.

The **CASCADE** option tells the system to drop all objects owned by the user as well as that user.

62. What would happen if you created a table and granted select privileges on the table to **public** ?

Ans. : Everyone could select from your table, even users you may not want to be able to view your data.

63. Is the following SQL statement correct ?

SQL> create user RON
identified by RON;

Ans. : Yes. This syntax creates a user. However, the user will acquire the default settings, which may not be desirable. Check your implementation for these settings.

64. Is the following SQL statement correct ?

SQL> alter RON
identified by RON;

Ans. : No. The user is missing. The correct syntax is

SQL> alter user RON
identified by RON;

65. Is the following SQL statement correct ?

SQL> grant connect, resource to RON;

Ans. : Yes. The syntax is correct.

66. If you own a table, who can select from that table ?
Ans. : Only users with the select privilege on your table.
67. In Oracle, how can you find out what tables and views you own ?
Ans. : By selecting from **USER_CATALOG** or **CAT**. The name of the data dictionary object will vary by implementation, but all versions have basically the same information about objects such as tables and views.
68. What types of information are stored in the data dictionary ?
Ans. : Database design, user statistics, processes, objects, growth of objects, performance statistics, stored SQL code, database security.
69. How can you use performance statistics ?
Ans. : Performance statistics suggest ways to improve database performance by modifying database parameters and streamlining SQL, which may also include the use of indexes and an evaluation of their efficiency.
70. What are some database objects ?
Ans. : Tables, indexes, synonyms, clusters, views.

Notes

Notes

Solved University Question Papers
Nov./Dec. 2014

Time : 3 Hours   2012 Pattern   Max. Marks : 70

1. (a) Explain good database design properties. With suitable example explain the consequences of bad designing. [5]
Ans.: Please Refer Article 4.1, 4.2, 4.3, on page no. 4.2 to 4.4
    (b) Explain with suitable example SQL aggregate functions. [5]
Ans.: Please Refer Article 6.9, on page no. 6.12 and 6.13

OR

2. (a) Define serializable schedule. Explain two forms of serializability. [5]
Ans.: Please Refer Article 8.2.5 and 8.2.6, on page no. 8.5 to 8.12
    (b) What is a relation ? What are the properties of relation ? Explain with example [5]
Ans.: Please Refer Article 3.2, on page no. 3.3 and 3.5

3. (a) Explain the following extended entity relationship features of E-R model. [5]
        (i) specialization (ii) generalization
        (iii) aggregation (iv) attribute inheritance
Ans.: Please Refer Article 2.6, on page no. 2.12 to 2.17
    (b) Explain rigorous two phase locking protocol. [5]
Ans.: Please Refer Article 8.3.1, on page no. 8.21 to 8.23

OR

4. (a) What is a deadlock ? Explain deadlock recovery techniques. [4]
Ans.: Please Refer Article 8.4.3, on page no. 8.39 to 8.41
    (b) Write the syntax for following SQL commands : [6]
        (i) create table   (ii) alter table   (iii) drop table
        (iv) insert   (v) delete   (iv) update
Ans.: Please Refer Article 5.3 and 5.4, on page no. 5.3 to 5.20

5. (a) Explain characteristics and advantages of distributed systems. [8]
Ans.: Please Refer Article 9.7, on page no. 9.13 to 9.15
    (b) Detail the procedure for connectivity of MongoDB with Java. [8]
Ans.: Please Refer Article 9.9, on page no. 9.16 to 9.19

OR

6. (a) Explain the need of data fragmentation and types of fragmentation. [8]
Ans.: Data can be stored in different computers by fragmenting the whole database intoseveral pieces called fragments. Each piece is stored at a different site.
Fragments are logical data units stored at various sites in a distributed database system.

- **Needs of Fragmentation**

Before we discuss fragmentation in detail, we list four reasons for fragmenting a relation

(i) Usage

In general, applications work with views rather than entire relations. Therefore, for data distribution, it seems appropriate to work with subsets of relation as the unit of distribution.

(ii) Efficiency

Data is stored close to where it is most frequently used. In addition, data that is, not needed by' local applications is not stored.

(iii) Parallelism

With fragments as the unit of distribution, a transaction can be divided into several sub queries that operate on fragments. This should increase the degree of concurrency, or parallelism, in the system, thereby allowing transactions that can do so safely to execute in parallel.

(iv) Security

Data not required by local applications is not stored, and consequently not available to unauthorized users.

- Horizontal Fragmentation
- Vertical Fragmentation
- Hybrid Fragmentation

- **Horizontal fragmentation**

It is a horizontal subset of a relation which contain those of tuples which satisfy selection conditions.

Consider the Employee relation with selection condition (DNO=5). All tuples satisfy this condition will create a subset which will be a horizontal fragment of Employee relation.

A selection condition may be composed of several conditions connected by AND or OR.

Derived horizontal fragmentation : It is the partitioning of a primary relation to other secondary relations which are related with Foreign keys.

- **Vertical fragmentation**

It is a subset of a relation which is created by a subset of columns. Thus a vertical fragment of a relation will contain values of selected columns. There is no selection condition used in vertical fragmentation.

Consider the Employee relation. A vertical fragment of can be created by keeping the values of Name, Bdata, Sex, and Address.

Because there is no condition for creating a vertical fragment, each fragment must include the primary key attribute of the parent relation Employee. In this way all vertical fragments of relation are connected.

- **Mixed (Hybrid) fragmentation**

A combination of Vertical fragmentation and Horizontal fragmentation.

This is achieved by SELECT-PROJECT operations which is represented by $\Pi_{Li}(s_{ci}(R))$.

If C = True (Select all tuples) and L ≠ ATTRS (R), We get a vertical fragment, and if C ≠ True and L ≠ ATTRS (R), we get a mixed fragment.

If C = True and L = ATTRS (R), then R can be considered a fragment.

    (b) Explain the speed-up and scale up issues with respect to parallelism. [8]

Ans.: Please Refer Article 9.6, on page no. 9.8 to 9.11

7. (a) Draw and explain basic building blocks of Hadoop. [8]

Ans.: Please Refer Article 11.3, on page no. 11.2 to 11.4

    (b) Describe XML data model. List the advantages of XML. [8]

Ans.: Please Refer Article 10.2, on page no. 10.3 to 10.5

OR

8. (a) Explain various components of Hadoop. [8]

Ans.: Please Refer Article 11.4, on page no. 11.5

    (b) Write a short note on : [8]

        (i) XQuery

Ans.: Please Refer Article 10.5.2, on page no. 10.8

        (ii) JSON

Ans.: Please Refer Article 10.7, on page no.10.9 to 10.12

9. (a) Draw and explain main components of data warehouse and its characteristics. [9]

Ans.: Please Refer Article 12.5, on page no.12.6 to 12.10

    (b) What are the characteristics of NoSQL cloud databases ? [9]

Ans.: Please Refer Article 7.4.3, on page no.7.9 to 7.10

OR

10. (a) What are the requirements of mobile databases ? List existing mobile dbs. [9]

Ans.: Please Refer Article 13.3, on page no.13.4 to 13.6

    (b) What is a decision support system ? Explain storage and data retrieval issues related to it. [9]

Ans.: Please Refer Article 12.4, on page no.12.5 to 12.6

DATABASE MANAGEMENT SYSTEMS (T.E. IT)   SOLVED UNIVERSITY QUESTION PAPERS

May 2015

Time : 2-1/2 Hours   **2012 Pattern**   **Max. Marks : 70**

1. (a) Explain ACID properties.   **[4]**

Ans.: Please Refer Article 8.2.2, on page no. 8.2 to 8.4

(b) Construct an E-R diagram for a car insurance company that has a set of customers each of whom owns one or more cars. Each car has associated with it zero to any number of recorded accidents.   **[6]**

Ans.: Please Refer Article 2.8, on page no. 2.23 Example no. 4

OR

2. (a) Explain different anomolies with example.   **[6]**

Ans.: Please Refer Article 4.7, on page no. 4.10 to 4.12

(b) What is cursor ? Explain cursor in PL/SQL with suitable example.   **[4]**

Ans.: Cursor : Oracle creates a memory area, known as context area, for processing an SQL statement, Which contains all information needed for processing the statement, for example, number of rows processed, etc.

A cursor is a pointer to this context area. PL/SQL controls the context area through a cursor. A cursor holds the rows (one or more) returned by a SQL statement. The set of rows the cursor holds is referred to as the active set. You can name a cursor so that it could be referred to in a program to fetch and process the rows returned by the SQL statement, one at a time. There are two types of cursors:

(i) Implicit cursors   (ii) Explicit cursors

(i) Implicit Cursors : Implicit cursors are automatically created by Oracle whenever an SQL statement is executed, when there is no explicit cursor for the statement. Programmers cannot control the implicit cursors and the information in it. Whenever a DML statement (INSERT, UPDATE and DELETE) is issued, an implicit cursor is associated with this statement. For INSERT operations, the cursor holds the data that needs to be inserted. For UPDATE and DELETE operations, the cursor identifies the rows that would be affected.

Example : By using the CUSTOMERS table which is displayed below :

Select * from customers ;

ID	NAME	AGE	ADDRESS	SALARY
1	Ramesh	32	Ahmedabad	2000.00
2	Khilan	25	Delhi	1500.00
3	Kaushik	23	Kota	2000.00
4	Chaitali	25	Mumbai	6500.00
5	Hardik	27	Bhopal	8500.00
6	Komal	22	Mp	4500.00

P.4

The following program would update the table and increase salary of each customer by 500 and use the SQL% ROWCOUNT attribute to determine the number of rows affected :

```
DECLARE
 total_rows number (2) ;
BEGIN
UPDATE customers
SET salary = salary + 500 ;
IF sql% not found THEN
    Dbms _ output. Put_line ('no customers selected ') ;
ELSIF sql% found THEN
    Total _rows : = sql% rowcount ;
    Dbms_output. Put _line (total_rows || ' customers selected ' ) ;
END IF ;
/
```

When the above code is executed at SQL prompt, it produces the following result :

6 customers selected

If you check the records in customers table, you will find that the rows have been updated :

Select * from customers ;

ID	NAME	AGE	ADDRESS	SALARY
1	Ramesh	32	Ahmedabad	2500.00
2	Khilan	25	Delhi	2000.00
3	Kaushik	23	Kota	2500.00
4	Chaitali	25	Mumbai	7000.00
5	Hardik	27	Bhopal	9000.00
6	Komal	22	Mp	5000.00

(2) Explicit cursors

Explicit cursors are programmer defined cursors for gaining more control over the context area. An explicit cursor should be defined in the declaration section of the PL/SQL Block. It is created on a SELECT Statement which returns more than one row.

The syntax for creating an explicit cursor is :

CURSOR cursor_ name IS select_ statement ;

Working with an explicit cursor involves four steps:
- Declaring the cursor for initializing in the memory
- Opening the cursor for allocating memory
- Fetching the cursor for retrieving data

- Closing the cursor to release allocated memory

Example : Following is a complete example to illustrate the concepts of explicit cursors:

```
DECLARE
    c_id customers. Id % type ;
    c_name customers. name% type ;
    c_addr customers. address% type ;
    CURSOR c_customers is
    SELECT id, name, address FROM customers ;
BEGIN
    OPEN c_customers ;
    Loop
        FETCH C-customers into c_id, c_name, c_addr ;
        EXIT WHEN c_customers % not found ;
        Dbms _output.put_line(c_id ||' '|| c_name ||' '|| c_addr) ;
END ;
/
```

When the above code is executed at SQL prompt, it produces the following result :

1. Ramesh Ahmedabad
2. Khilan Delhi
3. Kaushik Kota
4. Chaitali Mumbai
5. Hardik Bhopal
6. Komal MP

3. (a) Consider a relational database [8]

Supplier (Sid, Sname, address)

Parts (Pid, Pname, color)

Catalog (Sid, Pid, cost)

Write SQL queries for the following :-

(i) Find the names of suppliers who supply some red parts.

(ii) Find the names of all parts whose cost is more than Rs. 250.

(iii) Find name of all parts whose color is green.

(iv) Find numbers of parts supplied by each supplier.

Ans.: Please Refer Article 6.11, on page no. 6.18 to 6.26

(b) Write short note on Embedded SQL. [2]

Ans.: Please Refer Article 7.1, on page no. 7.1 to 7.3

OR

4. (a) When do dead lock happen ? How to prevent them, how to recover if dead lock takes place. [10]

Ans.: Please Refer Article 8.4.3, on page no. 8.39 to 8.41

5. (a) Why it is necessary to have client-server architecture for database management system. **[6]**

Ans.: Please Refer Article 9.3, 9.4 and 9.5 on page no. 9.3 to 9.8

(b) Explain and state difference between centralized and client-server architecture. **[8]**

Ans.: Please Refer Article 9.2 and 9.3, on page no. 9.2 to 9.8

(c) Explain different issues in design of parallel system. **[4]**

Ans.: Please Refer Article 9.6, on page no. 9.8 to 9.9

OR

6. (a) Explain need of partitioning techniques used in I/O parallelism. Explain techniques in detail. **[8]**

Ans.: Please Refer Article 9.6, on page no. 9.8 to 9.9

(b) What is distributed database. Discuss different approaches used for data storage in distributed database. **[8]**

Ans.: Please Refer Article 9.7 on Page no. 9.13 to 9.15.

Different approaches used for data storage :

Consider a relation 'r' that is to be stored in the database. There are two approaches for storing this relation in the distributed database.

1. Replication

The system maintains several identical replicas (copies) of the relation and stores each replica at a different site.

2. Fragmentation

The system partitions the relation into several fragments, and stores each fragment at a different sites.

1. Data Replication

If relation 'r' is replicated, a copy of relation 'r' is stored in two or more sites. In extreme case, a copy is stored at every site in the system, which is called as full replication.

Advantages of replication

(i) Availability : If one of the sites containing relation 'r' fails, then the relation 'r' can be found in another site. Thus, the system can continue to process queries involving 'r' despite the failure of one site.

(ii) Increased parallelism: Number of transactions can read relation 'r' in parallel. The more replicas of 'r' there are, the greater parallelism is achieved.

Disadvantage

- **Increased overhead on update :**

The system must ensure that all replicas of a relation 'r' are consistent; otherwise, erroneous computation may result. Thus, whenever 'r' is updated, the update must be propagated to all sites containing replicas. The result is increased overhead.

Example

In banking system, if particular account is replicated on various sites, then balance on all sites should be same all the time.

Thus, replication enhances the performance of read operations and increases the availability of data to read only transaction. However, update transactions incur greater overhead.

- **Data Fragmentation**

If relation 'r' is fragmented, 'r' is divided into a number of fragments $r_1, r_2 \ldots F_n$. These fragments contain sufficient information to allow reconstruction of the original relation 'r'.

- **Types of fragmentation**

(i) Horizontal fragmentation

In horizontal fragmentation, a relation 'r' is partitioned into a number of subsets, $r_1, r_2 \ldots r_n$. Each tuple of relation 'r' must belong to at least one of the fragments, so that the original relation can be reconstructed, if needed. In general, a horizontal fragment can be defined as a selection on the global relation 'r'. The predicate p_1 is used to construct fragment r_1.

$$R_1 = \sigma\, p_1\, (r)$$

We reconstruct the relation 'r' by taking the union of all fragments, i.e.

$$r = r_1 \cup r_2 \cup \ldots r_n$$

(ii) Vertical fragmentation

Vertical fragmentation splits the relation by decomposing the scheme R of relation 'r'. Vertical fragmentation of r (R) involves the definition of several subsets of attributes $R_1, R_2, \ldots R_n$ of the scheme R so that

$$R = R_1 \cup R_2 \cup \ldots R_n \cup$$

Each fragment η of 'r' is defined by

$$r_1 = \Pi\, R_i\, (r)$$

We reconstruct relation 'r' by taking the natural join; i.e.

$$R = r_1 \bowtie r_2 \bowtie \ldots \bowtie r_n$$

Example : Horizontal fragmentation :

Consider the account relation:

Account =(acc_no, branch_name, balance)

Then using horizontal fragmentation, the account relation is divided into several different fragments, each of which consists of tuplies of accounts belonging to a particular branch. If the banking system has only two branches –Hillside and Valley view. Then there are two different fragments :

Account1 = σ branch _name "Hillside" (account)

Account 2 = σ branch _name "Valkyview" (account)

Example : Vertical fragmentation

Consider a university database with a relation :

        Employee _info = (emp_id,name, designation, salary)

For privacy reasons, this relation may be fragmented into relations :

(1) employee-private_info = (emp_id, salary)

(2) employee... public..info = (emp_id,name, designation)

These fragments may be stored at different sites, again for security reasons.

    (c) What are internet databases. [2]

Ans.: Please Refer Article 9.8, on page no. 9.15 to 9.16

7. (a) Explain with example DTD. [6]

Ans.: Please Refer Article 10.4.1, on page no. 10.6 to 10.7

    (b) Discuss HBase data Model. [5]

Ans.: Please Refer Article 11.6 , 11.6.1 on page no. 11.8 to 11.9

    (c) Explain with syntax JSON data type and object. [5]

Ans.: Please Refer Article 10.5, on page no. 10.9 to 10.12

OR

8. (a) Write a short note on. [6]

      (i) X path

Ans.: Please Refer Article 10.5.1, on page no. 10.7

      (ii) X Query

Ans.: Please Refer Article 10.5.2, on page no. 10.8

    (b) What is Hadoop Framework and on what concept the Hadoop Framework works. [8]

Ans.: Please Refer Article 11.2, 11.3 and 11.4, on page no. 11.2 to 11.5

    (c) Explain NOSQL databases. [2]

Ans.: Please Refer Article 7.4, on page no. 7.7 to 7.11

9. (a) What is data preprocessing ? Explain data preprocessing techniques and its techniques. [8]

Ans.: Data Pre – Processing and techniques

Data pre-processing is an important and critical step in the data mining process and it has a huge impact on the success of a data mining techniques. Data pre-processing is a step of the Knowledge discovery in databases (KDD) process that reduces the complexity of the data and offers better conditions to subsequent analysis.

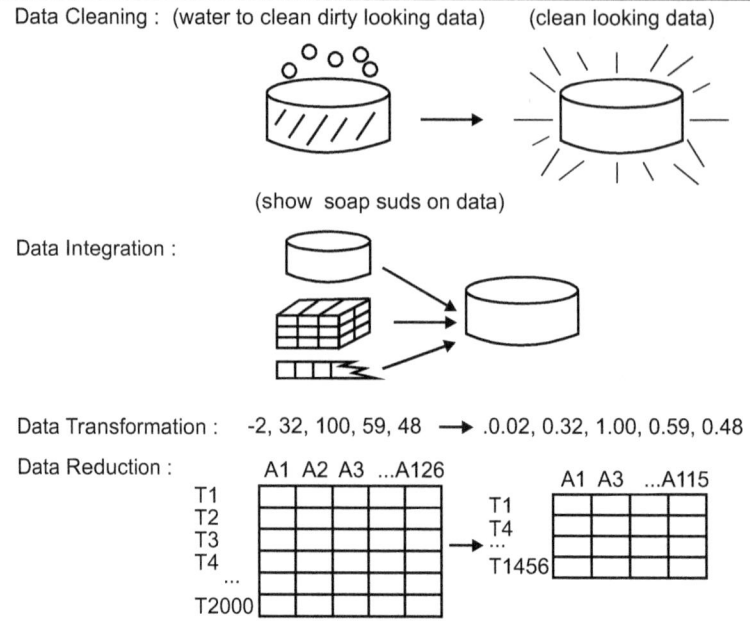

Fig. 1 : Forms of data preprocessing

Major Tasks in data preprocessing
1. Data Cleaning
2. Data Integration
3. Data Reduction
4. Data Transformation
5. Data Discretization

1. Data Cleaning :

Task work to"clean" the data by filling in missing values, smoothing noisy data, identifying or removing outliers, and resolving inconsistencies. If users believe the data are dirty, they are unlikely to trust the results of any data mining that has been applied. Furthermore, dirty data can cause confusion for the mining procedure, resulting in unreliable output. Although most mining routines have some procedures for dealing with incomplete or noisy data, they are not always robust. Instead, they may concentrate on avoiding over fitting the data to the function being modeled. Therefore, a useful preprocessing step is to run your data through some data cleaning routines.

Real-world data tend to be incomplete, noisy, and inconsistent. Data cleaning (or data cleansing) routines attempt to fill in missing values, smooth out noise while identifying outliers, and correct inconsistencies in the data.

Missing Values :

Imagine that you need to analyze the sales and customer data. You note that many tuples have no recorded value for several attributes such as customer income. How can you go about filling in the missing values for this attribute? Let's look at the following methods.

(i) Ignore the tuple : This is usually done when the class label is missing (assuming the mining task involves classification). This method is not very effective, unless the tuple contains several attributes with missing values. It is especially poor when the percentage of missing values per attribute varies considerably. By ignoring the tuple, we donot make use of the remaining attributes' values in the tuple. Such data could have been useful to the task at hand.

(ii) Fill in the missing value manually : In general, this approach is time consuming and may not be feasible given a large data set with many missing values.

(iii) Use a global constant to fill in the missing value : Replace all missing attribute values by the same constant such as a label like "Unknown" or $-\infty$. If missing values are replaced by, say, "Unknown," then the mining program may mistakenly think that they form an interesting concept, since they all have a value in common that of "Unknown." Hence, although this method is simple, it is not foolproof.

(iv) Use a measure of central tendency for the attribute (e.g., the mean or median) to fill in the missing value : With this approach, the mean value of the distribution is used to replace the missing value. This mean value can be obtained by plotting the normal distribution curve and measuring the mean of the curve.

(v) Use the attribute mean or median for all samples belonging to the same class as the given tuple : For example, if classifying customers according to credit risk, we may replace the missing value with the mean *income* value for customers in the same credit risk category as that of the given tuple. If the data distribution for a given class is skewed, the median value is a better choice.

(vi) Use the most probable value to fill in the missing value : This may be determined with regression, inference-based tools using a Bayesian formalism, or decision tree induction. For example, using the other customer attributes in your data set, you may construct a decision tree to predict the missing values for income.

2. **Data Integration :**

It is likely that your data analysis task will involve data integration, which combines data from multiple sources into a coherent data store, as in data warehousing. These sources may include multiple databases, data cubes, or flat files. There are a number of issues to consider during data integration. Schema integration can be tricky. How can like real-world entities from multiple data sources be "matched up"? This is referred to as the entity identification problem. For example, how can the data analyst or the computer is sure that customer _id in one database, and cust_number in another refer to the same entity? Databases and data warehouses typically have metadata - that is, data about the data. Such metadata can be used to help avoid errors in schema integration.

Redundancy is another important issue. An attribute may be redundant if it can be "derived" from another attributes. Inconsistencies in attribute or dimension naming can also cause redundancies in the resulting data set. Some redundancies can be detected by correlation analysis.

3. Data Reduction :
- A database/data warehouse may store terabytes of data
- Complex data analysis/mining may take a very long time to run on the complete data set.
- Data reduction is a process to obtain a reduced representation of the data set that is much smaller in volume but yet produce the same (or almost the same) analytical results.
- Data Reduction Strategies

(i) Aggregation   (ii) Sampling
(iii) Dimensionality Reduction   (iv) Attribute subset selection
(v) Data compression   (vi) Clustering

Data Reduction techniques can be applied to obtain a reduced representation of the data set that is much smaller in volume, yet closely maintains the integrity of the original data. That is, mining on the reduced data set should be more efficient yet produce the same (or almost the same) analytical results.

4. Data Transformation and Discretization :

In data transformation, the data are transformed or consolidated into forms appropriate for mining. Strategies for data transformation include the following:

(i) Smoothing, which works to remove noise from the data. Techniques include binning, regression, and clustering.

(ii) Attribute Construction (or feature construction), where new attributes are constructed and added from the given set of attributes to help the mining process.

(iii) Aggregation : where summary or aggregation operations are applied to the data. For example, the daily sales data may be aggregated so as to compute monthly and annual total amounts. This step is typically used in constructing a data cube for data analysisat multiple abstraction levels.

(iv) Normalization : where the attribute data are scaled so as to fall within a smaller range, such as -1.0 to 1.0, or 0.0 to 1.0.

(v) Discretization : where the raw values of a numeric attribute (e.g., age) are replaced by interval labels (e.g., 0–10, 11–20, etc.) or conceptual labels (e.g., youth, adult, senior).

The labels, in turn, can be recursively organized into higher-level concepts, resulting in a concept hierarchy for the numeric attribute. Figure 3.12 shows a concept hierarchy for the attribute price. More than one concept hierarchy can be defined for the same attribute to accommodate the needs of various users.

(b) Explain architecture of data mining system.   [8]

Ans.: Architecture of Data Mining

Data mining is described as a process of discover or extracting interesting knowledge from large amounts of data stored in multiple data sources such as file systems, databases, data warehouses etc. This knowledge contributes a lot of benefits to business strategies, scientific, medical research, governments and individual.

Business data is collected explosively every minute through business transactions and stored in relational database systems. In order to provide insight about the business processes, data warehouse systems have been built to provide analytical reports that help business users to make decisions.

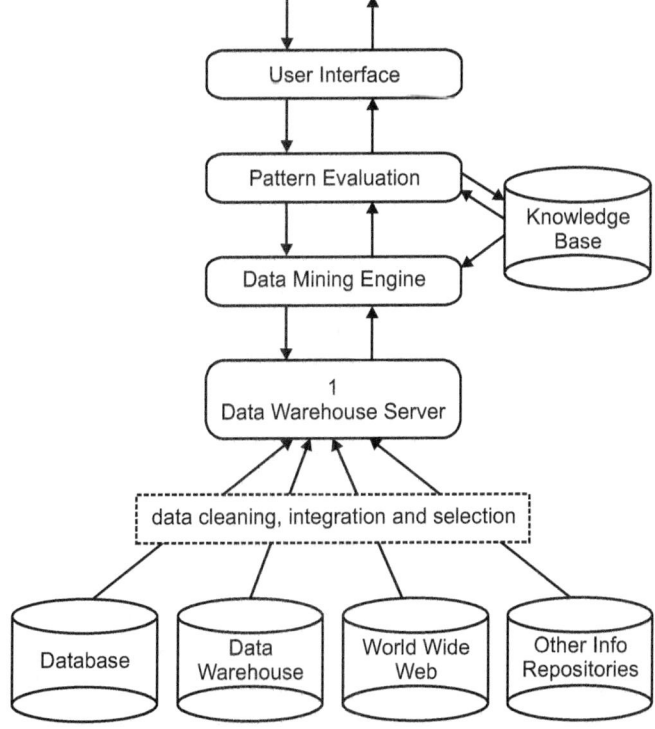

Fig. 2 : Architecture of a typical data mining

Based on this view, the architecture of a typical data mining system may have the following major components.

(i) Database :

Database, data warehouse, World Wide Web, or other information repository :

This is one or a set of databases, data warehouses, spreadsheets, or other kinds of information repositories. Data cleaning and data integration techniques may be performed on the data.

(ii) Database or data warehouse server :

The database or data ware house server is responsible user's data mining request.

(iii) Knowledge base :

This is the domain knowledge that is used to guide the search or evaluate the interestingness of resulting patterns. Such knowledge can include Con-cept hierarchies, used to organize attributes or attribute values into different levels of abstraction. Knowledge such as user beliefs, which can be used to assess a pattern's interestingness based on its unexpectedness, may also be included. Other examples of domain knowledge are additional interestingness constraints or thresholds, and metadata (e.g., describing data from multiple heterogeneous sources).

(iv) Data mining engine:

This is essential other data mining system and ideally consists of a set of functional modules for tasks such as characterization, association and correlation analysis, classification , prediction, cluster analysis, outlier analysis, and evolution analysis.

(v) Pattern evaluation module :

This component typically employs interestingness measures and interacts with the data mining modules so as to Focus the search toward interesting patterns. It may use interestingness thresholds to filter out discovered patterns. Alternatively, the pattern evaluation module may be into-grated with the mining module, depending on the implementation of the data mining method used. For efficient data mining, it is highly recommended to push the evaluation of pattern interestingness as deep as possible into the mining processso as to confine the search to only the interesting patterns.

(iv) User interface :

This module communicates between users and the data mining system, allowing the user to interact with the system by specifying a data mining query or task, based on Providing information to help focus the search, and performing exploratory data mining the intermediate data mining results. In addition, this component allows the user to browse database and data warehouse schemas or data structures, evaluate mined patterns, and visualize the patterns in different forms. From a data warehouse perspective, data mining can be viewed as an advanced stage of on-line analytical processing (OLAP). However, data mining goes far beyond the narrow scope of summarization-style analytical processing of data warehouse systems by incorporating more advanced techniques for data analysis.

OR

10. Write a short note on [16]

    (i) Machine learning for Big data

Ans.: Please Refer Article 11.1, on page no. 11.1 to 11.2

    (ii) Mobile databases

Ans.: Please Refer Article 13.3, on page no. 13.4 to 13.6

    (iii) Data Mart

Ans.: Please Refer Article 12.5, on page no. 12.10

    (iv) KDD

Ans.: Please Refer Article 12.6, on page no. 12.10 and 12.11

www.ingramcontent.com/pod-product-compliance
Lightning Source LLC
Chambersburg PA
CBHW060234240426
43663CB00040B/2663